Comparable Worth
and Wage Discrimination

Women in the Political Economy

a series edited by Ronnie J. Steinberg

Comparable Worth
and
Wage Discrimination:

Technical Possibilities
and Political Realities

Edited by

Helen Remick

TEMPLE UNIVERSITY PRESS

PHILADELPHIA

Temple University Press, Philadelphia 19122
©1984 by Temple University. All rights reserved
Published 1984
Printed in the United States of America

Library of Congress Cataloging in Publication Data

Main entry under title:

Comparable worth and wage discrimination.

(Women in the political economy)
Includes biographical references and index.
1. Equal pay for equal work—United States—Addresses,
essays, lectures.   2. Equal pay for equal work—Law and
legislation—United States—Addresses, essays, lectures.
I. Remick, Helen, 1942–   . II. Series.
HD6061.2U6C644   1984   331.2'1   84-41
ISBN 0-87722-345-9

62,409

This work is dedicated to my daughter, Elizabeth Remick—may the women of her generation reap the benefits of comparable worth—and to Judith Marrs, Michele Rudnick, Mary Lou Anderson Frey, and Patricia Ziobron, with regrets that clerical workers are still compensated for their contributions to such projects with acknowledgments and dedications rather than the dollars they so deserve.

Contents

Preface

HELEN REMICK

The concept of comparable worth—a policy of equal pay for work of comparable value—has the evocative power to move the former director of the Equal Employment Opportunity Commission to call it "the issue of the eighties" and a federal judge to say that it is "pregnant with the possibility of disrupting the entire economic system of the United States of America." The AFL-CIO has passed a resolution in its favor, and the Business Round-table has published a book opposing it. The Carter administration proposed enforcement regulations that would have mandated comparable worth for federal contractors; the Reagan administration rejected these regulations as too controversial.

The pattern of occupational segregation and its associated salary inequities are now well documented. Recent research by economists and sociologists indicates that the wage difference between men and women is only partly explained by worker or job characteristics (see Chapter 2). The remaining wage difference, about half of the total, is associated with the sex of the people doing the work. In fact, the sex of the workers performing a job is the best single predictor of the compensation for that job, surpassing in importance education, experience, or unionization.

Low wages are an issue not only for women, but for their families as well. Among families headed by working women, over one-third have incomes below the poverty level. As unemployment continues to be a problem, many married couples are discovering that the income of the wife, while adequate as a "supplement," is not sufficient to prevent economic disaster for the family when the husband becomes unemployed. The earnings ratio of women to men has shown no improvement over the past thirty years, and lower earning power during working years translates into poverty after retirement.

Efforts to improve women's earnings by integrating women into men's jobs have met with many obstacles. Only a few women have benefited, while most remain in traditional women's work. Men have not shown much enthusiasm for integrating women's jobs. To the degree that wages are determined by the sex of co-workers, it is obvious why many women seek men's jobs; it is equally obvious why men want to keep women out, why some women's professions are eager to attract men to their fields, and why men assiduously avoid women's work.

ix

Comparable worth addresses the sex difference in compensation that cannot otherwise be explained; when we advocate comparable worth, we mean that wages should be based upon the worth of the work, not upon the sex of the person doing it. This topic generates much heat and little light in part because it concerns one of the basic value systems of our culture: the manner in which compensation is assigned to work. Most men use their earnings as the primary measure of their self-worth; women tend to use other measures because by this measure they are nearly worthless and certainly worth less. A proposal to alter fundamentally the manner in which wages are assigned is therefore likely to arouse some emotion in virtually everyone.

Comparable worth is a policy in formation. It is the purpose of this book to present comparable worth in its full complexity in order to encourage the public discussion, research, and formation of legal strategies that are necessary for the formulation of new public policy. The contributing authors agree that salary disparities exist when male- and female-dominated occupations are compared and that these differences are based in large part on discrimination. The authors were chosen to represent a broad spectrum of perspectives on the issue, and they bring to this discussion of comparable worth the tools and assumptions of their respective fields. These differences in approach occasionally produce conflicting predictions or outcomes that beg for further study; often they complement one another, adding new dimensions to our picture of women at work.

Many discussions of comparable worth rely heavily on job evaluation as a means of measuring the value of a job and thus the differences in rates of compensation to men and women. For many years job evaluation systems have been applied by management to salary structures to justify existing policies; it has been only recently, with this new use of an old tool, that long-needed attention has been focused on how job evaluation systems work. While there are actually several broad types of job evaluation (see Chapter 4), as used in this volume the term refers to point factor job evaluation systems in which work is divided into *factors* (e.g., years of education needed, amount of precedent for decision making, or level of noise in the work environment), which are then assigned *points* for the degree the factor is present in the job. The total points assigned to a job represent its worth; in theory, at least, jobs with equal points or worth are compensated similarly. Analyses of job evaluation are inevitably technical in nature; yet comparable worth places such emphasis on it that one can hardly understand comparable worth without understanding some of the intricacies of job evaluation. As long as job evaluation in its many forms remains the central tool for measuring salary inequities, it holds the key to demonstrating and correcting this major form of discrimination; it is therefore too important to be left to management consultants and the faculties of business schools. Managers, union members, working women, politicians, and researchers must understand what is being measured and how because specific technical issues can have enormous effects on outcomes and incomes. Policies purporting to mandate comparable worth can be gutted by seemingly neutral technical decisions. Traditional applications of job evaluation systems also are in dire need of careful examination. The more job evaluation is studied, the better will be our understanding of salary-setting practices and wage inequities.

Some researchers use sophisticated mathematical techniques for salary analysis. Whether for good or ill, statistical models are now the major means of describing salary differences. The courts are joining this move, albeit reluctantly.[1] Potential plaintiffs and defendants as well as attorneys and judges need to learn to talk statistics, and soon. While authors were asked to make their articles as accessible as possible to a wide audience, some mathematics cannot be avoided when mathematical models are being described. As with job evaluation systems, the power to make public policy and bring about change belongs to those who understand the language.

This volume focuses on sex differences in wages. From overall wage data, we suspect that race is also a factor in salary setting, though not as large a factor as sex. Unfortunately, the major comparable worth studies to date

---

1. For example, in two recent and important discrimination cases brought under Title VII of the Civil Rights Act of 1964, the judges had this to say:

"This opinion has been written and rewritten, or equally accurate, has been calculated and recalculated, over the past year . . .: [T]he precisionlike mesh of numbers tends to make fits of social problems when I intuitively doubt such fits. I remain wary of the siren call of the numerical display and hope that here the resistance was adequate; that the ultimate findings are the product of judgment, not calculation. . . .

"Ultimately the findings of fact here are not numerical products and sums but a human judgment that the facts found are more likely true than not true. With that standard, stripped to essentials, and within the decisional limits placed upon me by higher courts, this is what I think happened, approximately" (District Judge Higgenbotham, *Vuyanich* v. *Republic National Bank of Dallas*, 24 FEP Cases 128.

"In closing, we add a note both rueful and cautionary. The bar is reminded that sound statistical analysis is a task both complex and arduous. Indeed, obtaining sound results by these means, results that can withstand informed testing and sifting both as to method and result, is a mission of comparable difficulty to arriving at a correct diagnosis of disease.

"We are no more statisticians than we are physicians, and counsel who expect of us informed and consistent treatment of such proofs are well advised to proceed as do those who advance knotty medical problems for resolution. Our innate capacity in such matters extends to the inexorable zero and perhaps, unevenly, somewhat beyond; but the day is long past—past at least since the Supreme Court's sophisticated analysis in *Casteneda* v. *Partida*—[citation omitted] when we proceed with any confidence toward broad conclusions from crude and incomplete statistics. That everyone who has eaten bread has died may tell us something about bread, but not very much [citation omitted]" (Circuit Judge Gee, *Wilkins* v. *University of Houston*, 26 FEP Cases 1230).

either have been conducted in jurisdictions with low minority populations, so that race segregation was not a major factor in employment patterns, or have not used race as a variable. Lacking adequate data, we will not discuss the effect of race on wages other than to suggest that minority status undoubtedly has a negative impact on earnings. We encourage researchers to include race as a factor in future studies.

This book begins by placing comparable worth in the continuum of equal employment policies. Comparable worth is related to, but different from, equal pay policies, which require that men and women receive the same pay for the same work. In her overview of comparable worth, Ronnie Steinberg discusses the policy context in which comparable worth is evolving and describes the nature of the problem it attempts to address. She discusses the characteristics of discriminatory pay policies that may lead to equal pay or comparable worth problems and introduces job evaluation as a means of measuring the extent of some kinds of discrimination.

The wage differential associated with occupational segregation is the condition that comparable worth attempts to correct. Paula England assesses the implications of a variety of economic and sociological theories posited as explanations of occupational segregation and wage disparities. England concludes that the persistence of occupational segregation is best explained by a melding of several of the theoretical models.

Patterns of occupational segregation can also be explained by psychological theories. Ann Viviano and Sharon Shepela maintain that there is a significant psychological component to wage setting and occupational segregation: "women are paid less because they are in women's jobs, and women's jobs are paid less because they are done by women. The reason is that women's work—in fact, virtually anything done by women—is characterized as less valuable." The authors' review of research in psychology lends credence to this hypothesis by demonstrating consistent patterns of undervaluation of work done by women.

Because of the importance of job evaluation to comparable worth, three chapters discuss major issues in this area. Richard and James Beatty describe major methods of assessing jobs and discuss the importance of job analysis (the description of work) to the process. They critique the various approaches and suggest future directions for job evaluation.

Donald Treiman demonstrates the effect that choice of factors and factor weights can have on the outcome of an application of a point factor job evaluation system. His data indicate that such choices are not neutral in effect and can serve as a source of sex bias.

Current pay practices are based on cultural values that are more implicit than explicit and thus are not always well thought out. Careful examination of salary structures for possible bias will inevitably uncover values that pertain to issues other than sex discrimination. Helen Remick uses the field of nursing to illustrate the conflicts that can arise as values are made explicit.

Overall salary data show that in segregated jobs work done by women pays less than work done by men. This fact alone gives no indication of *why* women earn less; perhaps they avoid responsibility, do not wish to use their education, and so on. Comparable worth advocates claim instead that women receive lower returns on their effort, skill, and responsibility than men do. Chapters 7 through 10 present four different models of measuring salary returns to workers. These chapters make it obvious that experts have not yet settled on a single approach to assessing or remedying the wage gap between men and women. Nonetheless, these various models all demonstrate sizable salary discrepancies between men and women in dollars received for comparable job demands and point to reasonable means of correcting salary inequities.

Helen Remick argues that salaries are set by a cultural value system, one that can be approximated with point factor job evaluation systems. She describes the results of the first comparable worth study, conducted in the state of Washington, and offers a definition of comparable worth that can be used to measure the effects of sex discrimination in salary policies.

David Pierson, Karen Koziara, and Russell Johannesson applied sophisticated statistical analysis to a select group of jobs in a state civil service system. They did so at the behest of a union, and here they discuss the special issues that arose in this somewhat unusual context. Women's jobs were found to be undervalued relative to male-dominated jobs, with one exception that points to a real drawback of this sort of analysis.

The federal government has evaluated many occupations according to their difficulty and complexity and the required characteristics of the workers. The evaluations are collected in a Department of Labor publication, the *Dictionary of Occupational Titles*. When these data were analyzed by Donald Treiman, Heidi Hartmann, and Patricia Roos, the authors found that 40 percent of the earnings gap between men and women is attributable to differences in job characteristics and 60 percent to differences, based on the sex of the worker, in the wages paid for these characteristics. Treiman and his colleagues describe four statistical models that could be used to correct the earnings gap and discuss the advantages and disadvantages of each.

Using economic models, Barbara Bergmann and Mary Gray describe how employer preference for males or females in particular jobs can result in salary differentials. When the marketplace at large exhibits such preference, individual employers may justify their patterns of segregation as merely reflective of a force beyond their control; Bergmann and Gray, however, argue that conformity to marketplace patterns of occupational segregation is economically unsound, thus demonstrating that employers choose to conform for motives other than profit maximization. The authors propose wage realignment as the only reasonable remedy to these illegal patterns of occupational segregation.

Antidiscrimination laws define a major arena for comparable worth. The concept is entering courts and government agencies as an extension of the equal pay for equal work doctrine and as a possible remedy for intentional occupational segregation. Under the Carter administration, federal enforcement agencies were taking the lead in discussions of action on comparable worth; the executive branch of the current administration, however, has done an about face in enforcement, leaving the courts and state enforcement agencies as the centers of action.

Implementation of comparable worth may not be as difficult or disruptive as some critics fear. Canada, for example, has adopted (with much apparent success) a comparable worth law covering employees under federal jurisdiction. This law, passed in 1977, mandates equal pay for work of equal value. Guidelines for implementation were developed only after consultation with managers, unions, and women's groups. Rita Cadieux describes the procedure followed after a complaint is filed and summarizes the settlements reached in some landmark cases. Even though several of the settlements have been costly, most have been resolved without recourse to Canadian federal courts.

Recent federal court decisions related to comparable worth under Title VII of the Civil Rights Act of 1964 and the Equal Pay Act of 1963 are reviewed by Mary Heen. Heen describes the burden of proof required in Title VII cases and outlines strategies for bringing successful cases. She concludes that future cases should be carefully selected to build the case law on which comparable worth cases can be won.

Labor unions and collective bargaining offer possibilities for implementation of comparable worth with or without reference to job evaluation. Labor unions have made comparable worth a collective bargaining issue in several jurisdictions, grounds for a strike, and the basis of several lawsuits; they are also modifying a longstanding antipathy toward job evaluation. Comparable worth is increasingly becoming an organizing tool in female-dominated segments of the workplace. Lisa Portman, Joy Ann Grune, and Eve Johnson explain the current position of labor regarding pay equity, describe the comparable worth activities of four unions, and predict future union activities.

Although most legal action on comparable worth has taken place in federal court, Virginia Dean, Patti Roberts, and Carroll Boone argue that state fair employment practice laws, equal rights amendments, and civil service laws present excellent opportunities for judicial review and action. They suggest criteria for choosing the strongest test cases appropriate for various legal systems and present tables summarizing state-by-state efforts to address comparable worth for state civil service workers. Collective bargaining laws for state workers are also reviewed, since collective bargaining is one of the major tools available for implementation of comparable worth.

Alice Cook looks at those jurisdictions where comparable worth laws have been successfully implemented and identifies the forces that brought about this outcome. Public employee unions and commissions on the status of women are shown to play important roles.

We have presented in this volume a picture of a policy in formation. Occupational segregation is now widely acknowledged, but we do not yet have a consensus on how to measure and correct the accompanying wage disparity. This disparity has implications for women far beyond the initial unfairness of receiving unequal return for work done. In a concluding chapter, Helen Remick and Ronnie Steinberg review the varying definitions of comparable worth offered in this volume. They discuss the merits of the major arguments against comparable worth and place the topic in the larger societal context. Lastly, they look at the steps involved in the transformation of comparable worth from an idea to a political policy.

A thorough exploration of comparable worth requires the expertise of persons in a wide range of fields. Sociologists, economists, and psychologists contribute the perspectives of their fields to document and explain occupational segregation patterns and the wage disparity between men and women. Measures of worth, necessary before comparisons can be made, have developed from business applications and statistical models. Whatever is documented and measured must fit into the legal framework of the courts and government enforcement agencies, and any movement for social change must take into account the political realities of governmental priorities and labor, management, and professional interests. From discussion of these various perspectives will emerge new social policy.

Whether viewed as a technical, legal, or political issue, comparable worth challenges existing norms. Its simple and straightforward premise that compensation should be free of sex bias is obviously just; it is also obviously in conflict with the way wages are now assigned. We hope that this volume will spur on the joint efforts that are needed in research, public education, political activity, labor, law, and, finally, formation of public policy. Working together we can make progress toward our goal of equity for women.

Comparable Worth
and Wage Discrimination

PART ONE

Introduction

1

"A Want of Harmony":
Perspectives on Wage Discrimination
and Comparable Worth

RONNIE J. STEINBERG

Miss Virginia Penny, who wrote in 1870 *How Women Make Money: Married or Single*, advised her readers that "we think, in the different departments of woman's labor, both physical and mental, there exists a want of harmony of labor done and the compensation" (Penny, 1870: xiii). She continued with a familiar comparable worth comparison: a gilder in a book bindery gets six dollars a week, or one dollar for a day of ten hours, which is equal to ten cents an hour. A girl at most mechanical employments receives for her sixty hours' labor three dollars a week, which is equal to five cents an hour (ibid.). Virginia Penny could have been writing today, for the "want of harmony" remains. Writing over a century later, in 1981, the National Research Council of the National Academy of Sciences (NRC/NAS) presented the same conclusion, generalizing that: "Not only do women do different work than men, but the work women do is paid less, and the more an occupation is dominated by women the less it pays" (Treiman and Hartmann, 1981:28).

One consequence of these differences in the relative wages of women and men is that the wage gap—among the oldest indicators of sexual inequality—remains wide. As of 1982 female workers earned, on average,

Acknowledgment: Cynthia Chertos, Lois Haignere, and Nancy Perlman offered extremely helpful comments on an earlier draft of this paper.

64 cents for every dollar earned by full-time year-round male workers.[1] Since 1955 women's earnings as a percentage of men's have stayed remarkably stable, especially in light of the dramatic increase over the last three decades in the proportion of women in the labor market. (see Table 1-1).

Moreover, as the NRC/NAS study established, some of the gap in wages can be accounted for by occupational sex segregation. The labor market has been and remains highly sex-segregated. Whether one calculates for 1900 or today or for some decade in between, fully two-thirds of all employed men and women would have to change jobs in order for sex-linked segregation to disappear (Hartmann and Reskin, 1983).[2] Indeed, the link between occupational segregation and labor market inequality is not unique to women. A similar relationship has been observed between the relative wages of minorities and nonminorities and occupational race segregation, although the relationship has not been found to be as pronounced as that observed for women.[3]

The policy goal of equal pay for work of comparable worth has evolved to rectify the sex and race discrimination that results from the link between the wage gap and occupational segregation. It is a type of discrimination thus far unaddressed in existing equal employment policy. Specifically, comparable worth concerns the issue of whether work done primarily by women and minorities is systematically undervalued because the work has been and continues to be done primarily by women and minorities. By "systematic undervaluation," we mean that the wages paid to women and men engaged in historically female or minority work are *artifically depressed* relative to what those wages would be if these jobs were being performed by white males.

This chapter introduces the concept of wage discrimination and the policy of comparable worth by discussing a number of background issues

1. *New York Times*, May 1982. This statistic on the wage gap is for the United States, but there is a significant wage gap in other advanced industrial democracies as well. Several of them, most notably Canada, Australia, and to a lesser extent the United Kingdom, have developed comparable worth policies as a component of their equal employment policies. A discussion of labor market inequality and comparable worth policy in other countries is, however, beyond the scope of this chapter. For a discussion, see Steinberg-Ratner (1980).

2. This finding is derived from a measure called the index of segregation. It "represents the proportion of workers of either sex who would have to move to an occupation dominated by members of the other sex for the occupational distribution of the two sexes to be identical" (Hartmann and Reskin, 1983:1).

3. The NRC/NAS study noted that the earnings difference between "men and women is greater than that between minorities and non-minorities" and that "the difference in earnings between minorities and non-minorities has declined." Its conclusion, however, is that "despite the apparently greater immediate relevance of the comparable worth issue to women than to minorities, our analysis is applicable whenever substantial job segregation between different groups exists and whenever particular jobs are dominated by particular groups" (Treiman and Hartmann, 1981:16).

Table 1-1
The Male-Female Wage Gap: 1955–1977

| Year | Median Earnings | | Women's Earnings as % of Men's | Wage Gap in Constant 1967 Dollars |
	Women	Men		
1977	$8,618	$14,626	58.9	$3,310
1976	8,099	13,455	60.2	3,141
1975	7,504	12,758	58.8	3,259
1974	6,772	11,835	57.2	3,433
1973	6,335	11,186	56.6	3,649
1972	5,903	10,202	57.9	3,435
1971	5,593	9,399	59.5	3,136
1970	5,323	8,966	59.4	3,133
1969	4,977	8,227	60.5	2,961
1968	4,457	7,664	58.2	3,079
1967	4,150	7,182	57.8	3,032
1966	3,973	6,848	58.0	2,958
1965	3,823	6,375	60.0	2,700
1964	3,690	6,195	59.6	2,696
1963	3,561	5,978	59.6	2,637
1962	3,446	5,974	59.5	2,790
1961	3,351	5,644	59.4	2,559
1960	3,293	5,417	60.8	2,394
1959	3,193	5,209	61.3	2,308
1958	3,102	4,927	63.0	2,108
1957	3,008	4,713	63.8	2,023
1956	2,827	4,466	63.3	2,014
1955	2,719	4,252	63.9	1,911

Source: U.S. Department of Commerce, Bureau of the Census, 1957–1977. "Money Income of Families and Persons in the United States," Current Population Reports. Washington, D.C.: Government Printing Office.

that set the stage for the focused case material in the subsequent chapters. I begin with an historical overview of comparable worth policy, placing it within the context of equal employment policy and identifying key events of the last five years which contributed to its evolution as a major national policy goal. I continue with an analysis of the nature of wage discrimination and its connection to the development of a comparable worth standard. This provides the basis for a brief discussion of the general methodologies currently available for identifying systematic undervaluation. I close by suggesting why the goal of comparable worth has, in its short history, engendered so much controversy.

Comparable Worth and Equal Employment Policy

Contemporary comparable worth activities activities are best treated as an outgrowth of the evolution of equal employment policy. This evolution took place over a one-hundred-year period in two broad stages. A lengthy first stage encompassed primarily state legislation and National War Labor Board orders. A more recent second phase was set into motion by several federal laws and regulations.

The development of equal employment and comparable worth is best explained from the perspective of political economy—that is, in terms of the intersection of political and economic institutions. Specifically, I regard the structure of the economy—both the organization of production and the ideology justifying it—and the distribution of political and economic power among interest groups in the labor market as profound and fundamental determinants of the parameters of social reforms and of the actual change in work organizations that can be brought about through policy implementation (Steinberg, 1983). For equal employment, entitlements were broadened and deepened gradually, primarily as a result of unions and civil rights and women's organizations building a critical mass of constituent support for their policy goals. They used, as a power resource to legitimize their demands, the growing body of social science research that captured with greater precision and insight the determinants of race and sex discrimination and the sources of the wage gap.[4]

Early History: State Legislation and National Orders

The goal of equal pay was first put forth in terms of equal pay for equal work in the late nineteenth and early twentieth centuries by the socialist movement, the trade unions, and the women's rights and suffrage movements (Cook, 1975). Equal pay for equal work has historically addressed a relatively narrow source of wage discrimination: that which is present when men and women or minorities and nonminorities perform identical work but are paid unequally for the performance of that work. The demand for equal pay recurrently surfaced in the United States and other countries, especially during World War I. It first became a widespread political demand during World War II, and several states, including New Jersey, Illinois, and New York, passed equal pay acts or fair employment practices acts prohibiting discrimination in compensation. During World War II proponents of equal pay—most notably trade unions—made progress through complaints to the National War Labor Board (WLB): over two thousand equal pay adjustments were reported to the WLB between November 1942 and October 1943 (Milkman, 1981:182). During its tenure, the WLB enacted some precedent-setting general orders, including the pathbreaking General Order No. 16, which established the principle of equal pay for equal work as

---

4. The definitive history of equal pay for work of comparable worth remains to be written. This overview of the first stage of its evolution draws heavily on Cook (1975), Milkman (1981), and Steinberg (1982). For a different reading of similar historical facts, see Williams and McDowell (1980).

board policy in late 1942, and a later decision in support of the broader concept of comparable worth.

General Order No. 16 addressed a dispute between the General Motors Corporation and the United Auto Workers. In its decision, the WLB ordered the company and the unions to include an equal pay clause in their contracts, which they did. The decision explicitly stated that it would be unacceptable to use "slight or inconsequential changes in a job as a reason for setting up a wage differential against women employees" (Milkman, 1981:182–83).

In a highly original study of equal pay activities during the war, Ruth Milkman identifies several unique aspects of the war years as significant in finally stimulating political activity and government support for equal pay. These included the wartime wage freeze and no-strike pledge, which made equal pay disputes before the WLB one of the few avenues available for increasing wages, and the New Deal orientation of the WLB and the society in general, which provided unions with the backing of government policy and public opinion in their efforts to constrain management discretion over the terms and conditions of work (Milkman, 1981:181). It is important to note that union support for equal pay at this time was stimulated primarily by the fear that women's entrance into male jobs would lead to a wartime and postwar reduction of the wage rates for these jobs. Theresa Wolfson, a prominent observer of the labor movement, summarized labor's reasoning in an article she wrote during World War II:

> Even though some members of trade unions balked at the entrance of women into their industry, they recognize that . . . wage differentials represent a serious bone of conflict in a possible postwar era of unemployment. Not out of altruism but out of pure self-preservation, many unions have insisted on the "equal pay for equal work" doctrine; for where an employer can get his work done by a labor force which costs less, he is less likely to concern himself with sex, race, or religion of that labor supply" (1943:50).

Getting government regulations is not the same as achieving equal pay in the workplace, however. Disputes subsequent to the one between General Motors and the UAW led to the second pathbreaking case: the 1945 suit brought by the United Electrical Workers of America (UE) against both General Electric and Westinghouse. Identified as "the first national-level case to establish the concept . . . known as 'equal pay for comparable worth'" (Milkman, 1981:185), these UE complaints developed out of long-term union efforts to narrow wage differentials between women's and men's work. The 1942 UE national agreement with Westinghouse, for example, included a clause reducing sex differentials by two cents per hour (ibid., p. 193), and the union regularly challenged management designations of new jobs as women's work, These progressive union policies were a response to the large proportion of female membership and to "the arbitrariness of the boundaries between men's and women's jobs in electrical manufacturing [which] had always been relatively transparent" (ibid., p. 194).

In its decision, the WLB indicated that this was not an equal pay case. Rather, it noted that the issue was "that the jobs customarily performed by women are paid less, on a comparative job content basis, than the jobs customarily performed by men," and "that this relative underpayment constitutes a sex discrimination" (ibid., p. 195).

Attacking the job evaluation systems used by GE and Westinghouse, the union explicitly cited discrimination in the assignment of unequal wages to jobs rated as equal in content. The companies in turn maintained that their own equal ratings obscured the fact that women performed jobs of lesser content. Both companies invoked the now famous "sociological factors" argument in justifying lower wages for women's work. As the Westinghouse wage administration manual stated:

> The gradient of the women's wage curve is not the same for women as for men because of the more transient character of the service of the former, the relative shortness of their activity in industry, the differences in environment required, the extra services that must be provided, overtime limitations, extra help needed for the occasional heavy work, and the general sociological factors not requiring discussion herein. (Ibid., p. 197)

The WLB accepted the UE's arguments on the inequitable wage structure and on 29 November 1945 issued a favorable decision that was ignored by the companies.[5] On 17 December the WLB issued a second lame-duck ruling requiring the companies "to raise women's pay by 4 cents an hour and to set aside a 2 cent per hour fund for each women employed, the distribution of which was to be determined by collective bargaining" (Milkman, 1981:99). While the ruling was never complied with because the WLB was no longer in operation, it did set a precedent for a 1946 UE strike settlement establishing the principle of flat-rate wage increases as a means of reducing wage inequities (ibid.).

After World War II it was assumed that women would leave the labor market. At the very least they, along with minorities, were expected to step

---

5. Two opponents of comparable worth, Robert E. Williams and Douglas S. McDowell, have concluded that the WLB arrived at a qualified decision, choosing "not to engage itself in job evaluation or job comparisons to determine whether specific job wage rates were the result of sex discrimination," but rather relying "upon the evaluations performed by the particular employees" (1980:211). Milkman, however, states that the unions presented Westinghouse's and General Electric's own evaluation plans as evidence of discrimination (1981:198). As indicated, the board accepted the union's arguments.

aside from the positions they held during the war to provide jobs for returning (white and male) war veterans. Instead, many women remained employed, if not in "male jobs," in lower-paid "women's jobs." Union women continued to press for equal pay legislation. Often they received the support of their unions. The demand for equal pay for equal work was carried to both state legislatures and Congress. A number of the more highly unionized states enacted equal pay laws or fair employment practices acts prohibiting "discrimination in compensation." (Chapters 14 and 15 in this volume argue that these laws may in the near future be reinterpreted or modified to encompass a comparable worth standard.)

Congressional efforts met with little success, however. In 1945 an equal pay bill was approved in committees of both houses but never came to a vote (Baker, 1964:415). In 1947 President Truman proposed that the Fair Labor Standards Act (FLSA) be amended to prohibit discrimination in employment, including wage discrimination on the basis of sex. Although the law was strongly supported by the Congress of Industrial Organizations (CIO), it made little headway (Rayback, 1966:405), in part because of the general antiunion backlash of the late 1940s and 1950s.

The 1960s: Federal Equal Employment Policy

The UE continued its comparable worth campaign after World War II. The 1946 settlement with Westinghouse, for example, included "a 19 cent across-the-board increase, plus a fund of one cent per hour per worker, to be applied to the equalization of women's rates." In the GE settlement, "UE . . . negotiated an additional 4 1/2-cent increase for two-thirds of the company's female employees," above the 18 1/2-cent across-the-board increase (Milkman, 1981:327). But, as Milkman notes, the power of the union was significantly reduced relative to its wartime strength, and gains were minimal.

The Women's Bureau of the U.S. Department of Labor provided sustained support to proponents of equal pay legislation after the war, as Alice Cook points out in Chapter 15. In 1952, for example, the bureau consolidated the activities of some twenty large national organizations into a united campaign for passage of a federal law. Yet these forces had to await a more favorable political climate to see their goal realized.

It was not until the early 1960s that an equal pay bill finally received serious attention in Congress. This shift in favor of federal legislation was the result of two changes in the political climate: first, the labor movement and the civil rights movement had delivered the critical margin of votes necessary for the Kennedy (and Democratic Party) victory in 1960. The political platforms of these movements were now treated with a seriousness not seen since the New Deal. Second, the contemporary women's movement was beginning to formulate and press for its own political priorities. Equal pay, long an issue associated with women's rights (albeit for reasons having to do with the anxieties of male workers), took on a new meaning consistent with the newly expressed interests of women (Steinberg, 1982).

In 1963 Congress passed the equal pay amendment to the Fair Labor Standards Act, one of the first federal laws requiring that women and men be paid the same wages for "equal work." This equal work standard was not the one originally proposed: the comparable worth standard was introduced into the 1962 bill considered by the House with the strong endorsement of the Kennedy administration and the support of women's and union groups.[6] The bill was amended several times after lengthy debate, however, to eliminate the comparable worth standard. Representative Goodell characterized the amendments as a:

> clear intention . . . to narrow the whole concept. We went from "comparable" to "equal," meaning that the jobs involved should be . . . very much like or closely related to each other. We do not expect the Labor Department people to go into an establishment and attempt to rate jobs that are not equal." (*Congressional Record* 9197 [1963], as quoted in Milkovich and Broderick, 1982:310)

The bill finally enacted by Congress in 1963 provided "for equal pay for equal work on jobs the performance of which requires equal skill, effort and responsibility and which are performed under similar working conditions" (Livernash, 1980: 217–18).

The 1964 Civil Rights Act prohibited discrimination in the terms and conditions of employment based on race, sex, religion, and national origin. The language of Title VII of the act, including its prohibition of discrimination in compensation, was modeled on the state fair employment practices legislation mentioned above. The passage of Title VII capped a thirty-year effort to obtain a national mandate to replace limited state statutes.

Executive Orders 11246 and 11375, issued respectively in 1965 and 1968, developed federal equal employment policy still further. They made it illegal for federal contractors to discriminate by race and sex in their employment policies or practices and required employers to take affirmative action to correct for such discrimination.

These first pieces of federal policy defined discrimination cautiously. As indicated above, the equal pay amendment restricted the definition of

---

6. The comparability concept had already been established in several international agreements directly endorsed or indirectly supported by the United States. These include Convention 100 of the International Labour Organization, promulgated in 1951, which stated: "each member shall . . . promote and . . . ensure the application to all workers of the principle of equal remuneration of men and women workers for work of equal value," and Article 119 of the Treaty of Rome, which in 1961 contained a nonbinding clause on equal remuneration (Steinberg-Ratner, 1980:30).

equality to wage rate comparisons between men and women performing identical or essentially similar work. The act provided, for example, that janitors and cleaning women could be paid the same wages if they are found doing similar work. Likewise, discrimination under Title VII was originally characterized as the intentional and conscious prejudice or bias of an individual employer against an individual woman or minority employee.[7] To some extent the watering down of the equal pay standard and the narrow definition of discrimination in Title VII reflected the power positions of interest groups supporting the 1962 bill and the lack of systematic (as opposed to anecdotal) information they could gather to support their arguments about the sources and consequences of labor market inequality.[8] As opponents of comparable worth are now quick to point out, "Congress examined and rejected in 1963 a theory of discrimination which would have allowed findings of discrimination to be based upon pay differentials for 'comparable' male and female jobs" (Williams and McDowell, 1980:212).

Although equal pay policy expanded slightly to allow for broader job comparisons, perhaps the most significant consequence of the first decade of enforcement of the federal laws and orders was a redefinition of what constitutes discrimination under Title VII.[9] Pivotal was the 1971 decision in

---

7. Prior to the enactment of Title VII, sex discrimination per se in most of the terms and conditions of employment was given almost no consideration. In contrast, sex-based wage discrimination was seriously and extensively examined prior to the enactment of the Equal Pay Amendments to the Fair Labor Standards Act (Williams and McDowell, 1980:212). Yet the decision to include sex discrimination in the prohibitions under Title VII was not made in a vacuum, and conservative congressmen may have gotten the idea from women lobbyists—for example, those from the National Women's Party. Its inclusion, Caroline Bird (1972) and other writers contend, was meant to discredit Title VII and hopefully to lead to its demise. Little did those conservatives know that the women's movement would indeed have the last laugh, in dead seriousness.

8. In a study of the rise and growth of six laws on wage and hour standards, I found that the weaker the power position of the advocates of a reform, the narrower the scope of coverage and the lower the standards legislated (Steinberg, 1982). For an intriguing history of the passage of the 1963 Equal Pay Act (although the authors oppose a comparable worth policy), see Williams and McDowell (1980:212–21).

9. Even the research programs carried out over this ten-year period shifted paradigmatically from an individualist to a structural perspective. Early researchers accounted for wage differences primarily by pointing to differences in "human capital" (or education and experience) brought into the labor market, in the choices made in relation to human capital, and in other responsibilities and roles. Whatever could not be accounted for was assumed to be at least partly the product of discrimination. To explain some of the variance, other researchers began to identify and incorporate into their models market characteristics that might explain wage differences by sex or race. One of these factors—occupational segregation—accounted for a considerable amount of the observed variation in wages, but these authors did not regard it as necessarily discriminatory. Rather, as Paula England notes in Chapter 2, the occupational segregation of female workers was viewed as a consequence of the

Griggs v. *Duke Power Company* (401 U.S. 424 3 EPD 8137), in which the Supreme Court "language . . . focuses . . . not on a 'series of isolated and distinguishable events . . . due to ill will' but to a description of the problem 'in terms of systems and effects'" (Robertson, 1980:133). Following this lead, the senate committee shaping the 1972 amendments to Title VII reported that:

> Employment discrimination as viewed today is a . . . complex and pervasive phenomenon. Experts familiar with the subject . . . describe the problem in terms of "systems" and "effects" . . . and the literature on the subject is replete with discussions of the mechanics of seniority and lines of progression, perpetuation of . . . discriminatory practices through . . . institutional devices, and testing and validation procedures. (Quoted in Robertson, 1980:131)

The legislative history behind the 1972 amendments made it clear that the focus of discrimination was no longer on employer behavior, but instead firm procedures and hiring, initial assignment, and promotion policies (Alvarez et al., 1979; Feagin and Feagin, 1978).

In the decade between 1965 and 1975, social scientists—particularly economists—brought forth a rich literature addressing the nature, scope, and parameters of employment discrimination (see, for example, Perlman and Ennis, 1980). Many of these studies contributed to the development of the schools of thought on job segregation and wage inequity discussed by Paula England in Chapter 2. These studies were influential as well in redefining discrimination in equal employment policy, as the preceding quotation suggests. In some instances, scholars testified directly in court or in legislative or administrative hearings. More frequently, their views were summarized in legal briefs or in the testimony of leaders of trade unions or civil rights or women's organizations (Bureau of National Affairs, 1973).

Comparable Worth: First Efforts

Title VII's systemic approach to discrimination provided the conceptual, if not yet the legal, foundation for efforts to achieve a comparable worth policy. By the mid-1970s one could identify a number of isolated activities aimed at rectifying that component of wage discrimination linked to pervasive sex and race segregation in the labor market. Two of the most

---

home responsibilities that forced them to accept a career pattern of intermittent employment. A second group of social scientists argued, on the contrary, that institutional and organizational characteristics were more important than human capital in understanding wage differences, contending as well that these were the consequence of discrimination resulting from pervasive sex and race segregation of occupations and industries.

important were set into motion by the government employees' union, the American Federation of State, County and Municipal Employees (AFSCME) and the International Union of Electrical, Radio and Machine Workers (IUE). First, in 1974, at the request of AFSCME, and with the cooperation of the Commission on the Status of Women, the state of Washington undertook a comparable pay study. (See Chapter 7 as well as Remick, 1980, for a case history and summary of the study.) The study, conducted by Norman D. Willis and Associates, found that female jobs received on average approximately 20 percent lower pay than male jobs with the same number of factor points.

Second, IUE continued the World War II efforts of UE in the electrical industries by forming a Title VII compliance program in 1972. Because of what IUE came to call "initial assignment discrimination," women were being denied the better-paying jobs. Women were assigned to traditionally female jobs and were paid less than men who were performing traditionally male jobs, even though male jobs required no greater skill, effort, or responsibility. Moreover, women were denied access to better-paying jobs through restricted career ladders (Newman and Vonhof, 1981; Newman and Wilson, 1981:326). Westinghouse was targeted and challenged by the union as part of this compliance program. Several Westinghouse plants revised their contracts through out-of-court settlements, and one of the campaigns resulted in *IUE* v. *Westinghouse Electric Corp* (CA 3, 1980, 23 FEP Cases 588), in which a U.S. court of appeals upheld the union's claim of intentional initial assignment discrimination (Bureau of National Affairs, 1981:7).

It was not until late 1977, however, when Equal Employment Opportunity Commission Chair Eleanor Holmes Norton identified the issue as a priority of her administration, that the comparable worth issue achieved national visibility. First, the EEOC contracted with the NRC/NAS to form a committee whose tasks included examining the feasibility of implementing a comparable worth policy. Norton's selection of the NRC/NAS to carry out the investigation appeared to be strategic and intentional: because she sensed that the issue was both complicated and controversial, she seemed to want to start slowly. She also, wanted if possible, the opinion of "organized science" in support of the existence of wage discrimination and the feasibility of implementing comparable worth. Later, in April 1980, prior to the release of the NRC/NAS report, the EEOC held hearings on wage discrimination and comparable worth. Over two dozen social scientists, lawyers, and representatives of unions, women's organizations, civil rights organizations, and businesses testified. The published transcript ran to over 1,200 pages (EEOC, 1980).

Perhaps most importantly, Norton's actions and commitment helped generate the formation of a national network of groups and individuals working to attain equal pay for work of comparable worth at the state or municipal level, in particular firms or agencies in the private or public sector.

Her efforts had a connection, for example, to the formation in 1981 of the National Committee on Pay Equity. In October 1979 representatives of almost a dozen organizations held a National Conference on Pay Equity, attended by over two hundred experts and activists. The proceedings of the conference formed the core of the *Manual on Pay Equity* (Grune, 1980), one of the first comprehensive resource books on comparable worth for policy-makers and organizers. One year later, this same group organized the founding convention of the National Committee on Pay Equity, a membership organization of over a hundred organizations and individuals, including labor unions, professional associations, women's and civil rights groups, and state and local government agencies. The committee's three functions are supporting ongoing pay equity initiatives, encouraging new ones, and assisting in strategy development among the diverse constituencies. (Joy Ann Grune, executive director of the committee, is a co-author of Chapter 13.) These efforts were paralleled by the development of comparable worth networks on the West Coast, including the Comparable Worth Project, a California-based clearinghouse. (Its original directors, Virginia Dean and Patti Roberts, have joined with Carroll Boone to contribute Chapter 14 on state laws.)

By 1980, comparable worth was a *visible* national demand supported largely by women's rights organizations, state commissions on the status of women, and trade unions. But the type of wage discrimination addressed by a comparable worth policy had yet to be institutionally acknowledged and legitimized through some policy or program that would lead to a re-evaluation of the actual wages paid to actual women workers.[10]

Comparable Worth: A Second Turning Point

Three events in 1981 contributed to the legitimacy of a policy of comparable worth. On June 9, 1981, the Supreme Court ruled in *County of Washington* v. *Gunther* (49 USLW 4623) that wage discrimination claims brought under Title VII are not restricted to claims for equal pay for substantially equal work. Although the Court was careful to emphasize that

---

10. A comparable worth policy was enacted in 1978 by the federal government of Canada. The Human Rights Act contained the first legal comparable worth standard. Covering federal employees and those engaged in interstate commerce, it provides for the comparison of dissimilar jobs. As part of its enforcement activity, the Human Rights Commission has developed a method for assessing the discriminatory bias of existing job evaluation schemes. These efforts proved influential in the United States, although many thought the types of comparisons being made for purposes of modifying wages for "women's" work were similar to those already established under the U.S. equal pay law. As a result, the act has served only as a limited precedent for a U.S. comparable worth policy. The Canadian approach and early cases are described by Rita Cadieux in Chapter 11.

the claim in *Gunther* was "not based on the controversial concept of comparable worth," it also indicated that the Court would be willing to regard certain explicit inequities between dissimilar jobs as constituting wage discrimination under Title VII. Thus, it set the stage for future court decisions, both articulating which forms of wage discrimination would be prohibited and setting forth a standard of comparable worth. (Mary Heen treats the influence of the *Gunther* and other decisions in the evolving comparable worth case law Chapter 12.)

A month later, in July, the public employees of San Jose went on strike over the issue of comparable worth even though public employee strikes are illegal in California. The city manager had previously hired a job evaluator to study the salaries for management positions and recommend adjustments. While the findings of this study were being implemented, AFSCME Local 101 pressured for a comparable worth study of nonexempt jobs. After considerable resistance, the manager and city council agreed to conduct a study and negotiate over its findings. The study, conducted by Hay Associates (perhaps the foremost management consultant on classification issues), found that female jobs received from 2 percent to 10 percent lower pay than the average rate for all jobs in the city.

Despite the agreement to negotiate, the parties made little headway in hammering out a strategy for making the wage adjustments warranted by the study findings. The union finally filed a complaint with the EEOC. Angered by this, the city manager refused to continue negotiations. Early in July 1981, the union voted to strike.[11] One week later, the parties reached a tentative agreement. While the agreement did not endorse the principle of comparable worth or incorporate it into the contract, it did provide salary adjustments for undervalued female-dominated job titles.

In the fall of that year, the Norton-commissioned NRC/NAS committee issued its long-overdue final report, *Women, Work and Wages Equal Pay for Jobs of Equal Value* (Treiman and Hartmann, 1981). Despite its cautious style, the study conclusions were crisp and to the point: "On the basis of the review of the evidence, our judgment is that there is substantial discrimination in pay" (p. 91), and "in our judgment job evaluation plans provide measures of job worth that, under certain circumstances, may be used to discover and reduce wage discrimination" (p. 95). While the report was essentially devoted to technical issues, it provided strong evidence of the distributive injustices suffered by women and men performing work historically associated with women. Moreover, by suggesting possible modifica-

---

11. Initially the union received approval from the local Labor Council to go out on strike in early May because of the lack of progress in negotiations. Just before the strike deadline, an agreement was reached to negotiate over the study findings during the general negotiations scheduled for the summer.

tions of job evaluation techniques, it undercut some of the strongest of the opponents' arguments against comparable worth. Although clearly not intended as such, the study's findings provided a useful power resource to comparable worth proponents and especially to women workers, the immediate beneficiaries of a comparable worth policy.

The comparable worth activities of the last half-dozen years represent a new and exciting stage in the long-term efforts to achieve labor market equality for women. In the late 1960s and early 1970s, more and more people came to understand that discrimination is not merely intentional but systemic—that it is, in other words, intrinsic to the operation of most work organizations and of the labor market as a whole. This critical support created an environment conducive to broadening the definition of discrimination through court decisions, strong and detailed administrative guidelines, and, finally, an amended Title VII. Successful reform of national and state legislation, in turn, provided the impetus to address other and new sources of discrimination. Indeed, among the major activities of the last half-dozen years has been general information gathering and the completion of comparable worth studies. Most state and municipal studies have been initiated by local unions, especially in the public sector, or by state commissions on the status of women. Funding for the studies has been provided in a variety of ways—through state funds under the Comprehensive Education and Training Act, legislative appropriations, governor-sponsored appropriations, or funds bargained for in labor-management contracts. All the studies have found substantial undervaluation of women's work.

The technical basis for estimating the extent of wage discrimination has been hotly debated by proponents and opponents of comparable worth, and many of the subsequent chapters address this issue. The next section of this chapter discusses the type of wage discrimination to be addressed through a comparable worth policy. It then presents a brief overview of the standards and techniques that are being used to assess the extent and scope of discrimination.

Occupational Segregation and Wage Discrimination

Comparable worth policy addresses that portion of the wage gap between women and men or minorities and nonminorities that is due to the systematic undervaluation of women's or minorities' work. A first question, then, is whether and to what extent such systematic undervaluation contributes to the observed wage gap. Answering this question was the major objective of the NRC/NAS Committee, which reviewed existing research and conducted original research when necessary both to determine the relationship between occupational segregation and the wage gap and to assess whether any of the observed relationship could be a function of discrimination. The committee determined that "women are systematically underpaid . . . [and] that the strategy of 'comparable worth' merits consideration as an alternative policy of intervention in the pay setting process" (Treiman and Hartmann, 1981:66–67).

Nevertheless, the wage gap associated with occupational segregation is not entirely a function of discrimination. Occupational segregation may translate into wage differences for two reasons. First, women and members of minority groups may be segregated into jobs that require less skill, effort, and responsibility than jobs filled by white males. Industrial psychologists and labor economists have come to call these job features "productivity-related job content characteristics" (Milkovich, 1980). If this is the case, wage differences are legitimately derived from differences in job prerequisites, requirements, and responsibilities. One study completed by the NRC/NAS staff did find that some small percentage of the difference in earnings could be accounted for by such job content differences as complexity and supervisory duties (Roos, 1981). The policy already embodied in Title VII exists to eliminate this source of the wage gap by using incentives and sanctions to increase the mobility of women and minorities into higher-paying white male jobs.

Second, women and minorities may be segregated into lower-paying jobs that require the equivalent amount of skill, effort, and responsibility as white male jobs. The NRC/NAS study also found that the percentage of female incumbents in a job was an important determinant of earnings. Some firm-level studies have reported the same finding. The state of Washington study, one of the first comparable worth projects completed, found that the job of a licensed practical nurse (an historically female job) required skill, effort, and responsibility equivalent to that of a campus police officer (an historically male job) (Remick, 1980). In 1978 the state of Washington paid a licensed practical nurse, on average, $739 a month. The campus police officer was paid, on average, $1,070 a month. These salary differences could not be justified in terms of productivity-related job content characteristics. The issue of comparable worth is concerned with this type of wage discrimination—that is, with differences that result from the systematic undervaluation of work performed predominantly by women and minorities.

Comparable Worth: A Standard and Technique for Assessing Relative Job "Worth"

Because a comparable worth policy involves identifying and correcting for the undervaluation of women's and minorities' work, it requires a technique for identifying and a standard for assessing the relative worth of jobs. In the words of the NRC/NAS Committee, "to adjust the pay rates of jobs . . . to remove what would be considered the discriminatory component . . . requires . . . development of a means for identifying whether and

what portion of pay differences in jobs within a firm are discriminatory"
(Treiman and Hartmann, 1981:69).

A Standard of Relative Job Worth

I indicated above that a comparable worth policy would not eliminate all
the differences in the wages paid for women's and men's and minorities' and
nonminorities' work because some are a function of actual job differences.
Comparable worth, then, is concerned only with eliminating those differences in wage rates that cannot be accounted for by productivity-related job
content characteristics. A standard can be *partly* based on market wages,
which are, after all, among the best available indicators of the value of work
to an employer on the so-called free labor market. While people work for
lots of different reasons, the essence of the labor contract—in theory, if not
in practice—is that employees are rewarded for the work they perform
because of the contribution (i.e., value) of that work to the employer. Yet,
comparable worth cannot be based solely on market wages, since, as the
NAS/NRC report stated, they reflect many factors other than the "marginal
productivity" of a job, including discrimination (ibid., p. 65). Moreover,
while there is considerable overlap in wage rates across firms, the overall
wage structure within a firm will differ from that of other firms as a function
of such factors as types of jobs, unionization, and characteristics of the
industry (Milkovich, 1980). A comparable worth policy must adopt a standard that takes into account these firm-based differences in wage structure.

For these reasons, the standards used in determining worth must be
both partly derived from market wages and, perhaps more importantly,
firm-based. Where there is no union representation, the standard has to be
determined by the employer. Where unions bargain with employers over
wages, it is necessary to take the perspectives of both management and labor
into account.

Consequently, there can be no absolute standard of comparable worth.
As the NRC/NAS Committee reasoned:

> Acceptance of a comparable worth approach—the attempt to measure
> the worth of jobs directly on the basis of their content—does not require
> an absolute standard by which the value or worth of all jobs can be
> measured. In the judgment of the committee, no such standard exists,
> nor, in our society, is likely to exist. The relative worth of jobs reflects
> value judgments as to what features of jobs ought to be compensated,
> and such judgments vary from industry to industry, even from firm to
> firm. Paying jobs according to their worth requires only that whatever
> characteristics of jobs are regarded as worthy of compensation by an
> employer should be equally so regarded irrespective of the sex, race, or
> ethnicity of job incumbents. (Ibid., p. 70)

Techniques for Measuring Relative Job Worth

An examination of wage discrimination for purposes of establishing comparable worth should ideally meet two objectives. First, it must determine whether the salaries associated with female- and minority-dominated job titles accurately reflect an explicit and consistently applied standard of value or whether they are artificially depressed because women and minorities fill the jobs. Second, it must pinpoint job titles that may be undervalued and then develop estimates of the potential costs of correcting for this wage discrimination. To meet these objectives, we need a technique that will describe job content or attributes (i.e., behaviors, tasks, and functions) comprehensively and consistently. We also need a technique for assigning a standard of value or worth to what is actually done on the job.

The combination of job analysis and job evaluation has historically offered one way to measure value or worth in terms somewhat independent of the wage rate. While both techniques go back almost a century, their use did not become widespread until World War II, when employers found them to be useful tools by which to establish a hierarchy of jobs as a basis for setting salaries (Treiman, 1979). Currently, many private firms, especially large firms, the federal government, many states, and some municipalities use formal systems to evaluate and classify jobs (Treiman and Hartmann, 1981). According to a Bureau of National Affairs report, Hay Associates, probably the largest and best-known job evaluation consultants in the United States, "numbers among its clients approximately 40 percent of the Fortune 500 companies" (1981:45).

The general purpose of *job content analysis* is to gather thorough and accurate descriptions of the range of tasks, behaviors, or functions associated with a job. As Richard and James Beatty note (Chapter 4), "job characteristics" may comprise such dimensions as skill, effort, responsibility, and working conditions, or they may be defined more specifically to include such items as job-related experience, length of formal training required, frequency of work review, the number of other workers an employee is responsible for, impact on and responsibility for budget, physical stress, time spent working under deadlines, time spent in processing information, and so on. Information typically is gathered through questionnaires (completed by job incumbents, supervisors, job analysts, or some combination of these) and job analysts' observations of a group of incumbents performing their jobs.

The purpose of *job evaluation* is to delineate standards of worth in terms of a set of job content criteria applied consistently to all job titles in a work organization for the purpose of ordering jobs according to these standards. Typically, jobs are assigned points depending on the weighting of these factors. These weights are derived either from classical job evaluation systems, as discussed in Chapter 7, or through a statistical analysis that is reviewed and can be modified by the parties to the labor contract, as discussed in Chapter 8. On the basis of the point value, wages are assigned to a job, and jobs are allocated over a wage structure.

When carried out by general classification consultants to design a wage structure within a firm, these techniques serve to legitimize salaries in terms of two dimensions of equity: internal equity, explained here by Richard and James Beatty as "related to the relative value of jobs within a firm," and external equity, related to "the value of each job with respect to prevailing labor market prices" (see Chapter 4). When used to examine a classification system for the purpose of assessing comparable worth, it is necessary to introduce a third dimension: gender and race equity. Operationally, this means comparing male- and female-dominated or minority- and nonminority-dominated jobs to determine whether job titles with the same total point value receive the same wages. Note that just as classification systems distribute highly dissimilar jobs along a wage structure using, in most circumstances, a point factor system, comparable worth research makes it possible to compare male and female or minority and nonminority jobs with very different characteristics. With point-factor-based job evaluation systems, jobs receiving the same total point value need not have identical or even very similar content. In a Minnesota study, for example, Registered Nurse, a female-dominated job title, received 275 points, the same total point value assigned to Vocational Education Teacher, a male-dominated title. The specific content characteristics of the two jobs are quite dissimilar, yet the types of prerequisites and the tasks associated with these jobs were found to be of equivalent worth to the state of Minnesota.

Introducing the dimension of gender or race equity into systems of job analysis and evaluation raises a number of thorny methodological complications that are only beginning to be addressed through research and analysis. The NRC/NAS final report highlights these complications (many of which were discussed at even greater length in the committee's interim report, *Job Evaluation: An Analytic Review* [Treiman, 1979]):

> A number of features of existing job evaluation systems make them less than optimal for use in the resolution of pay discrimination disputes. First, formal job evaluation systems order jobs by reference to a set of compensable factors—that is, factors thought to be legitimate bases of pay differentials. . . . The factors and their relative weights are often chosen in such a way as to closely replicate existing wage hierarchies. For that reason, they can hardly serve as an independent standard against which to assess the possibility of bias in existing pay rates. Second, it is possible that the process of describing and evaluating jobs reflects pervasive cultural stereotypes regarding the relative worth of work traditionally done by men and work traditionally done by women. These features of job evaluation systems make it probable that their use

as a standard of job worth understates the extent of differences in pay based on sex and perhaps on race or ethnicity. Third, most firms currently use more than one job evaluation plan, a practice that restricts comparisons between jobs to those within sectors of a firm—e.g., shop jobs, office jobs, or executive jobs. Finally, there are potentially serious technical shortcomings in the way regression procedures arc used to create job evaluation formulas. (Treiman and Hartmann, 1981:81)

Yet comparable pay studies have been and are being carried out primarily in the public sector. As of September 1982 the National Committee on Pay Equity estimated that over two dozen inquiries (including a half-dozen major studies) had been carried out in states and municipalities (Perlman and Grune, 1982). Using at least four different types of job analysis and job evaluation, these studies consistently reported that the female-dominated job titles commanded salaries 5 to 20 percent lower than male jobs with the same number of factor points. (Because of the small proportion of minority employees, the studies focused only on the under-valuation of women's work.) Along with the Washington and San Jose research mentioned above, these studies included a Connecticut study, completed in February 1980, which examined comparable worth and as-sessed the overall quality of the existing system of classification and compensation. It found that when jobs of equivalent worth are compared, individuals in "women's" jobs make from 81 to 92 percent of the salaries of individuals in "men's" jobs. (See Chapter 15 in this volume.)

In Idaho changes made in a 1975 merit system law instituted an objective job evaluation system based on the principle of equal pay for equal job content value. Although comparable worth was not a specific study objective, implementation of the plan resulted in larger salary increases for predominantly female classifications relative to traditionally male ones.

In Michigan in 1980 a preliminary investigation found pervasive sex segregation of state jobs. This stimulated a more comprehensive comparable worth study, in which two job evaluation approaches were used to assess undervaluation. The study, cautiously and with qualifications, found that the state classification systems contained some wage inequities based on sex appears to exist in the State pay systems and that the actual maximum pay rates for female-dominated jobs were lower than would have been the case based on the wages paid for comparable male jobs (Office of Women and Work, Michigan Department of Labor, 1981).

Finally, in Pennsylvania in 1980 the Comparable Worth Committee of Council 13 of AFSCME contracted with two industrial psychologists at the Center for Labor and Human Resource Studies at Temple University to carry out a comparable pay analysis on a small group of job titles on the lower end of the classification system. This study found that "for the jobs studied, differences existed in the wages paid for predominantely male and female jobs of comparable worth. The average difference between existing wages for female jobs and predicted wages for female jobs based on wages for male jobs was $1.10 per hour. This represents an annual amount of about $2,228" (Pierson and Koziara, 1981; see also Chapter 8).

Job Evaluation and Wage Discrimination

Job evaluation has been cautiously endorsed by the NAS/NRC as a technique for assessing wage discrimination. It has also been used in states and municipalities to measure the extent of undervaluation. Indeed, Helen Remick, in her chapter on the state of Washington study, (Chapter 7), operationally defines comparable worth as "the application of a single, bias-free point factor job evaluation system within a given establishment, across job families, both to rank-order jobs and to set salaries." A policy of comparable worth, then, would require that existing and newly developed classification systems in firms be based on such a single, bias-free system. A situation of wage discrimination would be said to exist in job evaluation systems where standards of worth are inconsistently applied or job content is inaccurately or incompletely assessed for jobs held by women or minorities. Let us illustrate each of these sources of wage discrimination.

Inconsistent Application of Values

IUE v. *Westinghouse* provides an excellent example of the inconsistent application of standards of worth. Westinghouse was one of a number of corporations that standardized wage rates in the 1930s. One job evaluation system was applied to all jobs. For the purpose of assigning wages, the jobs were first categorized by sex. Jobs primarily held by women paid approximately 80 percent of the rate for male-dominated jobs with the same job evaluation points. As the NRC/NAS Committee remarked, "the hourly wage rates were established in such a way as to pay all of the female labor grades less than the lowest male labor grade, despite the fact that the parallel male and female grades represented jobs of comparable worth according to the company's own criteria" (Treiman and Hartmann, 1981:57–58).

Negotiations between American Telephone & Telegraph and the Communications Workers of America over the classification of telephone operators offer a second example. AT&T uses separate job evaluation schemes for its nonmanagerial and managerial employees. The managerial job evaluation system assigns a high point value to customer contact. By contrast, telephone operators were given almost no points for customer contact, even though the company randomly screens the operators' calls to assess the quality of assistance. The job of telephone operator was recently upgraded to take into account the importance AT&T places on customer contact.

These examples represent the use by employers of two standards—one for predominantly male work and one for predominantly female work. Under a comparable worth standard, the women at Westinghouse would have received the same pay per job evaluation point as the men did, and telephone operators' customer contact would be as highly valued as that of managers.

Incomplete Assessment of Jobs

A study of the third edition of the *Dictionary of Occupational Titles* (Witt and Naherny, 1975) illustrates a second problem—incomplete assessment. The *DOT*, compiled by the U.S. Department of Labor, lists almost every job title along with a rating of the job in terms of a skill-complexity code. The code is built on the assumption that "every job requires a worker to function at some definable level with regard to Data, People and Things" (ibid, p. 24).

Witt and Naherny, researchers at the University of Wisconsin extension school, were disturbed by the ratings given to certain types of predominantly women's work. For instance, dog pound attendant and zoo-keeper were rated more highly than nursery school teacher or day care worker. They carried out an independent assessment of the predominantly female jobs and came up with ratings that differed substantially from those of the Labor Department.

Examining why the differences occurred, they found that the Labor Department had overlooked important characteristics of the female-dominated jobs, especially those associated with taking care of children. The evaluators did not regard these as job-related skills, but rather as qualities intrinsic to being a woman. In other words, the job evaluators were confusing the content and responsibilities of a paid job with stereotypical notions about the characteristics of the job holder. Under a comparable worth standard, it is assumed that people are rewarded in wages for what they do on a job, regardless of whether they have been trained in their duties prior to holding the job. Further, if white men are rewarded for these duties, women should also be rewarded.

We have defined wage discrimination as a situation where there is an inconsistent application of values or an inappropriate assessment of jobs. The values or standards in question are those of the employer as reflected in a firm's wage structure. Thus, comparable worth policy does not fly in the face of the market principle of basing wages on the productive contribution of a job to a firm. Rather, like other equal employment policies, it seeks to differentiate market-based values and standards from discrimination.

Conclusion: Why Comparable Worth Is Controversial

Comparable worth policy was once identified as the equal employment issue of the 1980s by Eleanor Holmes Norton of the EEOC (Cook, 1983). Since 1977, when the EEOC commissioned the NRC/NAS study to assess the feasibility of a policy of comparable worth, efforts to achieve such a policy have proliferated across the country. Alice Cook, in a study summarized in Chapter 15, has documented over eighty initiatives, primarily in the public sector (Cook, 1982; see also Dean et al., 1983).

Norton also predicted that comparable worth would prove to be the most controversial facet of equal employment policy. This prediction too has proven accurate. Indeed, activity in support of comparable worth has triggered considerable opposition to it, especially among business groups. For example, the Equal Employment Advisory Council, a lobbying arm of the Business Roundtable with a million-dollar annual budget, edited a $130,000 collection of commissioned essays highly critical of comparable worth policy (Livernash, 1980). The national board of the International Personnel Management Association voted to oppose a comparable worth policy, as did other personnel organizations, though many, including the IPMA itself, have since reversed their initial opposition.

This opposition is not surprising. The goal of equal pay for work of comparable worth is an especially sensitive social policy because it threatens to upset the way the labor market in particular and the society in general are organized in at least three ways. First, comparable worth appears to be a costly reform. I will argue in the concluding chapter that opponents overstate the cost of a comparable worth policy; still, one must acknowledge that upgrading women's work will add to the wage bill. This is not true of other equal opportunity reforms. For instance, changes in hiring and promotion procedures may carry an initial cost adjustment but they do not require employers to pay more for work performed, but rather to fill existing positions through a different and presumably more equitable process of recruitment and selection. The evolution of laws on wages and hours in the United States in the twentieth century reveals that employers have demonstrated the greatest resistance to reforms that threaten either to increase production costs or to curtail their discretion in establishing the terms and conditions of employment (Steinberg, 1982; see also Edwards, 1979).

Second, comparable worth policy challenges basic cultural assumptions about the relative value of the activities of different groups in society. As Shepala and Viviano point out in Chapter 3, women and men (and by extension minorities and whites) are viewed differently and unequally from birth. They report as well that "there are considerable anthropological and sociological data to indicate that the value of an activity or characteristic can be lowered simply through its association with women" or, one might add, minorities. In other words, conventional wisdom holds that what women and minorities do is less valuable than what white men do. By correcting for the systematic undervaluation of women's and minorities' work, comparable worth policy flies in the face of this pervasive cultural norm. Indeed, a secondary goal of the policy is to correct for this wider cultural "undervaluation." Because of this, it raises uncomfortable questions that encourage resistance to its implementation.

Finally, comparable worth policy would redistribute not only economic resources, but also labor market *power* to women workers. For, as wages are a proxy for the relative market power of an occupational group, the adjustment of wages among groups of employees is both a cause and a consequence of a change in their power position. Unionized workers, for example, earn on average 30 percent more than their nonunion counterparts (Steinberg and Cook, 1981): the power to bargain over certain terms and conditions of employment has resulted in higher wages. Similarly, to adjust the wages paid for female-dominated jobs relative to those paid for male-dominated jobs through comparable worth policy is to adjust as well the power position of women relative to men in the labor market.

The very emergence of the issue of comparable worth can be regarded as both a cause and a consequence of the change in women's power in the labor market. The progress that has been made since 1977 demonstrates the power women and minorities are able to command when they organize and press for legal and political change. Indeed, there has been a noticeable shift in the political arena, both in the terms of the comparable worth debate and in the institutional arena in which struggles are taking place. Early battles were fought primarily in the law courts. Under the Carter administration, government contractors were required to comply with federal comparable worth standards. These were rescinded in the first months of the Reagan administration, however, and the Reagan-appointed EEOC chair, Clarence Thomas, testified before Congress against EEOC backing of a comparable worth standard. Despite these setbacks, however, the policy has been making considerable headway at the state and municipal levels, as Chapters 14 and 15 report.

This book focuses largely on technical considerations in assessing wage discrimination and correcting it through an evolving policy of comparable worth. Yet comparable worth is less a technical than a political issue. Fundamentally, it is an issue of fairness. What most women and minorities might have considered a fair relative wage twenty years ago is now proving unacceptable to them. Even the NAS/NRC Committee understood that the comparable worth controversy is more one of value and values than of science and method. Its report concludes: "It must be recognized that there are no definitive tests of the 'fairness' of the choice of compensable factors and the relative weights given to them. The process [of job evaluation] is inherently judgmental and its success in generating a wage structure that is deemed equitable depends on achieving a consensus about factors and their weights among employers and employees" (Treiman and Hartmann, 1981:96). Comparable worth policy thus provides a vehicle for women and minorities to renegotiate the labor contract so as to gain their just reward for their valuable contribution to the U.S. political economy.

References

Alvarez, Rodolfo, and Kenneth G. Lutterman and Associates. 1979. *Discrimination in Organizations*. San Francisco: Jossey-Bass.
Baker, Elizabeth Faulkner. 1964. *Technology and Women's Work*. New York: Columbia University Press.
Bird, Caroline. 1972. *Born Female: The High Cost of Keeping Women Down*, rev. ed. New York: Pocket Books.
Bureau of National Affairs. 1973. *The Equal Employment Opportunity Acts of 1972*. Washington, D.C.: BNA, Inc.
Bureau of National Affairs. 1981. *The Comparable Worth Issue: A BNA Special Report*. Washington, D.C.: BNA, Inc.
Cook, Alice. 1975. "Equal Pay: A Multi-National History and Comparison." Manuscript.
Cook, Alice. 1982. *Comparable Worth: The Problem and States' Approaches to Wage Equity*. Honolulu: Industrial Relations Center, University of Hawaii.
Cook, Alice. 1983. "Comparable Worth: Recent Developments in Selected States." Paper presented to the Industrial Relations Research Association.
Dean, Virginia, et al. 1983. "State and Local Government Action on Pay Equity: New Initiatives." Paper commissioned by the National Committee on Pay Equity.
Edwards, Richard. 1979. *Contested Terrain: The Transformation of the Workplace in the Twentieth Century*. New York: Basic Books.
Equal Employment Opportunity Commission. 1980. *Hearings on Job Segregation and Wage Discrimination*. Washington, D.C.: Government Printing Office.
Feagin, Joe R., and Clairece B. Feagin. 1978. *Discrimination American Style: Institutional Racism and Sexism*. Englewood Cliffs, N.J.: Prentice-Hall.
Gross, Edward. 1968. "Plus ça change . . .? The Sexual Structure of Occupations over Time." *Social Problems* 16:198–208.
Grune, Joy Ann, ed. 1980. *Manual on Pay Equity: Raising Wages for Women's Work*. Washington, D.C.: Conference on Alternative State and Local Policies.
Hartmann, Heidi I., and Barbara Reskin. 1983. "Job Segregation: Trends and Prospectus." In *Occupational Segregation and Its Impact on Working Women: A Conference Report*, ed. Cynthia H. Chertos, Lois V. Haignere, and Ronnie J Steinberg, pp. 52–78. Albany, N.Y.: Center for Women in Government.
Livernash, E. Robert, ed. 1980. *Comparable Worth: Issues and Alternatives*. Washington, D.C.: Equal Employment Advisory Council.
Milkman, Ruth. 1981. "The Reproduction of Job Segregation by Sex: A Study of the Sexual Division in the Auto and Electrical Manufacturing Industries in the 1960's." Ph.D. dissertation, University of California at Berkeley.
Milkovich, George T. 1980. "The Emerging Debate." In *Comparable Worth: Issues and Alternatives*, ed. E. Robert Livernash, pp. 23–48. Washington, D.C.: Equal Employment Advisory Council.
Milkovich, George T. and A. Broderick. 1982. "Pay Discrimination: Legal Issues and Implications for Research." *Industrial Relations* 21:309–17.
Newman, Winn, and Jeanne M. Vonhof. 1981. "'Separate but Equal'—Job Segregation and Pay Equity in the Wake of *Gunther*." *University of Illinois Law Review*, pp. 269–331.
Newman, Winn, and Carole W. Wilson. 1981. "The Union Role in Affirmative Action." *Labor Law Journal*, pp. 323–42.
New York Times, May 1982.
Office of Women and Work, Michigan Department of Labor. 1981. "A Comparable

Worth Study of the State of Michigan Job Classifications: Technical Report."
Lansing, Michigan: Michigan Department of Labor.

Penny, Virginia. 1870. *How Women Can Make Money: Married or Single.* Springfield, Mass.: D. E. Fisk.

Perlman, Nancy D., and Bruce J. Ennis. 1980. "Preliminary Memorandum on Pay Equity: Achieving Equal Pay for Work of Comparable Worth." Working Paper no. 2. Albany, N.Y.: Center for Women in Government.

Perlman, Nancy, and Joy Ann Grune. 1982. "Comparable Worth Testimony of the National Committee on Pay Equity." Presented before the U.S. House of Representatives, Subcommittees on Civil Service, Human Resources and Compensation and Employee Benefits.

Pierson, David A., and Karen S. Koziara. 1981. "Study of Equal Wages for Jobs of Comparable Worth: Final Report." Philadelphia: Center for Labor and Human Resource Studies.

Rayback, Joseph G. 1966. *A History of American Labor.* Rev. ed. New York: Free Press.

Remick, Helen. 1980. "Beyond Equal Pay for Equal Work: Comparable Worth in the State of Washington." in *Equal Employment Policy for Women,* ed. Ronnie Steinberg-Ratner, pp. 405–48. Philadelphia: Temple University Press.

Robertson, Peter. 1980. "Strategies for Improving the Economic Situation of Women in the United States: Systemic Thinking, Systemic Discrimination and Systemic Enforcement." In *Equal Employment Policy for Women,* ed. Ronnie Steinberg-Ratner, pp. 128–42. Philadelphia: Temple University Press.

Roos, Patricia A. 1981. "Sex Stratification in the Workforce: male-female differences in economic returns to occupation." *Social Science Research* 10(3).

Steinberg, Ronnie J. 1982. *Wages and Hours: Labor and Reform in Twentieth Century America.* New Brunswick, N.J.: Rutgers University Press.

Steinberg, Ronnie J. 1983. "The Political Economy of Comparable Worth." Paper presented at the annual meeting of the Eastern Sociological Society.

Steinberg-Ratner, Ronnie, ed. 1980. *Equal Employment Policy for Women: Strategies for Implementation in the United States, Canada and Western Europe.* Philadelphia: Temple University Press.

Steinberg, Ronnie J., and Alice Cook. 1981. "Women, Unions and Equal Employment Opportunity." Working Paper no. 3. Albany, N.Y.: Center for Women in Government.

Treiman, Donald J. 1979. *Job Evaluation: An Analytic Review.* Washington, D.C.: National Academy of Sciences.

Treiman, Donald, and Heidi I. Hartmann. 1981. *Women, Work and Wages: Equal Pay for Jobs of Equal Value.* Washington, D.C.: National Academy Press.

U.S. Department of Commerce, Bureau of the Census. 1957–1977. "Money Income of Families and Persons in the United States: 1957 to 1977." Current Population Reports. Washington, D.C.: Government Printing Office.

Williams, Robert E., and Douglas S. McDowell. 1980. "The Legal Framework." In *Comparable Worth: Issues and Alternatives,* ed. E. Robert Livernash, pp. 197–249. Washington, D.C.: Equal Employment Advisory Council.

Witt, Mary, and Patricia K. Naherny. 1975. *Women's Work: Up From 878—Report on the DOT Research Project.* Madison: Women's Education Resources, University of Wisconsin-Extension.

Wolfson, Theresa. 1943. "Aprons and Overalls in War." *Annals* 229 (September):46–55.

2

Socioeconomic Explanations of Job Segregation

PAULA ENGLAND

Despite consistent increases in female employment (U.S. Bureau of the Census, 1978:398), occupational sex segregation persists. Even by 1970, about 70 percent of either men or women would have had to change occupational categories to achieve the same sex mix within each occupation that exists within the labor force (Blau, 1977: Ch. 1; U.S. Commission on Civil Rights, 1978:42). Although occupational segregation has decreased somewhat since 1900 (England, 1981a; Williams, 1976, 1979), a remarkable amount is still apparent.

This paper assesses the ability of several theories to explain the persistence of occupational sex segregation with logical consistency and fidelity to the available data: (1) sex role socialization theories; (2) neoclassical economics, including theories of human capital, tastes, monopsony, and statistical discrimination; (3) institutional economics, including theories of segmented and internal labor markets; (4) Marxist theories; and (5) theories of patriarchy. I will show that several supported explanations are complementary rather than mutually exclusive and, using insights gleaned from several theories, present a sketch of how segregation persists. I begin and end with a discussion of the relationship between segregation and comparable worth.

The type of discrimination at issue in the debate over comparable worth should be defined. This type of sex discrimination occurs when the sex composition of jobs influences what employers are willing to pay those who do the jobs, whether this influence is conscious or unconscious. The pay in predominantly female jobs is frequently lower than the pay in male jobs, and often the differentials are greater than can be explained by the skill levels, contribution to profit, or labor supply curves of the jobs or the qualifications of the jobs' incumbents. In such cases, it is reasonable to conclude that female jobs would have higher wages but for their sex composition. This type of wage discrimination is different from unequal pay for equal work and from those processes of market or premarket discrimination

Acknowledgment: Part of the research for this paper was funded by National Institute for Mental Health grant 5T 32 MH 14670 03 and National Science Foundation grant SES-810 7345. I thank Peter Lewin for comments on an earlier draft.

that contribute to occupational sex segregation. Yet comparable worth and occupational sex segregation are related. Without segregation, jobs would not differ greatly in their sex compositions, and so sex labels could not influence wages. Thus, segregation is a necessary but not sufficient condition of the sex discrimination at issue in comparable worth. Ending segregation is a sufficient but not necessary condition of abolishing such sex discrimination in wages. I will return to this relationship after considering the roots of occupational sex segregation.

Sex Role Socialization

When children or adults are asked their occupational aspirations, responses are usually sex-typed. (Regarding children, see Kirchner and Vondracek, 1973; Looft, 1971; O'Hara, 1962; Tyler, 1964.) How do people develop sex-typed preferences? Psychological theories of cognitive learning, role modeling, and reinforcement are all relevant here: people learn about, imitate, and are reinforced for sex-typical occupational choices.

Socialization also affects occupational segregation indirectly. Most people reach adulthood with traits and tastes compatible with occupations typical for their sex; thus, socialization indirectly perpetuates sex-typed occupational choices on the labor supply side. And because socialization develops different traits in males and females, employers use their knowledge of and preferences for these sex differences to decide whether men or women are more suited for particular jobs. In this case sex role socialization encourages demand-side hiring discrimination.

Five dimensions of sex role socialization are related to differences between predominantly male and predominantly female occupations. Females' socialization encourages (1) nurturant and helping orientations and (2) acceptance of responsibility for housework and child care and discourages (3) authoritativeness or aggressiveness, (4) quantitative or mechanical performance, and (5) physical strength. (For reviews of the evidence that females and males are differentially socialized on these dimensions, see Hetherington and Parke, 1979:566–603; Mischel, 1976:319–48; and Weitzman, 1979, particularly pp. 5–6 for Weitzman's critique of Maccoby and Jacklin, 1974.) When the sex composition of occupations corresponds with what is predicted by the content of traditional sex roles, this is evidence that sex role socialization helps perpetuate occupational sex segregation.[1]

---

1. I do not consider whether innate sex differences influence the occupational distributions of men and women. Socialization has undoubtedly magnified whatever sex differences in innate proclivities exist.

Nurturant and Helping Orientations

Table 2-1 shows that occupations involving nurturance—that is, those whose aim is to provide a service to a recipient with whom one has face-to-face contact—are disproportionately female: nursing, social work, teaching, counseling, and child care. Women constituted 73 percent of all

Table 2-1

Employment of Men and Women in Nurturant Occupations in 1970*

Occupational Title (Census Bureau's 1970 Detailed Classification	No. Men	No. Women	% Female
Librarians	22,047	100,160	82
Physicians, dentists, and related practitioners (except veterinarians)	474,739	44,733	9
Registered nurses	22,444	807,825	97
Therapists	27,631	47,603	63
Dental hygienists	942	14,863	94
Therapy assistants	1,093	2,122	66
Social workers	80,966	136,022	63
Recreation workers	29,481	20,478	41
Teachers, except college and university	817,002	1,929,064	70
Vocational and educational counselors	60,191	46,592	44
Bartenders	149,506	39,432	21
Food counter and fountain workers	39,405	118,981	75
Waiters (includes waitresses)	116,838	927,251	89
Health service workers (e.g., nurses' aides)	139,760	1,044,944	88
Airline stewardesses (includes stewards)	1,364	31,317	96
Attendants, personal service, not elsewhere classified	22,953	37,712	62
Baggage porters and bellhops	18,424	482	3
Barbers	159,557	7,861	5
Boarding and lodging housekeepers	2,099	5,304	72
Bootblacks	4,041	406	9
Child-care workers (not in private households)	9,684	126,667	93
Elevator operators	25,703	9,606	27
Hairdressers and cosmetologists	46,825	425,605	90
School monitors	2,576	23,538	90
Ushers	10,724	4,328	29
Welfare aides	3,634	11,764	76
Child-care workers, private households	7,215	263,165	97
Total: all nurturant occupations	2,296,844	6,227,825	73
Total: entire labor force	45,291,070	27,193,685	38

*Occupations that I have not considered nurturant, but that might be considered nurturant by some, include religious workers, clergymen, college and university teachers, personnel and labor relations workers, retail salesmen and sales clerks, receptionists, farm management advisors, home management advisors, and bank tellers. These were excluded because in each case some other goal seemed more fundamental to the occupational task than nurturance of people. However, these occupations taken as a whole are disproportionately female (50 percent), so that their inclusion would not substantially alter the conclusions reached.
Source: U.S. Bureau of the Census, 1973. *1970 Census of the Population*, vol. 1: *Characteristics of the Population*, Part 1, *U.S. Summary*, Section 2, Table 221.

workers in nurturant occupations in 1970, whereas they were only 38 percent of the labor force as a whole. While nurturant occupations provided employment for only 5 percent of all working males in 1970, they accounted for 19 percent of the employed females (U.S. Bureau of the Census, 1973).

Housework and Child Care

The National Longitudinal Survey data casts doubt on the contention that domestic responsibility makes women unsuitable for most male occupations. Among women in this 1967 sample, those who had never been married and had no children were as likely to be in predominantly female occupations as married women (England, 1982). This suggests that women's domestic work is not a crucial cause of the occupational distribution. Yet the finding is not decisive: since most women plan to marry, anticipation of domestic responsibility could keep even single women from jobs that would conflict with domestic roles. Thus, further probing of which male jobs conflict with women's domestic responsibility is worthwhile.

Time diary studies show that even when women are employed, they do most of the cooking, house cleaning, and tending of children in the evenings (Berk and Berk, 1979; Robinson, 1977). Jobs requiring more than forty to fifty hours of work a week or out-of-town travel are difficult to combine with these responsibilities. Such jobs include traveling sales work, factory jobs with required overtime, and time-consuming professional and executive jobs, all of which are predominantly male.

The allocation of child rearing to women accentuates the primacy of the male's career and discourages the funding of women's higher education by either parents or husbands (Freeman, 1975). Thus, more males than females have bachelor's and graduate degrees, though the gap is narrowing rapidly. Although the mean educational attainment of employed males and females is nearly identical at 12.5 years (Kreps and Leaper, 1976), since high school dropouts are predominantly male, females receive less specific vocational training than males, especially on the job (England et al., 1982; Lloyd and Niemi, 1979:141). Thus, women are concentrated in jobs requiring medium amounts of schooling and offering relatively little vocational training. Moreover, child-reading responsibility and the related primacy of the male career make it unlikely that women will fill jobs that demand geographical mobility. This helps explain the absence of women from elite professional and executive posts in which career progression requires mobility.

Yet the assignment of domestic responsibility to women does not explain their exclusion from *most* male jobs,[2] though it does contribute to the

---

2. I refer here to the objective demands on women's time and energy of domestic responsibility. Although these do not explain women's absence from a majority of male jobs, insofar as child rearing engenders nurturance, or the economic dependence of being a housewife engenders a subordinate stance, this will contribute to the types of segregation attributed above to female socialization to nurturance and nonauthoritativeness.

dearth of women in elite craft, executive, or professional careers which entail travel, geographical transfers, evening work, graduate education, or much on-the-job training. (To argue that the allocation of domestic responsibilities to women does not explain the absence of women in most male occupations is not to justify husbands' failure to share in homemaking and child rearing.)

Authoritativeness or Aggressiveness

Females are reared to be more compliant and pleasing and less aggressive and authoritative than males. Thus, women are underrepresented in occupations that involve the face-to-face exercise of power, particularly over men. In a recent national survey, women workers described their jobs as involving lower levels of authority over other workers than men reported for their jobs (Wolf and Fligstein, 1979).

One way of exercising power is persuading someone to accept a point of view in one's interest, as one does in the legal profession and commission sales work. In 1970 only 5 percent of lawyers were female (U.S. Bureau of the Census, 1973). In sales work, women are least prevalent in those categories in which self-interested persuasion is most important in determining rewards. The 1970 census showed only 6 percent of wholesale sales representatives, most of whom work on commission, to be female (ibid.). Most retail sales clerks do not work on commission, and 65 percent were women in 1970 (ibid.). Where women have entered commission sales work, it is frequently to persuade other women to buy (e.g., in the sale of real estate or cosmetics).

Supervisory and managerial jobs involve authority over other workers. Women are underrepresented in management and administration of all sorts; this occupational group was only 17 percent female in 1970 (ibid.). Even in nondurable goods industries that employ many female operatives, foremen were only 14 percent female. To be represented in proportion to their numbers in the labor force, women would have had to make up 38 percent of the work force in each of these jobs (ibid.).

Quantitative or Mechanical Performance

Males do better than females on tests of quantitative ability starting in adolescence (Maccoby and Jacklin, 1974:85–98). Does this difference in performance influence the division of occupations into male and female domains? That is, do predominantly male occupations require more quantitative or mechanical skill? Most occupations involving advanced mathematics are indeed predominantly male: mathematics, natural science, engineering, medicine, accounting, economics, and statistics. England et al. (1982) show that female occupations are less mechanical than male occupations, on average; they involve less manipulation of physical objects ($r = 0.46$) and require less spatial ability ($r = -0.33$).

Physical Strength

Women's lesser physical strength, undoubtedly reinforced by socialization, is reflected in occupational distributions. Jobs requiring physical strength are disproportionately male ($r = -0.37$). (See England and McLaughlin, 1979.)

Neoclassical Economics

Human Capital Theory

Human capital theorists (e.g., Becker, 1964; Mincer, 1974; Blau and Jusenius, 1976) contend that investments in humans yield monetary payoffs by making labor more productive. One's human capital appreciates through such activities as schooling or job experience. Earning power may decline if one's job skills get rusty from nonuse; this is depreciation of human capital.

Polachek (1976, 1978, 1979) contends that sex differences in human capital depreciation provide a supply-side explanation for occupational sex segregation. He starts from the observation that women's employment is intermittent because of their domestic responsibilities. Polachek points out that while women are out of the labor force, their job skills are depreciating rather than appreciating, as they would be in any job that involved training. He reasons that rational women who anticipate intermittent employment will choose occupations that require skills that do not depreciate rapidly from nonuse. In his view, segregation results from women's economically motivated choices; given their intermittent employment, women gain from segregation into jobs with low depreciation.

Human capital theory generates a different supply-side explanation of segregation than that offered by theories of sex role socialization. But Polachek's theory is complemented by one feature of sex role socialization: he assumes that women will stay home and rear children, an assumption that must be explained exogenously to his theory. Though he makes no reference to socialization, it is socialization that best explains why most child rearing is done by women in the home. If Polachek's theory is correct, the socialization that leads women to take on child rearing in the home is sufficient to cause economically motivated choices of female occupations; segregation can be explained without reference to other aspects of socialization, such as the development of traits and tastes appropriate to sex-typical occupations.

Polachek's explanation, however, conflicts with empirical evidence. If his thesis is correct, the wage penalty for depreciation should be less in predominantly female occupations than in male ones. Though Polachek (1979: tables 9.3, 9.8) has demonstrated a correlation between home time and wage loss, he has not demonstrated that predominantly female occupations subject women's human capital to less depreciation. Yet his theory depends on demonstrating that. With each of two data sets (Polachek, 1976,

1979), he calculates female atrophy rates for variants of the broad occupational groups defined by the Bureau of the Census. Atrophy is measured by the extent to which women's present earnings are lowered for every increment of time they have spent at home. When broad occupational groups are rank-ordered by the atrophy measures (Polachek, 1976: table 2; 1979: table 9.2), the ranks do not correspond closely with those obtained by rank-ordering the occupations according to percentage of females among their incumbents (though Polachek does not in fact present this latter ranking).

I have also tested the hypothesis that female occupations penalize women's intermittence less than male occupations. My empirical analysis differs from Polachek's in that I use more detailed occupational categories and code them according to their sex composition, the metric most relevant to his thesis. Two national data sets show that the penalty to current wages for past time spent out of the labor force is no less for women in predominantly female occupations than for women in male jobs (England, 1981b, 1982). In sum, neither Polachek's analysis nor mine finds female occupations to offer women lower penalties for intermittence than male occupations do.

Human capital theory also generates explanations of occupational sex segregation that focus on the appreciation, rather than depreciation, of human capital. The simplest of these posits that sex differences in job experience contribute to women's absence from jobs requiring much seniority. But this explanation of segregation does not go very far, since most fields are sex-segregated even at entry levels. Zellner (1975) has proposed another link between human capital accumulation and segregation. Her hypothesis hinges on the fact that occupations differ in their starting wages and rates of appreciation. Human capital theorists assume that jobs offering more wage appreciation will have lower starting wages because the earnings forgone in early years are an investment in on-the-job training that leads to wage appreciation. Zellner hypothesized that many women are not employed enough years to allow occupations with high appreciation rates to compensate for their lower starting wages. Thus, more women than men will maximize lifetime earnings by choosing occupations with high starting wages despite the disadvantage of their flat appreciation. To ascertain whether this thesis explains some sex segregation, I have used regression analysis to determine whether women make higher starting wages and can anticipate higher lifetime earnings if they are employed in predominantly female occupations (England, 1981b). Data from the national Panel Study of Income Dynamics do not support Zellner's thesis. In fact, at every level of experience, from starting wages to retirement, women make more if they are employed in predominantly male occupations.

These findings show that human capital theorists are incorrect in positing that pecuniary incentives lead women to segregate themselves into traditionally female jobs. To the extent that segregation is explained on the labor supply side, evidence suggests that it is more a result of sex role socialization, a phenomenon that encompasses what economists call "pre-market discrimination."

Monopsony

Another neoclassical model is proposed by Madden (1973, 1975, 1976), who sees men (whether husbands, workers, legislators, or employers) cooperating in sex discrimination because of the advantages to them of doing so. Madden observes that men have substantial power over women's decisions to accept jobs; women's options are limited by protective labor legislation that bars them from some jobs and by the patriarchal customs by which men dictate their family's place of residence. Such male power, which must be explained exogenously to Madden's monopsony model, is her point of departure. Hence the name of the model: because of the restrictions placed on them by men, it is as if women faced a single employer, a monopsonist, rather than having the option of many potential employers. This allows employers to increase profits by paying lower wages than they would if they were in competition for female labor. (For a related treatment, see Gordon and Morton, 1974).

Madden also assumes that male power over female labor leads to a lower wage elasticity of the female labor supply. Lower wage elasticity means that an increase in available wages does little to lure new entrants into employment, and that a decrease does little to deter employment. According to neoclassical theory, if many employers compete for female labor, a less elastic female labor supply does not, in itself, result in lower wages for females. But where women face a monopsonist, the lower the elasticity of their labor supply, the lower the monopsonist can keep female wages (Madden, 1975:152–53).

The main problem with Madden's formulation is that there are no empirical findings showing the wage elasticity of women's labor to be less than men's. Blau and Jusenius (1976) give an intuitive argument for the opposite hypothesis: women's disinclination to change employers because of male-defined residence (or other forms of male power) may be counterbalanced by their option to leave the labor market altogether because the occupation of housewife is socially acceptable for them. Male domicile lowers the wage elasticity of female labor; the option of housewifery raises it. We need an empirical estimate of which effect is stronger before Madden's model can be convincing.

A second criticism of Madden's monopsony model is that it does not have segregation as a logically necessary outcome. Employers can take advantage of their monopsony power by segregating women into low-paying jobs or by paying them lower wages than men within sex-integrated jobs. Madden (1975) suggests that employers choose the segregation strategy because it is encouraged by male workers, whose interests are better served by excluding women from well-paying jobs than by wage discrimination against women within integrated jobs, since the latter strategy would make visible to the employer his economic incentive to hire only women for such jobs. But Madden's theory does not explain how this "cartel" of males as husbands, workers, legislators, and employers is held together. As with all economic models of monopolies, group loyalty that conflicts with individual maximization has to be explained outside the model.

Tastes, Statistical Discrimination, and Error Discrimination

In a seminal treatise, Becker (1957) argued that race discrimination in hiring results from the indulgence of prejudices or "tastes" that are not economically motivated. This formulation contends that employers lose money by discriminating in hiring. Blacks must accept lower wages in order to find jobs, and the employers who hire blacks make relative gains from these lowered labor costs. Becker also argued that discrimination reduces total production and trade in an economy so that all workers, even the favored ones, may make less than they would in an economy with no discrimination.

To apply Becker's model to occupational sex segregation, we must adapt the theory in two ways. An aversion to hiring women (rather than blacks) must be posited, and the tastes for hiring men must be assumed to pertain only to certain occupations. Sex role socialization may form these tastes; indeed, Becker states that his is a theory about the economic consequences of tastes that must be explained by sociological or psychological theories (Becker, 1957:1).

Arrow (1972) has pointed out that for the competitive markets neoclassical economists usually assume, Becker's model implies that hiring discrimination will erode over time, since the lower labor costs of nondiscriminating firms give them an ever greater share of product markets. Becker's theory cannot explain the persistence of occupational sex segregation in a competitive market economy except as a vestige of unexplained tastes that the market has not yet completely weeded out. Thus, it is unsatisfactory as a theory to explain the persistence of segregation.

Several economists (Arrow, 1972:97; Blau and Jusenius, 1976; McCall, 1972; Phelps, 1972; Spence, 1974:104; Thurow, 1975:170–81) have suggested that employers may prefer to hire members of a certain group (e.g., whites, men) because, on the average, members of that group have more of the characteristics conducive to productivity, perhaps because of premarket discrimination or socialization. Statistical discrimination "occurs whenever an individual is judged on the basis of the average characteristics of the group . . . to which he or she belongs. . . . The judgments are correct, factual, and objective in the sense that the group actually has the characteristics that are ascribed to it, but the judgements are incorrect with respect to many individuals within the groups" (Thurow, 1975:172). The incorrectness arises because even if women have a lower mean score on some desired characteristic, there is usually a large overlap of male and female distributions such that some females have more of the desired characteristics than males.

Between the poles of taste and statistical discrimination lies what I call error discrimination. This is hiring discrimination based on *false* assumptions about sex differences in productivity-linked characteristics. It differs from taste discrimination in its economic motivation and from statistical discrimination in its basis in erroneous information about group averages (Lewin and England, 1982).

Phelps (1972) and Spence (1974) have argued that statistical discrimination differs from taste or error discrimination in that it can persist in competitive markets. But, in fact, the neoclassical model's assumptions lead to the conclusion that even statistical discrimination should erode in competitive markets because of the pecuniary advantage that accrues to nondiscriminators (Lewin and England, 1982). On the surface it appears that there is not much pecuniary advantage to ceasing statistical discrimination. Why should employers abandon a cheap source of information for estimating productivity and develop expensive screening devices in order to find individuals whose productivity is above the average for their sex? But employers gain in two ways by developing better screening operations. First, they obtain better work forces, and the benefits of this may exceed the costs of the new screening devices. Second, precisely because others are engaging in statistical discrimination, one can hire good workers (i.e., those whose productivity is above the average for their sex) for lower wages. Those who find more sensitive screening instruments than sex will gain in competitive economies at the expense of those who do not, much as with taste discrimination. Thus, the notion of statistical discrimination has to be taken out of the neoclassical framework to predict the persistence of segregation.

Of the many traits on which males and females in the labor market differ, women's greater propensity to quit, or "turnover," is the factor usually alleged to cause statistical discrimination. The reasoning is that employers will prefer to hire men in jobs where the costs of on-the-job training are relatively high, since these costs will be recouped only if the employee stays with the firm for quite a while. Consistent with this argument is the fact that women are less likely than men to be in jobs entailing on-the-job training (England et al., 1982; Lloyd and Niemi, 1979).

But are women's turnover rates really higher than men's? The evidence is equivocal (for a review see Price, 1977:40). Women are more apt than men to leave the labor force, usually to care for children, but men change firms more often (Barnes and Jones, 1974). Some studies find no sex difference in turnover when men and women in the same occupation are compared (Merchants and Manufacturers Association, 1970; Parrish, 1965; Women's Bureau, 1969). Those who "control" for occupation argue that

the relegation of women to low-paying jobs with little prospect of advancement makes their aggregate turnover rate higher than it otherwise would be.
Indeed, persons of both sexes are more apt to quit low-paying jobs (U.S.
Civil Service Commission, 1963). Yet it is only proper to control for a
variable that is causally prior to the dependent variable being examined, in
this case turnover (Blalock, 1972:442–50). If the difference in the propensity to turnover leads to differential occupational placement (through
women's choices or statistical discrimination), then controlling for occupation will lead to partialing out as due to occupation some of the difference
that is due to women's propensity to leave the labor force to rear children.
Thus, it is difficult to tell whether studies overestimate sex effects on
turnover when they fail to control for occupation or underestimate sex
effects when they control for it. If men and women have different turnover
propensities, such differences may lead to statistical discrimination against
women in jobs where turnover is expensive to employers. If the differences
are mythological, sex discrimination based on assumptions about turnover is
error discrimination.

The exclusive focus on turnover in discussions of statistical discrimination against women is misplaced. Other sex differences may also produce
statistical discrimination against women applicants for jobs requiring
mechanical, mathematical, authoritative or other skills that have traditionally been the province of males. The victims of statistical discrimination
will be those who have developed abilities and interests atypical for their sex
under current regimes of sex role socialization. Levinson (1975) has
documented such discrimination by having assistants make bogus phone
calls in response to job advertisements. Twenty-eight percent of the females
inquiring about traditionally male jobs and 44 percent of the males asking
about typically female jobs were told that persons of their sex would not like
or be good at the job.

Other evidence of statistical discrimination comes from interviews with
managers. Hakel and Dunnette (1970) asked managers who interview job
applicants to rank applicant characteristics on a seven-point scale from
unfavorable to favorable. The average manager saw female gender as
favorable for clerical applicants and male gender as favorable for applicants
for positions as managers, management trainees, and engineers. Summers
et al. (1976:41–42) also report on interviews with managers who decided *a
priori* whether to hire men or women for production jobs on the basis of
which sex they predicted to be more productive at the particular job. In sum,
there is substantial evidence of statistical discrimination in hiring despite the
fact that neoclassical theory predicts its gradual erosion.

Marxist Theories

Marxist explanations of occupational sex segregation assume that employers need always to be vigilant against the collective rebellion of workers

that threatens the capitalist system of ownership, control, and distribution. Marxists argue that capitalists employ a "divide and conquer" strategy against the workers (see Bowles and Gintis, 1976:184; Edwards et al., 1975: xiii–xiv; Gordon, 1972:71–78; Gordon et al., 1982; Humphries, 1976; Reich, 1981; Stevenson, 1978:94–95). While earlier Marxist literature posited an increasing homogeneity of the conditions of the working class, recent Marxist research emphasizes the division of jobs into clusters so that work that requires and rewards employee stability is clearly distinguished from work that does not. This job segmentation is seen by Marxists as a strategy to limit the extent to which those in desirable jobs identify with those in less desirable jobs. Segregation by race and sex further helps minimize solidarity among workers. Women are channeled into the less desirable jobs because their history of subordination makes them more likely to accept the authority of supervisors and employment that does not reward stability. (The preexisting power differences between men and women must be explained exogenously to the Marxist model.) Since sex has been made more salient by the combined processes of job segmentation and discrimination in placement, a sense of solidarity among workers is less likely. Hence, workers are less apt to unify in either revolutionary or reformist rebellions.

Arrow's (1972) questions about Becker's (1957) taste model can be applied to this Marxist model as well. If some employers limit women to undesirable jobs, why don't other employers take advantage of women's lessened bargaining power by hiring them for all jobs at lower wages than they would have to pay men? Wouldn't these lowered labor costs give the nondiscriminating employer a cost advantage? Marxists have an answer to these questions: if a firm hired women for all jobs, workers would be more apt to develop a common class consciousness and to act in concert to better their positions relative to management and the owners of capital.

Since most firms segregate by sex, how are we to know whether more worker solidarity would occur in the absence of such segregation? Since empirical research cannot address this question directly, the empirical evidence for the Marxist explanation of segregation consists mainly of historical accounts of employers' use of race or sex cleavages to weaken labor movements (Edwards et al., 1975; Gordon et al., 1982; Reich, 1981).

Institutional Economics: Segmented and Internal Labor Markets

The institutional school of economics focuses on the rigidities of administrative and customary arrangements in economic life rather than the smooth marginal adjustments of the neoclassical market. Two related developments within this school are the theories of segmented and internal labor markets.

Institutionalists have introduced the concept of a segmented, dual labor market characterized by primary and secondary jobs. Secondary jobs are menial, not connected to mobility ladders, and filled by persons with high turnover rates. Primary jobs have relatively good pay and working conditions, chances for advancement up institutional mobility chains governed by administrative rules, due process, and custom (Gordon, 1972; Harrison, 1972, 1977; Piore, 1975, 1977). A critical distinction between primary and secondary jobs is the attachment or nonattachment to institutionalized mobility ladders. Since only primary jobs are attached to internal labor markets, women entering a firm through a secondary job are unlikely to move up to a primary job.

A more complex model of segmentation is offered by Doeringer and Piore (1971) and applied to occupational sex segregation by Blau and Jusenius (1976). Internal labor markets are administrative units (such as firms) within which the pricing and allocation of labor is governed by a set of rules and customs rather than by the forces operating in the external labor market. Certain jobs are ports of entry, and all other jobs are on institutionalized mobility ladders leading up from the entry points. These latter jobs are less affected by factors in the external market, at least in the short run. Management adopts such mobility ladders to reduce training and turnover costs; employees favor the arrangement because of increased security and the promise of advancement.

Why would the prevalence of internal labor markets within firms encourage sex segregation of occupations? Recall that in this model employers' valuation of stability is a primary motivation for internal mobility lines between jobs, and that progression along these lines is characterized by rule-governed equity. Thus, if employers perceive women to have higher turnover rates, the strategic place for them to engage in statistical or error discrimination is at ports of entry. Segregation in jobs that are ports of entry leads to continued segregation by sex among cohorts of employees, since each job is on a predefined mobility ladder. Even when employers provide some mobility out of female jobs, the mobility ladders are often short (Grinker et al., 1970; Kanter, 1977:136).

Theories of segmented or internal labor markets all make use of notions of statistical or error discrimination or the Marxist "divide and conquer" theory to explain occupational sex segregation of entry jobs. The unique institutionalist contribution has been to turn attention toward the effects of structures such as the clustering of jobs into ladders and the nonattachment of some jobs to ladders. When female entry-level jobs are not on mobility ladders or are on short, sex-segregated ones, it becomes obvious how sex segregation at entry is perpetuated over time without the need for further overt sex discrimination.

Theories of Patriarchy

Theories of patriarchy see sex segregation as an attempt by men, acting individually or cooperatively, to maintain male dominance. (Madden's monopsony model assumes the causal primacy of patriarchy, though it is also neoclassical in its assumptions.) Few discussions of patriarchy have focused on the specific issue of occupational sex segregation.

According to most feminist thinkers, the assignment of domestic activities to women benefits men more than women (Chodorow, 1978; Mitchell, 1976). Men may seek to preserve this arrangement and thereby make it difficult for their wives to meet the demands of elite male occupations. Moreover, since predominantly female occupations have come to pay lower wages than are commensurate with their demands for skill and training (Blau, 1977; Bluestone, 1974; England and McLaughlin, 1979; England et al., 1982; Stevenson, 1975), men have an economic incentive to continue monopolizing their privileged enclaves. In these ways, most men have a material interest in continued sex segregation. Yet the male "cartel" sometimes breaks down, as when a man with a secure, well-paying job is not objectively threatened by the entrance of women into his occupation and has an economic interest in the ability of his wife to earn a good wage. To test the hypothesis that patriarchy maintains sex segregation, we need systematic observations of the responses of men (as workers, employers, and husbands) to efforts by women to enter their occupations, such as Hartmann's (1976) account of the behavior of male unions in the early twentieth century, most of which chose to exclude women rather than organize them.

Conclusion

Occupational sex segregation has no one parsimonious explanation; it is embedded in systems ranging from the psychological to the institutional level. I will summarize the critical assessment I have made of the several theories and offer an explanation of occupational sex segregation derived from the complementary relationship between those theories that predict segregation and have some empirical support.

Two theories were judged inadequate to explain occupational sex segregation because the deductive generation of segregation from the assumptions of the model is not convincing. Madden's monopsony model assumes that the wage elasticity of the female labor supply is lowered by male hegemony. This is not an obvious deduction from male power; as I noted above, the option of housewifery may increase the wage elasticity of female labor. Nor is it deductively obvious that employers would take advantage of their monopsonistic power by segregating rather than by paying women less than men within sex-integrated jobs. Becker's theory of taste discrimination can logically predict segregation, but not its persistence in the competitive economy his neoclassical theory assumes. Since nondiscriminators are presumed by the theory to have lower production costs than discriminators, those who segregate should lose ever more of their product market shares. Thus, segregation should erode if it is based on taste.

Theories of human capital and sex role socialization have overemphasized women's domestic responsibility as an explanation of their occupational distribution. Those who discuss sex role socialization have exaggerated the incompatibility of domestic responsibility with the demands of most male occupations. Intermittent employment and the ongoing domestic work of employed women do impede access to elite occupations in management, the professions, and the skilled crafts. But we must remember that the vast majority of men do not work in these fields, and yet their jobs are typically segregated male preserves with high wages relative to those earned by women. Polachek's human capital explanation assumes that domestic responsibility makes it rational for women to choose jobs in which the wage penalty for intermittence is low. Yet data fail to support his contention: predominantly female occupations do not penalize women's intermittence less than jobs containing more males do.

Those theories that generate segregation from their assumptions and have not been contradicted by empirical analysis are largely complementary in their explanations of segregation. By combining their insights, one obtains the following picture of why occupational sex segregation persists. The allocation of domestic responsibility to women, itself perpetuated by sex role socialization and male interest, makes it difficult for women to fill the most elite male occupations. Segregation in the remainder of the occupational hierarchy is aided by the socialization that both discourages sex-atypical occupational choices and makes people less qualified for sex-atypical occupations. Socialization steers females toward work which is more nurturant, and less authoritative, mathematical, mechanical, or physical. Average sex differences in interests and developed abilities lay the groundwork for statistical discrimination by employers, who use this illegal device to decrease information costs. Employers may also use sex-segregated job clusters to impede the formation of class consciousness and avoid unified attempts by male and female workers to improve their situation relative to managers and capital owners. Internal labor markets perpetuate sex segregation in entry-level jobs through structured mobility channels. The higher pay in male occupations gives men an interest in choosing such occupations and in trying to avoid female competition.

Until more empirical research is completed, this eclectic view is the most defensible explanation of the persistence of occupational sex segregation. It incorporates the major tenets of the explanations offered by several theories: sex role socialization, statistical discrimination, Marxism, institutional economics, and patriarchy. These theories about segregation have escaped fatal logical and empirical criticism, but none have received extensive empirical support. On global issues the theories are irreconcilable, but in their explanations of segregation they are logically complementary. Thus, empirical documentation of one explanation need not be a refutation of the others. Research should be directed at discovering which of the processes reinforce each other and which are the most serious impediments to occupational desegregation.

I conclude by returning to the question of the relationship between occupational sex segregation and comparable worth. Segregation is a prerequisite for the sex discrimination in wages that is at issue in discussions of comparable worth. Thus, many commentators have concluded that segregation is the real problem and that policies should focus on reducing segregation rather than directly attacking this newly conceptualized form of wage discrimination. But the foregoing review has shown how deeply segregation is embedded in systems from the psychological to the institutional level. This does not mean that segregation is immutable, but it implies that efforts to reduce it will be slow in their effects. Since the doctrine of comparable worth points to a type of wage discrimination engaged in after the fact of segregation, those interested in reducing discriminatory wage differentials will attend to these acts of wage discrimination as well as to the underlying pattern of segregation. Such a two-pronged attack should yield a more rapid erosion of the sex gap in earnings than a strategy that slowly lessens segregation but leaves discriminatory wage differentials between jobs untouched.

References

Arrow, Kenneth. 1972. "Models of Job Discrimination." In Anthony H. *Racial Discrimination in Economic Life*, ed. Anthony H. Pascal, pp. 83–102. Lexington, Mass.: D. C. Heath.

Barnes, William, and Ethel B. Jones. 1974. "Differences in Male and Female Quitting." *Journal of Human Resources* 9:439–53.

Becker, Gary. 1957. *The Economics of Discrimination*. Chicago: University of Chicago Press.

Becker, Gary. 1964. *Human Capital*. New York: Columbia University Press.

Berk, Richard, and Sara Fenstermaker Berk. 1979. *Labor and Leisure at Home*. Beverly Hills, Cal.: Sage.

Blalock, Hubert. 1972. *Social Statistics*. New York: McGraw-Hill.

Blau, Francine. 1977. *Equal Pay in the Office*. Lexington, Mass.: D. C. Heath.

Blau, Francine, and Carol Jusenius. 1976. "Economists' Approaches to Sex Segregation in the Labor Market: An Appraisal." In *Women and the Workplace*, ed. Martha Blaxell and Barbara Reagan, pp. 181–200. Chicago: University of Chicago Press.

Bluestone, Barry. 1974. "The Personal Earnings Distribution: Individual and Institutional Determinants." Ph.D. dissertation, University of Michigan.

Bowles, Samuel, and Herbert Gintis. 1976. *Schooling in Capitalist America*. New York: Basic.

Chodorow, Nancy. 1978. *The Reproduction of Mothering: Psycho-analysis and the Sociology of Gender*. Berkeley: University of California Press.

Doeringer, Peter, and Michael Piore. 1971. *Internal Labor Markets and Manpower Analysis*. Lexington, Mass.: D. C. Heath.

Edwards, Richard, Michael Reich, and David Gordon, eds. 1975. *Labor Market Segmentation*. Lexington, Mass.: D. C. Heath.

England, Paula. 1981a. "Assessing Trends in Occupational Sex Segregation, 1900–1976." In (ed.), *Sociological Perspectives on Labor Markets*, ed. Ivar Berg, pp. 273–95. New York: Academic.

England, Paula. 1981b. "Wage Appreciation and Depreciation: A Test of Neoclassical Economic Explanations of Occupational Sex Segregation." Paper presented at the annual meetings of the American Sociological Association, Toronto.

England, Paula. 1982. "The Failure of Human Capital Theory to Explain Occupational Sex Segregation." *Journal of Human Resources* 17:358–70.

England, Paula, and Steven McLaughlin. 1979. "Sex Segregation of Jobs and Male-Female Income Differentials." In *Discrimination in Organizations*, ed. Rodolfo Alvarez, Kenneth Lutterman, and Associates, pp. 189–213. San Francisco: Jossey-Bass.

England, Paula, Marilyn Chassie, and Linda McCormack. 1982. "Skill Demands and Earnings in Female and Male Occupations." *Sociology and Social Research* 66:147–68.

Freeman, Jo. 1975. "How to Discriminate against Women without Really Trying." In *Women: A Feminist Perspective*, ed. Jo Freeman, pp. 194–208. Palo Alto, Cal.: Mayfield.

Gordon, David. 1972. *Theories of Poverty and Underemployment*. Lexington, Mass.: D. C. Heath.

Gordon, David, Richard Edwards, and Michael Reich. 1982. *Segmented Work, Divided Workers*. New York: Cambridge.

Gordon, Nancy, and Thomas Morton. 1974. "A Low Mobility Model of Wage Discrimination—with Special Reference to Sex Differentials." *Journal of Economic Theory* 7:241–53.

Grinker, William, Donald Cooke, and Arthur Kirsch. 1970. *Climbing the Job Ladder: A Study of Employee Advancement in Eleven Industries*. New York: Shelley.

Hakel, Milton, and Marvin Dunnette. 1970. *Checklists for Describing Job Applicants*. Minneapolis: Industrial Relations Center, University of Minnesota.

Harrison, Bennett. 1972. *Education, Training and the Urban Ghetto*. Baltimore: Johns Hopkins University Press.

Harrison, Bennett. 1977. "Education and Underemployment in the Urban Ghetto." In *Problems in Political Economy: An Urban Perspective*, ed. David Gordon, pp. 252–62. Lexington, Mass.: D. C. Heath.

Hartmann, Heidi. 1976. "Capitalism, Patriarchy, and Job Segregation by Sex." In *Women and the Workplace*, ed. Martha Blaxall and Barbara Reagan, pp. 237–70. Chicago: University of Chicago Press.

Hetherington, E. Mavis, and Ross Parke. 1979. *Child Psychology*. New York: McGraw-Hill.

Humphries, Jane. 1976. "Women: Scapegoats and Safety Valves in the Great Depression." *Review of Radical Political Economics* 8 (1):98–121.

Kanter, Rosabeth. 1977. *Men and Women of the Corporation*. New York: Basic.

Kirchner, E., and S. Vondracek. 1973. "What Do You Want to Be When You Grow Up? Vocational Choice in Children Aged 3–6." Paper presented to the meeting of the Society for Research in Child Development.

Kreps, Juanita, and R. John Leaper. 1976. "Home Work, Market Work, and the Allocation of Time." In *Women and the American Economy*, ed. Juanita Kreps, pp. 61–81. Englewood Cliffs, N. J.: Prentice-Hall.

Levinson, Richard. 1975. "Sex Discrimination and Employment Practices: An Experiment with Unconventional Job Inquiries." *Social Problems* 22:533–43.

Lewin, Peter, and Paula England. 1982. "Reconceptualizing Statistical Discrimination." Paper presented to the annual Southwest Social Science meetings, San Antonio, Tex.

Lloyd, Cynthia, and Beth Niemi. 1979. *The Economics of Sex Differentials.* New York: Columbia University Press.

Looft, W. 1971. "Sex Differences in the Expression of Vocational Aspirations by Elementary School Children." *Developmental Psychology* 5:366.

McCall, John. 1972. "The Simple Mathematics of Information, Job Search, and Prejudices." In *Racial Discrimination in Economic Life*, ed. Anthony Pascal, pp. 205–44. Lexington, Mass.: D. C. Heath.

Maccoby, Eleanor, and Carol Jacklin. 1974. *The Psychology of Sex Differences.* Stanford: Stanford University Press.

Madden, Janice. 1973. *The Economics of Sex Discrimination.* Lexington, Mass.: D. C. Heath.

Madden, Janice. 1975. "Discrimination—a Manifestation of Male Market Power?" In *Sex Discrimination and the Division of Labor*, ed. Cynthia Lloyd, pp. 146–74. New York: Columbia University Press.

Madden, Janice. 1976. "Comment III." In *Women and the Workplace*, ed. Martha Blaxall and Barbara Reagan, pp. 245–50. Chicago: University of Chicago Press.

Merchants and Manufacturers Association. 1970. *Labor Turnover Handbook.* Los Angeles: Merchants and Manufacturers Association.

Mincer, Jacob. 1974. *Schooling, Experience, and Earnings.* New York: National Bureau for Economic Research.

Mischel, Walter. 1976. *Introduction to Personality.* New York: Holt, Rinehart and Winston.

Mitchell, Juliet. 1976. "Four Structures in a Complex Unity." In *Liberating Women's History*, ed. Berenice A. Carroll, pp. 385–99. Urbana: University of Illinois Press.

O'Hara, Robert. 1962. "Roots of Careers." *Elementary School Journal* 62:177–80.

Parrish, John. 1965. "Employment of Women Chemists in Industrial Laboratories." *Sciences* 148:657–58.

Phelps, Edmund. 1972. "The Statistical Theory of Racism and Sexism." *American Economic Review* 62:659–61.

Piore, Michael. 1975. "Notes for a Theory of Labor Market Stratification." In *Labor Market Segmentation*, ed. Richard Edwards, Michael Reich, and David Gordon, pp. 125–50. Lexington, Mass.: D. C. Heath.

Piore, Michael. 1977. "The Dual Labor Market: Theory and Implications." In *Problems in Political Economy: An Urban Perspective,* ed. David Gordon, pp. 93–96. Lexington, Mass.: D. C. Heath.

Polachek, Solomon. 1976. "Occupational Segregation: An Alternative Hypothesis." *Journal of Contemporary Business* 5:1–12.

Polachek, Solomon. 1978. "Sex Differences in College Major." *Industrial and Labor Relations Review* 31:498–508.

Polachek, Solomon. 1979. "Occupational Segregation among Women: Theory, Evidence and a Prognosis." In *Women in the Labor Market*, ed. Cynthia Lloyd, pp. 137–57. New York: Columbia University Press.

Price, James. 1977. *The Study of Turnover.* Ames: Iowa State University Press.

Reich, Michael. 1981. *Racial Inequality: A Political Economic Analysis.* Princeton: Princeton University Press.

Robinson, John. 1977. *How Americans Use Time: A Social-Psychological Analysis of Everyday Behavior.* New York: Praeger.

Spence, A. Michael. 1974. *Market Signaling.* Cambridge: Harvard University Press.

Stevenson, Mary. 1975. "Relative Wages and Sex Segregation by Occupation." In *Sex, Discrimination, and the Division of Labor*, ed. Cynthia Lloyd, pp. 175–200. New York: Columbia University Press.

Stevenson, Mary. 1978. "Wage Differences between Men and Women." In *Women Working*, Ann Stromberg and Shirley Harkness, pp. 89–107. Palo Alto, Cal.: Mayfield.

Summers, Gene, Sharon Evans, Frank Clements, E. M. Beck, and Jon Minkoff. 1976. *Industrial Invasion of Nonmetropolitan America*. New York: Praeger.

Thurow, Lester. 1975. *Generating Inequality*. New York: Basic.

Tyler, Leona. 1964. "The Antecendents of Two Varieties of Vocational Interests." *Genetic Psychology Monographs* 70:177–227.

U.S. Bureau of the Census. 1973. *1970 Census of the Population*, Vol. 1: *Characteristics of the Population*, Part 1, *U.S. Summary*. Washington, D.C.: U.S. Government Printing Office.

U.S. Bureau of the Census. 1978. *Statistical Abstract of the U.S.—1978*. Washington, D.C.: U.S. Government Printing Office.

U.S. Civil Service Commission, President's Commission on the Status of Women. 1963. *Report of the Committee on Federal Employment*. Washington, D.C.: U.S. Government Printing Office.

U.S. Commission on Civil Rights. 1978. *Social Indicators of Equality for Minorities and Women*. Washington, D.C.: U.S. Government Printing Office.

Weitzman, Lenore. 1979. *Sex Role Socialization*. Palo Alto, Cal.: Mayfield.

Williams, Gregory. 1976. "Trends in Occupational Differentiation by Sex." *Sociology of Work and Occupations* 3:38–62.

Williams, Gregory. 1979. "The Changing U.S. Labor Force and Occupational Differentiation by Sex." *Demography* 16:73–88.

Wolf, Wendy, and N. Flingstein. 1979. "Sex and Authority in the Workplace: The Causes of Sexual Inequality." *American Sociological Review* 44:235–52.

Wolf, Wendy, and Rachel Rosenfeld. 1978. "Sex Structure of Occupations and Job Mobility." *Social Forces* 56:823–44.

Women's Bureau, U.S. Department of Labor. 1969. *Facts about Women's Absenteeism and Labor Turnover*. Washington, D.C.: U.S. Government Printing Office.

Zellner, Harriet. 1975. "The Determinants of Occupational Segregation." In *Sex, Discrimination, and the Division of Labor*, ed. Cynthia Lloyd, pp. 125–45. New York: Columbia University Press.

3

Some Psychological Factors Affecting Job Segregation and Wages

SHARON TOFFEY SHEPELA AND ANN T. VIVIANO

We believe there is a significant psychological component to the relationship between occupational segregation and wage differentials. The hypothesis we offer is the following: Women are paid less because they are in women's jobs, and women's jobs are paid less because they are done by women. The reason is that women's work—in fact, virtually anything done by women—is characterized as less valuable. In addition, the characteristics attributed to women are those our society values less. In the workplace, the reward (wage) is based on the characteristics the worker is perceived as bringing to the task as well as on the "pure" value of the task to the employer.[1] The lower the value of those characteristics, the lower the associated wage.

The situation is cyclical and interwoven because the factors themselves may not be independent. It may be that "female" characteristics are valued less precisely because they are considered female. The same may be said of the lower value placed on female activities. There are considerable anthropological and sociological data to indicate that the value of an activity or characteristic can be lowered simply through its association with women (Broverman et al., 1972; Ortner, 1974). Margaret Mead (1974) has said that in all cultures, without any known exception, male activity is seen as achievement. Whatever women do, from seed gathering to skilled crafts, is valued less than those same tasks are when performed by men in a different culture: "When men cook, cooking is viewed as an important activity; when women cook it is just a household chore. And correspondingly, if an activity once performed by women becomes more important in a society, it may be

---

Acknowledgment: An earlier version of this paper was presented as part of a symposium—Can the Law Reach: Sex-Bias in Wage Compensation—held at the meeting of the Psychological Association, Los Angeles, August 1981. This analysis is based on Ruth Blumrosen's hypothesis in "Wage Discrimination, Job Segregation, and Title VII of the Civil Rights Act of 1964." The authors' contribution is equal.

1. Consider the case of an employer determining the bonus for the solution of a manufacturing problem. Clearly it will make a difference whether the solution is seen as resulting from the worker's intelligent involvement in the task or from the worker's stumbling onto it.

taken over by men. For example, midwifery, once a profession in which the female practitioners were both constricted and feared, has been taken over by male obstetricians" (quoted in Williams, 1979:56).

The Psychological Argument

The following is the sequence of arguments that has lead us to our hypothesis.

1. People view the sexes differently from birth on.
2. Part of that different view involves differential evaluation of characteristics and work, with male work and characteristics more highly valued.
3. The different view includes differential attributions regarding the reasons for success and failure for women and men.
4. Studies on reward allocation in a simulated business setting show that differential rewards are based more on attributions than on gender, although the two are separated only with some difficulty.
5. The attributions that are more highly rewarded are those associated with males.
6. Gender-based occupational segregation may be related in part to these perceived attributes.
7. Therefore, if a job is perceived as a woman's job, associated with female attributes, it will be paid less, and if a woman is doing a neutral or male-dominated job, she will be seen as bringing to that job her female attributes, and the tendency will be to want to pay her less for the same job.

Different Views

That the sexes are viewed differently from birth has been well documented. Rubin, Provenzano, and Luria (1974) demonstrated parents' differential perception of female and male first-borns. They asked thirty pairs of parents (parents of fifteen girls and fifteen boys) to describe their infants before leaving the hospital, using an adjective checklist. The parents of the girls rated their infants as significantly smaller, finer-featured, softer, and less attentive than did the parents of the boys, despite the fact that there were no significant differences in length, weight, or physical condition between the babies at birth. The fathers' sex-typed ratings of both sons and daughters were more extreme than the mothers', although both mothers and fathers agreed on the direction of the difference. We see what we expect to see.

In another experiment, women who were themselves mothers were asked to interact with the same six-month-old child, who was identified to half of them as a male and to the rest as a female. The "girl" child was offered different toys than was the "boy" child, and the women described the child as typical of the sex they thought it to be (Will, Self, and Datan,

1974).[2] Seavey, Katz, and Zalk (1975) got similar results with male and female nonparent volunteers.

Condry and Condry (1976) videotaped an eighteen-month-old child and showed the same tape to adults. The same behavior was interpreted as "angry" if the adult subjects thought the child a boy and "afraid" if they thought the child a girl.

While adults' perception of children is influenced by the gender of the child, there appear to be few consistent gender-dependent patterns in parents' actual interaction with children, except that parents provide gender-typed toys and discourage children, especially boys, from engaging in activities they believe appropriate only for the opposite sex (Fling and Manosevitz, 1972; Maccoby and Jacklin, 1974; Rothbart and Maccoby, 1966).

The schools take up the message. Studies of textbooks show extremes of stereotyping. In a content analysis of 2,760 stories in 134 elementary school readers, Women on Words and Images (1975) discovered that males were shown in 147 different occupations and females in 26. The study found only three working mothers. Girls were found rehearsing their domestic roles 166 times to boys' 50. Passivity, docility, and dependence were attributed to girls six times as often as to boys: Tommy builds a playhouse; Sally stands and admires it. The positively valued characteristics of courage, exploration, and imagination were overwhelmingly attributed to males (216 to 68 instances), while industry, problem solving, courage, and strength were attributed selectively to males with similar ratios. As the grade level increased from first to sixth grade, the difference increased. Not only were girls perceived differently, but girls and women tended to disappear altogether from textbooks and this was especially true for science and math books. In the original 1972 study of 134 textbooks, the ratio of male-centered to female-centered stories was five to two; in 1975 it was seven to two. Weitzman and Rizzo (1974) found that the representation of women in illustrations in science textbooks dropped from 36 percent in the second grade to 18 percent in the sixth grade. One second-grade science series had no adult women in 99 of 100 pictures. Key (1975), summarizing over a dozen studies on this topic, reports that the findings are remarkably similar. While some positive changes have been made, and both male and female characters are more human, considerable stereotyping is still evident in textbooks (Morse, 1982). Whereas Mark once commented about Janet: "Look at her. She is just like a girl, she gives up," Pedro now makes the same comment about Nina, and our children learn that bias knows no cultural bonds.

In addition to presenting children with stereotypical images, the schools view and treat girls and boys differently. Serbin and O'Leary (1979) found

---

2. These same subjects strongly asserted that they did not treat their own children differently according to gender.

that nursery school teachers' differential responses to good and bad behavior by girls and boys actually resulted in more misbehavior by the boys.
Sears and Feldman (1974) found similar differences in teachers' perceptions
of and reactions to boys and girls.

Broverman et al. (1972), in a now classic study on sex role stereotypes,
found widespread agreement across age, sex, educational level, and marital
status on the reality and desirability of different characteristics for women
and men.

Differential Evaluation

"Different" does not necessarily imply "better" or "worse"; yet
perhaps one of the most consistent findings in the research on sex differences
is that males and females are evaluated differently. Both men and women
tend to value men and male attributes more highly than women and female
attributes (Broverman et al., 1972; Kitay, 1940; McKee and Sheriffs, 1957;
Smith, 1939). There is research indicating that male products are rated more
highly than female products, even when the quality of the actual products is
constant (Deaux and Taynor, 1973; Goldberg, 1968; Pheterson et al., 1971).
The Goldberg paradigm best illustrates these studies. An identical piece of
work—article, abstract, even art object—is attributed to John T. McKay
with one group of subjects and to Joan T. McKay with another. Each group
is asked to evaluate the work on a number of dimensions. The standard,
replicable result is that any work by a man is evaluated more favorably than
the identical work by a woman. This prediction fails only when the woman's
work has been independently highly rated, as when it has won an award.

In a work setting, the performance and credentials of women are rated
less favorably than those of an equivalent man (Cohen and Bunker, 1975;
Dipboye et al., 1977; Etaugh and Kasley, 1981; Francesco and Hakel, 1981;
Piacente et al., 1974; Rosen and Jerdee, 1974a and 1974b). In the Etaugh
and Kasley (1981) study, 184 female and 184 male college students read a
completed job application and an article written by a "person recently hired
as a newswriter for a local paper." Subjects were told that the study concerned the prediction of job success and were asked to answer eight evalua-
tive questions regarding the competence of the applicant and the merits of
the article. The manipulated factors were the sex and the marital and
parental status of the applicant. On all eight questions females were significantly devalued by both male and female subjects, but particularly by males.
Male applicants were rated as more professionally competent and dedicated
to the journalistic profession had a higher professional status, and greater
job success was predicted for them. The article, when ostensibly written by a
male, was more highly valued by the reader, was more influential in changing subjects' opinions, was judged better written, and got a higher overall
grade. Each subject rated only one applicant, so these data do not result
from a conscious comparison of men and women job applicants, although

they do represent a strong bias against women. Etaugh and Kasley suggest that the differences in the salaries of women and men may be due in part to these differences in perceived competence, and that this effect may be exacerbated by the fact that the vast majority of managers and administrators in the United States work force are male, the sex that in this study showed the greatest tendency to devalue women.

The pervasiveness of this sex bias appears even in situations in which equality between the sexes in a work environment seems to have been realized. In a recent organizational analysis of several large eastern corporations, women managers who perceive themselves to be equal to their male cohorts in a large, integrated organization were shown to have significantly less power (defined in terms of budget and personnel responsibilities), even when their slaries were equivalent (Harlan and Weiss, 1981).

Attributional Bias

Attributional bias is yet another manifestation of the phenomenon that men and women are viewed differently. The differential perceptions of males and females persist even when success and failure are to be explained. That is, the reasons offered for the success and failure of a male are different from the reasons offered for the success and failure of a female.

The research of Pheterson et al. (1971) demonstrated that specific information regarding the quality of performance eliminates sex-linked biases in the evaluation of that performance. This research has generated additional questions about whether observers attribute identical causes to identical performances. According to Deaux and Emsweller (1974), they do not. In their study, males' performance was more likely to be attributed to ability, whereas females' performance was more likely to be attributed to luck. This difference in attribution of cause was particularly evident when the task performed was masculine in nature. Subsequent research in this area showed that male success, which is expected, is attributed to ability, a stable explanation, whereas female success, which is unexpected, is attributed to the unstable explanation of luck (Deaux and Farris, 1977; Etaugh and Brown, 1975).

Deaux (1976) suggests that the choice of these attributions reflects the stereotypical assumption that men are more competent and women incompetent. That is, competence or success is explained differently in men and women because it is expected in men but unexpected in women. When failure is to be explained, the findings continue to show the same pattern. In the research of Feather and Simon (1975), failure by a man was attributed to unstable, external causes such as bad luck, whereas the failure of a woman was attributed to stable, internal causes such as lack of ability. According to Weiner et al. (1971), we attribute performance to stable factors when we expected that performance and expect it to recur in the future and to unstable factors when it was unexpected and we do not expect it to recur.

Therefore, the consistent attribution of women's success to luck reflects the unexpectedness of that success to the evaluators and their anticipation that it will not recur.

Results of recent research has shed further light on these findings. Garland and Price (1977) gave male subjects descriptions of a successful or unsuccessful female manager and asked them to rate each of four possible causes for the success or failure: two internal variables (ability and effort, or the lack of them) and two external variables (luck and the easiness or difficulty of the job). Effort received the highest rating for explaining success and lack of effort received the highest rating for explaining failure.

Stevens and DeNisi (1980) replicated the Garland and Price study and included both male and female subjects. In their study, men attributed a woman's success to the internal but unstable factor of effort, whereas women attributed it to either the internal stable factor of ability or the internal unstable factor of effort. Men attributed women's failure to either lack of ability, which is internal and stable *or* task difficulty, which is external and unstable; women attributed failure primarily to the internal, stable factor of lack of ability. Men's attributions are thus similar to those found by Garland and Price (1977). However, an interesting difference emerged: women added the possibility that women succeed because of a stable factor, and men added the possibility that women fail because of an unstable factor.

The trend of all the results reported above is that people explain the success and failure of men and women differently. Men's success is internal and stable; it was expected, and it will occur again. Women's success is external and unstable; it was unexpected, and it will not recur.

Practical Consequences of Attitudinal and Attributional Biases

Rose and Stone (1978) suggest that widely shared sex role stereotypes may result in performance decisions based on unwarranted performance inferences. Hence, employees, despite good performance records, risk being discriminated against and having their careers disrupted when organizational rewards are distributed.

Indeed, several studies have shown that identical performances by males and females result in different rewards. In an early study of the consequence of sex role stereotypes, Rosen and Jerdee (1974a) asked ninety-five male bank managers to assume the role of a personnel manager and to make four decisions. The results were as follows: a male applicant was recommended for promotion to branch manager significantly more often than a female; the male applicant received significantly higher ratings for both customer and employee relations; and, when an employee was chosen to attend a conference, a highly promotable female was preferred only slightly more than an employee with less potential, whereas a highly promotable male was strongly preferred over an employee with less potential.

In a later study, Rosen and Jerdee (1974b) asked subjects to take the role of a consultant to a clothing manufacturer who had to fill four executive positions. Female applicants were selected significantly less often; males received significantly higher ratings for technical potential, potential for long service to the organization, and potential for fitting in; and females were rejected for the most demanding job significantly more often than the males. Similar results were obtained by Dipboye et al. (1975) for more demanding jobs. The pattern that this research has identified is, as Rose and Stone suggest, that organizational rewards are distributed inequitably on the basis of gender alone.

Terborg and Ilgen (1975), in an attempt to understand this phenomenon more thoroughly, examined the effects of sex role stereotypes on two types of discrimination: access and treatment. Access discrimination refers to pre-job-related limitations and rejection based on these reasons: for example, discrimination involving the decision to hire and starting salary. Treatment discrimination refers to invalid differential treatment once a person has been hired—discrimination in, for example, employee development, employee evaluation, delegation of assignments, and promotion.

In their study, personnel administration undergraduates were asked to complete an in-basket exercise that included rating the resumes of three applicants for an engineer's job. They were asked which, if any, of the applicants were unacceptable, to set a starting salary, and to evaluate the applicants' past performance. The results indicated that the woman's performance was seen as due to luck more than was the man's. Furthermore, perhaps as a result of this differential evaluation, the female applicant was assigned a significantly lower starting salary and second-year salary than the identical male applicant. Analysis of the treatment variables reveals that the likelihood of being sent to training programs correlates with how lucky a woman is viewed to be, rather than with ability or effort, whereas both task assignment and size of bonus correlate with how much ability a man is seen to possess. The authors suggest that a less ostentatious form of discrimination occurs when the applicant is rated as acceptable but, because of sex or minority group status is offered a lower starting salary.

Some research has focused on the sex context of the situation, which includes the sex of both the evaluatee and his or her subordinates. Rose and Stone (1978) asked business students to make career decisions about four managers. Male managers managing females received significantly higher salaries than male managers managing males, but female managers' salaries did not depend on their subordinates' sex. In addition, male managers were expected to remain with the organization longer than female ones.

The pattern that these studies reveal is that women, because they are women, are less likely to be hired or promoted and more likely to receive lower starting salaries. Thus, the devaluation of women and their products discussed above has been shown to have practical consequences in terms of hiring, salaries, and promotion.

Some recent research has illustrated that it is not gender per se that causes these differential perceptions, attributions, and rewards, but rather expectations about men and women and responses to the traits, behaviors and characteristics associated with them. A study that provides evidence supporting this view was conducted by Heilman and Souivatari (1979). They suggest that physical attractiveness exaggerates perceptions of gender-related attributes, thus enhancing sex bias in reward. In their study, attractiveness in a male always led to higher evaluations and stronger recommendations to hire than unattractiveness. But attractiveness benefited females only when they were applying for nonmanagerial jobs. Unattractive female applicants for managerial jobs received higher evaluations of their qualifications and stronger recommendations to hire than attractive applicants. The authors conclude that the more attractive a woman is, the less suitable she will be judged for a job that is thought to require male characteristics. That is, since a female is already seen as possessing fewer managerial traits (Shein, 1973, 1975), the more attractive she is, the greater the incongruity between her gender and the job.

Heilman and Guzzo (1978) suggest that it is the causal attributions made about the success of men and women that result in discriminatory behavior. In their study, male and female MBA students were given "supervisors'" evaluations of subordinates. These evaluations were varied along the luck/ability continuum for both males and females. The subjects were asked to make salary and promotion decisions about four employees, all identified as either male or female. Their results indicate that success attributed to ability or effort received higher pay in both males and females than success attributed to luck. In addition, promotions were more strongly favored for able employees than for those exhibiting either effort or luck. Since ability is typically attributed to males, it appears likely that they will receive higher rewards than females, whose performance, though comparable, is attributed to luck when its cause is left to inference.

Probably the most interesting finding of this study was that females were preferred significantly more often for promotion than were males when ability as the cause of performance was held constant. Perhaps ability is so unexpected in females that it is highly rewarded when found. This interpretation is partly supported by Heilman and Guzzo's (1978) further finding that subjects were more likely to attribute characteristics typically considered requisite for high-quality management to employees whose success derived from ability. Since a vast body of research has indicated that these managerial traits are identical to traits attributed to men (Shein, 1973, 1975), ability in a woman is considered highly unusual.

A recent study (Wittig et al., 1981) confirmed the results obtained by Heilman and Guzzo (1978). Subjects awarded a significantly greater proportion of a reward to themselves when the experimenter attributed their performance to effort rather than to luck.

Mai-Dalton, et al. (1979) compared the effects on perceived effectiveness and likelihood of promotion of behavior consistent or inconsistent with female stereotypes. They gave male and female banking executives of equal rank a scenario describing a male and female manager dealing with an incident in an emotional (angry) or unemotional (calm) manner. Calm and unemotional behavior was rated significantly more effective and appropriate. Furthermore, the calm manager was seen as significantly more likely to be promoted, regardless of gender, than the angry manager. As in the Heilman and Guzzo study, the behavior expected of women received poorer responses than the behavior expected of men, and women who behaved as the men did received the same reward.

That we do still expect men and women to act differently was confirmed by Locksley et al. (1980), who found that a target's behavior (assertive or passive), and not his or her gender, determined whether he or she was viewed as masculine or feminine. Furthermore, in the absence of any other information, significantly more assertiveness was attributed to males than females, and subjects believed that a significantly greater proportion of males than females were assertive. Finally, they found that prior beliefs about the proportion of assertive males and females correlated with judgments of the probable assertiveness of subjects when no behavioral information about assertiveness was given.

The studies reported in this section indicate that we still have expectations of men and women that are consistent with traditional stereotypes and that the behavior consistent with the female stereotype receives lower rewards than that consistent with the male stereotype, regardless of the gender of the person exhibiting the behavior.

Summary

We have proposed that women earn less money than men because women are culturally devalued and their work is devalued as a result. Some of the alternative arguments are that women lack certain key credentials, such as tenure; they have interrupted their careers; they have different qualifications; and they tend to work part-time. If these variables were truly the explanation for lower pay, then we would predict that women who had the same tenure, had not interrupted their careers, had worked full-time, and so on should make the same money as a comparable man. However, studies show this not to be the case, and even when individual women *do* make the same money as a comparable man, their power and control are not the same.

Our review has clearly indicated that women earn less money because they are in women's jobs, because the attributions made about women in general are extended to what they do on their jobs, and, finally, because anything associated with women is worth less in our society than things associated with men.

What are the implications of this research for policy decisions regarding compensation systems? We have shown that there are deeply ingrained, pervasive psychological biases that affect decisions made about the competence and work of women. Women's work is everywhere devalued. The subtle forces that we hypothesize to be in part responsible for continued gender-based wage discrimination will be difficult to eradicate, but their effects have been well documented. Those trying to develop equitable compensation systems must assume that bias will be in operation and control its effects as best they can.

References

Broverman, I., S. Vogel, D. Broverman, F. Clarkson, and P. Rosenkrantz. 1972. "Sex-Role Stereotypes: A Current Appraisal." *Journal of Social Issues* 23: 59–78.

Cohen, Stephen, and Kerry Bunker. 1975. "Subtle Effects of Sex-Role Stereotypes on Recruiters' Hiring Decisions " *Journal of Applied Psychology* 60:566–72.

Condry, John, and Sandra Condry. 1976. "In the Eye of the Beholder." *Child Development* 47:812–19.

Deaux, Kay. 1976. "Sex: A Perspective on the Attribution Process." In *New Directions in Attribution Research*, Vol. 1, ed. Ickes and Kidd, pp. 335–52. New York: Erlbaum.

Deaux, Kay, and T. Emsweller. 1974. "Explanations of Successful Performance on Sex-Linked Tasks: What Is Skill for the Male Is Luck for the Female." *Journal of Personality and Social Psychology* 29:80–85.

Deaux, Kay, and Elizabeth Farris. 1977. "Attributing Causes for One's Own Performance: The Effects of Sex, Norms, and Outcome." *Journal of Research in Personality* 11:59–72.

Deaux, Kay, and Janet Taynor. 1973. "Evaluation of Male and Female Ability: Bias Works Two Ways." *Psychological Reports* 32:261–62.

Dipboye, R. L., R. D. Arvey, and D. E. Terpstra. 1977. "Sex and Physical Attractiveness of Raters and Applicants as Determinants of Resume Evaluations." *Journal of Applied Psychology* 62:288–94.

Dipboye, Robert L., Howard L. Framkin, and Kent Wilback. 1975. "Relative Importance of Applicant Sex, Attractiveness, and Scholastic Standing in Evaluation of Job Applicant Resumes." *Journal of Applied Psychology* 60:39–43.

Etaugh, Claire, and Barry Brown. 1975. "Perceiving the Causes of Success and Failure of Male and Female Performers." *Developmental Psychology* 11:103.

Etaugh, Claire, and Helen C. Kasley. 1981. *"Evaluating Competence: Effects of* Sex, Marital Status, and Parental Status." *Psychology of Women Quarterly* 6:196–203.

Feather, N. T., and J. G. Simon. 1975. "Reactions to Male and Female Success and Failure in Sex-Linked Occupations: Impressions of Personality, Causal Attributions and Perceived Likelihood of Different Consequences." *Journal of Personality and Social Psychology* 31:20–31.

Fling, S., and M. Manosevitz. 1972. "Sex Typing in Nursery School Children's Play Interest." *Developmental Psychology* 7:146–52.

Francesco, Anne Marie, and Milton Hakel. 1981. "Gender and Sex as Determinants of Hireability of Applicants for Gender-Typed Jobs." *Psychology of Women Quarterly* 5:747–57.

Garland, H., and K. Price. 1977. "Attitudes Toward Women in Management and Attributions for Their Success and Failure in a Managerial Position." *Journal of Applied Psychology* 62:29–33.

Goldberg, P. A. 1968. "Are Women Prejudiced against Women?" *Trans-Action* (April): 28–30.

Harlan, Anne, and Carol Weiss. 1981. "Moving Up: Women in Managerial Careers." Working Paper. Center for Research on Women, Wellesley College, Wellesley, Mass.

Heilman, M. E., and R. A. Guzzo. 1978. "The Perceived Cause of Work Success as a Mediator of Sex Discrimination in Organizations." *Organizational Behavior and Human Performance* 21:346–57.

Heilman, Madeline E., and Lois R. Souivatari. 1979. "When Beauty Is Beastly: The Effects of Appearance and Sex on Evaluations of Job Applicants for Managerial and Nonmanagerial Jobs." *Organizational Behavior and Human Performance* 23:360–72.

Key, Mary R. 1975. "The Role of Male and Female in Children's Books—Dispelling All Doubt. In *Women: Dependent or Independent Variable?* ed. Rhoda Unger and Florence Denmark, pp. 55–70. New York: Psychological Dimensions.

Kitay, P. M. 1940. "A Comparison of the Sexes in Their Attitudes and Beliefs about Women." *Sociometry* 34:399–407.

Locksley, Anne, Eugene Borgida, Nancy Brekke, and Christine Hepburn. 1980. "Sex Stereotypes and Social Judgement." *Journal of Personality and Social Psychology* 39:821–31.

Maccoby, Eleanor, and Carol Jacklin. 1974. *The Psychology of Sex Differences.* Stanford: Stanford University Press.

McKee, J. P., and A. C. Sheriffs. 1957. "The Differential Evaluation of Males and Females." *Journal of Personality* 25:356–63.

Mai-Dalton, R. R., S. Feldman-Summers, and T. R. Mitchell. 1979. "Effect of Employee Gender and Behavioral Style on the Evaluation of Male and Female Banking Executives." *Journal of Applied Psychology* 64: 221–26.

Mead, Margaret. 1974. "On Freud's View of Female Psychology." In *Women and Analysis*, ed. J. Strouse. New York: Grossman.

Morse, Tracey, 1982. "The Same Old Story in a Variety of Covers: Sex-Role Stereotypes in Children's Resources." Manuscript prepared for Psychology 102, Hartford College for Women, Hartford, Conn.

Ortner, Sherry. 1974. "Is Female to Male as Nature Is to Culture?" In *Women, Culture and Society*, ed. Michelle Rosaldo and Louise Lamphere, pp. 67–87. Stanford: Stanford University Press.

Pheterson, G. I., Sara B. Kiesler, and Phillip A. Goldberg. 1971. "Evaluation of the Performance of Women as a Function of Their Sex, Achievement, and Personal History." *Journal of Personality and Social Psychology* 19:114–18.

Piacente, B. S., L. A. Penner, H. L. Hawkins, and S. L. Cohen. 1974. "Evaluation of the Performance of Experimenters as a Function of Their Sex and Competence." *Journal of Applied Social Psychology* 4:321–29.

Rose, G., and T. Stone. 1978. "Why Good Job Performance May (Not) Be Rewarded: Sex Factors and Career Development." *Journal of Vocational Behavior* 12:197–207.

Rosen, B., and T. Jerdee. 1974a. "Influence of Sex-Role Stereotypes on Personnel Decisions." *Journal of Applied Psychology* 59:9–14.

Rosen, B., and T. Jerdee. 1974b. "Effects of Applicants' Sex and Difficulty of Job on Evaluations of Candidates for Managerial Positions." *Journal of Applied Psychology* 59:511–12.

Rothbart, M., and Eleanor Maccoby. 1966. "Parent's Differential Reaction to Sons and Daughters." *Journal of Personality and Social Psychology* 4:237–43.

Rubin, J. Z., F. J. Provenzano, and Z. Luria. 1974, "The Eye of the Beholder: Parents' Views on Sex of Newborns." *American Journal of Orthopsychiatry* 44: 512–19.

Sears, P., and D. Feldman. 1974. "Teacher Interactions with Boys and with Girls." In *And Jill Came Tumbling After: Sexism in American Education*, ed. J. Stacey, S. Bereaud, and J. Daniels, pp. 149–58. New York: Dell.

Seavey, C. A., P. A. Katz, and S. R. Zalk. 1975. "Baby X: The Effect of Gender Labels on Adult Responses to Infants." *Sex Roles* 1:103–9.

Serbin, Lisa, and K. Daniel O'Leary. 1979. "How Nursery Schools Teach Girls to Shut Up. In *Psychology of Women: Selected Readings*, ed. Juanita Williams, pp. 183–87.

Shein, Virginia Ellen. 1973. "The Relationship between Sex-Role Stereotypes and Requisite Management Characteristics." *Journal of Applied Psychology* 57: 95–100.

Shein, Virginia Ellen. 1975. "Relationships between Sex Role Stereotypes and Requisite Management Characteristics among Female Managers." *Journal of Applied Psychology* 60:340–44.

Smith, S. 1939. "Age and Sex Differences in Children's Opinions Concerning Sex Differences." *Journal of Genetic Psychology* 54:12–25.

Stevens, G., and A. DeNisi. 1980. "Women as Managers: Attitudes and Attributions for Performance by Men and Women." *Academy of Management Journal* 23:355–61.

Terborg, James R., and Daniel R. Ilgen. 1975. "A Theoretical Approach to Sex Discrimination in Traditionally Masculine Occupations." *Organizational Behavior and Human Performance* 13:352–76.

Weiner, B., I. Freize, A. Kukla, L. Reed, A. Rest, and R. Rosenbaum. 1971. *Perceiving the Causes of Success and Failure*. Morristown, N.J.: General Learning Press.

Weitzman, Lenore, and Diane Rizzo. 1974. "Images of Males and Females in Elementary School Textbooks." Manuscript and slide presentation. Department of Sociology, University of California, Davis.

Will, J., P. Self, and N. Datan. 1976. "Maternal Behavior and Perceived Sex of Infant." *American Journal of Orthopsychiatry* 46 (1):135–39.

Williams, J. 1979. *Psychology of Women: Selected Readings*. New York: Norton.

Wittig, Michele A., Gary Marks, and Gary A. Jones. 1981. "Luck versus Effort Attributions: Effect on Reward Allocations to Self and Other." *Personality and Social Psychology Bulletin* 7(1):71–78.

Women on Words and Images. 1972. *Dick and Jane as Victims: Sex-Stereotyping in Children's Readers*. Princeton: Princeton University Press.

Women on Words and Images. 1975. *Dick and Jane as Victims: Sex-Stereotyping in Children's Readers*. 2d ed. Princeton: Princeton University Press.

PART II

Technical Issues in Job Evaluation

4

Some Problems with Contemporary Job Evaluation Systems

RICHARD W. BEATTY AND JAMES R. BEATTY

How wages are determined is receiving renewed attention as organizations seek ways to explain their compensation policies to employees. Historically, the systems for allocating pay have been kept secret, even while organizations profess their relatedness to attracting, maintaining, and motivating the best available workers from the labor market. Much research has been conducted concerning how organizations should use pay as a motivator for achieving organizational objectives. There has been a paucity of research, however, on how organizations use compensation to attract and maintain a work force.

Basically, compensation practices address internal equity, external equity, and individual equity. Internal equity determines the relative value of jobs within a firm; external equity the value of each job with respect to prevailing labor market prices; and individual equity the compensation given an individual employee for that employee's output (i.e., merit pay). This chapter focuses primarily upon internal equity (i.e., the job evaluation practices in organizations), reviewing and critiquing current practices, noting the advantages and disadvantages of alternative methods, and reviewing research on the validity of job evaluation. It concludes with a discussion not only of the limitations of job evaluation systems, but also of ways to improve them.

Job evaluation has not been widely studied in personnel/human resources research (Schwab, 1980). It has been practiced by consultants whose methodologies have been kept confidential to protect "trade secrets," which had led to considerable mysticism, if not occasional deception, on the part of consultants in the compensation area. We do not attempt to review all approaches to job evaluation here, but rather the major ones, to give the novice an idea of current methods and their problems.

One purpose of job evaluation is to develop an internal hierarchy of job worth (i.e., job structure), which denotes the value of the job, as seen by the firm, relative to other jobs within that firm. The job is to be evaluated, not the employee in that position. Thus, most job evaluation methodologies focus upon job content to determine a job's worth, which is then compared with external labor market prices to assess the correspondence between the internal valuing of jobs and the labor market value. Traditionally, the internal valuing of jobs has been driven by the external valuing; the internal values assigned to jobs were generally expected to mirror labor market pricing with respect to salaries. Thus, much of the current controversy over job evaluation is limited by the fact that the "value" of jobs is generally determined (or dictated) by the labor market, which in turn dictates most internal evaluation methodologies (Schwab, 1980). If this is the case, then job evaluation may not be the total solution hoped for by comparable worth advocates, as discussed elsewhere in this volume, in that traditional job evaluation methodologies are generally based upon market prices and not upon an independent, internal system of values developed by an organization, its compensation committee members, society at large, and so on.

The original purpose of job evaluation was to develop a surrogate to price jobs where there was inadequate labor market information. Where adequate labor market data existed, prices were obtained from the market and used to assign wages, thereby avoiding much of the "hocus-pocus" of job evaluation. Organizations have always been concerned about the equity of job pricing with respect to the market, but the concept that *internal* equity should determine the worth of a job (or a class of jobs) relative to others within the organization became a reality only because there existed little data for establishing external equity.

Job Analysis

Job evaluation programs follow a fairly fixed pattern: job analysis and description; determination of compensable factors; job evaluation; and compensation structure. Almost invariably, job evaluation systems begin with some form of job analysis, or field audit of positions, in order to ensure that job content is adequately captured. The collection of job evaluation data may differ from traditional job analysis in that some job evaluation systems collect information only on compensable factors, as determined by their relevance to the labor market. Thus, in many organizations traditional job analysis is not used for job evaluation, and more than one job analysis is conducted; that is, one job analysis is conducted for job descriptions, performance appraisals, and selection criteria, while another is conducted for job evaluation, in which only information relative to determining a job's value is sought.

There are many methods of job analysis, only a few of which will be discussed here. Reference to the federal government's "Uniform Guidelines on Employee Selection Procedures" (1978) will be made; not to recognize these regulations in an arca fraught with controversy and litigation potential would be shortsighted. For any job evaluation system to work, job content should be exhaustively examined; too often it is overlooked or not effectively assessed in the development of job evaluation instruments.

The purpose of job content identification is to enable the job analyst to identify the tasks, personal characteristics, or behaviors that are required on the job. These points are clearly demonstrated in the following statement from the "Guidelines," which is almost always introduced by plaintiffs in employment discrimination cases:

> *Job analysis or review of job information.* A description of the procedure used to analyze the job or group of jobs, or to review the job information should be provided (essential). Where a review of job information results in criteria which may be used without a full job analysis, . . . the basis for the selection of those criteria should be reported (essential). Where a job analysis is required a complete description of the work behavior(s) or work outcome(s) and measures of their criticality or importance should be provided (essential). The report should describe the basis on which the behavior(s) or outcome(s) were determined to be critical or important, such as the proportion of time spent on the respective behaviors, their level of difficulty, their frequency of performance, the consequences of error, or other appropriate factors (essential). (1978:38300–38301)

This quotation focuses attention on the nature of the job itself and on the methods used to capture information. The key point is to seek specific information about the job. The types of information sought have been described by McCormick (1976) and reproduced in Figure 4-1. In practice most job analyses capture some information about the work to be performed and some information about the worker's personal characteristics, often through a loosely structured interview or survey. The purpose of any job evaluation effort should dictate the method or methods chosen to collect data for each job. A job analysis including all of the items mentioned in Figure 4-1 from a single job would easily capture commonly cited differences in jobs in terms of skill, effort, responsibility, and working conditions.

Many approaches to gathering information about jobs are available. They are discussed in some detail here because most reports on job evaluation seem to ignore much about this critical step. Basically, job analysts interview incumbents, observe incumbents, examine the work environment and equipment used, study previous job descriptions and other job informa-

Figure 4-1
Worker and Worker-Oriented Data
Compared through Job Analysis

1. Work activities

   Task-oriented activities (description of the work activities performed, expressed in "job" terms, usually indicating what is accomplished, such as galvanizing, weaving, cleaning, etc. Sometimes such activity descriptions also indicate how, why, and when a worker performs an activity; usually the activities are those involving active human participation, but in certain approaches they may characterize machine or system functions)

   • Work activities/processes
   • Procedures used
   • Activity records (films, etc.)
   • Personal accountability/responsibility

2. Worker-oriented activities

   A. Human behaviors (behaviors performed in work, such as sensing, decision making, performing physical actions, communicating, etc.)
   B. Elemental motions (such as used in methods analysis)
   C. Personal job demands (human expenditures involved in work, such as energy expenditure, etc.)
   D. Machines, tools, equipment, and work aids used
   E. Job-related tangibles and intangibles

      • Materials processed
      • Products made
      • Knowledge dealt with or applied (such as law or chemistry)
      • Services rendered (such as laundering or repairing)

   F. Work performance

      • Work measurement (i.e., time taken)
      • Work standards
      • Error analysis
      • Other aspects

   G. Job context

      • Physical working conditions
      • Work schedule
      • Organizational context
      • Social context
      • Incentives

   H. Personnel requirements

      • Job-related knowledge/skills (education, training, work experience, etc., required)
      • Personal attributes (aptitudes, physical characteristics, personality, interests, etc., required)

Source: E. J. McCormick, 1976 "Job and Task Analysis," in *Handbook of Industrial and Organizational Psychology*, ed. M. D. Dunnette, pp. 652–53. Chicago: Rand McNally.

tion, use a structured (quantitative) job analysis questionnaire, or perform some combination of these techniques. A task-oriented approach is used in the military (Cristal, 1964) and in several civilian settings (Chalupsky, 1962), and a worker-oriented approach has been suggested by McCormick, Jeanneret, and Mecham (1972) and by Fleishman (1972, 1975). Other, less widely used models include dimensions of human motivation (Hackman and Oldham, 1975), critical behaviors (Flanagan, 1954), and physiological data and numerous industrial engineering factors (Salvendy and Seymour, 1973). Each of these stresses a different aspect of work. We have selected five specific information-gathering methods for discussion here: the functional job language technique, the critical incident technique, the job inventory technique, the job element technique, and the Position Analysis Questionnaire (PAQ).

Qualitative Methods

The *functional job language technique* (U.S. Department of Labor, 1972 and 1974) derives job information by interviewing incumbents and requesting that forms be completed describing what is done on the job. The emphasis here is on identifying worker activities, as is done in the *Dictionary of Occupational Titles* (U.S. Department of Labor, 1977), also known as the *DOT*, which gives descriptive information on over 35,000 jobs. A coding system enables analysts to describe the functions and complexity of each job in terms of working with data, people, and things. The *DOT* can thus be helpful when beginning a job analysis. It should be noted, however, that functional job analysis is used to summarize dimensions of job duties in a qualitative manner and may have limited use for job evaluation because of the *DOT*'s very general job specifications.

The *critical incident technique*, another qualitative model, requires job incumbents to be surveyed to ascertain what activities are critical to effective or ineffective performance (Flanagan, 1954). Employees are asked to describe situations that made a difference in effective work performance. Rather than identifying all relevant worker functions, as is done in the functional job language technique, this model identifies only those critical to effective performance.

Quantitative Methods

In the *job inventory technique*, predetermined lists of job content are given to incumbents and/or supervisors, who are to note the frequency or importance of a job's tasks. A final list of job content dimensions is created from this list. Such a procedure avoids the questions about reliability that arise with nonquantitative methods that may not use the same words to describe the same job dimensions contained in different jobs. Where there are several incumbents, multiple ratings can easily be obtained and checked for reliability; the ratings can also be compared to supervisory reports to gauge supervisor-subordinate agreement.

These systems are usually referred to as job inventory or task inventory methods of "scored questionnaires" (American Society for Personnel Administration and American Compensation Association, 1981), and consist of a list of tasks relevant to all job titles within an organization. These methods are similar to "checklists," although the term "checklist" may be inappropriate because it implies a "checking" of items, whereas most job inventories require more complex responses, such as rating the importance of each job content item on the list. Well-designed job inventories usually consist of statements of activities, omitting obvious cues as to expected outcome.

A major contributor to the development of job inventory techniques has been the Personnel Division of the U.S. Air Force Human Resources Laboratory (Cristal, 1964). Other military services have adopted them as well, and at least a few other organizations—private and governmental—have used some form of job inventory for research or operational purposes.

Another example of a quantitative procedure is the *job element technique*, which questions job "experts" about important work activities (Primoff, 1974). Each expert is to respond to four questions about a job element to determine its importance. It should be noted that job elements are usually human qualities or traits and not behaviors or tasks. The form used to collect job content information requires a very complex scoring procedure.

The *Position Analysis Questionnaire* (PAQ) is a worker-oriented, quantitative approach that is attractive for job analysis. It assumes that although diverse jobs may contain an infinite number of unique activities, all activities can be characterized in terms of a finite number of common, underlying process elements that capture the entire "world of work." The PAQ consists of 186 items on a standard questionnaire that can be used to build a profile of any job and rank it relative to others on such broad categories as interpersonal activity or job situation and context. It is perhaps its standardization and ability to rank jobs that have made it popular. The PAQ is a statistically derived instrument resulting from several years of research into the nature of work. Certainly one considerable problem in job analysis—reliability—can be solved with the PAQ. As a worker-oriented approach, it is also easier to administer because it can be compiled in a single booklet and simultaneously administered to all incumbents and across all jobs.

Any of these techniques can help a job analyst specify the behaviors or activities that encompass a particular job. Once this information is gathered, education, training, and experience levels or other requirements can be developed. For large organizations the best approach to job analysis may be quantitative. To develop a quantitative job analysis system, job analysts could use existing job content information such as job descriptions or previous performance appraisals; or they could use the functional language technique and the *DOT* to collect basic data on job content. Once a list of tasks is obtained, it can be distributed to all job incumbents to identify which of their tasks—usually ten to twelve—are most important, most frequently performed, or most critical. A system for scoring these tasks can then be devised, and once the tasks are identified for each job title, a system for evaluating each job can be devised as well. Such a system should meet at least the minimal expectations of the "Guidelines" for the capture of job content information.

The PAQ, and the numerous other quantitative job analysis methodologies all provide useful approaches to job analysis, although questions have been raised about their reliability (Milkovich, 1980; Schwab, 1980). There are also difficulties in deciding what levels of job analysis should be pursued (e.g., task, position, job, occupation, or family level). These are difficult and still unresolved issues (Pearlman, 1980). There is also the possibility that the sex of the job analyst may interfere with the accurate assessment of job content (Schwab, 1980). These issues will be further explored later.

The Assessment of Job Analysis

The courts' assessment of the adequacy and importance of job analysis seems to be inconsistent, but they have generally been lenient in their requirements for the analysis of job content. Thirty-one cases of performance appraisal litigation were reviewed by Kleiman and Faley (1978). In only eleven did defendants conduct job analysis: for example, *Bridgeport Guardians* v. *Police Department* (16 FEP 486), *Chance* v. *Board of Examiners* (Appeals, 4 FEP 556), *Davis* v. *Washington* (5 FEP 293), *Commonwealth of Pennsylvania* v. *Flaherty* (11 EPD 10,624), *Jones* v. *New York Human Resources Administration* (11 EPD 10,664), *Shield Club* v. *City of Cleveland* (13 FEP 533), *U.S.* v. *City of St. Louis* (Appeals, 14 FEP 1486), and *Western Addition Community Organization* v. *Alioto* (Appeals, 6 FEP 85).

In the twenty other cases, the court assumed knowledge of the job or relied on either expert testimony or pre-existing information, such as job descriptions or specifications that were developed for other purposes. Despite the fact that job analysis is essential to validity, the study found that the absence of formal job analysis had little effect on the rulings. In only three cases—*Kirkland* v. *Department of Correctional Services* (7 FEP 694), *Vulcan Society* v. *Civil Service Commission* (6 FEP 1945) and *Western Addition Community Organization* v. *Alioto* (4 FEP 772)—did a judge rule against a defendant for failure perform an adequate job analysis. Kleiman and Faley concluded that "in the vast majority of cases, . . . the courts failed to consider the issue" and that the courts' evaluations were based upon whatever job information was available, regardless of how it was obtained.

What basis do the courts use, then, to evaluate job analysis? It appears that job analysis may be accepted if it is done in "good faith" or by obtaining a statement of the duties by consulting with a subject matter expert (e.g., job incumbents, job analysts, and supervisors) to determine the most significant responsibilities of the job. Thus, it appears as if the courts are not presently following the "Guidelines" for job analysis requirements in their performance appraisal decisions and may not do so in job evaluation cases; but to deviate too far from the "Guidelines" may prove to be dangerous in the future.

A joint publication by the American Society for Personnel Administration and the American Compensation Association entitled *Elements of Sound Base Pay Administration* (1981) advocates that whatever the method of job analysis used, descriptions should describe the nature (principle duties) and the level of skill and responsibility of the work performed, the types and amounts of mental and physical effort required, and the general physical conditions under which the work is performed. They summarize job description requirements for job evaluation as follows:

1. A job identification section including job title, department or location, company, date of completion, and an area for approval.
2. A general summary or job purpose statement.
3. A list of principal duties and responsibilities of the incumbent(s). It is not necessary to list every conceivable task. Rather, major responsibility areas should be highlighted. In addition, some indication of priority of duties or percent of time spent on each can be most helpful . . . including some or all of the following information, either in the description itself or in some other document:

   1. The minimum levels of knowledge, skill, *and* abilities required to perform the work adequately.
   2. Relevant scope data, such as budget, sales or profit responsibility, number of people supervised, etc.
   3. The nature and extent of supervision received and given.
   4. The physical and mental effort required.
   5. The physical working conditions under which the work is performed.
   6. A disclaimer clause, stating that the job description is not necessarily all inclusive in terms of work detail. (p. 12)

We have demonstrated some of the limitations of various analysis methods. Effective job evaluation requires that pains be taken in capturing information about job content.

Job Evaluation

Many considerations influence an organization's allocation of pay. These include the importance of pay to the organization and the organization's pay philosophy (e.g., training and developing versus hiring fully proficient employees), ability to pay, the financial consequences of employee withdrawal (in the form of turnover, absenteeism, and tardiness) due to dissatisfaction with pay, government regulations regarding pay systems (e.g., minimum wage and discrimination laws), the motivational uses of pay (performance and retention), the extent of unionization, industry practices, and tradition. These considerations cause variances in compensation across jobs in organizations.

There are numerous methods for designing an internal wage structure based on the "worth" or "value" of each job relative to other jobs with the objective of providing equal pay for jobs of equal worth or importance, and differentials between jobs not of equal value. The rationale is that jobs are not all equally valuable to an organization and therefore are not compensated the same. For example, some jobs are in high demand and others in low demand, some have high status and others low, some call for large amounts of responsibility and others little, some are boring and others interesting, some are risky and others safe, some demand a high degree of specialized training or education and others do not. The term "job evaluation" has come to mean the *overall* process of developing an organization's job worth hierarchy.

Perhaps the most common approach to establishing the worth of a job is market pricing: using market data to determine the price and, therefore, the worth of each job. Market pricing is, in essence, "job evaluation" without an evaluation of the job's content, in that no internal standard or value for the job is determined. The hierarchy of job worth is established entirely by market prices.

This is obviously a relatively simple method of pricing, since it ignores job content, unlike the other methods to be described. If an analysis of job content is available, however, the job's content should be scrutinized to confirm that the job does, in fact, match the job title found in the salary survey data and to reconcile the job's perceived value to the organization with external labor market prices. Reconciliation may be difficult; some jobs may be valued by the labor market far in excess of a firm's valuation, or vice versa. The problem with market pricing—beyond its failure to evaluate job content—is that it is difficult to price any job not readily found in salary survey data. The choice of market data rather than a job content approach usually depends on the number of distinct jobs, the organization's competence in compensation, and the funds available to design, install, and maintain a system. Whichever approach is followed, organizations are usually faced with determining the relative worth of some jobs on the basis of job content alone because no survey information is available for a position as the organization has described the job.

The literature on job content approaches to job evaluation cites several traditional job evaluation systems or methods, dating as far back as the 1880s, when Frederick W. Taylor designed a formal, systematic way of assigning pay to jobs (which became known as "job evaluation") for a steel company. The 1923 Federal Classification Act, an initial attempt by Congress to establish a pay system for federal white-collar employees, encouraged formal compensation systems using methods for analyzing relative job value. The first "point factor" evaluation plan was designed by Merrill R. Lott about 1920, followed in the late 1930s or early 1940s by the "factor comparison" method of evaluation, developed by Edward N. Hay, Eugene

I. Benge, and Samuel L. H. Burke. There are a number of "unconventional" methods (e.g., "time-span of discretion" [Jacques, 1964]; "decision-banding" [Paterson, 1972a, 1972b]; "direct consensus" [Livy, 1975]), but these are variants of conventional methods and will not be reviewed here. In practice, there is an almost limitless variety of evaluation methods emphasizing job content because organizations tailor systems to their own needs, but most are modifications or derivatives of the basic methods. We will review two classes of job evaluation methods here: qualitative and quantitative.

Qualitative Methods

Qualitative methods determine the relative worth of jobs on the basis of an overall or global assessment of the job's content; the quantitative methods, in contrast, analyze segments or factors in job content on a factor-by-factor basis. Qualitative methods do not yield a numerical score for each job evaluated; they do, however, ordinally sequence jobs to provide a job structure. Three qualitative methods are discussed here: ranking, classification, and slotting.

Ranking

The ranking method is probably the oldest, fastest, and easiest of the qualitative methods. Because it is quick, it is inexpensive and therefore frequently chosen by small firms. Evaluators rank jobs by overall worth or value to the organization. The job that the evaluators believe to be worth the most is placed first, the one that they believe to be worth the least is ranked last, and so on, to produce a job hierarchy. Variations of this method involve the consideration of certain job attributes in the rankings. One approach, paired comparison, compares each position with all other positions one at a time and develops a "score" (i.e., overall rank) based on the number of times a position is deemed more important than another position.

Without factor-by-factor ranking, the subjective judgments of evaluators may be problematic. Moreover, rankings are easily outmoded by changes in job content. The method provides no explanation of why one job is valued more than another and no measure of how much more value one job has than another, and it prohibits ranking jobs equally. A change in the duties of one job may necessitate a change in its rank, the rankings of other jobs, and, thus, the job evaluation system. Basically, ranking systems are a comparison of jobs with respect to an ambiguous criterion of "worth" and are usually not held in high repute as a method of job evaluation (International Labour Organisation, 1960; Lanham, 1955).

Classification

The classification system was originally developed by the federal government to establish its pay program (General Schedule, or GS, ratings) by specifying a number of grades for which broad descriptions are written for various "types" of jobs. Jobs are compared with the grade description and placed within the "appropriate" grade. For example, ten grades may be established, each defined by certain characteristics of the jobs in it. Grade III might include those jobs in which people perform tasks without direct supervision; Grade I might contain those jobs in which people perform tasks under constant supervision. Evaluators do not define each factor and then compare jobs on a factor-by-factor basis, as in the factor-comparison method to be described later; rather, they compare the whole job. Usually, the higher the grade, the more education, skill, and so on are required. Expert judgment is heavily relied on, and the chances of bias or inconsistency are reasonably high, but the system is relatively easy to implement. Basically, classification requires an idealized hierarchical structure to be predetermined, with categories based on factors such as skill or responsibility. The classification of the U.S. Civil Service Commission is probably the best-known classification system. Eighteen grades are defined by eight factors, and each job is assigned a GS level for pay purposes. A problem is that jobs high on one level but low on another (e.g., high educational qualifications but no supervisory responsibility) may not easily fit the grade, and therefore arbitrary decisions must be made (International Labour Organisation, 1960).

Slotting

The final qualitative technique is a system that slots jobs. This is similar to the classification system, in which evaluators compare descriptions of jobs already in the structure and place the new jobs with the most similar ones. Often a matrix is used with grades on the vertical axis and departments or job families on the horizontal axis to facilitate comparisons across organizational lines. Often called "benchmark" or "key" jobs, these are similar enough to those in other organizations that they can serve as market "anchor" points. Such jobs should be important elements in the organization's internal hierarchy, usually with many incumbents; represent many organizational levels; be widely found in the labor market; and generally be believed to be fairly priced with respect to labor market phenomena (i.e., an abundance or scarcity of supply should not exist). Other positions are paid ("slotted") with respect to these jobs.

Rating, classification, and "market-slotting" systems suffer from a lack of explicit criteria and reliability because little detail is provided to guide decision-makers. Classifying also tends to "force" jobs into rigid classes and prevent the legitimate movement of a job from one class to another in order to protect a system that may, in fact, have no consistent rules for internal decisions.

Quantitative Methods

The quantitative approach to job content evaluation has three primary methods: factor comparison, point rating (or point factor), and quantitative job analysis. Each method evaluates the content of jobs factor by factor and yields numerical scores for each factor and each job evaluated.

Factor Comparison

The factor comparison approach requires a series of specific and somewhat complex steps. One selects ten to fifteen benchmark jobs that are assumed to be fairly priced because of the job's widely accepted definition and adequate supply and demand. Benchmark jobs should show variations in such traditional job worth factors as skill, physical effort, responsibility, mental complexity, and working conditions (or subfactors thereof). Usually no fewer than four or more than seven factors are used (Livy, 1975). Each benchmark job is ranked on each factor, often by paired comparison. Each job is then evaluated on each factor, using a dollar continuum with evaluators assigning a "factor" dollar worth to each job.

Because of its complexity, and because it is time-consuming, highly subjective, and difficult to explain to employees, the factor comparison system is not widely used (Akalin, 1970; Livy, 1975). It also requires considerable training of evaluators; it cannot change rapidly with dollar changes in the labor market; and it requires difficult evaluation judgments to determine the "key" jobs. However, it clearly increases the reliability of evaluation and addresses internal and external equity simultaneously.

The Point Factor Method

By far the most popular of the major methods of job evaluation is the point factor method (Akalin, 1970). The point factor method requires the evaluator to rate each job on a series of factors (e.g., physical effort, complexity of tasks, education, risk) presumed to contribute to overall job worth. Points are assigned to "degrees" of each factor to indicate the extent to which a job possesses the factor. Job descriptions are often used to develop statements associated with the degrees. Total points for each job are computed in order to compare relative worth and eventually assign salary levels. Job prices are assigned by grouping jobs into job families and into similar point totals within job families. Key jobs are then selected within each group and pay data sought from salary surveys. The pay philosophy selected by the organization (e.g., survey midpoint plus 10 percent for the key job) is then used to price all jobs within this job group.

Point systems have advantages over other methods in that they are potentially more reliable, are immune from market fluctuations, are relatively easy to use, require little evaluator training, and can measure differences between jobs (although usually not with ratio scales). However, they are expensive and time-consuming and raise serious validity questions (see Remick, 1981; Schwab, 1980). In contrast with factor comparison, the range of points is constant across jobs, which makes the system administratively simpler, but causes excessive rigidity (Benge, 1943). Nevertheless, this method probably has the best chance of attaining job evaluation objectives because jobs can be reliably differentiated and the system is simple enough to explain to employees.

Because point factor systems are the basis for many discussions of comparable worth, it is important to understand basic terms used in this method of evaluation. A *factor* is a broad category of job content, qualifications, and so on that can be used to group jobs (e.g., education, training, physical demands). Each broad factor may have several subfactors. A *weight* is the maximum relative value of each factor compared to other factors, usually on a scale of 1 to 100 (e.g., education—weight 65; physical demand—weight 15). The weights do not always sum to 100. The *degree* refers to the relative amount of each factor a job requires. For example, there may be four "degrees" of the factor education. Degree 4 could require a doctorate; degree 3, completion of master's level work; and so on. The relative worth of each degree is designated in *points*, with the highest number of points given to the highest degree. For example, degree 4 of education may be worth 65 points, while degree 3 is only worth 20, as a doctoral degree is significantly more difficult to attain than a master's.

Quantitative Job Analysis

In using quantitative job analysis (e.g., PAQ), job elements are identified and grouped in clusters for specific jobs; the scores are then correlated with market prices, permitting the construction of a wage structure (see Taylor, 1978; Taylor and Colbert, 1978). This method should afford considerable reliability, but its validity will be questioned, as with other methods, because of its use of market prices for the determination of job worth. Scores may also be regressed against the *DOT* worker function ratings of data, people, and things. Low scores in the middle three digits of the *DOT* code represent more complex data management and broader responsibilities on more complicated tasks. Thus, jobs with lower numbers in the middle three digits are generally expected to be more highly valued (i.e., priced) in the labor market (see, for example, Chapter 9).

Quantitative job analysis has many of the advantages and disadvantages of point methods. However, because the procedure usually requires incumbents and supervisors to respond to questionnaires about their jobs, questions concerning the adequacy and uniformity of job content capture may be minimized. The major problem is in regressing job content scores against prevailing labor rates to obtain job prices (or against the *DOT* codes as a surrogate for validity).

Problems with Job Evaluation Methods

Problems in Contemporary Practice

Several limitations of job evaluation practices should be noted. First, organizations often want only to make the wage determination process easier, and are not concerned about the reliability and validity of job evaluation systems. In fact, equity, reliability, and validity usually are not researched—or even considered—since organizations often believe that labor market functioning resolves these issues. They simply use job evaluation to price jobs when they feel "uncomfortable" with current practices or as a *post hoc* rationalization of the prices paid. Thus, it is easy for sex bias to enter the wage determination process.

Second, the choice of a method is based on ambiguous criteria at best, and the method once chosen, tends to be inflexible. Whether salary policy is implicit (i.e., the wage and salary people feel "comfortable" with it) or explicit and developed from a standard evaluation method, job prices appear to be fairly resistant to change except when labor market changes are dramatic and obvious. The pay for "women's jobs" may thus be unlikely to change even with market changes because such movement violates "the system."

Third, the actual methods used to determine job structures and job families are seldom consistent or explicit. Job structures are influenced by job titles, technical specialties, points, the number of jobs in the system, line versus staff position, reporting relationships, career pathing, and so on. The choice of key jobs to price these structures suffers from the same problem. These issues—the determination of job structures and key jobs—should not be underemphasized, because these subtle decisions greatly influence job pricing and thus women's pay.

Technical Problems

Beyond these problems of contemporary practice, job evaluation suffers from numerous technical difficulties, some of which have been outlined above, in job analysis, compensable factor selection, validity, and administration. Tenopyr and Oeltjen (1982), in their review of industrial and organizational psychology, state that the measurement and valuation of a job skill cannot be accomplished with any scientific rigor and involve "so many value judgments that it probably can have no completely satisfactory answer" (p. 586). It is with similar skepticism that we begin our critical examination of the steps involved in the job evaluation process and its potential for sex bias.

The job analysis methods described earlier all present measurement problems. These problems actually begin with the selection of the unit to analyze. Some of the methods take a "micro" focus to job content by examining the job's tasks or elements within tasks; others analyze jobs at the "macro" level: that is, at the level of position, job classification, or occupation (Milkovich, 1980). There is no theoretically defensible reason for the "micro" approach to job content examination other than the fact that it permits a more finite gradation or differentiation of jobs, thus permitting more finely tuned pricing policies. The precision of gradation is always subject to question, but it can hardly be disputed that pricing decisions would be more complex if the level of analysis chosen were the position, job title, or occupational level. Women stand to gain from the systems that use a micro approach because of the greater chance that their tasks will be found similar to men's; this is unlikely to happen when job titles or job functions are compared.

Once the level of analysis is selected, a way to measure job content must be designed. The methods noted all present difficulties with reliability and validity. The decision-making process may be biased by the choice of persons to participate in the data collection and analysis. Some argue that incumbents should not participate in job evaluation because they attempt to enhance their job descriptions to gain higher pay (Arvey et al., 1982). In the face of such fears, trained job analysts are often employed to "field audit" jobs by visiting incumbents and collecting information. Such procedures are subject to reliability problems themselves, often impossible to control because auditors discuss their results and reach consensus before finalizing a job description. Not only may this "consensus" be merely compliance or conformity, but some evaluation items may be omitted because the process does not require independent job content capture and reporting. Rater/ evaluator bias in observing and documenting behavior is also possible (Bernardin and Cardy, 1982; Borman, 1978; Spool, 1978), in that people may be inaccurate observers or may base their ratings on factors that are not consistent with the purposes of the rating task (see, for example, Chapter 3; Cooper, 1981; Feldman, 1981; Kelly and Michela, 1980). Job content capture using outside or "expert" raters may have face validity but be fraught with measurement error and easily sex-biased. Thus, it may be useful to use more than one method of job analysis—for example, questionnaires as well as observations—and several sources of data, such as incumbents, supervisors, subordinates, and peers. Because of the many problems noted here, the reliability of job analysis has often been questioned (Milkovich and Broderick, 1982; Schwab, 1980; Treiman, 1979). It offers fertile ground for research as well as critical examination by practitioners.

Macro approaches requiring the correct matching of jobs with external labor market positions can cause problems, especially when market pricing is used. Improper slotting of jobs can be costly to employees. For example, placing a director of nursing with nursing classifications rather than managerial ones could cost that employee several thousand of dollars in salary every year. Thus, accuracy in content capture is essential both in obtaining a job's market price and in "grouping" the job once a market price is established for job groups.

Micro job content procedures are also open to serious error. First, if the compensable factors used in a plan are selected *a priori*, obvious bias may occur. Most factors commonly used in internal equity systems are highly correlated with labor market prices and therefore reflect characteristics of "male" jobs; for example, physical effort/exertion is often used, while fine motor skill usually is not. Micro approaches—and any approaches that use job content factors—are usually based on prevailing labor rates. In fact, it would be economically imprudent not to allow prevailing labor rates (i.e., external equity) to influence the price paid for human resources, just as market rates influence the price of other organizational resources.

The operationalization of compensable factors may further bias results. For example, an interpersonal skill factor might include negotiating (e.g., "conflict resolution" in largely male jobs) and counseling (e.g., "helping" in women's jobs). Both are interpersonal skills, but they may earn different points, the difference being based on traditional (i.e., male) norms rather than the contribution of the activities to the organization's goals. The compensable factor bias is maintained even if factors are chosen by policy capturing, which employs the external market to dictate an organization's internal values.

Job evaluations are also biased by the weights assigned to compensable factors (Eyde, 1981; Remick, 1979; Treiman, 1979). Factors are often weighted *a priori*, and sex bias may result. On the other hand, with policy capturing, the bias in the marketplace is captured. The use of "women's" compensable factors or heavier weights for these factors may not necessarily solve the problem.

The choice of key, or benchmark, jobs is another major problem. As noted earlier, key jobs are traditionally well defined in the labor market (in terms of tasks required, qualifications, and so on), are relatively stable with respect to salary, represent various hierarchical levels, and are thought to be "fairly priced" by the labor market. These criteria ignore any biases in the market that might be reflected in job evaluation results (Milkovich and Broderick, 1982). Policy-capturing techniques do not identify the value of jobs to the organization or indicate whether jobs that do not meet key job criteria produce value in the same way as key jobs. Clearly, if key jobs are sex-linked, their use will bias wage structures.

Other questions deal with the construct validity of the job structure, which links job evaluation data to salary survey data. There are two major problems with the use of salary survey data. The first is that the survey data are not randomly collected, limiting statistical inferences and thus the accuracy of an organization's prices. The second is the incompleteness of the compensation data; critical comparisons cannot be made because the data do not include information on the effects of benefits, overtime, training expenditures, and incentive pay. Benefit costs average 40 percent of payroll and are increasing; employer practices with respect to supplemental pay and benefits differ across industry, region, and job type and are not accounted for in wage data used in the job evaluation/wage-setting process. An employee's supplemental pay may therefore reduce or amplify sex-linked wage inequity. Further, even if these survey problems could be ignored, survey wage data still reflect only the market value of the job and not the value of the job to the organization. Wage determinants are known to include a number of factors irrelevant to the job itself, especially industry and location (for a review of economic determinants of job value, see Wallace and Fay, 1981). The choice of any survey statistic to use as the market criterion (e.g., median, average, average maximum, weighted mean salary, average minimum) may change the relative values of jobs in an organization, depending on the salary distributions in the market and the market statistics chosen for the key jobs in question, further indicating the subjectivity to which job pricing is vulnerable.

Also often overlooked is the influence on the market of turnover and job vacancy. If an organization has frequent turnover in a job or long-term vacancies, prices should increase irrespective of job evaluation. If prices do not move despite high vacancy rates, then discrimination may in fact be occurring; that is, discrimination may be suspected when the law of supply and demand does not work for positions primarily staffed by women (e.g., nursing positions).

Another source of error is the use of several job evaluation systems in an organization, with different factors and/or factor weights. The mere use of multiple systems makes it likely that jobs valued under a different system will not meet pay equity comparable worth criteria. The prior descriptions of job evaluation systems and selection of compensable factors should make this obvious.

Finally, the models used to link job evaluation points to survey data are typically linear regression models. The statistical assumptions required for such models (e.g., the independence of factors used to "predict" wages) are probably violated. In fact, when one compares compensable factors with one another, most factors (e.g., Hay factors) have very high intercorrelations. Even if the statistical assumptions are met, nonlinear models may be more appropriate (see Bloom and Killingsworth, 1982).

Summary and Recommendations

Job evaluation is a process fraught with problems: questions about the reliability of the evaluation process itself (including the wage data used as criteria in the process), the administrative use of multiple job evaluation systems for different sets of jobs, and the relatively long-term difficulties of adjusting to supply and demand issues. Even if such problems could be minimized, job evaluation methods that rely on market data do not address the value of a job to an organization. If organizations wish to measure the contribution of jobs, they should explore new methods of assessing internal equity: for example, ways of measuring common contributions such as sales, production, profitability, cost reductions, or the long- and short-term financial impact on the organization if the job was not performed. These values could then be assessed against prevailing rates to guide prudent purchases of job skills, and if skills were making a substantial impact or were in short supply, prices would be "bid up."

Clearly one of the major impediments to pay equity for women is the inadequacy of current measurement systems. In fact, the best hope for equity, may lie in serious research in this very murky area. Job evaluation can offer an acceptable and equitable system of measuring a job's value in an organization, despite the many simultaneous influences on pay practices (e.g., skills required, supply and demand, industry differences, ability to pay, and discrimination).

Despite the many criticisms of job evaluation cited above, job evaluation systems can and do provide guidance in making pay decisions and can be helpful in resolving pay discrimination allegations. In order to use job evaluation for the best and most equitable results the following should be seriously considered:

1. Exhaustive job analysis using several methods (e.g., interviews and questionnaires) and sources of input.
2. Use of compensable factors that are not redundant, represent the value of jobs to an organization, and demonstrate a correspondence with labor market prices for a majority of jobs.
3. Job evaluation systems that have demonstrated reliability in developing job structures, whether in building job families through classification or designing hierarchies through quantitative systems.
4. Constant monitoring of pricing practices to ensure that survey methods and the statistics used to determine prices within the hierarchy are consistently applied across all jobs.
5. An assessment of all pricing practices (i.e., job analysis, compensable factor selection, job structure development and assignment, survey adequacy and comparability, key job determination, and assignment of job prices) to ensure that the influence of sex differences has been eliminated.

These steps may require considerable research efforts and a level of self-examination presently uncommon in organizations, but if pay equity and economic survival are organizational objectives, the investment should be not only returned over time, but enhanced as more efficient and equitable pay systems are developed.

References

Akalin, M. T. 1970. *Office Job Evaluation.* Des Plaines, Ill: Industrial Management Society.

American Society for Personnel Administration and the American Compensation Association. 1981. *Elements of Sound Base Pay Administration.* Berea, Ohio: American Society for Personnel Administration.

Arvey, R. D., G. A. Davis, S. L. McGovern, and R. L. Dipboye. 1982. "Potential Sources of Bias in Job Analysis Processes." *Academy of Management Journal* 25:618–29.

Benge, E. J. 1943. *Job Evaluation and Merit Rating*. New York: National Foremen's Institute.

Bernardin, H. J., and R. L. Cardy. 1982. "Appraisal Accuracy: Ability and Motivation to Remember the Past." *Public Personnel Management Journal*, 11:352–57.

Bloom, D. E., and M. R. Killingsworth. 1982. "Pay Discrimination Research and Litigation: The Use of Regression." *Industrial Relations* 21:318–39.

Borman, W. C. 1978. "Exploring Upper Limits of Reliability and Validity in Performance Ratings." *Journal of Applied Psychology*, 63:135–44.

Chalupsky, A. B. 1962. "Comparative Factor Analyses of Clerical Jobs." *Journal of Applied Psychology* 46:62–67.

Cooper, W. H. 1981. "Ubiquitous Halo." *Psychological Bulletin* 90:218–44.

Cristal, R. E. 1964. "The United States Air Force Occupational Research Project." JSAS *Catalog of Selected Documents in Psychology* 4:61.

Eyde, L. D. 1981. "Evaluating Job Evaluation: Emerging Research Issues for Comparable Analysis." Paper presented to the American Psychological Association.

Feldman, J. M. 1981. "Beyond Attribution Theory: Cognitive Processes in Performance Appraisal." *Journal of Applied Psychology* 66:127–48.

Flanagan, J. C. 1954. "The Critical Incident Technique." *Psychological Bulletin* 51:327–58.

Fleishman, E. A. 1972. "Systems for Describing Human Tasks." *American Psychologist* 37:821–34.

Fleishman, E. A. 1975. "Toward a Taxonomy of Human Performance." *American Psychologist* 30:1127–49.

Hackman, J. R., and G. R. Oldham. 1975. "Development of the Job Diagnostic Survey." *Journal of Applied Psychology* 60:159–70.

International Labour Organization. 1960. *Job Evaluation*. Geneva: International Labour.

Jacques, Eliot. 1964. *Time-Span Handbook*. London: Heinemann.

Kelly, H. H., and J. L. Michela. 1980. "Attribution Theory and Research." *Annual Review of Psychology*, 31:457–501.

Kleiman, L. S., and Faley, F. 1978. "Assessing Content Validity: Standards Set by the Court." *Personnel Psychology* 31:701–13.

Lanham, Elizabeth, 1955. *Job Evaluation*. New York: McGraw-Hill.

Livy, Bryan. 1975. *Job Evaluation: A Critical Review*. New York: John Wiley.

McCormick, E. J. 1976. "Job and Task Analysis," In *Handbook of Industrial and Organizational Psychology*, ed. M. D. Dunnette, pp. 651–96. Chicago: Rand McNally.

McCormick, E. J., P. R. Jeanneret, and R. C. Mecham. 1972. "A Study of Job Characteristics and Job Dimensions as Based on the Position Analysis Questionnaire (PAQ)." *Journal of Applied Psychology* 56:347–67.

Milkovich, George T. 1980. "Wage Differentials and Comparable Worth: The Emerging Debate." In *Comparable Worth: Issues and Alternatives*, ed. E. R. Livernash, pp. 23–47. Washington, D.C.: Equal Employment Advisory Council.

Milkovich, G. T., and R. Broderick. 1982. "Pay Discrimination: Legal Issues and Implications for Research." *Industrial Relations* 21:309–17.

Paterson, T. T. 1972a. *Job Evaluation, Vol. 1: A New Method*. London: Business Books.

Paterson, T. T. 1972b. *Job Evaluation, Vol. 2: A Manual for the Paterson Method.* London: Business Books.

Pearlman, K. 1980. "Job Families: A Review and Discussion of Their Implications for Personnel Selection." *Psychological Bulletin* 87:1–28.

Primoff, E. S. 1974. How to Prepare and Conduct Job Element Examinations. Washington, D.C.: U.S. Government Printing Office.

Remick, Helen. 1979. "Strategies for Creating Sound, Bias Free Job Evaluation Plans." In *Job Evaluation and EEO: The Emerging Issues*, pp. 85–112. New York: Industrial Relations Counselors, Inc.

Remick, Helen. 1981. "The Comparable Worth Controversy." *Public Personnel Management.* 10:371–83.

Salvendy, G., and W. D. Seymour. 1973. *Prediction and Development of Industrial Work Performance.* New York: Wiley.

Schwab, Donald P. 1980. "Job Evaluations and Pay Setting: Concepts and Practices." In *Comparable Worth: Issues and Alternatives*, ed. E. R. Livernash, pp. 49–77. Washington, D.C.: Equal Employment Advisory Council.

Spool, M. D. 1978. "Training Programs for Observers of Behavior: A Review." *Personnel Psychology* 31:853–88.

Taylor, L. R. 1978. "Empirically Derived Job Families as a Foundation for the Study of Validity Generalization. Study I: The Constructions of Job Families Based on the Component and Overall Dimensions of the PAQ." *Personnel Psychology* 31:325–40.

Taylor, L. R., and G. A. Colbert. 1978. "Empirically Derived Job Families as a Foundation for the Study of Validity Generalization. Study II: The Construction of Job Families Based on Company-Specific PAQ Dimensions." *Personnel Psychology* 31:341–53.

Tenopyr, M. L., and P. D. Oeltjen. 1982. "Personnel Selection and Classification." In *Annual Review of Psychology*, ed. M. R. Rosenzweig and L. W. Porter, 33:581–618. Palo Alto: Annual Reviews, Inc.

Treiman, Donald J. 1979. "Job Evaluation: An Analytical Review." Interim Report to the Equal Employment Opportunity Commission. Washington, D.C.: National Academy of Sciences.

"Uniform Guidelines on Employee Selection Procedures." 1978. *Federal Register*, 25 August 43:38290–315.

U.S. Department of Labor. 1973. *Dictionary of Occupational Titles.* 3d ed. Washington, D.C.: Government Printing Office.

U.S. Department of Labor. 1974. "Guide to Writing Class Specifications." Washington, D.C.: U.S. Government Printing Office.

U.S. Department of Labor, Bureau of Employment Security. 1977. *Dictionary of Occupational Titles.* 4th ed. Washington, D.C.: Government Printing Office.

U.S. Department of Labor, Manpower Administration. 1972. *Handbook for Analyzing Jobs.*

Wallace, Marc J., Jr., and Charles H. Fay. 1981. "Job Evaluation and Job Worth: Towards a Model of Organizational Judgement of Job Value." Working Paper no. BA72. Lexington: Office of Research, College of Business and Economics, University of Kentucky.

5

Effect of Choice of Factors and Factor Weights in Job Evaluation

DONALD J. TREIMAN

In the United States today, many large private companies, the federal government, and many state governments make use of some kind of formal job evaluation as an aid to establishing pay rates for jobs. Although job evaluation systems differ in details of design and implementation, almost all conform to a common methodology and underlying logic: all the jobs in the unit being analyzed are described; the descriptions are then rated or evaluated according to one or more "compensable factors" (job features identified as legitimate bases for pay differentials); the ratings are weighted in some way and summed to create a total score, sometimes called a "job worth score"; and the scores are used—sometimes alone and sometimes with other information—to assign jobs to pay classes.[1]

It has variously been suggested that the choice of measured factors and factor weights matters a good deal or not much at all. That is, it is sometimes asserted that the choice of factors and the weights assigned to included factors can have a substantial effect on the total scores created by summing factor scores, and that different choices of factors and weights can produce scales that are only weakly correlated. On the other hand, both job evaluation experts and psychometricians point to practical experience in asserting that the choice of factors and factor weights or, more generally, the choice of weights for summative scales, usually makes little difference, in the sense that the resulting scales are usually highly correlated.

As I have shown elsewhere (Treiman, 1979:62–63), the degree of intercorrelation among alternatively weighted summative scales depends upon the degree of intercorrelation among the factors included in the scale. When the factors making up a scale are highly correlated, the choice of factor weights will make very little difference. But when the factors are only weakly correlated, scales produced by various weightings of the component variables may themselves be only weakly correlated. For example, if a two-variable scale is constructed two ways—(1) by weighting the two com-

Acknowledgment: This is a revised version of a paper originally prepared for the Committee on Occupational Classification and Analysis, National Academy of Sciences. June Price provided excellent research assistance.

1. The properties of job evaluation systems are described in more detail in Treiman (1979) and Treiman and Hartmann (1981).

ponent variables equally and (2) by weighting one variable four times as much as the other—it can be shown that the correlation between the resulting scales will be $.5 + .5r_{AB}$, where A and B are the two component variables. Then, for example, if $r_{AB} = .9$, the correlation between the two scales will be .95; but if $r_{AB} = -.2$, the correlation between the two resulting scales will be .4, a very low correlation between two versions of the same scale. What such a low correlation implies is that many jobs that score high on one scale would not score high on the other.

The importance of this is twofold. First, because jobs are often assigned to pay grades on the basis of their points on an enterprise's job evaluation scale, it matters a great deal how many points each job receives. Changing the weights assigned to various factors could substantially alter the pay relationships between jobs, unless the factors are very highly intercorrelated.

Second, beyond their impact on particular workers, alterations of job evaluation scales could change the relative advantage or disadvantage of particular race or sex groups. Because male and female workers and white and minority workers tend to work at different jobs, it is quite possible for the choice of measured factors and factor weights to differentially affect entire classes of workers. For example, black males tend disproportionately to work at jobs entailing heavy physical effort but requiring little education. A job evaluation scale that gives heavy weight to physical effort would hence tend to give high scores to jobs done by black men, thus improving the pay position of black men relative to other workers. On the other hand, a job evaluation scale that gives heavy weight to the educational requirements of jobs would tend to give low scores to jobs done by black men and thus lower their pay position relative to other workers.

Unfortunately, we do not know enough about the distribution of job content by race and sex to be able to predict in any clear way what the impact would be of including some factors rather than others or differentially weighting factors. While there is reason to suspect that some choices would be advantageous for men and others for women, some for whites and others for minority workers, it is not obvious whether the effect of differential weighting would be large or small nor which categories of workers would be relatively advantaged or disadvantaged by particular factor weights.

As a straightforward approach to this question, in this paper I simulate a comparison of differential factor weights by creating a series of job evaluation scales differing only in the relative weight accorded each factor and study shifts in the mean job worth scores of white and black males and females.

Data

It would have been desirable to utilize data derived from an existing job evaluation plan applied to the jobs in a specific enterprise. This proved impossible, however, since I was unable to obtain access to data for individual enterprises that simultaneously included information on the sex and race composition of each job classification and scores for a set of job evaluation factors.

Accordingly, I made use of data from the April 1971 *Current Population Survey* to simulate a job evaluation scheme and its application. The *CPS* is a monthly survey of adult members of approximately 60,000 households, chosen in such a way as to be representative of the U.S. labor force (U.S. Bureau of the Census, 1978:2, 6). A variety of information is collected by the *CPS*, including the occupation and labor force status of the respondent, industry, age, education, race, and sex. Ordinarily, occupational data are coded according to the detailed occupational classification of the U.S. Bureau of the Census, which consisted of 441 categories in 1970. The April 1971 survey is of special value for the present purpose because in that month occupational descriptions were also coded using the nine-digit codes of the third edition of the *Dictionary of Occupational Titles* (U.S. Department of Labor, 1965, 1967). The *DOT* classification consists of about 12,000 occupational categories and thus comes much closer than the census classification to representing the sort of detail ordinarily found in the job classifications of specific enterprises.

In addition to the occupational classification, the *DOT* includes measures of forty-six occupational characteristics, known as Worker Traits and Worker Functions. The variables used here are a subset of Worker Traits and Worker Functions from the fourth edition of the *DOT* (U.S. Department of Labor, 1972, 1977). The fourth-edition characteristics were added to the April 1971 *CPS* data tape by Lloyd Temme, then of the U.S. Bureau of the Census. In addition to the standard *CPS* variables, this tape contains the third-edition *DOT* occupation codes, a selection of Worker Traits and Worker Functions from the third edition, the fourth-edition *DOT* occupation codes, and the entire array of Worker Traits and Worker Functions collected for the fourth edition.[2]

Because some job evaluation schemes are administered on an industry-wide basis (e.g., the CWS plan of the steel industry), I considered whether the *DOT* data could usefully be disaggregated to the industry level. The answer is no, since even with approximately 60,000 cases the sample is too small to sustain the necessary degree of disaggregation. I have, however, restricted the analysis to full-time, employed, civilian wage and salary workers, on the ground that this is the part of the labor force that is most

---

2. These data are described in greater detail in Miller, et al. (1980) and in Cain and Treiman (1981). The tape is available from the Inter-University Consortium for Political and Social Research, University of Michigan, P.O. Box 1248, Ann Arbor, MI 48106, and from the National Technical Information Service, 5285 Port Royal Road, Springfield, VA 22161. Inquiries should refer to the "April 1971 Current Population Survey augmented with DOT Characteristics."

subject to job evaluation and for which job evaluation is most appropriate. I also excluded those cases for which fourth-edition *DOT* occupation codes were not available.[3] To reduce the cost and facilitate data processing, I based the analysis on a 10 percent subsample of the cases meeting the above restrictions.[4]

The Variables

Given my interest in simulating a generic job evaluation, I chose for analysis five variables that are broadly representative of the kinds of variables most frequently included as factors in job evaluation scales: measures of skill, responsibility, effort, and working conditions. These variables, shown in Figure 5-1, are the complexity of worker functions in relation to data, people, and things; the amount of strength required to do the job; and the unpleasantness of the job environment. These variables can be interpreted as follows. "Data" is an index of the skill requirements of jobs. It is highly correlated with measures of educational requirements (GED) and training time (SVP). "People" is an index of the responsibility entailed in jobs. There is no direct measure of supervisory responsibility among the *DOT* variables, and "people" is used as a surrogate for that sort of variable. "Things" is an index of responsibility for materials and equipment, another variable widely utilized in job evaluation systems and not otherwise indexed in the *DOT*. "Strength" corresponds closely to measures of effort commonly found in job evaluation scales. Likewise, "environment" corresponds closely to commonly used measures of working conditions. Together, these variables include most of the nonredundant factors typically found in existing job evaluation scales.

As Table 5-1 indicates, these variables are on the whole not highly correlated. Of the ten correlations only two are substantially positive: the correlation of .56 between "data" and "people" and the correlation of .58

---

3. This includes a number of cases for which the occupational descriptions provided by the interviewers were inadequate to permit assignment of third-edition *DOT* codes, as well as a number of cases for which no match between third- and fourth-edition codes was possible because illegal third-edition codes had been recorded through coding or keypunching error.

4. The Census Bureau routinely assigns variable weights to data collected in its sample surveys, both to permit estimation of population characteristics from the sample data and to correct for differential nonresponse. To ensure a representative sample, I utilized the weighted data. However, to permit computation of confidence intervals, I divided each case by the mean weight for the sample to achieve a weighted sample of the same size as the unweighted sample. This does not take account of the relative inefficiency of cluster samples compared to simple random samples. Since I was unable to ascertain the size of the design effect for this sample, I compensated by utilizing a conservative critical value, $\alpha = .01$, two-tailed, in tests of significance.

Figure 5-1
Description of Variables

Complexity of Worker Functions in Relation to:

Data	People	Things
7. Synthesizing	9. Mentoring	8. Setting up
6. Coordinating	8. Negotiating	7. Precision working
5. Analyzing	7. Instructing	6. Operating-controlling
4. Compiling	6. Supervising	5. Driving-operating
3. Computing	5. Diverting	4. Manipulating
2. Copying	4. Persuading	3. Tending
1. Comparing	3. Speaking-signaling	2. Feeding-offbearing
	2. Serving	1. Handling
	1. Taking instructions-helping	

Strength
5. Very heavy work
4. Heavy work
3. Medium work
2. Light work
1. Sedentary work

Environment (sum of conditions present)
Extreme cold with or without temperature changes
Extreme heat with or without temperature changes
Wet and/or humid
Noise and/or vibration
Hazards
Unpleasant atmospheric conditions

Source: U.S. Department of Labor (1977).

between "strength" and "environment." Of the other eight, six are negative. Hence, summative scales formed from these variables but based on differing configurations of weights will be only weakly positively correlated—or, indeed, negatively correlated.

Procedure

As noted, we wish to determine whether different weightings of the five variables favor or disfavor particular race or sex groups. To do this, I constructed a number of scales, each a different weighted sum of the five

Table 5-1
Correlations, Means and Standard Deviations among Variables

Variable (type)*	Data	People	Things	Strength	Environment
Data (skill)	1.00	.56	−.04	−.43	−.27
People (responsibility)		1.00	−.32	−.36	−.27
Things (responsibility)			1.00	.13	.24
Strength (effort)				1.00	.58
Environment (working conditions)					1.00
Mean	3.86	2.94	3.64	2.23	.514
Standard deviation	1.85	2.04	2.55	.975	.973

*The term in parentheses refers to the general class of job evaluation factors that the variable represents.

variables, and compared the mean scale scores for white and black males and females. Since these four groups tend to do jobs that differ with respect to these characteristics, we have reason to suspect that they will differ with respect to the resulting scale scores as well. Table 5-2 shows the means and standard deviations on each of the five variables for each of the four race-sex groups. Inspecting the table, we see that blacks tend to work at jobs with less favorable environments than the jobs whites work at and that males tend to work at jobs with less favorable environments than the jobs females work at. Hence, a scale that gives heavy weight to the environment factor would, all else being equal, give higher scores to blacks than to whites and to males than to females. By contrast, a scale that gives heavy weight to the data factor would, all else being equal, give the highest scores to white males and the lowest scores to black females.

To construct a set of weighted scales, I first produced a set of variables with identical weights by dividing each variable by its standard deviation to create standardized scores. Scale 1 was created by simply summing these standardized scores. Scales 2 through 9 were created by multiplying each standardized score by the weight shown in Table 5-3 and then summing.

Scales 2 through 6 successively give each variable 10 times the weight of the remaining variables. Lest it be thought that a weight of 10 is excessive, note that in the Factor Evaluation System used to classify positions in the General Schedule (the federal job evaluation scheme for white-collar jobs), Factor 1, "knowledge required by the position," has a range (and hence potential weight) 41 times that of Factor 8, "physical demands," and Factor 9, "work environment" (Treiman, 1979:140). Similarly, in the Hay Associ-

Table 5-2

Means and Standard Deviations of Variables by Race and Sex

Variable	White Males	White Females	Black Males	Black Females
	Means			
Data	4.12	3.63	3.27	2.92
People	3.04	2.92	2.51	2.51
Things	3.59	3.73	3.90	3.37
Strength	2.41	1.81	2.81	2.14
Environment	.659	.210	.882	.340
	Standard Deviations			
Data	1.95	1.56	1.97	1.65
People	2.14	1.92	1.95	1.68
Things	2.65	2.40	2.53	2.28
Strength	1.00	.786	.951	.784
Environment	1.07	.652	1.10	.778
N	2,115	1,162	213	182

Table 5-3

Weighting Factors to Create Alternative Scales

	Scale								
*Variable**	*1*	*2*	*3*	*4*	*5*	*6*	*7*	*8*	*9*
Data	1	10	1	1	1	1	10	1	1
People	1	1	10	1	1	1	10	1	1
Things	1	1	1	10	1	1	1	1	10
Strength	1	1	1	1	10	1	1	10	10
Environment	1	1	1	1	1	10	1	10	10

*Variables with unit variance were created by dividing each original variable by its standard deviation.

ates' evaluation of Idaho state personnel, the accountability factor has a range (and hence potential weight) 42 times that of the working conditions factor.

Scale 7 weights the data and people variables each 10 times as heavily as the remaining variables. I have interpreted these variables as representing skill and supervisory responsibility, and accordingly would expect professional and managerial jobs—and white males, who tend to hold such jobs—to score high on this scale.

Scale 8 weights the strength and environment variables each 10 times as heavily as the remaining variables. Given the kinds of jobs blacks tend to do in American society, I would expect them to score high on this scale. Also, given the sex distribution of job content, I would expect men to score higher than women. Scale 9 is similar to scale 8, except that I have also given "things," which I interpret as representing responsibility for materials and equipment, a weight of 10. This should increase the sex difference but decrease the race difference, since skilled craft jobs tend to score highest on "things" and these jobs are held mainly by white males.

Results

As expected from the pattern of intercorrelations among the component variables, the weighted scales vary widely in their degree of intercorrelation (Table 5-4). Scales emphasizing "data" and/or "people" tend to be negatively correlated with scales emphasizing "strength" and/or "environment." Scales emphasizing "things" tend to be relatively unrelated to other scales, although they show more affinity to the strength/environment cluster than to the data/people cluster. All in all, the large number of negative and weak positive correlations suggests that the choice of factor weights can have a very strong impact on the resulting scales.

How do race and sex groups fare under these alternative weights? The top panel of Table 5-5 shows the mean scores for white and black males and

Table 5-4

Correlations among Alternative Scales

	1	2	3	4	5	6	7	8	9
Scale 1	1.00	.56	.48	.62	.59	.72	.48	.66	.73
Scale 2		1.00	.64	.17	−.14	.01	.90	−.14	−.09
Scale 3			1.00	−.07	−.11	.00	.90	−.12	−.18
Scale 4				1.00	.32	.42	−.02	.36	.70
Scale 5					1.00	.68	−.22	.92	.83
Scale 6						1.00	−.08	.91	.86
Scale 7							1.00	−.24	−.25
Scale 8								1.00	.91
Scale 9									1.00
Mean									
Standard	7.76	26.5	20.7	20.6	28.3	12.5	39.4	33.1	45.9
deviation	2.15	10.0	9.83	10.2	10.1	10.4	16.8	17.3	21.4

females on each of these scales. Inspecting these data, we see that the relative advantage of the four groups changes depending upon which factors are emphasized. That is, some weightings tend to give higher scores to the jobs white males do than to the jobs other workers do, while other weightings tend to give higher scores to jobs done by other classes of workers. Interestingly, none of the weighting schemes gives higher average scores to the jobs women do than to the jobs men do, although some schemes— notably those that emphasize complexity of work with "people" and "things"—result in similar averages for white males and females.[5] However, Scales 2 and 7, which emphasize skill alone and skill and supervisory responsibility together, are more favorable to whites, while Scales 5, 8, and 9, which emphasize various combinations of effort and working conditions, are more favorable to blacks. It should be noted that this perhaps anomalous result—which shows blacks to work at more highly evaluated jobs than those whites work at—is strictly a consequence of the heavy weight put on the effort and working conditions factors. As I have shown elsewhere (Treiman, 1979), in most extant job evaluation plans, effort and working conditions factors receive very little weight.

---

5. I have not presented significance tests for differences between pairs of means. However, it is possible to compute such tests using the information contained in Tables 5-2 and 5-5. The appropriate formula is:

$$t = \frac{\bar{X}_1 - \bar{X}_2}{\sqrt{\dfrac{s_1^2}{N_1} + \dfrac{s_2^2}{N_2}}}.$$

As indicated above (footnote 4), it would be judicious to use a .01 level of significance to compensate for the (unknown but probably substantial) design effect.

Table 5-5

Means and Standard Deviations of Alternative Scales by Race and Sex

	White Males	White Females	Black Males	Black Females
	Means			
Scale 1	8.27	6.92	8.31	6.67
Scale 2	28.3	24.6	24.2	20.8
Scale 3	21.7	19.8	19.4	17.7
Scale 4	21.0	20.1	22.1	18.6
Scale 5	30.5	23.6	34.2	26.4
Scale 6	14.4	8.86	16.5	9.82
Scale 7	41.6	37.4	35.2	31.9
Scale 8	36.6	25.5	42.4	29.6
Scale 9	49.3	38.7	56.2	41.5
	Standard Deviations			
Scale 1	2.26	1.60	2.31	1.73
Scale 2	10.4	8.44	10.9	9.08
Scale 3	10.1	9.42	9.52	8.48
Scale 4	10.9	8.90	10.5	8.90
Scale 5	10.4	7.93	9.52	7.60
Scale 6	11.5	6.76	11.8	8.02
Scale 7	17.3	15.4	17.2	15.2
Scale 8	18.6	12.0	17.5	12.4
Scale 9	23.9	14.1	21.6	14.0

It is instructive to consider the effect of these alternative weighting schemes for different kinds of jobs. To do this, I computed the mean scale scores for two subsets of occupations: nonmanual occupations, which include professional, technical, managerial, clerical, and sales occupations; and manual occupations, which include processing, machine trades, benchwork, and structural work occupations. In this exercise I excluded service, agricultural, and miscellaneous occupations. To avoid problems associated with small sample size, and to facilitate the clarity of the comparison, I restricted this analysis to white workers. The results are shown in Table 5-6.

Two aspects of these results are particularly striking. First, the impact of alternative weightings on the relative advantage of male and female workers varies substantially between manual and nonmanual jobs. Second, some weightings do produce scales that are advantageous to female workers compared to males, but only in nonmanual jobs. Every one of the nine alternative weightings shows the manual jobs men do to be "worth" more on average than the manual jobs women do, which suggests that—as measured by these five variables—the manual jobs men do tend to entail more skill, more effort, more responsibility, and more difficult working conditions than the manual jobs women do. For nonmanual jobs the situation is much more complex: the scales emphasizing skill, responsibility for things, and unfavor-

Table 5-6

Means and Standard Deviations of Alternative Scales by Sex and
Occupational Group for White Workers

	Nonmanual Occupations*		Manual Occupations†	
	White Males	White Females	White Males	White Females
	Means‡			
Scale 1	8.05	7.96	8.91	6.30
Scale 2	36.2	33.1	24.3	15.4
Scale 3	28.4	29.8	17.6	12.5
Scale 4	16.9	15.0	26.3	19.7
Scale 5	22.3	25.4	36.4	28.2
Scale 6	8.91	8.05	20.0	12.4
Scale 7	56.5	55.0	33.0	21.6
Scale 8	23.2	25.5	47.5	34.3
Scale 9	32.0	32.6	64.9	47.7
	Standard Deviations			
Scale 1	1.73	1.19	2.46	2.16
Scale 2	5.28	4.25	10.8	8.78
Scale 3	11.5	11.3	7.46	6.18
Scale 4	9.94	6.89	9.82	8.83
Scale 5	6.59	6.67	8.70	7.61
Scale 6	4.32	1.56	12.7	11.5
Scale 7	13.0	13.1	14.7	12.7
Scale 8	8.54	6.81	17.7	15.7
Scale 9	14.5	10.9	20.3	17.9
N	682	269	949	200

*DOT major groups 0–2. Includes professional, technical, managerial, clerical, and sales occupations.
†DOT major groups 5–8. Includes processing, machine trades, benchwork, and structural work occupations.
‡The difference between the means for males and females in nonmanual occupations is not statistically significant at the .01 level, two-tailed (see footnote 4).

able working conditions (scales 2, 4, and 6) give more points on average to the jobs men do; the scales that emphasize effort (scales 5 and 8) give more points on average to the jobs women do; and the remaining scales show no significant difference by sex. It is of considerable interest to note that the nonmanual jobs done by women tend on average to require more strength than those done by men.

Conclusion

The conclusion to be drawn from this exercise is unambiguous: the choice of factors included in job evaluation schemes and the relative weight accorded these factors can have very substantial consequences for the ordering of jobs with respect to their relative worth and hence relative pay.

Certain weighting schemes are likely to be relatively advantageous to particular social categories—men versus women, whites versus blacks, and so on. Because of this, job evaluation practices and procedures require close scrutiny and careful negotiation to ensure, first, that there is consensus between workers and management and among various categories of workers as to what should be valued in jobs and, second, that job evaluation procedures as implemented actually reflect such consensus. The choice of factors and factor weights in job evaluation schemes should not be regarded as a technical issue beyond the purview of affected parties but rather as an expression of the values underlying notions of equity and hence as a matter to be negotiated as part of the wage-setting process.

References

Cain, Pamela, and Donald J. Treiman. 1981. "The *Dictionary of Occupational Titles* as a Source of Occupational Data." *American Sociological Review* 46:253–78.

Miller, Ann R., Donald J. Treiman, Pamela S. Cain, and Patricia A. Roos, 1980. *Work, Jobs, and Occupations: A Critical Review of the Dictionary of Occupational Titles*. Washington, D.C.: National Academy Press.

Treiman, Donald J. 1979. *Job Evaluation: An Analytic Review*. Washington, D.C.: National Academy of Sciences.

Treiman, Donald J., and Heidi I. Hartmann, eds. 1981. *Women, Work, and Wages: Equal Pay for Jobs of Equal Value*. Washington, D.C.: National Academy Press.

U.S. Bureau of the Census. 1978. "The Current Population Survey: Design and Methodology." Technical Paper 40. Washington, D.C.: Government Printing Office.

U.S. Department of Labor. 1965. *Dictionary of Occupational Titles: Definitions of Titles*. Vol. 1. 3d ed. Washington, D.C.: Government Printing Office.

U.S. Department of Labor. 1967. *Suffix Codes for Occupational Titles in the Third Edition DOT*. Washington, D.C.: Government Printing Office.

U.S. Department of Labor. 1972. *Handbook for Analyzing Jobs*. Washington, D.C.: Government Printing Office.

U.S. Department of Labor. 1977. *Dictionary of Occupational Titles*. 4th ed. Washington, D.C.: Government Printing Office.

6

Dilemmas of Implementation: The Case of Nursing

HELEN REMICK

As a group of workers comes to believe that it is underpaid, it calls attention to what it does. This attention, sometimes accompanied by comparisons with other groups, causes a focus on the nature of work in general. The use of job evaluation systems to measure relative job worth further encourages us to see work as composed of groups of elements, such as effort, skill, responsibility, and working conditions. Such scrutiny can give us insight into the nature of work and how we choose to assign compensation, but the insight can also make explicit and force us to deal with issues with which we may or may not be prepared to deal. The ensuing conflict can be both external, involving a specific group of workers and the outer culture, and internal. Current trends in nursing illustrate these various processes.

Nursing and the Outer Culture

The field of nursing is obviously in a state of crisis. Although new students are still entering the field and there are more than enough registered nurses, there is an acute shortage of persons willing to do the work for the going wage under existing working conditions. In the Seattle area hospitals find themselves overly dependent upon temporary nursing services, to the detriment of patient care. The problem now appears to be coming under control only because the poor state of the economy has left many persons without access to health insurance and therefore health care and has encouraged women otherwise unemployed to continue nursing. As the economy recovers, we should expect the shortage to reappear.

Why do many nurses refuse to practice the vocation for which they were trained? The reasons are many. The nursing profession has always been relatively low-paying; hospitals have their historical roots in charitable organizations, and nurses were called upon to donate a large part of their time as charitable work (doctors, of course, were not and are not expected to make similar monetary sacrifices). The rewards for nurses were to come in the form of good feelings for having been helpful. Working conditions have always been difficult, with long hours, weekend and night work (even when women were "protected" from night work in most other fields), heavy lifting, exposure to death and disease, cranky patients, and an authoritarian hospital structure in which nursing often seems unappreciated. Nurses are expected to be nurturant, feminine, kind, and supportive and do error-free work in an efficient and competent manner, while never complaining and never, never confronting a doctor.

Nursing, like most other areas in the health care field, has changed drastically over time. Nursing specialties, for example, can make extensive use of electronic monitors, involve significant amounts of teaching, and/or require sophisticated diagnostic work. Unfortunately, the work of nurses is not always visible to the patient, in part because of stereotypes about nurses and women in general. In a well-publicized example, after the attempted assassination of President Reagan, he recalled the nurse who had been so comforting to him while he was in the intensive care unit and conducted a search to thank her. Giving comfort was one of her least important duties in terms of his survival; she was constantly monitoring his vital signs for change and was fully competent to initiate emergency procedures should the situation have called for it. Responsibility for the well-being and survival of the president of the United States would hardly have been turned over to a nurse if all she could do was offer comfort. But since many people expect only comforting from nurses, that is all they see. They are also likely to think that a low salary for nurses is justified if they perceive the job as requiring only nurturance, which they may believe to be innate to women and therefore requiring no learning.

This tendency to undervalue and underestimate what women do is, of course, not limited to nursing. The literacy requirements of clerical work, the teaching skills of day care workers, and the skills and responsibilities of mothering are similarly overlooked and therefore undercompensated and undervalued. Unfortunately, since women are not only workers in these fields but also participants in the culture at large, they often share the undervaluation of women's work, whether done by themselves or by other women.

For nursing, as for other female-dominated fields, change will require education of the public on what nurses do, what skills are involved, how the responsibility compares to that required for other jobs, and what working conditions are like. Personnel officers, hospital administrators, doctors, and nurses themselves will need special attention in order to bring about change.

Nursing within the Health Care System

Nursing exists as a profession and as part of a community composed of physicians, nurses, and other health professionals. Major issues that arise in these contexts and must be confronted by job evaluation include the nature of nursing education; the relative worth of specialties; and the relative value of health care versus medical care. These issues are already the focus of much discussion; widespread application of job evaluation systems would force resolutions.

Nursing Education

Nursing education is the subject of lively debate in the nursing community. There are three major routes into nursing: two-year community college programs; three-year hospital training programs; and four-year baccalaureate degrees. All three result in identical licensing as a registered nurse. Three-year hospital programs have been on the wane for the last fifteen years.

Advocates of each of the three systems argue variously for and against a differentiation in title and salary among their graduates. The B.S., or four-year degree, is often a requirement for promotion into supervision and management and for entry into master's level programs leading to specialization and teaching. Advocates of differentiation argue that the broader preparation of a four-year degree, with its greater emphasis on science courses and theoretical material, makes for better nurses. Two-year advocates, on the other hand, maintain that the importance of on-the-job training leaves no basis for differentiation by educational program, especially after several years of work.

Hospital personnel administrators, as they make salary recommendations for nurses, enter the fray and say that neither group should have higher starting salaries than four-year liberal arts graduates like themselves, although they concede that engineers and business administration graduates should earn more. From the standpoint of the nature and intent of nursing education, I think a strong argument can be made that the proper comparators for four-year nursing programs are engineering and business administration rather than liberal arts degrees. Engineering, business, and nursing curricula are all designed to produce practitioners—people with specific skills readily applicable to specific jobs. Likewise, a three-year hospital program can be compared to a crafts apprenticeship program; both combine intensive on-the-job training in specific skills with supplementary classroom work, and their graduates assume journey-level status after four years.

I think the nursing profession does itself an injustice by focusing on the relative worth of graduates of the various degree programs when the far more significant differentiation is between nursing as a whole and comparable male-dominated fields. Engineering, the crafts and trades, and nursing all have in common that most workers remain at the journey level with little opportunity for advancement and that training is specific and is not generalizable to other fields. Engineering and the crafts compensate workers for these limitations with relatively high but narrow-ranged journey-level salaries; nursing offers relatively low and narrow salary levels.

The nursing profession needs also to look at the nature of nursing education. Critics, especially older nursing students, claim that nursing education is characterized by excessive demands for "good girl" behavior; they say that teachers are intolerant of assertiveness and reward passivity, thus denying students an intellectually challenging experience and needed skills. While these lessons may produce students who are "less trouble" and instill behaviors with high survival value in hospital bureaucracies, they are anachronistic in view of the levels of competiveness and competency needed by women in other fields and even within nursing in the battle (often led by nursing faculties) to gain recognition for the worth of nurses. The critics may be overstating their case, but they point to the need for women to examine their role in their own subjugation. Education teaches more than is found in textbooks.

Job evaluation systems will differ in their approaches to educational level and on-the-job training. Nurses, administrators, and consultants will have to face the issue of the relative worth of the various degree programs at the time a system is implemented. Are there substantive differences? What are the politics of making or not making the differentiation? How important is on-the-job training? How long does this training period last? What is the role of formal or informal continuing education? Is the training period the same for all specialties?

Specialties

In many hospital settings, nurses specialize their work. Nurses in intensive care, emergency rooms, surgery, psychiatric wards, and obstetrics, for example, get extra training in these specialties, both on the job and in the classroom. These specialists are not interchangeable: specialization in intensive care does not make one a better psychiatric or surgical nurse. Nurses can specialize in doing procedures or in teaching others to do them, and teaching roles can be as diverse as practical specialties, covering infant care, how to perform one's own dialysis, proper procedures after a colostomy, or basic sanitation, diet, and health care. Nurses in primary care hospitals specialize in dealing with patients with a wide range of needs; while they do not work with kidney transplant patients, they must understand the needs of patients after tonsilectomies, serious accidents, bouts with pneumonia, and so on.

Consideration of differentials among medical specialties gives some hint of underlying values in the medical community. High-technology fields (e.g., neurosurgery or cardiosurgery) have the highest status and earnings and the fewest females, while those dealing with women and children (e.g., family medicine and pediatrics) have the lowest status and earnings and the most females. (Gynecology is seen in the medical field as a surgical specialty and therefore is accorded higher status.) There is no such differentiation among nursing specialties. Why not? Would such differentiation be desirable?

Nurses' assignments vary greatly on such dimensions as number of patients; direct responsibility for the well-being of those in their care; need for independent action (e.g., initiating emergency procedures and administering needed medications); levels of stress; decision-making power; level of dexterity required; teaching of other health workers; and teaching of patients. Hospitals seem to compensate for some kinds of responsibility by lowering patient loads; intensive care nurses, for example, may be responsible for the well-being of only one or two patients.

Salary differentials do not appear to be the rule. Hospital administrators may wish to avoid salary differentiation in order to maintain the illusion of low and interchangeable skill levels. Nurses themselves seem unsure of the real value of their skills; after all, if they really know something, why are they paid so poorly? When asked to do work outside their specialty, they seem more often to focus on the skills they lack rather than the ones they have (Carol Barickman, personal communication, 1982); thus, they apologize for not knowing everything instead of demanding recognition for their areas of expertise, whether gained through schooling or experience.

Are all of these specialties and working conditions of equal worth? They are usually paid as though they are. How would job evaluation systems approach these jobs? Can the chosen system differentiate among the jobs? Should it differentiate? If so, on what dimension? What is the proper wage spread among the specialties relative to routine nursing (if there is such a thing)? What do nurses want? What do administrators want? What will insurance companies accept, and are insurance companies the appropriate agency to set the standards by which we value work?

Health Care versus Medical Care

In a draft of this chapter I referred to nursing as part of the medical community. I was corrected in no uncertain terms: nurses are part of the health care community, which stresses prevention and wellness and has an emphasis on the patient as a whole. Doctors, on the other hand, are the main body of the medical community. Their training emphasizes the detection and correction of things that are wrong; they focus on intervention and taking action. These distinctions, I now know, are reflected in educational philosophies and in licensing procedures. In the state of Washington, for instance, this separation is institutionalized by having medical and nursing licensing regulated by separate state boards.

While there are obvious differences in function between physicans and nurses, there are also obvious overlaps. The state of Washington's definition of medical doctor includes the following actions: diagnose, cure, advise, prescribe or administer drugs, and sever or penetrate the tissues of human beings. The definition of nursing includes: observe, assess, diagnose, counsel, teach, maintain health, prevent illness, delegate, and, under general direction of a physician, administer medications, treatments, tests, and inoculations. (See the Appendix below for the actual texts.) According to these regulations, nurses can do virtually anything under the "general direction of a licensed physician . . . whether or not the severing or penetrating of tissues is involved and whether or not a degree of independent judgment and skill is required."

Let us add a third category of worker to this discussion: physician's assistants. Physician's assistant programs came to the fore in the beginning of the 1970s to accommodate veterans who had served as medics in Vietnam and wished to be credentialed to continue such work in the United States. These programs acknowledge previous practical experience and provide the missing theoretical framework and breadth of knowledge. Interestingly, these programs provided students, almost all men, with greater recognized decision-making responsibilities and often higher pay than nurses. They are now used as much by nurses wanting formal recognition of their ability to work independently as by former service men and women.

In the state of Washington, regulations on physician's assistants are included as part of the section on physicians. The law reads as follows:

"Physician's assistant" means: (a) A person who is enrolled in, or has satisfactorily completed, a [medical] board approved training program designed to prepare persons to practice medicine to a limited extent; or (b) A person who is a university medical graduate of a foreign medical school or college. (RCW 18.71A.010)

Physician's assistants are registered to specific physicians, who must supervise their work in a general way. Physician's assistants are authorized to write prescriptions for all but controlled substances for patients of the physician to whom they are assigned. Registered nurses can prescribe medication only after receiving additional certification (30 hours of pharmacology and an examination).

I wonder what a job analyst would find in a comparison of the actual tasks of physicians, nurses, and physician's assistants. I suspect that there are more structural similarities than differences. Schools have traditionally emphasized different philosophies for nursing and medicine, and these differences no doubt modify to some degree one's approach to patients and health/medical care. They have certainly colored the cultural and worker valuations of the work done by these people. But while there are differences in labels, are there really differences in what is done or in the final outcome to the patient? Is there a real difference in how a physician's assistant with his/her medical model treats a patient as compared to a nurse using her/his health care model?

The dichotomy between medical and health care is similar to that found in other fields and in our culture in general. For example, dentists and dental hygienists divide dentistry along similar lines, with dentists doing the corrective work and hygienists the preventive. This division is considered a basic one: men build buildings and make war, and women take care of the family and raise the children. Issues of power underlie this division as well. Physicians and dentists remain adamant that only they can make reasonable business decisions and work independently; they spend large sums of money lobbying against legal changes that would allow nurses and dental hygienists to work independently. How then can we explain physicians' support for greater autonomy for physician's assistants than for nurse practitioners? The most obvious reason is that one group of workers is predominantly male and the other predominantly female. Is this also the main difference between medical and health care? Is the perceived difference actually in the training and approach of the workers or in the attributed characteristics of the workers based upon their sex?

I do not wish to deny that there may be real differences in the training of nurses and physician's assistants. On a personal note, for example, I have only recently come to understand some limitations in my childhood learning. I am the older of two daughters in a family with no sons. As a child I worked with my father on a variety of projects. While I grew up feeling that I had learned many skills, I now realize that I do not know how to do most of the tasks I worked on. Rather, I am a good assistant: I know when and how to hold the end of a board being cut on a table saw, but I do not know how to use the saw. I know which tools to hand someone, but not how to use them. I was lovingly taught, but within the constraints of appropriate male and female roles. Have nurses, dental hygienists, clerical workers, and other daughters been similarly trained as helpmates rather than doers? Have we been subtly and not so subtly denied the secrets, the essence of knowledge, being given only as much as others thought we needed to know? Is this another form of protection without which we would be better off?

How can job evaluation sort out real differences in work from cultural stereotypes of what is appropriate for the sex doing the work? How should worth be assigned to comparator jobs in the health and medical fields?

Job Evaluation in a Health/Medical Setting

Job evaluation systems are faced with other difficulties in the health/ medical care setting. Most systems have been designed for manufacturing or other product-oriented businesses. Many factors present in this sector are not found in nursing, and many in nursing are not found in manufacturing. Further, most occupations in the health care field are female-dominated and low-paying, so comparator positions are hard to find. Since the important factors in nursing seem to be unique, one must either devise systems using the appropriate factors (and somehow determining appropriate weights), apply existing systems as best one can, or conclude that the task is inappropriate or impossible.

A new system would require intensive examination of what it is that nurses actually do. Weights might be assigned by analogy. For example, many evaluation systems measure responsibility only in fiscal terms. Nurses clearly have very responsible jobs, but the responsibility is for people rather than things or money. While one might choose to enter into a philosophical debate on the value of a human life, I would suggest that instead one might be able to use as a measure of responsibility the malpractice cost of an error on the nurses' part. Use of malpractice costs would also allow for comparisons between physicians and nurses and among health/medical workers in general.

Just as job evaluation systems will have difficulties with nursing, so will nursing have difficulties with job evaluation. The close inspection of nursing will expose internal squabbles; if nursing professionals do not agree ahead of time on how such issues as education and specialization should be dealt with, then personnel specialists and management consultants will decide the issues for them. Control would pass from those within the profession to outside technocrats. Those of us who advocate comparable worth as part of a feminist philosophy must take care that our actions increase, or at least do not decrease, the power of the groups we wish to help.

Comparable worth not only addresses salary issues but also provides a framework for looking at society, work, and training. I chose to focus on nursing because it is illustrative of the treatment of women's work in general. Virtually all women's work suffers from the cultural perceptions that its main purpose is to help, not to do, and that there need to be men around to tell women what to do. These beliefs lead naturally to an assumption that women's work deserves little compensation; any woman could do it (with a little help from a man), and it is inherently rewarding.

We must make these and similar cultural assumptions explicit so that we can evaluate them for their truthfulness and relevance, with the ultimate goal of realizing the full potential and worth of indiviuals within our society regardless of their sex.

Appendix

A person is practicing medicine if he does one or more of the following:

1. Offers or undertakes to diagnose, cure, advise or prescribe for any human disease, ailment, injury, infirmity, deformity, pain or other condition, physical or mental, real or imaginary, by any means or instrumentality;
2. Administers or prescribes drugs or medicinal preparations to be used by any other person;
3. Severs or penetrates the tissues of human beings;
4. Uses . . . in the conduct of any occupation or profession pertaining to the diagnosis or treatment of human disease or conditions the designation "doctor of medicine," "physician," "surgeon," "M.D.". . . (Revised Code of Washington [RCW] 18.71.011)

The practice of nursing means the performance of acts requiring substantial specialized knowledge, judgment and skill based upon the principles of the biological, physiological, behavioral and sociological sciences in either:

1. The observation, assessment, diagnosis, care or counsel, and health teaching of the ill, injured or infirm, or in the maintenance of health or prevention of illness of others.
2. The performance of such additional acts requiring education and training and which are recognized jointly by the medical and nursing professions as proper to be performed by nurses licensed under this chapter and which shall be authorized by the board of nursing through its rules and regulations.
3. The administration, supervision, delegation and evaluation of nursing practice. . . .
4. The teaching of nursing.
5. The executing of medical regimen as prescribed by a licensed physician, osteopathic physician, dentist or chiropodist. (RCW 18.88.030)

A registered nurse under her or his license may perform for compensation nursing care (as that term is usually understood) of the ill, injured or infirm, and in the course thereof, she or he is authorized to do the following things which shall not be done by any person not so licensed, except as provided for licensed practical nurses:

1. At or under the general direction of a licensed physician, dentist, osteopath or chiropodist (acting within the scope of his or her license) to administer medications, treatments, tests and inoculations, whether or not the severing or penetrating of tissues is involved and whether or not a degree of independent judgment and skill is required.
2. To delegate to other persons engaged in nursing, the functions outlined in the preceding paragraph.
3. To perform specialized and advanced levels of nursing as defined by the board.
4. To instruct students of nursing in technical subjects pertaining to nursing. (RCW 18.88.285)

Note: the chapter on physicians uses "he" throughout, even though much of it has been revised since 1975. The chapter on nurses uses "he or she," while that on licensed practical nurses avoids singular pronouns altogether.

PART III

Four Approaches to Assessing Wage Discrimination

7

Major Issues in *a priori* Applications

HELEN REMICK

Comparable worth can best be understood and discussed in the context of salary-setting policies and practices. Practice does not always coincide with policy (see, for example, Schwab, 1980), and there can be a great difference between what people think or say they are doing and what they are actually doing. While wage-setting mechanisms are traditionally assumed to be fair because they are based upon marketplace forces (Hildebrand, 1980, summarizes these arguments), studies of actual practices demonstrate clear and persistent patterns of sex bias (Treiman and Hartmann, 1981). Comparable worth is, for many, a vague concept aimed at correcting this systemic sex bias in wages.

As Milkovich (1980) and Schwab (1980) have complained, proponents have not yet put forward a clear definition of comparable worth. While I think avoidance of definition can be a wise course, especially for a politically loaded concept in the process of formation, I nonetheless put forth the following operational definition: "the application of a single, bias-free point factor job evaluation system within a given establishment, across job families, both to rank-order jobs and to set salaries." (Remick, 1981).

Those familiar with job evaluation will see this definition as a new use of old tools. In fact, as defined here, job evaluation and comparable worth differ in very few ways. Most important politically, but least important technically,[1] they differ in intent. The traditional use of job evaluation is to justify existing salary practice or simplify salary setting, whereas comparable worth is used to remedy sex discrimination. Sometimes there is also a difference in the scope of jobs covered; traditional applications are often limited in the number of job families (e.g., managers, clericals, or crafts) evaluated, or use different evaluation tools and/or salary scales for each job family, whereas comparable worth applications include all job families. Initially, only comparable worth applications looked for and corrected sex bias in the evaluation systems, although good traditional applications now also look for this source of bias. The methodology of application is identical, though comparable worth applications are more likely to include the use of evaluation committees including employee representatives.

This definition has a number of immediately obvious limitations. First, a bias-free evaluation system probably does not yet exist. This limitation does not have to mean that comparable worth cannot be applied until such a system does exist. Rather, it can serve as a reminder that bias should be eliminated wherever possible and minimized elsewhere. Since job evaluation systems and prevailing wages are based on cultural value systems that are forever changing (see the discussion that follows), a perfect job evaluation system, good for all time, is impossible. Therefore, existing systems can be used with bias minimized as new and better systems, reflecting new values, evolve.

Second, because of its dependence on job evaluation systems, this definition is based solidly on the marketplace. As Remick (1979), Schwab (1980), and others have pointed out, job evaluation systems are designed to reflect prevailing wages in their choice of factors, weighting of factors, and salary-setting practices. To the degree that people disagree with the fundamental values underlying current salary-setting practices, they will dislike this definition. The use of prevailing wages in the marketplace perpetuates whatever bias exists there.

Third, this model will work best in application in large firms where the majority of employees are men whose jobs are distributed across the full range of points for the given application. If a firm employs mostly men at the top and middle levels and women at the bottom (as in insurance companies, for example) or employs mostly women overall, even with men in the few top positions (as in banks and hospitals), a sex-balanced salary line will be

---

1. The term "technical" refers to methodological decisions made by specialists on salary administration in the privacy of their own personnel department. Technical choices are based on tradition or theoretical preference. When these procedures are exposed to outside groups, through discussion with management, in collective bargaining, in civil service systems, and so on, seemingly neutral technical decisions take on "political" aspects reflecting the relative importance of their acceptibility to various groups.

harder to establish. Firms should also be large enough to have sufficient benchmark or key classes[2] for which prevailing-wage data can be gathered and a salary line established.

Fourth, this definition does not address the political or economic ramifications of changes in salary-setting methods. Nor are some technical issues solved. These problems are addressed more fully in Chapter 6 and in the discussion of the state of Washington study in this chapter.

Fifth, comparable worth, as an abstract concept, can be implemented through collective bargaining or employer initiative without resort to a formal job evaluation plan. Enough data now exist to give unions and management a good idea of where undervaluation (underpayment) is present, and salary increases can be negotiated or granted to remedy problems.

These limitations do not alter the importance of comparable worth studies, nor do the results of such applications differ significantly from those using other methods (see Chapters 8, 9, and 10). The 1974 Washington State study provides an excellent example for a discussion of the technical issues involved in a comparable worth study as defined above. Because the study was conducted in the public sector, the process has been more open to scrutiny than would be the case in the private sector; it has also been more susceptible to political pressures. Choices among technical options have often been determined, and will no doubt continue to be determined, by political considerations. Therefore, though this chapter has technical considerations as its focus, I will comment on the political aspects where appropriate. The study is instructive, not only for the now familiar findings of undercompensation of women's work, but also as a basis for the discussion of several issues: what job evaluation systems actually measure and how that relates to the marketplace; possible sources of sex bias in job evaluation; and ways in which technical decisions can alter the outcome of such studies.

The State of Washington Study

In 1973 the top management of the state of Washington (e.g., agency directors and associate directors) asked the governor to fund for the application of a job evaluation system to their positions. Job evaluation has the dual purpose of establishing internal alignment and tying jobs to the outside market; the purpose of this request was not so much to address internal alignment as to argue for salary increases to bring state salaries more in line with outside wages. Washington is, or should be, notorious for its tight-

---

2. Prevailing wage surveys are conducted on a sample of jobs, not all positions. The sampling is done by selecting positions with large numbers of incumbents and with counterparts in other firms. These positions are called "benchmark" or "key classes."

fisted policies toward state workers. The governor approved the project; a local firm was hired; and the top 242 management positions were evaluated, including those of 6 elected officials. The study uncovered two facts, both reflective of cultural values: managers in the public sector are noticeably underpaid relative to the private sector, and elected officials are underpaid relative to appointed ones. The consulting firm recommended sizable salary increases for these employees, and the legislature approved a smaller but substantial one. This salary system is still in place for these appointed and elected officials.

In 1974 the now retired head of the largest state employees' union, the Washington Federation of State Employees (American Federation of State, County and Municipal Employees, AFL-CIO), approached the governor, asking that a study be done comparing the salaries of sex-segregated positions. The Washington State Women's Commission was also involved in pushing for the study. The governor approved this landmark study. Jobs were chosen for evaluation which represented sizable numbers of employees and in which incumbents were predominantly (at least 70 percent) of the same sex.

Because this study is so often referred to, the methods used are worthy of description. Willis and Associates, the firm used for the management study, also conducted the comparable worth study. Their point factor system, similar to that of Hay and Associates, was not modified for this new application. Because of political considerations, an Advisory Committee was appointed by the governor to represent the interests of business, labor, the governor's office, the personnel systems, and women in the overall formulation of the study. An Evaluation Committee, the working group that actually assigned rankings to the jobs, was composed of 11 state employees and two appointees from the private sector. Additionally, at the request of the Advisory Committee, Willis hired a female consultant to work on the project.

Position questionnaires were sent to a sample of 1,600 employees in the jobs to be evaluated, and approximately half of these persons were also interviewed. The questionnaires, as supplemented or not by interviews, became the basis for the evaluation of the jobs. The Evaluation Committee assigned levels of knowledge and skills, mental demands, accountability, and working conditions in accordance with standard practices in the personnel field. Evaluated points were then compared to existing wages within the state civil service system. Salaries for state workers were then (and still are) based upon the results of elaborate salary surveys of employers throughout the state, so that results are generalizable to the state at large.

The results of the study were startling to many. There was virtually no overlap in average salary in any given point range for male- and female-dominated jobs (Figure 7-1). Overall, the average rate of compensation for female-dominated jobs was only about 80 percent of that for male-

Figure 7-1
1974 Washington State Study

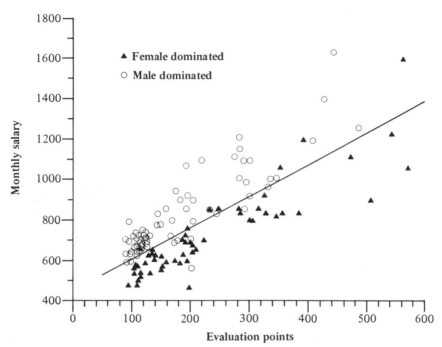

dominated jobs. Examples bring the issue to life. A Food Service Worker I, at 93 points, earned an average salary of $472 per month, while a Delivery Truck Driver I, at 94 points, earned $792; a Clerical Supervisor III, at 305 points, earned an average of $794. A Nurse Practitioner II, at 385 points, had average earnings of $832, the same as those of a Boiler Operator with only 144 points. A Homemaker I, with 198 points and an average salary of $462, had the lowest earnings of all evaluated jobs.

The comparable worth study generated much discussion. To many women's groups, it demonstrated what they had suspected all along: that women were paid less because they were women. Others charged that the study and the evaluation system were biased in favor of women because the state and marketplace would not discriminate so blatantly against women (keep in mind that this was the same system that had just been implemented and is still in effect for appointed officials). The legislature did not accept the results. The governor authorized a follow-up study in 1976 and, as he left office, included $7 million dollars in his proposed budget for partial implementation of the study. The new governor had campaigned on a platform including implementation of the study, but once in office, she removed the comparable worth item from the budget, saying that comparable worth was like "comparing apples, pumpkins, and cans of worms."

In 1977 the Washington Federation of State Employees succeeded in getting the following language included in the instruction for the biennial salary survey:

> The [personnel] board shall furnish the following supplementary data in support of this recommended salary schedule: . . . (5) A supplemental salary schedule which indicates those cases where the board determines that prevailing rates do not provide similar salaries for positions that require or impose similar responsibilities, judgment, knowledge, skills, and working conditions. This supplementary salary schedule shall contain proposed salary adjustments necessary to eliminate any such dissimilarities in compensation. Additional compensation needed to eliminate such salary dissimilarities shall not be included in the basic salary schedule but shall be maintained as a separate salary schedule for purposes of full disclosure and visibility. (State Senate Bill 2383, 1977)

These supplementary data have been prepared for the 1979, 1981, and 1983 legislative sessions for consideration in the biennial budget process. An update study was conducted in 1980, expanding the number of jobs evaluated. Figure 7-2 shows the July 1982 relationship between evaluation points and prevailing rates in the state (actual salaries of state workers average 15 percent below these figures). There is no discernible improvement in the relationship of salaries between male- and female-dominated positions.

In 1981 AFSCME filed a complaint with the U.S. Equal Employment Opportunity Commission on behalf of all women employees of the state of Washington, alleging that:

> The State of Washington has and is discriminating on grounds of sex in compensation against women employed in *state service* by establishing and maintaining wage rates or salaries for predominantly female job classifications that are less than wage rates or salaries for predominantly male job classifications that require equal or less skill, effort and responsibility. The State maintains these lower rates or salaries for predominantly female classifications although a study commissioned by the State itself establishes that many predominantly female jobs are discriminatorily underpaid. (Charge of Discrimination, *AFSCME and AFSCME Council 28* v. *State of Washington*, September 1981; emphasis in original)

In the 1982 legislative session, a bill was introduced that committed the state to comparable worth but included no appropriation. In an election year right after the discovery of the "gender gap," the bill passed many committees and the state senate with virtually no negative votes or discus-

Figure 7-2
1982 Washington State Study

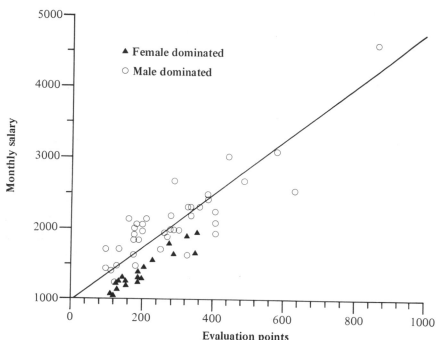

sion, only to die at the end of the session before a vote was taken in the house; no one had to vote no, but the bill did not pass.

The November 1982 elections gave the leadership in both houses to Democrats. In July 1982, AFSCME filed a suit against the state based on its EEOC complaint, and in November 1982 3,000 clerical workers at the University of Washington voted to affiliate with the Service Employees International Union (SEIU) District 925, becoming one of the largest bargaining units in the state. These events, combined with strong lobbying by women's groups and some unions (particularly AFSCME, the Washington State Nurses Association, and SEIU), created a new atmosphere more favorable to comparable worth in the legislature. The 1982 bill was reintroduced by a female Republican senator, while a female Democratic representative inserted $1.5 million to begin comparable worth implementation into the appropriations bill. Passage was not easy (see Remick, 1983), and media coverage was most often negative. Yet both bills were signed into law in June 1983.

Washington State is now committed to full implementation of comparable worth by 1993, although "full implementation" is not defined in the legislation. The initial appropriation provides for a $100 per year salary increase for those benchmark jobs falling at least 20 percent below the average-worth line (see Figure 7-2) and for jobs whose salaries are related to these benchmarks. Affected employees for this first adjustment include virtually all clerical workers, registered nurses, licensed practical nurses, physical therapists, telephone operators, and laundry workers.

In August 1983 *AFSCME* v *State of Washington* went to trial. The trial was not, the judge said, over whether comparable worth was a reasonable means of setting salaries—the legislature had already passed legislation saying it was—but whether the State's present and past practices were discriminatory. At the end of the liability phase, the judge concluded that the State was guilty of intentional and pervasive discrimination. Intent was obvious from such acts as use of sex-segregated want ads as late as 1973, with no apparent efforts made after that date to overcome the effects of such practices. The State's comparable worth studies were important for demonstrating its failure to act in the face of evidence of disparate impact of salary setting practices and as a measure of the extent of the impact. The judge has appointed a special master to oversee resolution of the case, including specifics of salary adjustments and calculations of back wages. The State is appealing the ruling, and final resolution will be years away if it comes in the courts. Political pressure is already mounting for an out-of-court settlement, possibly with limited back wages and a phase-in of salary increases. The future of this case is difficult to predict but guaranteed to be interesting.

Washington State was the third state to appropriate funds for comparable worth. New Mexico did so in April 1983 ($7 million for a very small work force), with no formal study and by increasing salaries for the lowest-paid workers; 86 percent of the beneficiaries are women, and most of the remaining workers are Hispanic or Native American. In May 1983 Minnesota appropriated $21.7 million for their 1983–85 biennium to be distributed through the collective bargaining process to occupations identified by a job evaluation study. California was the first state to pass enabling legislation, but by the end of 1983 it has not yet entered a cycle of collective bargaining.

Sex Bias in Existing Systems

As states begin to fund comparable worth based on results of job evaluation studies, these studies need to be scrutinized for fairness. *A priori* job evaluation systems are designed to capture existing salary practices; they therefore are likely to capture existing discriminatory practices as well. Some sex bias can be eliminated by careful application with awareness of where discrimination is most likely to occur. The four major points at which bias may enter an application are the following:

1. *Choice of factors*. Are factors found primarily in women's jobs missing from the system? Men's and women's jobs have often been found to

differ on the following dimensions: light versus heavy work; full-body movement versus repeated use of only a few muscles; freedom to move about versus confinement to small spaces; presence of speed and fine motor requirements; importance of sensory decisions; level of physical danger; responsibility for tangible property versus responsibility for persons; levels of decision making and analysis; fiscal responsibility; amount of interruption and simultaneous processing; interpersonal skill requirements; level of schooling; on-the-job training versus pre-existing skills acquired at one's own expense; credit given for literacy; nature of negative work conditions; compensation for deviation from standard work week; and compensation for newness of technology (Remick, 1979; Rohmert and Rutenfranz, 1977). Many systems include most of the factors found primarily in men's jobs, but omit some of those found primarily in women's jobs. When one buys a "canned" system, choice of factors is the responsibility of the consultants, though the firm using the system will be held responsible for the resulting salary inequities. Use of multiple regression techniques to "capture" salary policies does not eliminate this problem area (see Chapter 8).

2. *Weighting of factors.* Are nondiscriminatory factors present but given less than equitable weight? Again, consulting firms will determine these weights for prepackaged systems, and regression studies will merely reflect market discrimination.

3. *Application.* Systems can be fair, but applications biased. Are job descriptions for all groups equally complete? Are predetermined values biasing assignment of points? If an employee committee is used, are all job groups represented, and is the committee representative of employees by race, sex, and job groups? Since women tend to use "weaker" verbs, do word choices by employees unduly influence judgments? For example, what is the difference between managing and supervising, interpreting and using, organizing and doing?

4. *Salary setting.* What exceptions are made to salary grade assignments? What is the sex and race composition of the incumbents in the exceptional jobs? How many salary scales are used? If more than one scale is used, do any scales apply to job groups that are held primarily by members of one race or sex?

The "perfect" job evaluation system may be impossible to achieve, since consensus on values is unlikely. It is in any case a long way off. The imperfections of job evaluation systems are now being catalogued (e.g., Remick, 1979; Treiman, 1979; Schwab, 1980; and see Chapter 4). Yet I do not think that the flaws being discovered mean that all systems should be thrown out. Salaries must, after all, be set somehow, and explicit standards certainly seem preferable to implicit ones. Job evaluation systems reflect value systems, which are now in flux; the evaluation systems need to respond to the changing values so that they more accurately reflect current thinking. We must keep in mind that many people thought the Equal Pay Act of 1963 was revolutionary—that it would bankrupt thousands of businesses; yet the equal pay principle is now generally accepted. Similar adjustments can take place in job evaluation systems through reinterpretation of existing factors.

Techniques of Implementation

What does it mean to implement comparable worth? This question is at once economic, political, and technical, and the answer will depend on the funds available, the relative power of concerned groups, and the exact methodology chosen. All of these variables will have an impact on the relief given to underpaid workers.

These issues also go to the heart of salary administration. What is good salary administration? What is politically feasible, as compared with what is theoretically desirable? Listed below are major decision points in the application of a job evaluation system and some of the technical and/or political questions likely to arise.

1. Internal alignments are determined.

(a) A job evaluation system is selected. For ease of application the system selected is usually one offered by a consulting firm rather than one developed internally or derived from a policy-capturing model. Who should decide which system to choose? What is superior: *a priori* systems or policy-capturing techniques? How aware are the designers of the potential for built-in bias, and how willing are they to modify their system to minimize it? Employers should carefully screen systems for bias, since they will be held liable if sued for any bias therein, even if they did not design the systems themselves.

(b) Evaluation committees are usually set up to conduct the evaluations. The ratio of management to worker representation varies widely, but reasonable worker participation is associated with higher acceptance of results. Who should be on the evaluation committee(s)? Is the committee representative of the work force by sex, race, age, and occupational group? What is the desired role of employee organizations?

(c) Evaluations are conducted, which may or may not include employee interviews, individual questionnaires, or ratings based on written job descriptions. Points are assigned, based on the effort, skill, responsibility, and working conditions associated with the positions. These points form the basis for establishing the relative worth of the positions and therefore their salaries. What method should be used to evaluate jobs? Should all jobs be evaluated? While it is cheaper to limit evaluation to a few classes, maintaining traditional alignments of classes, the eventual evaluation of all occupations is a good idea: one does a comparable worth study precisely because one is questioning traditional alignments. If all positions are to be evaluated, can the evaluations be phased in over time? If so, how should priorities be established?

2. Relative salaries must now be translated into actual salaries.

(a). Usually not all jobs are surveyed for salary data. Instead, a few, often called key or benchmark jobs, are selected by some set of standards. Decisions are made about the firms to be surveyed in terms of size, nature of the business, and geographical location: what are the appropriate choices on these dimensions? Which jobs should be the basis for the salary survey and the salary line that will describe the relationship between survey results and evaluation points? On which dimensions should they be representative of the total work force: by the nature of the work (e.g., clerical or crafts or accounting), by the number of employees either in that class or in the jobs related to it for salary-setting purposes, by the race and sex of the incumbents, or by all of these? Data from studies to date show that male-dominated jobs receive a much higher rate of return (salary) for evaluation points than do female-dominated jobs, so that having larger numbers of male- or female-dominated positions included among the surveyed classes will affect the salary line and therefore the compensation for all workers.

(b) Prevailing salaries are plotted against assigned points. A salary line is constructed, usually using the statistical line of best fit, which represents the average rate of compensation for given points. In application, this line is then modified into salary steps, with a range of points simplified to a single step. Each step is assigned a range of salaries to reflect seniority and/or merit (see Figure 7-3). The line used to set salaries may deviate from the line of best fit if the policy of the organization is to pay above or below market rates. Is the policy to pay less than the market rate for jobs held by women and minority males but at or above it for those held predominantly by white males?

How should the evaluated jobs be weighted when drawing the salary line? The salary line can be constructed with one "vote" per job, one "vote" per incumbent in surveyed classes, one "vote" per employee of the organization whose salary is related to the surveyed job, one "vote" per employee of the other firms included in the salary survey data, or in some other manner. In the civil service system of the state of Washington, predominantly female classes tend to have large numbers of incumbents, while primarily male ones represent fewer workers. Since female-dominated jobs are compensated at a lower rate, the salary line and rate of return to each worker is higher when the line is drawn with each job receiving equal weight and lower with each state incumbent receiving equal weight.

How should the sex of incumbents be considered in the construction of the salary line? Existing studies show that present salary structures might best be described by two separate and unequal salary lines, one for male-dominated jobs and one for female-dominated jobs, with few cases where men's jobs at given point ranges earn as little as the best-paid women's job of similar value. A salary line constructed from all jobs combined falls at the low end of compensation for men and the high end for women, thus

Figure 7-3
Relationship of Salary Line, Grade, and Range

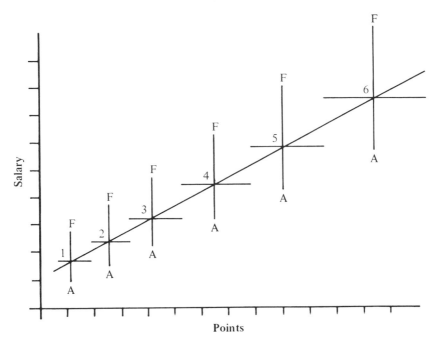

Salary lines show the relationship between the "worth" of a job and its salary. The worth is assessed in terms of points received for level of effort, skill, responsibility, and working conditions. For each additional point, or increase in the value of the job, the salary increases. In practice, the continuous salary line is converted into grades and ranges. Points are grouped into ranges for ease of salary administration; for example, 80 to 100 points might be assigned to grade 1, 101 to 130 points to grade 2, and so on. Here these grades are labeled 1 to 6. Salaries vary for persons within each grade depending on seniority and/or merit; here, these ranges are labeled *A* to *F*. As points increase, the intervals between grades usually increase, and ranges are often divided into steps based on percentage increases. The "salary line" is used as a shorthand notation for describing this more complex relationship between points and salary.

describing neither very well, but deviation from this combination could be costly to the employer in terms of salary or turnover.

(c) The salary line is used to assign salaries to surveyed and nonsurveyed jobs. How should the salary line be implemented? If the average salary line is used, bringing jobs below the line to the line would result in substantial salary increases for many jobs, most of which have female incumbents. What, then, is to be done with the jobs receiving rates of compensation above the line? It is possible to leave them at the values of salary survey results, while paying others at the average salary line. But in some ways this solution perpetuates a dual salary structure because in actual application women's jobs would be paid at an average rate and men's jobs above the average. Lowering the jobs above the average to the average would, over time, save some money but would have a very high political cost, since it would alienate organized labor and all workers receiving above-average compensation; it might also result in recruitment and retention problems for these jobs, or their feminization. Using the salary line that describes male-dominated jobs as the overall rate of compensation would be similar to the Equal Pay Act requirement that salaries be raised, not lowered, to bring about equity. It seems likely that there would be less resistance by workers in male-dominated jobs to putting all jobs on the male average, since any downward adjustments would be relatively small. However, this solution is obviously the most costly, thus detracting from its acceptability.

Because of the cost involved, how can such results be phased in over time? (This question will, of course, be moot if employers are successful in suits against employers, since such a result would probably require immediate implementation *and* back wages.) The phase-in could begin with the worst cases, the lower salary grades, percentage increases, step increases, and so on. Jobs above the salary line could receive the exact amount indicated by the salary survey, the overall average increase indicated by the survey, or an amount less than the average (thus bringing them to the line over time). What should be the role of employee organizations, other employers, and, in the public sector, taxpayers in making these decisions?

(d) A few jobs (e.g., computer programmers and football coaches) may need upward salary adjustments to respond to special market conditions. If exceptions are to be allowed to the assignment of a case to a salary grade, what will be the criteria used? No equity will be gained if women are paid by the rules and most men's jobs are made exceptions and paid more. If supply and demand arguments are made for salary exceptions, these arguments should be translated into measurable criteria. For example, excessive demand might be looked at in terms of retention problems, which could be measured by turnover rates. However, if excessive turnover rates are a signal for salary adjustments for some job classes, then rates over a certain level should be a signal for all classes. Adjustments also need a "sunset" clause, so that they are re-evaluated periodically. A permanent salary exception violates the workings of the market, wherein supply, over time, increases to meet demand, and a new equilibrium is achieved.

(e) Systems are maintained by conducting periodic salary surveys for selected classes and adjusting the entire salary grid as necessary through across-the-board increases. Merit and seniority adjustments are separate.

How should the system be maintained? Once the jobs below the line have reached the rate of compensation of whichever salary line is chosen, how shall the steady state be maintained? On subsequent salary exercises, all employees might receive increases equal to the overall average for survey results; but which jobs will be surveyed? New salary lines could continue to be created periodically. In the most simple case, salaries could be adjusted according to the Department of Labor figures for all workers in the appropriate geographical area or industry.

Many of these questions are not limited to comparable worth but should be asked in any job evaluation application. Their emergence has coincided with that of comparable worth because comparable worth has come to our attention as an issue in the public sector, where personnel decisions are open to discussion and will undergo even closer public scrutiny in the courts. Job evaluations, on the other hand, have taken place most often in the privacy of the private sector, though they too will be closely reviewed as court cases increase.

What Do Job Evaluation Systems Measure?

Whatever job evaluation system is used, and however fairly, questions remain as to what is being measured and how this is related to our cultural concept of wages. In many ways the state of Washington study is most remarkable for the high correlation ($r = 0.75$) between job evaluation points and prevailing salaries for a wide range of occupations.[3] Such a high correlation indicates that there is some logic to salary practices and that this logic can be approximated with job evaluation systems. Job evaluation systems are nothing more than attempts to make explicit the usually implicit factors determining salaries; as such, they are good indicators of the cultural values upon which salaries are based. Of the systems I have seen, not one asks questions about the supply of, or demand for, workers in the jobs being evaluated. Rather, the questions concern the number of employees supervised, years of education and/or training required, freedom to make decisions, financial responsibility, kind of interaction with other people, impact of errors, noise in the environment, amount of heavy lifting, and so on. These factors are usually variants of effort, skill, responsibility, and working conditions. In the Washington study, the factors of "knowledge and skills," "mental demands," and "accountability" correlate with one another at $r =$

---

3. Correlation measures the relatedness of two variables. If the variables are perfectly related (as one value increases, so does the other at a constant proportional rate), then the correlation (r) $= 1$. If the data are perfectly random, $r = 0$. The correlations reported here range from very high ($r = 0.70$) to extraordinarily high ($r = 0.95$). All are statistically significant, that is, not likely to occur by chance alone; stated in plainer English, the two variables are highly related in all cases.

0.94. (For nonstatisticians, a correlation of this magnitude indicates that the three factors are so closely related that they can be considered to be virtually identical.) The fourth factor, "working conditions," contributes little to total points, leaving a single factor, perhaps "effortskillresponsibility," that nonetheless is highly predictive of prevailing wages. Such correlations with the marketplace are not unusual. For example, in an application at the University of Washington for professional and managerial positions only, pre-existing wages set by individual negotiation correlated with evaluation points at $r > 0.85$; this system has six relatively independent factors.

On the basis of these results, I posit that job evaluation systems primarily measure how cultural values are compensated in the marketplace, with the few supply-demand problems treated as exceptions for salary-setting purposes. Wages are important to workers as determiners of material well-being and as measures of status, power, and self-worth. They are also important to employers, who must make judgments on how much to pay to attract the kind of employee they want while still managing an acceptable profit margin. Workers expect to earn a certain amount for doing various kinds of work, and employers expect to pay within certain ranges.

The psychological or cultural component of wages appears to be at least as important as the economic one, and it influences workers and employers alike. Sociologists have found high agreement by members of a wide variety of groups on ratings of socioeconomic status of various occupations. These status ratings show high correlations with actual salaries when male-dominated and female-dominated occupations are considered separately; females show consistently lower salaries associated with status level (England, 1979). Status ratings also correlate highly with job worth, as shown by point scores on at least one job evaluation system (Marrs, 1983). Other statistical studies show the sex of the workers to be the single most important predictor of wages (for an excellent review, see Treiman and Hartmann, 1981). We must conclude that one of our values is to pay less for women's work.

Values of work are also rated to specific aspects of the required tasks. Supervisors, for example, make more than those they supervise. Many find it enigmatic that someone who is very good at something must at some point stop doing that thing and supervise others doing it in order to make more money; there is a ceiling on the amount of money we will pay for doing a given thing well. The value system is not static; rather, it changes with technology, laws, and other forces. Manual labor, when many jobs required it, received low compensation; now that relatively few jobs require it, a bonus for hard physical labor is said to be needed to attract workers. Computers have also changed our value system. To most persons, computers are mysterious and frightening; workers have therefore demanded higher wages when their jobs were computerized, even though the computer may in fact have simplified their tasks.

Unions have introduced the concept of a living wage: the idea that no man should be expected to work full-time for less money than he needs to provide the basic necessities for himself and his family. This amount appears to be considerably above minimum wage, even for such entry-level jobs as laborer or custodian. The definition of a living wage varies with the expected life style of the person doing the work. Thus, a man entering middle management is expected by both employer and employees to maintain a life style requiring a certain income level, and this level is different from the amount required to maintain the expected life style of a blue-collar worker.

Women are apparently expected to need less to live on, to be dependent on someone else as their principal source of income, or to maintain a lower standard of living. Most women earn less than the average wage of men, and women make up the bulk of workers making the minimum wage. In the past, many women have focused on the intrinsic rewards of their work than on salary; when maximization of salary is not possible, opting for interesting work makes good sense. The movement for comparable worth represents a major shift in the women's value system, from stressing intrinsic rewards to expecting monetary return for services rendered. I have heard this shift criticized as sullying the more noble values previously exhibited by women (even if not by choice), and the criticism is sometimes accompanied by advice on protecting women from malelike avarice. I think women need more protection from poverty than from greed.

Women's demands for increased wages are sometimes seen as unreasonable on other grounds as well. Male tree trimmers for the city of Denver, interviewed for a television report on the efforts of nurses in that city to raise their wages, repeatedly said that they thought tree trimmers deserved a higher salary because their work was more "difficult," "dangerous," and "dirty" (Gregg Pratt, personal communication, 1981). Their choice of terms illustrates how cultural values invade our concepts of jobs—and efforts to conduct bias-free job evaluations. It would seem fair to conclude that the tree trimmers are referring to the physical difficulty of climbing trees and ladders, the danger of physical labor at heights and with certain machinery, and the dirt of outdoors work. They, and many others, do not see the difficulty of work in intensive care units, the danger of dealing with disease and psychotic patients, or the dirt of vomit. I find their use of "dirty" especially interesting. Apparently, to most men and women alike, dirty jobs are those where no attempt is made to keep the work environment clean, and the dirt shows, under your fingernails, after work hours; axle grease is dirty. Many nurses I have talked to see their job as clean, in part because of the constant effort to make the environment sterile, in spite of their exposure to vomit, urine, feces, blood, pus, dead people, disease, and so on. Garbage collectors do dirty work, while food service workers, producing the garbage, do clean work. "Clean" environments are seen as more pleasant and therefore deserving of lower rates of compensation.

Still, many men are coming to support increased wages for women as they see that poor wages paid to their wives, sisters, daughters, and mothers affect the economic well-being of the entire family. Winn Newman, special counsel for AFSCME, has observed that the "dual-income family" should more correctly be called the "1.59 income" family, since women working full-time make only fifty-nine cents for each dollar earned by men working full-time. A fair return for their wives' work outside the home is seen by increasing numbers of men as a reasonable and necessary compensation for the loss of the wives' services within the home and the concomitant increase in their own workloads there.

This argument for the importance of cultural values does not deny that the marketplace is involved in the setting of salaries under job evaluation systems: factors and factor weights are at some time derived from the pre-existing market rates; and point factor systems produce only rank-orderings of jobs, which must be related back to wages through surveys of prevailing wages for selected positions. It is, in fact, a widely held value that wages are or should be set by marketplace mechanisms, and references to the marketplace are often used to justify existing salary practices. Yet many of the factors said to be important in setting wages are either unmeasured or unmeasurable. Few employers, for instance, have reliable means of measuring the quality of job applicants (witness the difficulty employers have in validating pre-employment testing), in part because most jobs have not been analyzed to identify the skills needed for given levels of performance, and because no one has devised a way to measure these skills and to determine whether someone has too little or too much of them. Instead, we guess what proxies might be used: level of schooling, previous job experience, character references, hobbies, military experience, age, sex, race, marital status, and all of the other items seen on application forms or asked about in job interviews.

Retention and other recruitment issues present similar measurement difficulties. Few employers actually measure their turnover rates; fewer still know what to make of the numbers they get. Rather, employers choose to tolerate high turnover rates in some jobs but not others, and apparently their reasons are based on economics, politics and cultural stereotypes. Computer programmers and engineers, for example, seem to be valued highly enough in many firms that wages will be increased in order to recruit and retain them. In contrast, a high turnover in clerical and custodial positions is often tolerated or welcomed as a way of saving on salaries (delay in replacing clerical workers in some settings, for example, causes temporary inconvenience to individual units but can result in considerable salary savings overall), or as an unavoidable characteristic of the available workers, not of the jobs themselves (see Chapter 3 for further discussion). In the latter case, women, minorities, and lower-class people have attributed to them the characteristics of low job commitment and instability, and salary increases that would produce no decrease in turnover or increase in productivity would be seen as wasted money.

As a further complication, our stereotypes about the persons likely to be hired color how we design, or at least describe, occupations. Thus, clerical jobs are seen as requiring low levels of on-the-job training and high levels of interchangeability, desirable characteristics if one assumes that the workers will have low tenure on the job. These aspects of the job then limit promotional opportunities; one does not bother to build promotional ladders for workers who will not stay long enough to use them or who have so little investment in their jobs that promotion would be of no interest. Such expectations become self-fulfilling prophecies: ambitious workers will not stay in jobs offering no growth and no opportunity for promotion. These stereotypes are so strong that it is difficult to ascertain whether the jobs have been structured to match the stereotypes of likely workers or whether they are in fact substantially different from their official descriptions and the characteristics are incorrectly attributed to the job as well as the workers.

Prevailing wage data as gathered by a salary survey can override turnover information. Recently a large employer in the Seattle area experienced high turnover in clerical positions. The employer conducted a salary survey of other large employers in the area and found that his wages were competitive with the others; therefore no salary increase was given, *even though* the other employers were also experiencing recruitment and retention difficulties. Crafts positions in this same firm are given higher-than-average salary increases in spite of amazingly low turnover and very high unemployment in the geographical area because lower salaries *might* result in recruitment or retention problems. Both the artificially low wages to clericals and the artificially high wages to crafts workers prevent market forces from working freely.

Schwab (1980) and Treiman and Hartmann (1981) discuss many other imperfections of the marketplace and salary-setting mechanisms. Most workers are not well informed about salaries within their own employing firm and are even less likely to have information about other firms and other occupations. Additionally, in large firms internal structures become more important than external force, with only a few general occupations serving as bridges to the market. Job evaluation systems allow employers to establish pay relationships among jobs for which outside data are either not collected or not possible to collect. The value system used to establish these salary relationships is either that of a consulting firm (when a fixed package is used) or that of the firm itself (when a policy-capturing statistical model is employed).

Values are not bad and need not—cannot—be avoided. Any salary structure is based upon a value system, either a system of paying everyone the same or a system compensating some work more than others. Every compensation plan and every collective bargaining contract reflects the relative values of jobs. What we want to avoid are values that discriminate among persons according to perceived group characteristics. In employment, group discrimination can occur not only in hiring, when individuals may be deemed unsuitable or suitable because of perceived group character-istics, but also in assigning salaries to jobs held by certain groups of workers. Equal opportunity laws have focused to date on the first kind of discrimina-tion. Comparable worth is an attempt to understand and, if necessary, correct the second kind of discrimination. Nondiscrimination laws do not require that an employer place no value on aspects of work or criteria for selection, only that the values and criteria be bias-free. Since our culture does not encourage paying everyone the same salary, employers can and should be discriminating in how they set salaries, but their reasons for differentiating should not be influenced by the race or sex of incumbents and applicants.

The application of an *a priori* evaluation system to a diverse sample of civil service positions gives us clear evidence of differential rates of return for male-and female-dominated jobs. Job evaluation systems hold out the promise of quantitative corrections to sex bias in compensation; however, many technical, political, and cultural issues will arise as we move toward comparable worth. In the process, salary administration practices will undergo close scrutiny, and longstanding policies and practices will take a beating. We should emerge from this exercise with a better understanding of the nature and value of work in our culture.

References

England, Paula. 1979. "Women and Occupational Prestige: A Case of Vacuous Sex Equality." 5(2):252–65.

Hildebrand, George. 1980 "The Market System." In *Comparable Worth: Issues and Alternatives*, ed. E. R. Livernash, pp. 79–106. Washington, D.C.: Equal Employment Advisory Council.

Marrs, Judith. 1983. Unpublished study.

Milkovich, George T. 1980. "The Emerging Debate." In *Comparable Worth: Issues and Alternatives*, ed E. R. Livernash, pp. 23–47. Washington, D.C.: Equal Employment Advisory Council.

Remick, Helen. 1979. "Strategies for Creating Sound, Bias-Free Job Evaluation Systems." In *Job Evaluation and EEO: The Emerging Issues*, pp. 85–112. New York: Industrial Relations Counselors, Inc.

Remick, Helen. 1981. "The Comparable Worth Controversy." *Public Personnel Management* 10:371–83.

Remick, Helen. 1983. "An update on Washington State." *Public Personnel Management* 12:390–94.

Rohmert, W. and J. Rutenfranz. 1977. Abbreviated English version of "Federal Government Report on the Application of Article 119 of the EEC Treaty." Bonn: Bundesminister für Arbeit and Sozialordnung.

Schwab, Donald P. 1980. "Job Evaluation and Pay Setting: Concepts and Practices." In *Comparable Worth: Issues and Alternatives*, ed. E. R. Livernash, pp. 49–77. Washington, D.C.: Equal Employment Advisory Council.

Treiman, Donald J. 1979. *Job Evaluation: An Analytic Review*. Washington, D.C.: National Academy of Sciences.

Treiman, Donald J., and Heidi I. Hartmann, eds. 1981. *Women, Work and Wages*. Washington, D.C.: National Academy of Sciences.

8

A Policy-Capturing Application in a Union Setting

DAVID PIERSON, KAREN SHALLCROSS KOZIARA,
AND RUSSELL JOHANNESSON

Equal pay for jobs of comparable worth is one of the most significant compensation issues currently confronting employers. Comparable worth is also extremely controversial, and it has been the subject of considerable discussion and debate. Much of this debate centers on the question of whether or not employers should be required to pay equal wages for jobs segregated by sex but of comparable worth to an employer. In contrast, relatively little attention has been paid to operationally defining and measuring comparable worth.

Both the definition and the measurement of comparable worth are extremely important to the development of the comparable worth issue. Regardless of whether comparable worth is pursued in the courts, at the bargaining table, or through legislation, its operational definition and measurement will be critical.

This chapter presents the issues involved in measuring comparable worth. It then illustrates the handling of these issues in one comparable worth study.

Critical Issues in Studying Comparable Worth

Five major issues must be resolved during any study of comparable worth. Particular emphasis here is placed on studies conducted within a single wage-setting unit. Studies using data aggregated across wage-setting units might be useful for ascertaining the extent to which overall wage inequities exist (see Chapter 9), but they cannot determine the extent to which equal wages are not paid for comparable jobs within a particular setting. These general studies thus cannot guide organizational decision-makers.

The first, and perhaps most important, issue is defining comparable worth in measurable or operational terms. Proceeding without a definition agreed to by all principals involved in the study will lead either to ambiguous results or to disagreement about the meaning of the results. The parties' financial stake in the results increases the importance of a mutually agreed upon definition.

Second, the specific jobs to be studied or compared must be chosen. The choice should be made early in the study so that peculiarities of the jobs are considered. As this principle implies, it is difficult to generalize results beyond the particular jobs studied.

The choice of jobs has implications for the entire study. One useful approach is to use three job categories. One category includes jobs held primarily by women. These will probably be predominantly clerical positions, but may include other jobs, such as nursing and teaching, if these are found within the organization. A rule of thumb is that at least 75 percent of the incumbents of each job should be women. The second category includes jobs held predominantly by men. Again the 75 percent rule can be used. Skilled craft jobs, managerial jobs, and perhaps heavy labor jobs will commonly fit here. The last category includes jobs not dominated by either men or women. The number of jobs chosen depends on the methodology of the study. The greater the number of jobs, the more generalizable the study's results will be.

Third, specific dimensions for comparing jobs must be determined. These dimensions should be consistent with the operational definition of comparable worth. Since comparable worth involves comparing dissimilar jobs, it is crucial that dimensions common to all jobs be chosen or a method of determining them be agreed upon. These dimensions should be important to employers as well as employees to help ensure that the study results are acted on by decision-makers and accepted by employees.

Fourth, a method of obtaining information on the common dimensions must be determined. This issue is crucial, since the quality of information is highly dependent on its source and manner of collection.

Finally, the criterion issue, or the manner in which dollars are attached to the various dimensions, must be addressed. Jobs will be compared on the common dimensions identified in the fourth step. The criterion issue involves the manner in which the dimensions are scaled and the weights attached to the dimensions. Alternatives include judgments made by experts and reference to a single, nonarbitrary, pricing mechanism applicable to all jobs in the study. The choice of criterion significantly influences the study's relevance, and therefore the criterion should reflect the specific environment the organization confronts.

Apart from the technical problems outlined above, a comparable worth study can result in political tensions for the parties involved. All the workers whose jobs the study covers will have concerns about its results. Women concentrated in low-paying jobs will anticipate wage increases, particularly if the study shows their jobs to be undervalued when compared to men's jobs. People in other jobs will worry that wage adjustments for low-paid female jobs may come at the expense of wage gains by other workers.

These anticipations and concerns have the potential to create problems for employers and unions undertaking comparable worth studies. The internal political pressures will probably be clearest to union leaders because members look to them to represent their interests to employers. Employers, however, face similar pressures, not only because wage increases are cost increases, but because wage structure changes resulting from comparable worth adjustments, like other changes in internal equity, can affect worker satisfaction and motivation.

These problems are more easily described than avoided. One way to reduce them, however, is to develop a consensus supporting the desirability of having wages reflect comparable worth before undertaking a study. Education and open communication are necessary in developing this consensus. Open communication also permits the inclusion of many viewpoints in the study design. This in turn should help gain acceptance, or at least understanding, of comparable worth and its implications.

It is crucial to remember that comparable worth studies are unlike most other studies conducted by behavioral scientists within organizations. The results of a comparable worth study can have a major influence on people's wages and the organization's internal wage equity. Few issues could have as great an impact.

Case Study

The comparable worth study we conducted in a public employment setting illustrates the issues outlined above. This approach will, we hope, provide ideas for further comparable worth studies. Field investigations such as this one are crucial in developing a valid and useful methodology for measuring comparable worth.

Setting

The study was conducted at the request of a public sector union representing most state employees of a large industrial eastern state. A statewide convention of the union had passed a resolution establishing a comparable worth committee to determine the extent to which the existing state wage structure provided for equal wages for jobs of comparable worth.

The twenty-member committee consisted largely of local presidents, although it included several staff members as well. Eighteen members were women. All members of the committee seemed convinced that certain women's jobs were underpriced compared to both men's jobs and lower-level management jobs.

We were responsible to this committee. Although state administrators provided some cooperation during the course of the study, they were not involved. Since wages are a mandatory bargaining issue and since the study directly investigated wage-setting practices, the committee felt that the results could be used at the bargaining table and therefore that state support and involvement in the study were unnecessary. A subcommittee of the twenty-person committee directly guided the study and served as a source of information. Much of the study's success was due to the persistent efforts and continual support of this committee.

Defining Comparable Worth

Defining comparable worth is the first task of a comparable worth study. We define comparable worth as existing when the empirical relationship between job content and wages is the same for male- and female-held jobs. When job content is rewarded differentially in male and female jobs, wages are not equal for jobs of comparable worth by this definition. This definition can be extended to the actual wage determination process used by an employer. If the relationship between job content and wages differs for traditionally male and female jobs, using the content/wage relationship of one class of jobs to compute wages for the other class will produce estimated wages that differ from those actually paid by the employer. If noncomparable wages are paid for male and female jobs matched on job content, wages predicted for traditionally female jobs using the male content/wage relationship should be more than the actual wages for female jobs. Conversely, wages for male jobs estimated using the female content/wage relationship should be less than those actually paid.

Focusing on empirical job content to compare jobs rather than labor market influences or job holders' characteristics overcomes several problems. Segregated labor markets are often cited as the reason for the existing and widening gap in male and female wages. Employers maintain that the wage gap exists not because of overt discrimination against women, but because labor markets have established relatively low wages for traditionally female jobs. Employers insist that they are merely responding to labor market influences in setting wages.[1]

If labor markets for male and female jobs are segregated, relying on markets to assign values to jobs will result in comparable wages across employers for either male or female jobs. But the comparability will not extend to male and female jobs within a single firm, because these jobs are seldom in the same job family. This observation, coupled with the fact that wages are indeed an indication of job worth, suggests that comparable worth is best assessed by using the job content/wage relation existing in one category of jobs to assess the wages paid in the other category.

Choice of Jobs

Jobs were chosen from all three categories noted in the earlier section: predominantly female jobs, predominantly male jobs, and jobs shared

---

1. Similar reasoning was found in the early civil rights cases. Although employers argued that they did not intend to discriminate, the courts ruled that *de facto* discrimination, regardless of intent, was illegal.

equally by women and men (or "general" jobs). The final choice was made by the comparable worth committee and the researchers. Care was taken to include jobs with a high number of incumbents for two reasons. First, organizational impact is enhanced if important jobs are included. Second, the study's methodology necessitated a large number of respondents per job. The general jobs were included to check for any systematic differences between what men and women told us they did on their jobs. Five female jobs, six male jobs, and two general jobs were chosen. The specific job titles are listed in Table 8-1.

Relying on a committee to choose the jobs to be studied presents certain dangers. Political interest or self-interest may influence the choices: the members may happen to represent a number of people in these jobs, or they may hold the jobs themselves and feel that they are underpaid. The researcher must be careful to maintain objectivity throughout the process. In this case, the committee was continually reminded that the anticipated results of the study should not guide its design.

Job Comparison Dimensions

Jobs can be compared on a variety of dimensions. The choice of dimensions is crucial and, though subjective, should not be made arbitrarily. The definition of comparable worth that guided this research stipulates that job content be used to compare the jobs. Other dimensions, such as worker characteristics or labor market conditions, were excluded.

Table 8-1
Number of Women and Men Respondents by Job Class

Job Classification	Men	Women	Total
Female Jobs			
Clerk II	24	79	103
Clerk III	14	77	91
Clerk Typist I	2	110	112
Clerk Typist III	3	91	94
Clerk Stenographer III	1	92	93
LPN II	8	72	80
Male Jobs			
Safety Inspector	68	0	68
Laborer	105	5	110
Equipment Operator	61	0	61
Carpenter	99	0	99
Utility Plant Operator	85	0	85
General Jobs			
Purchasing Agent	9	16	25
Activity Aide	4	45	49
Totals	483	587	1,070*

*Sixteen respondents did not indicate their sex.

Two alternative approaches, both relying on job content dimensions, are possible. The first is an *a priori* approach that specifies in advance the particular job factors to be studied. Traditional job evaluation, based on either a point system or factor comparison, uses this approach. This is an appropriate vehicle in a policy-setting study, since it specifies the factors that policy-makers feel are important when evaluating jobs. The second approach derives factors from job content. Here jobs are specifically described in detail, and factors emerge that are empirically common to the job descriptions. Common factors can be economically determined by a factor analytic type method.

The second approach was used in this study for several reasons. First, the study was not undertaken on behalf of administrative policy-makers, and it would therefore have been difficult to reflect their judgments in the choice of job factors. Second, wages are determined in the study setting by collective bargaining, with no explicit set of factors used to compare jobs. Third, the initial assignment of jobs into labor grades was accomplished by an unknown job classification system; the factors implicit in the classifications were therefore also unknown. Finally, most traditional job evaluation methods use trained analysts to describe the jobs. For a variety of reasons—some political, some practical, and some financial—trained analysts could not be used.

Method of Data Collection

Data were collected by using a self-report quantitative job analysis questionnaire. The source instrument for the final questionnaire used was the Job Activity Preference Questionnaire (JAPQ). Based substantially on the original Position Analysis Questionnaire (PAQ) (R. C. Mecham, personal communication, 1980), the JAPQ taps individual preferences for specific work characteristics. It is self-administered, a prerequisite for this study, and the reading level is thought to be below that of the PAQ (ibid.).

A number of changes had to be made in the JAPQ for use in the present study. First, since the study was concerned with what people did rather than what they preferred to do, all JAPQ response formats were altered to reflect descriptions rather than preferences. Second, JAPQ items include parenthetical examples to help the reader understand the items' meanings. Additional examples were added to ensure that items were meaningful to incumbents of both male and female jobs. Take, for example, an item such as: "How important is setting up or adjusting equipment (setting up a lathe or drill press, adjusting an engine carburetor, etc.)?" A person in a female job might not respond to it, because the examples relate only to traditionally male-held jobs. This item was changed by adding behaviorally similar examples that were less sex-biased and became: "How important is setting up or adjusting equipment (attaching devices to patients, setting up a lathe or drill press, adjusting office equipment)?"

Third, some items were altered to more closely reflect the jobs sampled in this study, and some wording was changed to make items more understandable to the respondent sample.[2] Finally, in order to get a more global picture of people's jobs, fifteen items from Hackman and Oldham's (1975) Job Diagnostic Survey (JDS) were added. Again some wording was changed to make it more understandable. A section of demographic information completed the instrument.

Although a number of changes were made in the JAPQ, its essence was preserved. Fully 83 percent (125 of 150) of the original JAPQ items were retained, with examples altered when necessary as noted above. Ten other JAPQ items were combined, and fifteen items were deleted because they had no relevance to the jobs studied in this research. Only six new items were added to more fully capture the content of the jobs under consideration.

The final questionnaire is a self-administered, quantitative, job-content-oriented,[3] job analysis instrument based substantially on the JAPQ. It probes particular job activities, sources of information, interactions with people, equipment used, and job situations. All items were thoroughly reviewed for content appropriateness and understandability by the union subcommittee with whom we worked. Questionnaire development required close and intense interaction with the subcommittee. This was the area in which the committee's job knowledge, as well as its knowledge of potential respondents, was most important. Mailed questionnaires give researchers only one opportunity to collect data. Consequently, it is imperative that the questionnaire be both exhaustive and understandable.

Questionnaires were sent to a stratified random sample of 2,005 individuals in the thirteen jobs listed in Table 8-1. This sampling procedure ensured coverage of specific bureaus and geographic areas. Each participant received an initial questionnaire, along with cover letters from the investigators and a union official. A follow-up post card and another questionnaire were also sent. It was explained that all participants received the follow-up material because responses were completely anonymous. A total of 1,125 questionnaires were completed, for a response rate of 56.1 percent. Thirty-nine questionnaires were eliminated because job class could not be identified. The number of male and female respondents in each job is shown in Table 8-1.

---

2. The instrument's instructions are written at the 6.3 grade level according to the Raygor readability estimate. The instructions of the JAPQ are written at the 10.6 grade level.

3. Only three items were included that did not tap specific job content material. One dealt with education, another with experience, and the third with the training needed to do the job. While this is a minor violation of our strict job content approach, these items were taken directly from the JAPQ.

To determine the factor dimensions, the responses were subjected to a principal components analysis with varimax rotation to the questionnaire. Successive rotations of five- to twelve-factor solutions showed the eight-factor solution to be the most meaningful.

Factor reliability was assessed by computing Cronback's alpha for each factor, using unit weighting for all items with a factor coefficient greater than 0.40. Table 8-2 shows the names given to the eight factors, the variance each accounts for, reliabilities, and intercorrelations.[4]

Next, the ability of the refactored job analysis questionnaire to discriminate among jobs was established with a one-way multiple analysis of variance (MANOVA) (Lissitz et al., 1979). The thirteen jobs were used as the independent effect, and the eight scale scores from the job analysis instrument made up the dependent vector. Unit weighting was used to calculate scale scores. The strong MANOVA effect for job ($F_{96,6872} = 46.35$, $p < .001$) demonstrated the discriminant validity of the instrument for the jobs in the study.

The questionnaire was specifically designed to tap the content of the jobs included in this study. The extent to which questionnaire results mirror job content determines the instrument's content validity. The greater its validity, the greater the reliance that can be placed on the results.

While construct validity is difficult to establish for any questionnaire (Smith and Hakel, 1979), several steps were taken to help ensure it. First, an established questionnaire was used as the source document. Second, reading level was consistent with the sample. Third, people knowledgeable about the jobs analyzed helped construct the final questionnaire. Fourth, scale reliability was established, as was the questionnaire's ability to discriminate among jobs. As a final demonstration of construct validity, individuals were asked to indicate the proportion of their job that the questionnaire covered. Seventy-five percent of the respondents stated that one-half or more of their job was represented by their questionnaire responses. Forty-eight percent indicated that 70 percent or more of their job was covered. Given that most people feel that any form of job analysis taps only part of their job, these results seem to be well within the acceptable range.[5]

---

4. An objective of the study was a parsimonious solution with a limited number of factors. It should be noted, however, that the eight factors used here compare favorably with those found in earlier factor analyses of the total PAQ and account for approximately the same amount of variance (McCormick et al., 1972). In comparison, Krzystofiak et al., (1979) used sixty factors to account for approximately 55 percent of the variance in their quantified job analysis instrument.

5. The underlying assumption is that the job elements not measured by the questionnaire are related to wages in the same way as the job elements measured. This assumption is particularly important when the male and female jobs are compared, since it could be a source of bias. Incumbents of the male and female jobs studied here did not significantly differ in the extent to which they reported that their

Table 8-2
Factor Characteristics

Factor	No. of Items	Eigen Value	Variance Explained — As % of Total Variance	As % of Explained Variance	Std. Alpha	Intercorrelations by Factor No. — 2	3	4	5	6	7	8
1. Cognitive judgment	32	18.14	12.5	27.6	.945	.42	.48	-.02	.23	.30	.41	.53
2. People-orientation	9	6.00	4.2	9.3	.871		.22	.45	.42	.36	.23	.23
3. Complexity	13	5.19	3.5	7.7	.802			.15	.21	.10	.22	.20
4. Physical demands	36	22.63	15.6	34.4	.952				.59	.29	.24	-.06
5. Machine tending	14	3.76	2.6	5.7	.858					.33	.14	.29
6. Working conditions	7	3.16	2.2	4.9	.733						.20	.26
7. Word and paper processing	10	4.28	3.0	6.6	.835							.27
8. Reading and listening	3	2.54	1.7	3.8	.555							
			45.3	100.0								

Mean factor scores for each of the six female jobs and five male jobs reflect common conceptions of the jobs. This supports the instrument's construct validity. (See Table 8-3.) Laborers, carpenters, and equipment operators have the most physical jobs. Safety inspectors and higher-level clerical jobs involve the most cognitive judgment. Licensed Practical Nurse II (LPN II) is the most people-oriented job. Lower-level clerical jobs apparently involve the most paperwork but only limited interaction with people. Safety inspectors, carpenters, and higher-level clerical workers have the most complex jobs. Utility plant operators do extensive machine tending. LPN II's report the most difficult working conditions, including distractions, irritations, and adverse physical surroundings. Finally, purchasing agents, safety inspectors, LPN II's, and clerical workers do the most reading and listening.

As noted, two jobs with approximately equal numbers of men and women were included to check for systematic differences in reporting job content. Only the purchasing agent job had enough responses for analysis. Using a one-way MANOVA design with sex of the respondent as the independent effect, we found no significant differences between men and women ($F_{8,12} = 1.56, p = .236$).

Establishing the Criterion

A weighting mechanism had to be applied to the dimensions used to compare the jobs in the study, as it cannot be assumed that all the dimensions are of equal value. Once the weights for the dimensions are established, the overall importance of the jobs can be determined by simply multiplying the measured value on each job dimension by the dimension's weight and then summing these results across all dimensions for each job.

The initial criterion used in this study was the relationship between the job content and actual wages for the six male jobs. One of the reasons comparable worth is an issue is that employers have traditionally set wages separately for each major job family (e.g., managerial, clerical, and production and technical jobs). Employers develop separate programs for the job families for a variety of reasons, including the fact that separate, and often independent, labor sources are accessed for entry-level workers in each family. Since employers wish to maintain competitive wages for these entry-level jobs, and internally equitable wage structures for each job family, they are careful to ensure that the entry wages reflect labor market conditions within these separate labor markets. A consequence of these practices is that different relationships between job content and wage rates probably exist in different job families.

---

jobs were measured by the questionnaire. This eliminates the source of potential bias that would result from one type of job being measured less completely than the other.

Table 8-3

Factor Scores

Job Class	Cognitive Judgment	People-Orientation	Com-plexity	Physical Demands	Machine Tending	Working Conditions	Word/Paper Processing	Reading/Listening
Female Jobs								
Clerk II	1.50	.54	3.67	.77	1.02	1.33	1.28	2.47
Clerk III	1.89	.46	4.00	.61	.95	1.35	1.21	2.63
Clerk Typist I	1.75	.73	3.54	.77	.98	1.32	2.14	2.44
Clerk Typist III	2.27	.66	4.31	.75	.98	1.14	2.10	2.39
Clerk Stenographer III	2.61	.69	4.44	.75	.94	1.06	2.52	2.43
LPN II	2.52	3.55	4.54	1.77	1.64	1.81	1.11	2.67
Male Jobs								
Safety Inspector	2.91	.45	4.50	1.51	1.13	1.32	.50	2.79
Laborer	1.23	1.20	3.52	2.52	1.42	1.36	1.45	1.59
Equipment Operator	1.18	1.26	3.58	2.68	1.99	1.09	1.32	1.64
Carpenter	1.18	.89	4.64	2.71	1.08	1.29	2.35	1.90
Utility Plant Operator	1.33	.98	4.35	2.30	3.27	1.37	1.45	1.61
General Jobs								
Purchasing Agent	2.76	.49	4.73	.73	1.05	1.02	1.37	2.95
Activity Aide	2.42	3.06	4.40	1.80	1.40	1.92	1.54	2.21

Our choice of the job content/wage relationship in male jobs as the criterion reflects our operational definition of comparable worth. Male and female jobs would be comparably paid if their job content was rewarded equally. Since employers establish separate wage-setting practices by job family and job families are often sex-segregated, it is necessary to decide whether to use the content/wage relationship for male or female jobs. We initially chose to use the male relationship as the criterion because proponents of comparable worth usually insist that male jobs are more highly paid than comparable female jobs. As a check on the validity of our results, we also used the female job content/wage relationship as the criterion by which value was established for the job content dimensions.

Two wage measures were collected and used as criterion variables. Participants were asked to give their current salaries. Additionally, a scheduled wage based on job category was supplied for each respondent. Both wage measures were used as dependent variables because of their potential relationship to job content. The only determinants of salary in the organization studied are job classification and seniority. Because people may assume more discretionary responsibility within their job as they gain experience, reported job content may vary by experience in the job. Since we are interested in relating job content to wages, and since content can vary in this way, we used both scheduled wages, reflecting classification, and individual wages, reflecting length of service as well as classification.

Regression analysis was used to establish the weight or value for each job dimension. The scores of the eight job factors were regressed against both wage variables for male job incumbents. The model for this analysis is as follows:

$$W_m = \text{CONST} + B_{m_1}X_{m_1} + B_{m_2}X_{m_2} + \ldots \qquad (1)$$
$$+ B_{m_8}X_{m_8} + e$$

where: W_m = Wages paid to male job incumbents
            B_{m_i} = Weight obtained for the ith factor for the male jobs
            X_{m_i} = Value of the ith job factor for male job incumbents
       CONST = Constant

The regression coefficients for the eight job dimensions obtained in these analyses reflect the relationship between job content and wages for the male jobs. The unit of analysis is the individual position, not the job. As noted earlier, job content may vary from incumbent to incumbent. Analyzing content aggregated by job obscures this potential variance.

Roberts (1980) argues that to the extent that measurement errors exist in predictor variables and the wages for male jobs are greater than those for female jobs, regression analysis will necessarily result in a significant effect for a male/female job variable. Measurement errors obviously cannot be eliminated, and women's jobs are indeed typically paid less than men's jobs; this is the heart of the comparable worth issue.

Table 8-4

Regression Results for Male Jobs

Job Factors Used as Independent Variables	Dependent Variable			
	Reported Wages		Scheduled Wages	
	Regression Coefficient	t-value	Regression Coefficient	t-value
Cognitive Judgment	.570***	8.33	.403***	9.46
People-orientation	−.428***	−4.43	−.345***	−5.07
Complexity	.467***	6.56	.397***	8.90
Physical demands	−.398***	−3.57	−.348***	−4.98
Machine tending	−.212***	−4.05	−.117***	−3.57
Working conditions	.044	.61	.053	.20
Word and Paper Processing	−.000	.01	.002	.05
Reading and Listening	.059	1.08	.142***	4.29
(Constant)	5.567***	17.45	5.254***	26.71
Number	341		359	
R^2 (adjusted)	.522		.643	

* $p < .05$
** $p < .01$
*** $p < .001$

In this study, *individual* wages reported by incumbents of the selected female jobs do not significantly differ from wages paid to incumbents of the selected male jobs. Average *scheduled* wages for these male-job incumbents, however, are $0.19 per hour, or 3 percent, greater than average scheduled wages for the female-job incumbents. To the extent that Roberts' arguments apply to the method used in this study, they would limit the conclusions drawn from the analysis of scheduled wages only, not individual wages.[6]

Results of the regression analysis of job content on both wage variables for the male jobs are reported in Table 8-4. Cognitive judgment, people-orientation, complexity, and physical demands are most highly associated with both reported and scheduled wages for male jobs. The negative coefficients indicate that male jobs involving more people-orientation and greater physical demands as well as machine tending have a relatively lower wage associated with them. The eight scales account for about 64 percent of the scheduled wage variance and 52 percent of the reported wage variance. Additional wage variance could be explained by including additional predic-

---

6. The difference in scheduled but not individual wages indicates that female job incumbents are, on the average, in higher steps within their respective salary grades than are male job incumbents. The ratio of actual wages to grade midpoints, a form of compa-ratio, supports this conclusion. The ratio is significantly greater for female job incumbents than for male job incumbents.

tor variables not specifically measuring job content. However, the intent of the study is not to explain as much wage variance as possible, but rather to utilize job content as a measure of comparable worth common to both traditionally male and traditionally female jobs.

As was noted, either male or female wages could be used to determine the value to be placed on the job dimensions. As a type of validity check, regression weights were determined for each job dimension using the wages paid to the female jobs. These weights are determined in a way directly analogous to the determination of weights from the male wages. Here the questionnaire results from the female jobs are used to determine job dimension scores on each of the eight job dimensions. These scores are then regressed against the two wage variables for the female job respondents to determine job dimension weights. Table 8-5 shows the results of regressing female job content on female job wages. Cognitive judgment, people-orientation, complexity, and machine tending are most highly associated with actual and scheduled wages. Interestingly, the model is fairly similar to the male job content/wages model. The job factors account for 29 percent of the schedule variance and 23 percent of the actual wage variance.

Determining Whether Comparable Wages Are Paid for Male and Female Jobs

The final step of the study is determining whether the employers' wage structure results in comparable wages for the male and female jobs being

Table 8-5
Regression Results for Female Jobs

| | Dependent Variable | | | |
| | Reported Wages | | Scheduled Wages | |
Job Factors Used as Independent Variables	Regression Coefficient	t-value	Regression Coefficient	t-value
Cognitive Judgment	.447**	5.05	.321***	6.39
People-orientation	−.299***	−3.03	−.188***	−3.35
Complexity	.227***	3.36	.153***	3.97
Physical demands	−.246***	−1.35	−.031	−.30
Machine tending	−.255*	−2.15	−.242***	−3.56
Working conditions	−.055	−1.00	−.046	−1.47
Word and Paper	−.022	.37	.019	.57
Processing	−.057	−1.34	−.042	−1.73
Reading and Listening	5.56***	21.90	5.42	37.70
(Constant)				
Number	376		398	
R^2 (adjusted)	.233		.287	

* $p < .05$
** $p < .01$
*** $p < .001$

analyzed. Difference scores were used to make this analysis. Using the job dimension weights calculated for the male jobs, we calculated the wages that would be paid for the female jobs if comparable job content were paid equally. Predicted wages for each of the female jobs were calculated by multiplying the job factor scores obtained from each female job incumbent by the regression coefficients obtained from the analysis of male jobs. The model is as follows:

$$\hat{W}_f = \text{CONST} + B_{m_1}X_{f_1} + B_{m_2}X_{f_2} + \ldots + B_{m_8}X_{f_8} \tag{2}$$

where $\hat{W}_f$ = Predicted wage for each female job incumbent
        X_{f_i} = Value for the ith job factor for the female job incumbents
        CONST and B_{m_i} are derived from (1)

A difference score, W_{dif}, the difference between predicted wages and actual wages for female job incumbents ($W_{dif} = \hat{W}_f - W_f$), indicates the extent to which female-job incumbents are undercompensated for jobs of comparable worth.

The absolute and relative differences between the average predicted and actual wages for the female jobs are reported in Table 8-6. With the exception of the LPN II job, all differences are positive, indicating that the predicted wage is greater than the actual wage. If equal wages were paid for comparable jobs, five of the six female jobs would be paid higher wages.

The wage differences are greatest for the lower-level clerical jobs, Clerk Typist I and Clerk II. These jobs are the most underpaid in terms of equal pay for comparable worth. The negative wage differences for LPN II indicate that this female job is overpaid according to the comparable worth criterion for this limited sampling of jobs. LPN IIs report an extremely high value for the people-orientation factor. However, people-orientation has a negative regression coefficient from the male regression analysis, indicating that male jobs reporting high values for this factor receive relatively low wages. The predicted wage for LPN II is thus depressed by the high people-orientation score.[7]

Male wages were then predicted from the relationship of female job content to wages paid for female jobs. This analysis is the reverse of that just noted and provides a check on the results given above. Table 8-7 shows the absolute and relative differences in the predicted and actual male wages. All of the differences are negative, indicating that wages paid for the male jobs are greater than they would be if the relationship between female job

---

7. This rationale for the negative LPN II wage difference was analyzed by recomputing wage differences without the people-orientation scale. This analysis resulted in wage differences for the other female jobs highly similar to those found in the initial analysis. The LPN II wage difference, however, became positive, indicating that the original results were due to the dominance of people-orientation in the job.

Table 8-6
Differences between Predicted and Actual Wages
by Female Job Class

Job Class	Difference Based on Reported Wages		Difference Based on Scheduled Wages	
	Absolute	*Relative*	*Absolute*	*Relative*
Clerk II	$1.55*	25%	$1.31*	23%
Clerk III	$1.14*	16%	$1.05*	16%
Clerk Typist I	$2.17*	40%	$1.65*	31%
Clerk Typist III	$1.06*	15%	$ .92*	14%
Clerk Stenographer III	$ .96*	13%	$ .87*	13%
LPN II	−$ .65*	− 9%	−$ .59*	− 9%
Average	$1.04	18%	$ .87	15%

* $p < .01$

content and wages were imposed on the male jobs. These results are highly consistent with the wage differences found for female jobs.

The union committee for whom this study was conducted was particularly interested in knowing what wages would be paid if the wage structure negotiated with the state paid all jobs comparably. The results of the analysis just presented give this information in a straightforward fashion. An alternative analysis would involve combining male and female jobs into a single analysis and assessing the effect of a male/female job categorical or dummy variable. This analysis would statistically control for any differences in job content between male and female jobs and determine the effect on one's wages of having a male, as opposed to a female, job. Such an analysis of the data in this study found that with job content held constant, incumbents of male jobs received on the average $0.90 per hour, or 13.4 percent, more than incumbents of female jobs in terms of individual wages ($p < .001$). They also received $0.80 per hour, or 12.4 percent, more on scheduled wages ($p < .001$).

Implications

This study has several implications. According to a definition of comparable worth that focuses on job content, four of the five female jobs studied were not paid wages that reflect equal pay for comparable worth. The 15 to 20 percent differential is similar to that reported in other studies using quite different methodologies. The most direct implication of this study, then, is that the contract negotiated between the union and the state did not compensate job content comparably (as defined in this study) for at least the jobs included in this sample. Since the jobs are representative of other jobs and have numerous incumbents, these results can tentatively be generalized to other jobs and employers with similar wage-setting practices.

Table 8-7

Differences between Predicted and Actual Wages
by Male Job Class

Job Class	Difference Based on Reported Wages		Difference Based on Scheduled Wages	
	Absolute	*Relative*	*Absolute*	*Relative*
Safety Inspector	−$2.04*	−23%	−$2.34*	−28%
Laborer	−$ .05	− 1%	−$ .37*	− 7%
Equipment Operator	−$ .88*	−14%	−$ .77*	−13%
Carpenter	−$1.62*	−22%	−$1.53*	−22%
Utility Plant Operator	−$1.30*	−20%	−$1.59*	−25%
Average	−$1.15	−16%	−$1.32	−19%

*p < .01

A variety of methodological implications also can be drawn from this research. Quantitative job analysis represents an excellent method of capturing the wage-setting practices of an organization. Since job dimensions are not established *a priori*, the dimensions that do emerge from the study can be used to compare jobs along common dimensions. Thus, quantitative job analysis allows researchers to study jobs without a set of preconceived job dimensions. An important advantage of this approach is that the resulting job dimensions will be job-specific. Federal guidelines on discrimination explicitly note the importance of basing employment decisions on job-specific criteria. Quantitative job analysis helps meet this stipulation, since job dimensions flow from the jobs themselves.

If job specificity is to be ensured, however, it is important that quantitative job analysis items specifically reflect activities and responsibilities germane to the jobs studied. Researchers must carefully consider item content in any existing job analysis questionnaire before using it. To be content valid, the items must at least be inspected by individuals familiar with the jobs to be studied. The items must also be examined to eliminate any implicit sex bias. As much as possible, the items must relate to jobs regardless of whether they are typically held by men or women.

It is also important to consider the use of regression analysis to determine the weights to be applied to the various job factors. This study was conducted to capture policy, not to set it. It determined the extent to which existing policies and procedures rewarded male and female jobs comparably. Weights therefore were first established for the job factors that reflected the wage-setting practice for male jobs. These weights were then applied to female jobs. Regression analysis is particularly appropriate for this purpose.

Regression analysis can also be used by employers to set weights in a policy-setting mode. Two methods can be used. First, a set of internal wages that the employer is confident are correctly set can be used to establish the weights, which are then applied to other jobs. For comparable worth considerations, the jobs chosen should include both male and female jobs as well as jobs not typically associated with either sex. Coefficients resulting from regressing the job evaluation scores against these wage rates would constitute the weights to be used for all other jobs. Second, external wage rates associated with specific key jobs can be chosen to set the weights. Again both male and female jobs as well as non-sex-typed jobs should be chosen. The regression proceeds in the same way as in the first alternative. The important distinction between these methods is in the unit of comparison. Employers usually wish to reflect labor market conditions in their wage-setting practices. The latter alternative allows this to occur without violating comparable worth standards because the same wage-setting mechanism is used for both male and female jobs.

The study uncovered a dimension of the comparable worth issue that needs further comment. The LPN II job was found to be overpaid because of its strong people-orientation, a factor negatively weighted in the male jobs and the other female jobs. The implication is that relatively unique jobs that load heavily on a factor not found in the other jobs, be they male or female, will be undervalued by a policy-capturing method such as the one used here. Several other important issues arise from this situation.

First, the more jobs that are included in the study, the less likely it is that any single job will be as unique as LPN II was here. In this case male jobs with greater people-orientation would have made the LPN II job less unique.

Second, if the female jobs and male jobs contain truly unique factors, then the method used here will most likely undervalue the female jobs. As noted earlier, the method we used is conservative in this respect. Using factor analysis to identify the job dimensions reduces the likelihood of this undervaluation, but if highly sex-linked factors remain, they should perhaps be eliminated from the rest of the analysis. Even though less of the job will be covered in the analysis, the jobs will be compared on common dimensions. The advice given by designers of *a priori* systems—choose only factors common to all jobs (Belcher, 1974)—reflects this concept. Thus, the problem is of concern in policy-setting as well as policy-capturing techniques.

Third, it could be argued that more professional jobs, such as LPN II, will most likely contain unique dimensions. This is because professional jobs are more influenced by standards imposed by the profession than those imposed by the organization. Wage-setting procedures for these jobs are thus more likely to be market-oriented, and internal comparisons will be less important in establishing wages.

The study described here was conducted for a union. Cooperation between behavioral scientists and unions is too rare (Gordon et al., 1978), and the reason is that behavioral scientists have typically done research and consulting at the behest of management. The term "hired gun" comes quickly to mind. Behavioral scientists are professionally interested in the world of work, however, and unions are important in many work situations. The potential therefore exists for a beneficial working relationship between unions and behavioral scientists. We were fortunate as researchers in that the union approached us to do the study and consequently we did not have to overcome undue skepticism. We carefully communicated from the outset that an objective stance would be maintained throughout the study, the same objectivity that should exist with managerially sponsored research.

Political realities occasionally became a concern during the study, since each committee member owed his or her leadership position to constituents. Yet managers owe their positions to superiors, and many of the same political difficulties would arise with any client. In the end the committee assumed ownership of the study to a great extent and therefore wanted it to be conducted professionally. Without a doubt the study benefited from their concern and input.

Unions often react negatively to job evaluation as a management tool (James, 1979), and experts often say that unions will not abide its use. This is not necessarily the case. Job evaluation in and of itself is a value-free technique. Values are added when factors are chosen, weights assigned, and jobs evaluated. These decisions are made by the individual designers of the system according to their own value systems and the perceived organizational norms of the sponsoring body. Including employee representatives in the job evaluation design team helps ensure that employee values are also reflected in the final job evaluation system.

A careful explanation of the technique used in this study satisfied the union committee's initial doubts. A bigger problem arose from our use of quantitative job analysis. Job incumbents often feel that the analysis does not completely capture their jobs. Quantitative job analysis can be very exhaustive, however, and therefore the resulting evaluation tends to be accepted as reflecting most of people's jobs than an evaluation based on typical job analysis results.

Several other observations flow from this study. Perhaps the most important effect of the comparable worth issue is that it brings wage and salary considerations out of the closet for many employees. Employees are beginning to ask some very difficult questions of people making wage decisions, including employers and union officials. Women in typically female jobs are comparing their salaries with those for other jobs. Other employees are asking variations of the same questions. In the past, wage decisions have often been made secretly and without relying on a rational system. The hard questions put to employers force them to reconsider the systems and programs they use and to revamp them so that they can stand the test of employee scrutiny.

References

Belcher, D. 1974. *Compensation Administration*. 3d ed. Englewood Cliffs, N.J.: Prentice-Hall.

Gordon, M. E., L. S. Kleinman, and C. A. Hanie. 1978. "Industrial-Organizational Psychology: 'Open Thy Ears O House of Israel.'" *American Psychologist* 33: 893–905.

Hackman, J. R., and G. R. Oldham. 1975. "Development of the Job Diagnostic Survey." *Journal of Applied Psychology* 60:159–70.

James, H. D. 1979. "Union Reviews on Job Evaluation." *Personnel Journal* 58: 80–85.

Krzystofiak, F., J. M. Newman, and G. Anderson. 1979. "A Quantified Approach to Measurement of Job Content: Procedures and Payoffs." *Personnel Psychology* 32:341–57.

Lissitz, R. W., J. L. Mendoza, D. J. Huberty, and H. V. Markos. 1979. "Some Further Ideas on a Methodology for Determining Job Similarities/Differences." *Personnel Psychology* 32:517–28.

McCormick, E. J., P. R. Jeanneret, and R. C. Mecham. 1972. "A Study of Job Characteristics and Job Dimensions as Based on the Position Analysis Questionnaire (PAQ)." *Journal of Applied Psychology* 56:347–68.

Roberts, H. V. 1980. "Statistical Biases in the Measurement of Employment Discrimination." In *Comparable Worth: Issues and Alternatives*, ed. E. R. Livernash, pp. 173–95. Washington, D.C.: Equal Employment Advisory Council.

Smith, J. E., and M. D. Hakel. 1979. "Convergence among Data Sources, Response Bias and Reliability and Validity of a Structured Job Analysis Questionnaire." *Personnel Psychology* 32:677–708.

9

Assessing Pay Discrimination Using National Data

DONALD J. TREIMAN, HEIDI I. HARTMANN,
AND PATRICIA A. ROOS

The concept of "comparable worth"—equal pay for work of equal (or comparable) value—raises important questions about the structure of rewards in the labor market. Comparable worth advocates claim that women's jobs (that is, jobs held mainly by women, such as nursing and secretarial work) are not rewarded for their skill, effort, responsibility, and working conditions in a way commensurate with men's jobs. The assertion is that male-dominated and female-dominated jobs have fundamentally different earning structures (i.e, different returns to such pay-related factors as years of schooling, years of experience, complexity of the job, physical effort required, working conditions, etc.). The remedy proposed is to reward women's jobs in the same way as men's jobs—that is, to give women's jobs the same return on such factors as men's jobs. In this chapter, we examine the claim that women's and men's occupations have different earnings structures; estimate the proportion of the pay differential that can be attributed to differences in the rate of return on various job characteristics and the proportion that can be attributed to differences in the characteristics of men's and women's jobs; and illustrate some alternative correction strategies.

Previous research has confirmed that average occupational earnings vary inversely with the proportion of women among the incumbents (Fuchs, 1971; Treiman and Terrell, 1975). Surprisingly little attention has been paid, by either sociologists or economists, to the causes of this phenomenon, even in studies that attempt to assess the extent of differences due to discrimination. Typically studies of discrimination are carried out at the level of the individual worker, rather than the occupation. Human capital variables (e.g., education and experience) are generally the explanatory variables. An overview of these studies reveals, however, that occupational differences have substantial and persistent importance in earnings equations and, in particular, in accounting for the wage gap between men and women (Treiman and Hartmann, 1981). In those studies where the occupational range is restricted (university professors or scientists, for example), differences in human capital variables between men and women often account for a substantial portion of the gap, reducing the unexplained residual (often called discrimination) to near zero. Moreover, in labor-force-wide studies that include detailed occupations or occupational groups as explanatory variables, the remaining unexplained residuals are reduced relative to studies that do not include occupational variables. In studies that do neither, however, human capital variables explain at best half the gross difference in earnings between men and women. Hence, the evidence is strong that occupations do not reward human capital characteristics equally, particularly for women and men. Findings such as these have underscored the importance of occupation as an intervening factor in the relationship between human capital and earnings.

A few studies have looked directly at the characteristics of jobs within establishments, attempting to show that earnings structures differ for jobs held mainly by men and those held mainly by women. The Washington State study (see Chapter 7) is a good example of this genre. Studies such as this support the claim that men's and women's jobs are paid differently for similar requirements.

Here we replicate the methodology of studies of earnings differences among jobs in firms, using data on occupations in the economy as a whole (detailed occupations from the 1970 census are used). Our indications of job worth are of two types: characteristics of occupations as determined by the

Dictionary of Occupational Titles, or *DOT* (U.S. Department of Labor, 1977), and human capital characteristics of the incumbents of occupations. The purposes of this exercise are to examine the validity of the claim that women's and men's jobs are not rewarded similarly in accordance with their worth; provide estimates of the extent to which women's jobs are underpaid relative to men's; and suggest ways of adjusting salaries to achieve equity.

The Study

The present exercise is intended mainly to illustrate the feasibility of our approach. For this reason we felt free to use an available data set that differs somewhat from the data to which such procedures would normally be applied. Whereas assessment of the relative worth of jobs would ordinarily be restricted to jobs within a single firm, for the present illustrative exercise we make use of 1970 census data for the entire U.S. labor force (the 1980 data were not yet available). Specifically, our sample consists of the 499 occupational categories included in published tabulations of the *Subject Report on Occupations* (U.S. Bureau of the Census, 1973b) for which complete data are available.[1] These are, of course, not jobs but rather occupations practiced in a wide variety of contexts, and hence they are subject to variability in earnings due to characteristics of work settings, firms, industries, and labor markets. If anything, this should reduce our ability to predict average earnings from a small set of worker characteristics.

Variables. In order to take account of the fact that occupations vary in their requirements and in the qualifications or characteristics of their incumbents, we include four job characteristics and two individual characteristics among our predictors of income. In addition, for some purposes we use a measure of the sex composition of each occupational category. The dependent variable is a measure of the average earnings of incumbents of each occupation.

Job characteristics. To estimate the requirements of jobs, we made use of the wealth of data collected by the U.S. Department of Labor for the *DOT*. In work reported elsewhere (Miller, et al., 1980: Ch. 7 and appendix F), scales measuring four dimensions of occupations have been developed from the forty-four occupational characteristics collected for the *DOT* and scores assigned to each detailed census category. The four dimensions are: substantive complexity (designated *F1*), motor skills (*F2*), physical demands (*F3*), and unfavorable working conditions (*F4*). These four dimensions

---

1. These categories correspond to the three-digit 1970 census occupational classification, except that some categories are subdivided on the basis of industry, and among managers and administrators a further distinction is made between self-employed and salaried workers. Our analysis is restricted to wage and salary workers.

correspond reasonably well to three of the four types of factors generally included in job evaluation plans: skill, effort, and working conditions. Unfortunately, we do not have adequate measures of responsibility.

Individual characteristics. Education is measured by the mean years of schooling completed by incumbents of each occupation (designated E). Extent of previous work experience (designated X) was, unfortunately, not measured directly by the census. For males, an adequate proxy can be computed in a straightforward way: mean years of work experience is estimated by mean age minus mean years of school completed minus 6. That is, we assume that, on the average, men start school when they are six years old and work every year subsequent to completing their schooling. While this assumption cannot be completely correct—if only because it ignores the fact that some men have military experience of several years' duration and many have periods of unemployment—it is quite a close approximation (Corcoran and Duncan, 1978:18) and is conventionally used in the economic literature (e.g., Mincer 1974; Oaxaca, 1973).

For women, by contrast, such a proxy is inappropriate because large numbers of female workers leave the labor force after marriage and still larger numbers leave during the child-bearing years. To achieve a reasonable estimate of the average labor force experience of women in each occupation, we therefore use an alternative estimation procedure, viewing the average labor force experience of women in each occupation as a function of the average age of women in the occupation. (See Appendix.)

Finally, to derive an experience measure for incumbents of both sexes in each occupation, we simply compute a weighted average of the estimates for males and females, with the weights equal to the proportion of incumbents of each sex. Note that this variable probably understates the amount of labor force experience of incumbents of female-dominated occupations, since our estimate of the mean years of experience of *women* in the average occupation is 9.3 years, compared to an estimate of about 13 years for individual women derived from the Panel Study of Income Dynamics (Corcoran and Duncan, 1978:18).[2] Hence, our estimates of the extent to which earnings differences between occupations can be accounted for by differences in the labor force experience of incumbents should be regarded as high.

Percent female. At some points in the analysis, we will measure the sex composition of occupational categories by the percentage of women among incumbents (designated W).

---

2. The female experience estimates based on age-specific rates are no doubt too low because the key assumption required for the estimate—that the participation rate can be equated with the length of labor force experience of the average *woman*—understates the labor force experience of *women who work*. Some women never work, and other women work throughout their adult lives. The former do not appear in our data and should be regarded as irrelevant when estimating length of labor force experience; yet our estimation procedure precludes this possibility.

Earnings. Our earnings variable (designated Y) is the weighted average of the median earnings of female and male workers (means are not available), adjusted to take account of occupational differences in average hours worked per year. We make this adjustment in recognition of the fact that a possible reason for the lower earnings of women's occupations is that they are more likely to be performed on a part-time basis; in so doing, we also assume that part-timers are paid less than full-time workers for the same work. To create the adjusted variables for males and females, we multiplied median annual earnings for each by 2,080 divided by the product of the mean hours worked per week times the mean weeks worked per year. The constant 2,080 is an estimate of the hours worked per year by full-time, year-round workers, on the assumption that such workers work 40 hours per week and 52 weeks per year. Our final variable, sometimes referred to below as "annualized mean earnings," is just the weighted average of the adjusted variables for male and female workers.

Our basic procedure involves (1) regressing mean earnings of occupations on job and worker characteristics, (2) using the estimated coefficients to compute expected earnings, and (3) comparing actual with expected earnings. We use two basic models, one excluding and the other including percent female as a predictor variable, and we estimate these models both for all occupations in the sample and for three subgroups specified on the basis of their sex composition. Male-dominated occupations are defined as those with at least 90 percent of incumbents male. Of our 499 occupations, 182 (36 percent) are male-dominated by this criterion, and they average 4.3 percent female. The advantage of choosing such a low cutting point is that these occupations are unambiguously "men's work" and hence appropriate for use as a standard for assessing earnings functions in the absence of discrimination. Female-dominated occupations are defined as those at least 70 percent female. Thirteen percent of all occupations are in this category ($N = 65$). Since the average occupation is only 28 percent female, it seemed to us that occupations at least 70 percent female would be generally perceived as "women's work." These occupations average 87 percent female. The remaining 252 occupations (51 percent of all occupations) are regarded as mixed. They average 31 percent female.

The first task in our analysis is to establish for these data the extent to which occupational earnings differences are associated with sex composition. We do this by comparing the average earnings of workers in occupations dominated by males, mixed occupations, and occupations dominated by females. The top row of Table 9-1 shows the mean of the average earnings variable for all occupations and for each of the three categories (male-dominated, mixed, and female-dominated occupations). Note that these are means of means—they indicate the average earnings in the average occupation in each category, not the average earnings of all workers in the category, since we are averaging over occupations and not over individuals. This

Table 9-1

Means and Standard Deviations for Variables Included in the Analysis, for All Occupations and Three Sex-Type Subgroups

Variable	All Occupations		Male-Dominated Occupations (≤10% female)		Mixed Occupations (10<% female <70%)		Female-Dominated Occupations (≥70% female)	
	Mean	S.D.	Mean	S.D.	Mean	S.D.	Mean	S.D.
Y: mean annualized earnings	$6,978	$2,652	$7,985	$2,594	$6,874	$2,491	$4,564	$1,585
E: mean years of school completed	12.5	2.34	12.3	2.17	12.8	2.58	12.2	1.63
X: mean years of labor force experience	17.3	6.55	21.5	5.28	16.2	5.76	9.69	3.39
F1: substantive complexity	4.130	2.410	4.260	2.330	4.240	2.580	3.350	1.720
F2: motor skills	4.920	1.720	5.270	1.650	4.610	1.730	5.170	1.720
F3: physical demands	2.010	2.200	3.250	2.580	1.340	1.560	1.160	1.560
F4: undesirable working conditions	.483	1.110	.575	1.060	.470	1.200	.278	.855
W: percent female	28.5%	28.4%	4.29%	2.75%	30.9%	16.4%	86.7%	9.13%
N	499		182		252		65	

is a deliberate choice: our analysis focuses on characteristics of occupations, not characteristics of workers; hence, each occupation is weighted equally.

When one inspects the table, it is evident that workers in male-dominated occupations earn more on the average than workers in other occupations. These differences are very substantial: pay rates in mixed occupations average 86 percent, and in female occupations 57 percent, of those in male occupations. The effect of the sex composition of occupations on earnings can be seen graphically in Figure 9-1, which presents the regression of average annual earnings on percent female for all 499 occupations. Average earnings decrease $42.39 for each percentage point increase in females. As a result, the expected level of average earnings in 1970 for occupations with no female incumbents is $8,185, while for entirely female occupations the expected earnings are only $3,946.

The data presented here leave no doubt that "women's work" is paid less than "men's work." The question remains, however, to what extent the observed differences are due to differences in job requirements or in the qualifications of workers in male jobs and female jobs. From Table 9-1 it is evident that male-dominated occupations, mixed occupations, and female-dominated occupations differ substantially with respect to both job requirements and worker characteristics. Workers in male-dominated occupations tend to have the most labor force experience, and workers in female-dominated occupations the least; female-dominated jobs tend to be less

Figure 9-1
Relationship between Percent Female and
Mean Annualized Earnings of Occupations

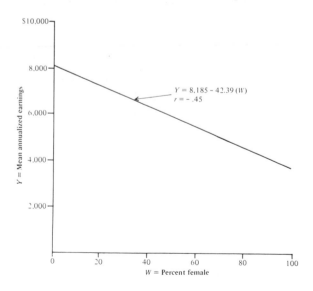

$$Y = 8,185 - 42.39\,(W)$$
$$r = -.45$$

complex and have more desirable working conditions than other occupations; and male-dominated occupations tend to be more physically demanding than other occupations. To the extent that these characteristics determine the pay rates of occupations, we would expect the average pay rates of the three job groups to differ.

Table 9-2 shows that these characteristics do account for a substantial portion of the variation in earnings among occupations. The table gives coefficients for two regression models of income determination, computed over all occupations and separately for male-dominated, mixed, and female-dominated occupations (the correlations among variables in the model are shown for all occupations and for male-dominated occupations in Table 9-3). For the moment our interest is in Model I. For the labor force as a whole, over 70 percent of the interoccupational variance in average earnings can be attributed to differences in the four job characteristics and two worker characteristics in the model. As we can see from the left-hand column in the bottom panel, by far the most powerful predictor is the average educational attainment of incumbents; labor force experience and the substantive complexity of jobs are also important. In a gross way, the same pattern holds for each of the sex-type subgroups, although some variations are of interest. In particular, within female-dominated occupations (but not the other two groups) earnings do not depend on substantive complexity but do depend on motor skills and physical demands. This may reflect the tendency for blue-collar occupations done by women to pay better than clerical jobs.

Differences and similarities in regression coefficients do not, however, tell the whole story, since it would be quite possible for men's and women's jobs to have identical regression slopes and quite different average earnings (the differences would appear in the intercept); in such a case we would regard the earnings structures as different. There are several ways of assessing this possibility.

First, we simply add an indicator of the sex composition of occupations to the earnings quotation. Model II in Table 9-2 is identical to Model I except that in addition it includes percent female as a predictor variable. The coefficient associated with percent female can be interpreted as a direct measure of discrimination. It tells us how much we could expect two occupations to differ in average income if they were identical in average educational attainment and labor force experience of incumbents and in the four job characteristics, but differed in their sex ratios. The coefficient computed for all occupations is -27.5, which means that two occupations differing in their sex composition by 10 points but identical with respect to the remaining variables would be expected to differ by \$275 in annual income. It is useful to contrast this coefficient with the coefficient for sex composition shown in Figure 9-1. There we noted that the gross cost of each additional percent female is \$42.39. Taking account of differences in the composition of

Table 9-2

Coefficients of Two Models of Earnings Determinants for All Occupations and Three Sex-Type Subgroups (standard errors in parentheses)

Variable	All Occupations I	All Occupations II	Male-Dominated Occupations I	Male-Dominated Occupations II	Mixed Occupations I	Mixed Occupations II	Female-Dominated Occupations I	Female-Dominated Occupations II
Metric coefficients								
E: education	793 (65.4)	681 (61.6)	705 (133)	739 (130)	705 (76.0)	663 (71.9)	893 (120)	891 (124)
X: experience	150 (11.7)	75.2 (13.5)	81.6 (26.4)	76.2 (25.8)	99.0 (15.7)	65.4 (15.9)	122 (41.0)	121 (42.1)
$F1$: complexity	217 (61.4)	217 (61.4)	299 (118)	244 (116)	162 (72.6)	139 (68.5)	34.1 (109)	34.9 (110)
$F2$: motor skills	73.2 (56.7)	82.4 (34.7)	124 (77.3)	101 (75.6)	-23.1 (47.2)	6.36 (44.7)	250 (75.4)	251 (76.5)
$F3$: physical demands	95.3 (39.6)	-9.25 (36.6)	37.2 (56.4)	-33.6 (59.1)	-106 (62.4)	-218 (62.0)	183 (75.4)	183 (78.6)
$F4$: undesirable working conditions	85.4 (66.1)	23.6 (34.0)	-31.8 (126)	39.9 (125)	94.2 (80.2)	104 (75.5)	268 (77.4)	264 (157)
W: percent female	—	-27.5 (2.98)	—	-158 (48.6)	—	-29.2 (5.11)	— (145)	-1.08 (13.9)
Constant	-7,011	-3,341	-4,441	-3,515	-4,205	-2,122	-9,189	-9,069
R^2	.707	.751	.622	.644	.769	.796	.718	.718
Standard error	1,444	1,334	1,621	1,579	1,212	1,141	884	892
Standardized coefficients								
E: education	.700*	.601*	.590*	.618*	.730*	.687*	.919*	.917*
X: experience	.370*	.186*	.166*	.155*	.229*	.151*	.261*	.260*
$F1$: complexity	.197*	.197*	.268*	.219*	.168*	.144*	.037	.038
$F2$: motor skills	.048	.054*	.079	.064	-.016	.004	.272*	.273*
$F3$: physical demands	.079*	-.008	.037	-.033	-.067	-.137*	.180*	.181*
$F4$: undesirable working conditions	.036	.010	-.013	.016	.045	.050	.180*	.142
W: percent female	—	-.294*	—	-.167*	—	-.191*	.145	-.006

*Metric coefficient is at least twice its standard error.

Table 9-3

Correlations among Variables Included in the Analysis (all occupations above diagonal; male-dominated occupations below diagonal)

Variable		Y	E	X	F1	F2	F3	F4	W
Y:	mean annualized earnings		.721	.211	.754	−.049	−.165	−.231	−.454
E:	mean years of school completed	.742		−.259	.861	−.177	−.418	−.307	−.029
X:	mean years of labor force experience	−.061	−.339		−.004	.074	.261	−.011	−.611
F1:	substantive complexity	.748	.861	−.114		−.052	−.354	−.372	−.152
F2:	motor skills	.047	−.081	−.018	.040		.160	−.074	−.007
F3:	physical demands	−.360	−.521	.126	−.456	.194		.362	−.346
F4:	undesirable working conditions	−.279	−.270	−.042	−.386	−.071	.254		−.086
W:	percent female	−.120	.118	−.147	−.019	−.208	−.357	−.279	

occupations with respect to earnings determinants, the net cost is $27.50, or about two-thirds of the gross cost. That is, by this estimate only about one-third of the gross sex composition effect can be explained without invoking discrimination.[3]

Our second strategy is to use the characteristics of male-dominated occupations as a standard for assessing the adequacy of the wage rates of other categories of occupations. Specifically, we substitute the means on the independent variables for each of the other two subgroups into Model I estimated for male-dominated occupations to determine the average earnings that could be expected for the other occupational groups if those occupations had the same return on their education, experience, and job characteristics as male occupations. The difference between actual and expected mean earnings is taken as an indicator of over- or under-payment. This approach is based on the assumption that for male-dominated occupations the average wage is an acceptable indicator of job worth. We also assume that, for this subset of occupations, existing wage differences are outcomes of the operation of market forces that are legitimate determinants of wage differentials, whereas we are unwilling to make this assumption for all occupations.

Table 9-4 gives the results of this exercise. Whereas female-dominated occupations actually pay an average of 57 percent as much as male-dominated occupations, they would pay an average of 83 percent as much if they were rewarded in the same manner as male-dominated occupations; the remaining difference is due to the different characteristics (on the average) of female occupations. In all, about 40 percent of the earnings gap between male- and female-dominated occupations can be attributed to differences in job characteristics and 60 percent to differences in the rate of return on these characteristics. Similarly, whereas mixed occupations actually pay an average of 86 percent as much as male-dominated occupations, they would pay an average of 97 percent as much if they were

---

3. Birnbaum (1979) has argued that simple reliance on a coefficient for sex (or sex composition) to measure discrimination may be misleading, since it is possible to generate statistically significant coefficients relating sex and earnings even under a single factor model in which sex, earnings, and "merit" (legitimate determinants of pay differences) are all determined by an underlying "quality" dimension but are otherwise uncorrelated. He proposes as a test for discrimination that both of the following relations hold: $\beta_{YW \cdot M} < 0$ and $\beta_{MW \cdot Y} > 0$, where Y and W are defined as before and M is a measure of "merit" (in the present case, let M = the expected earnings predicted from Model II, estimated for all occupations, with W omitted). Discrimination is clearly present under this criterion, since $\beta_{YW \cdot M} = -.294$ and $\beta_{MW \cdot Y} = .201$. That is, it is true both that, holding constant differences among occupations in the educational attainment and experience of incumbents and the four occupational characteristics, the higher the percent female the lower the average earnings; and that, holding constant average earnings, the higher the percent female the higher the overall level of the factors that predict earnings.

Table 9-4

Decomposition of Average Earnings Differences
between Subsets of Occupations

Mean Annualized Earnings	Male-Dominated Occupations	Mixed Occupa-tions	Female-Dominated Occupations
Actual			
Earnings	$7,985	$6,874	$4,564
Percentage of mean			
for male occupations	100%	86%	57%
Male occupations as standard			
Adjusted for composition			
Earnings*	$7,985	$7,748	$6,614
Percentage of mean			
for male occupations	100%	97%	83%
Percentage of gap explained by			
occupation†	—	21%	40%

*The mean earnings for each group of occupations is computed on the assumption that all groups have the earnings structure empirically observed for male-dominated occupations (Model I for male-dominated occupations in Table 9.3). The means for each of the other two subgroups are substituted into this equation to derive estimates of the mean earnings to be expected if the only difference between the groups was due to their different means on the independent variables.
†This is estimated by determining the ratio of the adjusted group differences to the actual group differences: for example, (7,985–7,748)/7,985–6,874).

rewarded in the same manner. In all, only 21 percent of the earnings gap between male and mixed occupations can be attributed to differences in job characteristics and 79 percent to differences in the rate of return on these characteristics.

Since in both cases the bulk of the earnings gap is due to differences in the rate of return on characteristics that account quite well for occupational differences in earnings within groups (and for all occupations taken together), the inference is strong that a discriminatory process is at work: occupations are paid best when they are dominated by men and worst when they are dominated by women.[4]

4. In exercises of this kind, the choice of standards is to some extent arbitrary. While we would argue that on substantive grounds it is most sensible to use male occupations as the standard—since we would expect this subset of jobs to be least subject to discriminatory processes—it is useful to confirm that the use of other standards would not lead to different results. Substituting means for male-dominated occupations into Model I computed for female-dominated occupations and estimating an expected value for the earnings variable leads to the conclusion that 41 percent of the gap between the average earnings of these two groups of occupations can be attributed to differences in composition and 59 percent to differences in the rate of return for occupational characteristics. Comparisons involving mixed occupations yield similar results, regardless of which equation is used as the standard. Hence, the "index problem" is not a problem in the present case.

This inference is, of course, open to challenge on the ground that we have failed to measure other factors that legitimately create earnings differences. Procedures that define "discrimination" as a residual component are always open to this sort of challenge. But it should be noted that for additional variables to further "explain" the earnings gap, they must be correlated with both earnings levels and percent female in jobs and *uncorrelated* with the explanatory variables already included; that is, their additional explanatory power is reduced to the extent that they are correlated with variables already in the model. We pose the search for additional explanatory variables as a challenge to those who wish to dispute the interpretation of the residual effect as "discrimination."

Correcting Discriminatory Pay Differences

Having determined the probable existence of sex discrimination in pay rates, we need to consider procedures for correcting it. In this section we describe four statistical adjustment procedures that exploit the analysis already presented. Many other procedures can be imagined, but these are sufficient as vehicles to explore some of the strengths and weaknesses of alternative approaches.

The first approach is simply to use Model I (computed over all occupations) as a formula to derive a pay rate for each occupation. This is formally analogous to the use of conventional job evaluation procedures to derive pay rates (e.g., the GS system for federal white-collar jobs), in that the pay rate for each job is determined by a weighted sum of a set of "compensable factors." Indeed, many job evaluation systems derive the factor weights in precisely this manner—by regressing pay rates on the factor scores (Treiman, 1979).

The disadvantage of this approach is that since the factor weights are derived in such a way as to maximize the prediction of existing pay rates and since pay rates are strongly correlated with the sex composition of occupational categories, those factors most strongly correlated with the sex composition of occupational categories will tend to receive the heaviest weight. To this extent, then, the predicted earnings levels for each job will tend to be correlated with actual earnings levels, and any sex bias in pay rates will tend to be unaffected. To overcome this difficulty two procedures are available.

First, the equation for male-dominated occupations can be used as a standard. Since discriminatory processes presumably do not affect the relative earnings of occupations at least 90 percent male, the factors that predict earnings differences among such jobs could be used as a standard for all jobs. Appropriate earnings levels for each job could be computed by using Model I (computed for male jobs) as a formula. This approach has the advantage of bringing all pay rates up to a level commensurate with the highest returns currently offered, which is probably psychologically preferable, but has the corresponding disadvantage of increasing the cost of the total pay package (unless, of course, the pay rates for all jobs are reduced by some constant).

Alternatively, the weights associated with the compensable factors could be computed holding sex composition constant. This, in fact, is what Model II (computed over all occupations) does. For example, the coefficient for years of school completed gives the predicted increment in earnings for each year of additional average schooling *among occupations that have identical proportions female.* To compute pay rates from compensable factors adjusted to remove the effect of sex composition, Model II (for all occupations) is used as the computing formula, except that the coefficient for percent female is evaluated at the mean and added to the constant.

The three procedures discussed so far have in common the complete determination of earnings from a weighted sum of compensable factors. In this sense they are all versions of a comparable worth approach derived from job evaluation procedures. However, an employer may feel that such an approach is overly deterministic. After all, a variety of idiosyncratic factors might legitimately create pay differences between occupations, and, it could be argued, these ought not to be ignored or arbitrarily omitted. Hence, we offer a final approach that preserves differences in the pay rates of jobs— *insofar as the unmeasured idiosyncratic component of pay differentials is uncorrelated with sex composition.* We do this by using the coefficient of percent female from Model II (computed over all occupations) as an adjustment factor, adding to the existing mean pay rate of each occupation a constant equal to $-b(W)$ (in the present case, 27.5(W)). That is, we add $27.50 to the annual pay rate of each occupation for each additional percent female. The result of such an exercise is to reduce the net effect of sex composition to zero. Of course, since the legitimate compensable factors typically will be (and in the present case are) correlated with sex composition, the zero-order correlation between sex composition and earnings will not be entirely eliminated.

Table 9-5 summarizes the effect of each of these procedures by showing the correlation between sex composition and adjusted earnings and also the average adjusted earnings for each subgroup. The conclusions to be drawn from this table are quite straightforward. The simple simulation of job evaluation (row 2) improves the relative earnings of mixed and female-dominated occupations somewhat, but the other three procedures are much more effective in doing so, mainly because they statistically remove the discriminatory component of the relation between sex composition and earnings. On average, these latter procedures create nearly equivalent average earnings for male-dominated and mixed occupations—as they should, given the essential similarity between these two groups of occupations with respect to their characteristics (Table 9-1). They also reduce the earnings gap between male dominated and female-dominated occupations

Table 9-5

Effect of Various Adjustment Procedures on Sex Discrimination in Earnings

Adjustment	$r_{\hat{Y}W}$*	Expected Mean Earnings			Percentage of Mean for Male-Dominated Occupations	
		Male-Dominated Occupations	Mixed Occupations	Female-Dominated Occupations	Mixed Occupations	Female-Dominated Occupations
Actual earnings	−.454	$7,985	$6,874	$4,564	86	57
All occupations as standard	−.365	7,595	6,957	5,336	92	70
Male occupations as standard	−.229	7,985	7,750	6,613	97	83
All occupations, adjusted to remove effect of percent female	−.211	7,182	7,080	6,046	99	84
Increment by coefficient of percent female	−.176	8,103	7,724	6,947	95	86

*$\hat{Y}$ refers to the various adjustments; W = percent female.

by about two-thirds—again as they should, given (as we have seen) differences in average levels of the compensable factors that account for about one-third of the gap.

Summary

This chapter has been an exercise in the application to actual data of a variety of procedures for identifying and correcting sex discrimination in pay rates. Using available economywide data on occupations as a proxy for firm-specific data on jobs, we first showed that the sex composition of occupations has a strong effect on earnings that cannot be attributed to differences in occupational requirements (measured by four factor-based scales derived from *DOT* data) or in the educational qualifications or labor force experience of their incumbents. From these results we inferred that there is substantial sex-based discrimination in pay rates. We then illustrated a variety of procedures for reducing the discriminatory component of pay differences between occupations, including some that pay occupations strictly on the basis of their compensable features and one that adjusts pay rates to remove the net effect of sex composition but otherwise permits unmeasured factors to influence pay rates.

While these procedures show considerable promise, a great deal of work still needs to be done to explore the full implications of implementing them in particular cases. It is probable that a tradeoff will have to be made between psychological and economic considerations. Minimizing worker resentment would seem to require raising pay rates for underpaid jobs rather than reducing them for "overpaid" jobs; yet such a solution could add substantially to a firm's labor costs. These and a host of other specific issues demand full exploration—a task that we ardently encourage.

Appendix

ESTIMATING THE LABOR FORCE EXPERIENCE OF WOMEN

We estimate the average labor force experience of women in each occupation from age-specific rates of female labor force participation adjusted by the age distribution of women in each occupation. We do this by taking advantage of the availability of information on labor force participation rates by age, collected by the U.S. Census for the period 1920–1970 (U.S. Bureau of the Census, 1933, 1943, 1953, 1964, 1973a, 1973b). From the available information we can construct an historical profile of labor force participation for five-year birth cohorts by five-year age intervals. Assuming that the proportion of women in the labor force at the census date is equal to the proportion of the time the average woman was in the labor force during the interval including the census date, we can estimate the amount of labor force experience for women of a given age by summing the participation rates over age intervals for each cohort. By making the further assumption that the average amount of labor force experience for women in each occupation is equal to the estimated labor force experience of women of the age equal to the average for the occupation, we estimate the average labor force experience for the occupational category. Although this method of estimating female experience would not be appropriate for individuals, the fact that we are using occupations as the unit of analysis makes the use of category averages tenable.

As an example of our estimating procedure, consider an occupation in which the average age of female incumbents in 1970 was 41.5 years. To estimate the average labor force experience of women in this occupation, we first construct a labor force participation profile for women aged 40–44 in 1970, utilizing data from the census publications cited above.

Census Year	Cohort Age	Participation Rate (%)	Average Years Experience
1970	40–44	52.1	2.61
	35–39	44.3	2.22
1960	30–34	35.5	1.78
	25–29	33.8	1.69
1950	20–24	43.2	2.16
	14–19	20.7	1.24

In this table, the participation rates for noncensus years are simply the average of the rates for the same age group in the preceding and following census year. Thus, the participation rate for 35–39-year-olds is the average of the rates for 35–39-year-olds in 1960 and 1970. Average years of experience is the participation rate times the number of years included in the interval, which is six for the youngest age interval and five for each of the remaining intervals. Thus, the average number of years of experience for this cohort during the period in which its members were 35–39 was 2.22 [experience = $(44.3/100)(5)$]. The sum of the years of work experience up to age 40 is 9.09. Since the years of experience during the period when the cohort was 40–44 is 2.61, we estimate the experience of women in an occupation with an average age of 41.5 years as $9.09 + ((41.5 - 40)/5)(2.61)$, or 9.87 years. This last calculation adjusts for the fact that the women in this particular occupation, who on the average are 41.5 years old, have not yet lived through the entire age period 40–44. A similar computation is completed for each occupation.

References

Birnbaum, Michael H. 1979. "Procedures for the Detection and Correction of Salary Inequities." In *Salary Equity: Detecting Sex Bias in Salaries among College and University Professors*, ed. T. R. Pezzullo and B. E. Brittingham, pp. 121–44. Lexington, Mass.: Lexington Books.

Corcoran, Mary, and Greg J. Duncan. 1978. "A Summary of Part I Findings." *Five Thousand American Families—Patterns of Economic Progress*, ed. Greg J. Duncan and James N. Morgan. Vol. 6: *Accounting for Race and Sex Differences and Other Analyses of the First Nine Years of the Panel Study of Income Dynamics*, pp. 3–46. Ann Arbor, Michigan: Institute for Social Research, the University of Michigan.

Fuchs, Victor R. 1971. "Differences in Hourly Earnings between Men and Women." *Monthly Labor Review* 94 (May): 9–15.

Miller, Ann R., Donald J. Treiman, Pamela S. Cain, and Patricia A. Roos, eds. 1980. *The Dictionary of Occupational Titles: A Critical Review*. Final Report of the Committee on Occupational Classification and Analysis to the U.S. Department of Labor. Washington, D.C: National Academy of Sciences.

Mincer, Jacob. 1974. *Schooling, Experience, and Earnings*. New York: Columbia University Press.

Oaxaca, Ronald. 1973. "Sex Discrimination in Wages." In *Discrimination in Labor Markets*, ed. Orley Ashenfelter and Albert Rees, pp. 124–51. Princeton: Princeton University Press.

Treiman, Donald J. 1979. *Job Evaluation: An Analytic Review*. Interim Report by the Committee on Occupational Classification and Analysis to the Equal Employment Opportunity Commission. Washington, D.C.: National Academy of Sciences.

Treiman, Donald J., and Heidi Hartmann. 1981. *Women, Work and Wages*. Washington, D.C.: National Academy Press.

Treiman, Donald J., and Kermit Terrell. 1975. "Women, Work and Wages: Trends in the Female Occupational Structure since 1940." In Social Indicator Models, ed. Kenneth Land and Seymour Spilerman, pp. 157–99. New York: Russell Sage Foundation.

U.S. Bureau of the Census. 1933. *Census of the Population: 1930*. Vol. 5: *General Report on Occupations*. Washington, D.C.: Government Printing Office.

U.S. Bureau of the Census. 1943. *Census of the Population: 1940*. Vol. 3: *The Labor Force*. Part 1: *U.S. Summary*. Washington, D.C.: Government Printing Office.

U.S. Bureau of the Census. 1953. *Census of the Population: 1950*. Vol. 2: *Characteristics of the Population*. Part 1: *U.S. Summary*. Washington, D.C.: Government Printing Office.

U.S. Bureau of the Census. 1964. *Census of the Population: 1960*. Vol. 1: *Characteristics of the Population*. Part 1: *U.S. Summary*. Washington, D.C.: Government Printing Office.

U.S. Bureau of the Census. 1973a. *Census of the Population: 1970*. Vol. 1: *Characteristics of the Population*. Part 1, Section 2: *U.S. Summary*. Washington, D.C.: Government Printing Office.

U.S. Bureau of the Census. 1973b. *Census of the Population: 1970*. Final Report PC(2)-7A: *Occupational Characteristics*. Washington, D.C.: Government Printing Office.

U.S. Department of Labor. 1977. *Dictionary of Occupational Titles*. 4th ed. Washington, D.C.: Government Printing Office.

10
Economic Models as a Means of Calculating Legal Compensation Claims

BARBARA R. BERGMANN AND MARY W. GRAY

In *County of Washington* v. *Gunther*,[1] the Supreme Court decided that Title VII of the 1964 civil rights act prohibits sex discrimination in wages in situations other than those involving equal work. If an effective remedy for such discrimination is to be devised, consideration must be given to the way in which wages are set and the ways in which courts may ensure that sex does not play a role in the process, as it may have done in *Gunther*. We propose that any company that segregates its work force and pays those in predominantly female jobs at a lesser rate that those in predominantly male jobs should be forced to realign its pay structure. Such a realignment would be based on estimates of a non-discriminatory wage structure.

One problem in the way of court-ordered realignment of occupational wage structures within firms is the fact that judges may believe that firms' decisions on pay are conditioned by market factors, and that these market factors are outside the firms' control. There is a "market" for executive trainees and a "market" for secretaries, and these two markets are thought to "dictate" that different wages be paid to these two classes of employees. The conditions in these markets are conceived of as reflecting the forces of supply and demand. Judicial intervention under Title VII in this supposedly impersonal process of wage setting may be viewed as a penalization of the firm for something other than that firm's acts in violation of Title VII, and a violation of the "laws" of economics to boot.

In this chapter we undertake the task of exploring the connection between the firm's behavior in assigning applicants to jobs and setting the wages for each job and the events outside the firm that constitute part of the economic environment in which the firm functions. We explore the relationship between the generalized practices of a majority of employers and the compulsions on particular employers in the face of these common practices.

We suggest that firms practicing sex segregation that violates Title VII are inflicting on their segregated employees a penalty in the form of low

---

1. 452 U.S. 161 (1981).

wages. In setting such wage levels, they are taking advantage of the poor labor market alternatives these persons face as a result of the discriminatory practices of other employers. We further argue that when an employer is shown to have violated Title VII by segregating workers by sex, the realignment of that employer's occupational wages is appropriate as a remedy on legal grounds and makes economic sense. The strong precedent against displacing male employees from their jobs and substituting for them females who have been discriminated against means that wage realignment is the only way of making such victims whole. We also assert that it is possible to develop a set of principles guiding that realignment that would be in accord with economic principles governing competitive, nondiscriminatory labor markets.

In developing the argument, we use a greatly simplified example to spell out the economic consequences of segregating men and women. Next, we discuss the legal remedies that Title VII might offer to employees of individual firms. Finally, we relax the simplifying assumptions and discuss how similar principles apply to more realistic and, therefore, more complex cases.

The Effect of Sex Segregation on Market Wages

In a labor market in which employers disregard sex in deciding whom to hire and which jobs to assign to which individuals, the supply of workers who can perform in a particular occupation in an individual firm will be influenced by the productivity such workers would have if they worked for other employers, by the length and cost of training programs required to produce a worker who can perform in that occupation, by the proportion of workers who have the innate talent to profit from the training, and by the pleasantness or unpleasantness of the work. Where sex is considered in hiring, assignment, and promotion decisions by all employers or a high proportion of them, this fact will also importantly affect the supply of labor of each type of worker to each firm in the labor market. If employers are in the habit of refusing to consider women for all but a very small number of occupations, then the supply of women to these occupations, which we may label the "women's occupations," is increased by the number of women who would, in the absence of discrimination, have been employed in the "men's occupations." By the same action, the supply of labor to the men's occupations is decreased accordingly. These changes affect the wages of these occupations as changes in supply normally operate—increasing the wage in occupations to which the supply of labor has been diminished and decreasing it in occupations in which the supply has been increased.

In order to explore the effect of sex segregation on wages, we shall consider a greatly simplified case in which differences in training, native abilities, and taste for different kinds of work are assumed to play no part.

We shall analyze a labor market with just two occupations, in both of which men and women are initially assumed to be equally welcome. We will also initially assume that anyone in the labor market is capable of doing either job and likes one job as well as the other.

It is most convenient and sacrifices no generality to consider the argument in terms of a numerical example. Table 10-1 gives in numerical form hypothetical demand schedules for the two occupations, which represent the number of workers employers would hire for those jobs at various wage levels. For example, at a wage of $200 per week, employers in this labor market are assumed to be willing to hire 14,000 workers in Occupation A. At the same wage in Occupation B they are assumed to want to hire 4,000, for a total of 18,000. At higher wages, employers would want to hire fewer, and at lower wages it is assumed that they would want to hire more.

At this point it is worth remarking that under the conditions we have stipulated, market forces would be expected to eliminate any difference in wages between Occupation A and Occupation B. If any difference in wages did show up, workers in the lower-paid occupation would try to shift to the higher-paid occupation. We are assuming that there would be no bar to such movement due to lack of training or skill, to any distaste for the occupation, or to custom. Nor are employers assumed at this point to impede the flow of workers by excluding anyone for reasons of sex. The attempt of workers to enter the higher-paying occupation would increase the supply of workers to it and decrease the supply of workers to the lower-paying occupation. This process would go on until the wages in the two occupations were once again equal.

Since wages in the two occupations can, under our assumptions, be presumed to be the same except for temporary lapses, it makes sense to compile a "Total Demand" schedule, which is the total amount of labor

Table 10-1
Demand Schedules

Occupation A		Occupation B		Total Demand Assuming Equal Wages	
Weekly Wage	No. of Workers Demanded (thousands)	Weekly Wage	No. of Workers Demanded (thousands)	Weekly Wage	No. of Workers Demanded (thousands)
$300	8	$300	0	$300	8
250	11	250	1	250	12
200	14	200	4	200	18
150	17	150	7	150	24
100	20	100	10	100	30

Table 10-2

Supply Schedules

Males		Females		Total Supply	
Weekly Wage	*No. of Workers Supplied (thousands)*	*Weekly Wage*	*No. of Workers Supplied (thousands)*	*Weekly Wage*	*No. of Workers Supplied (thousands)*
$300	12	$300	10	$300	22
250	11	250	9	250	20
200	10	200	8	200	18
150	9	150	7	150	16
100	8	100	6	100	14

employers would be willing to hire at various wage levels, with identical wages in the two occupations. This schedule is displayed in the last two columns of Table 10-1.

Hypothetical supply schedules are displayed in Table 10-2, which shows the numbers of men and women who would offer their labor to employers at various wage rates. If wages do not differ by sex, the total supply of people to employers at each wage is shown on the right as the "Total Supply" schedule.

In the hypothesized case, because there is competition across sexes for jobs, and across jobs for labor, the considerations of supply and demand would suggest that the wage in both occupations and for both sexes would be $200 a week. This is the wage at which the number of workers sought by employers would be equal to the number of workers who wanted jobs in each occupation and in the labor market as a whole. This solution is shown diagrammatically in Figure 10-1. There would be 14,000 people in Occupation A and 4,000 in Occupation B, and the wage would be the same in both jobs. Both men's and women's wages would be $200. In such a labor market, we would expect to see men and women in both occupations.

Now consider a labor market with the same two occupations in which employers for some reason have decided to restrict women to jobs in Occupation B. Since we have by hypothesis eliminated issues of skill and workers' preferences for one job over another, we must assume that employers are following tradition, or that they believe that mixing men and women in the same occupation would be disadvantageous to the employer. Whatever the reason for the segregation, the supply and demand situation would be very different from that in the labor market under our previous hypothesis. The demand schedule for Occupation A would become purely and simply the demand for male workers, and, similarly, the demand schedule for Occupation B would become the demand for female workers. It would no longer be appropriate to add up either the demand schedules or

Figure 10-1
Unsegregated Wage Equilibrium

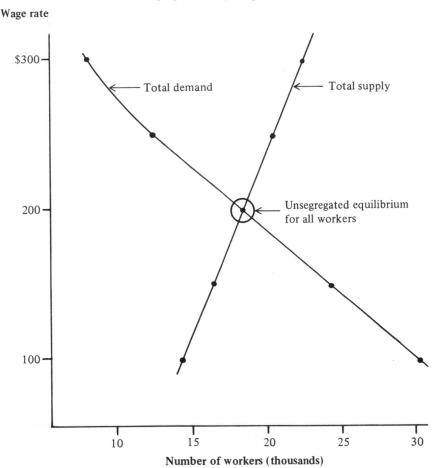

the supply schedules, because there would now be separate men's and women's labor markets, with independent solutions. In fact, the supply and demand conditions now assumed to be in force would dictate that the market for men would be cleared at an average wage of $250 per week, and the market for women cleared at $150. These solutions are displayed in Figure 10-2.

This result would not be materially affected if employers were to permit men to enter Occupation B while maintaining the prohibition of Occupation A to women. Few men would be tempted to enter Occupation B because of its relatively low wage.

It is interesting to note that in our example, had women been assigned to Occupation A and men to Occupation B, women would be more highly paid

Figure 10-2
Segregated Wage Equilibriums

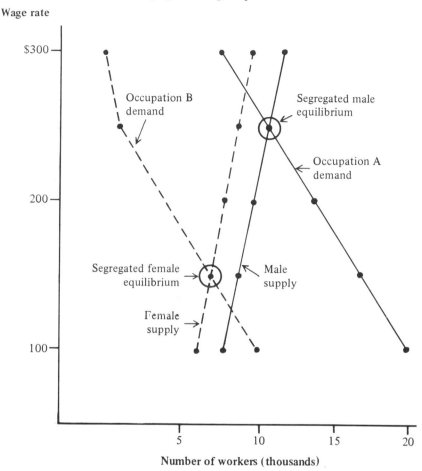

than men. To maintain a wage differential in favor of men requires not only segregation, but also the relegation of women to a relatively overcrowded territory.

While we usually think of occupational segregation as the cause of sex-based wage differentials, an alternative explanation is that wage differentials are the cause of occupational segregation. For example, suppose a woman is qualified both for a well-paying position that has potential for advancement to management and for a lower-paying position. If she is given an opportunity to take the better position, the other may go unfilled, as men can do better elsewhere. Thus, she is directed by personnel procedures into the lower-paying job. A series of such hiring decisions will result in a segregated work force, with women in what have become the women's jobs being paid less than similarly qualified males in the men's jobs.

The "Market Wage" in Wage Setting

Our analysis has thus far encompassed the labor market as a whole. At this point, let us shift the focus to the individual employer and inquire how this employer participates in the labor market and is affected by it.

An employer whose operations include particular jobs will keep cognizant of the "market wage" for workers considered to be acceptable for performing those jobs. The employer will keep abreast of what other employers are paying such workers and use that information in setting the firm's wage. We may note here that to an employer who practices sex segregation, being of the correct sex is required for "acceptability," along with an ability to do the job.

The reason for an employer's use of information on what other employers are paying "acceptable" workers lies in the employer's own interest. If an establishment sets a wage much below what other employers are offering, few "acceptable" workers may apply, and the best ones it has may leave. If an establishment's wage is set much above the market wage—the average others are paying—costs may be driven above, and profits below, what they might otherwise have been.

There are occasions when an establishment will want to depart from the market wage. Sometimes the offer of a wage similar to the market wage brings too few "acceptable" applicants, and the firm must then consider whether the productivity of this type of worker is high enough to make it profitable to offer a higher wage. In the opposite case, where there is an oversupply of good applicants, a lower wage may be set, at least for new entrants. It is episodes like this that change the levels of market wages and make them responsive to changes in conditions of supply of workers to firms and demand by firms for workers.

In the presence of competition, it makes economic sense for employers to pay attention to the market wage when setting their own wages, and, in the absence of discrimination, it is generally conducive to economic efficiency that firms operate in this way.

Let us now consider how individual firms might react to market wages, when, as in the example given in the previous section, these wages are the result of other employers' segregation of male and female workers. Let us first consider the Jones Company, which has entry jobs in Occupations A and B to fill. Let us assume, as above, that all men and women in the labor market from which the company draws its workers are capable of doing all of the jobs and, given equal pay, would be indifferent to which job they had.[2]

---

2. There may be a few traditionally male entry-level jobs that there will not be enough women to fill, either because of the physical strength requirements or because socialization has kept women from developing even the rudimentary skills that are needed. However, there are an enormous number of jobs for which this is not the case—plumber's helper, assembly line worker, and so on.

Let us assume that the Jones Company is the exception to the general practice of sex segregation and, unlike other employers, does not take into account the sex of the applicant in deciding whether to hire and where to place that applicant. We may now ask what wages the Jones Company might reasonably set. One possibility would be to ascertain market wages for both occupations, and to set wages accordingly. This behavior would set the jobs held in other companies by males (Occupation A) at a higher rate of pay than jobs held by females in other companies (Occupation B). The Jones Company would end up with both males and females in Occupation A—the male-type jobs—and all or mostly females in Occupation B—the female-type jobs. Males applying to Jones who were not offered A jobs could probably do better elsewhere, and few would accept employment by Jones in B jobs. As time went on, the females employed by Jones in B jobs would ask for transfers to the A jobs in Jones, and if they were given preference over outside applicants, these jobs would also become all-female.

A second, and more reasonable, possibility for the Jones Company would be to set wages of all entry jobs at the same level. If it followed the procedure outlined above, raising or lowering wages according to the supply of acceptable applicants, it would set them close to the "market" level of wages in B jobs. This would be profit-maximizing behavior.[3] In this case, we would see very few men in any of Jones's entry jobs. If for some reason Jones set the uniform wage at something near the market wage in A jobs, we would expect to see men and women scattered at random throughout all entry jobs. No matter how Jones set its wages, however, we would expect that if we saw males doing certain jobs, we would also see females doing those jobs in numbers at least proportional to their representation in the applicant flow.

We now come to consider the Jones Company's position with respect to Title VII. It can be argued that however Jones set its wages, the situation in the entry jobs would not seem to support a Title VII claim of discrimination. Some of its occupations may be integrated, and some would be all-female (males rejecting employment opportunities with the company because of the low wages it paid). There would be no difference in the way the firm treated males and females, and no adverse impact on the females. While Jones's wage setting would be influenced by market wages, it would probably find it profitable to depart from the wage structure typical of discriminating employers.

Let us contrast the situation of the Smith Company, all of whose entry jobs could be done by all members of the labor force, but whose A jobs are all or virtually all held by males and whose B jobs are entirely held by females. The Smith Company decides on its wages by amassing information

3. In fact, the company's failure to follow this profit-maximizing behavior could be taken as *prima facie* evidence of discrimination.

on wages paid in A and B jobs by other companies, the vast majority of whom look more like Smith than Jones with respect to their pattern of use of male and female workers.

Under our assumptions, we must conclude that the Smith Company (like other firms with the same staffing patterns) *is* paying attention to the sex of its applicants in deciding which entry job to place them in. Its exclusive assignment of women to B jobs would be said to have an adverse impact on women because of the fact of the segregation itself, even if the firm set equal wages for Occupations A and B. If, in addition to the segregation, the firm has assigned the B jobs a lower wage than the A jobs, the assignment of women predominantly to the former affects adversely their present income. This effect is additional to the adverse effect of their segregated status, which, for example, may deny to women male-type jobs with training opportunities that lead to still higher wages. The segregation, in addition, allows the employer to pay men and women different wages under color of merely following the market.

The Jones Company example suggests that a nondiscriminatory employer who was rational and profit-maximizing would not have a wage structure that resembles the one adopted by discriminating employers. It further suggests that the Smith Company's wage structure is part and parcel of its segregationist behavior.[4]

Occupational Segregation and Wage Realignment

Why does occupational segregation require wage realignment? Consider the policies of the Smith Company as described above. The company can truthfully say that it has followed the market in its wage-setting practices. However, Smith will go on to say that it has done what supply and demand dictate. This is quite untrue, as we have shown, since the maximization of profit by a nondiscriminatory firm would require entirely different behavior. What is true is that the supply of and demand for labor have been deeply and importantly affected by the practice of excluding women from all jobs in Occupation A, and this has affected wage structures in discriminating

---

4. The courts are not yet clear on this issue. See, e.g., the language of the decision in *IUE* v. *Westinghouse Electric Corp.*, 455 F. Supp. 392, 396 (N.D.W.V. 1977), *rev'd* 23 FEP Cases, 588 (3d Cir. 1980):

> Thus, one reason for requiring equal work in order to invoke the Equal Pay Act was to preclude any massive job reevaluation by the Government in the Federal Court forum. Such a criteria [*sic*] is laudable for that purpose, as the Federal Courts should not be involved in "second-guessing" economic decisions better left to management and labor.

Reversal was based on an interpretation of the Bennett Amendment similar to that of the Court in *County of Washington* v. *Gunther*, 452 U.S. 161 (1981).

firms. Smith has excluded women from such jobs and is certainly liable on this account under Title VII.[5] The question, however, is what might be the appropriate remedy within the firm for this violation.

We might say that the only remedy was to permit women to apply for future openings in A jobs, and to try to find women who had been turned away from such jobs in this firm in the past.[6] Obviously, this would do little or no good for the women within the firm who occupied jobs in B.[7] Under our assumption, they were as capable of doing A jobs as were the men who were given those jobs in the first place, and they continue to be as capable. To leave them at a lower wage would be to allow the employer to continue to treat them worse than people who, under Title VII, should have been indistinguishable from them.

The wage structure in the Smith Company results from discrimination—from Smith's discriminatory behavior in mimicking the discriminatory behavior of others. A realignment of Smith's wage structure to fit the economic facts of the postulated case and eliminate the effects within the company of discrimination would establish equality of wages in the two occupations. This realignment would produce a wage structure identical with the structure produced in the absence of discrimination.

Indeed, when all employers have been forced or persuaded to give up their practice of excluding women from Occupation A, the wages in every establishment will reflect the wage structure of a nondiscriminating market, which in this case would mean equality of wages in both occupations. Requiring the particular employer under suit to realign its wages merely requires it to do what all employers will sooner or later be forced or induced to do.[8]

---

5. See, e.g., *Shultz* v. *Wheaton Glass Co.*, 421 F.2d 259 (3d Cir.), *cert. denied*, 398 U.S. 905 (1970); *Wetzel* v. *Liberty Insurance Co.*, 508 F.2d 239 (3d Cir.), *cert. denied*, 421 U.S. 1011 (1975).

6. In devising a remedy, courts have traditionally required that access to all jobs be opened to workers of both sexes, but any wage realignment has been limited to that resulting from a determination that the men's and women's jobs involved equal work and hence required equal pay. For example, in *Laffey* v. *Northwest Orient Airlines*, 567 F.2d 429 (D.C. Cir. 1976), the requirement that pursers (male) on international flights be responsible for customs documents was insufficient to make their job unequal to that of a stewardess (female), especially in view of the fact that pursers were also paid more on domestic flights; the airline was required to pay stewardesses at the higher rate, since the Equal Pay Act forbids a remedy that would lower the pay of the higher-paid group.

7. They would, of course, have the same remedies available to them as those not employed by the firm; if they had been turned away from A jobs or discouraged from applying, they would be eligible for future openings. However, that would probably require them to give up acquired seniority as well as the skills developed in Occupation B in order to start at the beginning in Occupation A, and therefore they would be disadvantaged in comparison to the men who have advanced to higher wages on the basis of their experience in Occupation A.

8. We may compare the situation of a firm that shares its labor market with firms practicing race and sex discrimination with that of a firm that shares its labor market

A further consideration in suggesting that remedies include wage realignment in addition to improved future access is that the cost to the employer of merely providing future access to all jobs is minimal, if not nonexistent, so that the access remedy alone has virtually no deterrent effect.[9]

The Bearing of *Gunther* and *Westinghouse*

The case of *Gunther versus the County of Washington* concerns salaries paid to male and female jail attendants. The County of Washington had conducted a survey of wages for jobs in the community comparable to those of men and women jail attendants, the latter of whom were also assigned certain clerical duties. Although the county's own evaluation showed that

---

with firms violating the minimum wage law. A firm in the latter situation would be violating the law if it based its wages on what its fellow employers were paying. Such a firm, should it refrain from following the "market wage" set by "supply and demand," would undoubtedly suffer competitive disadvantage by refraining from violating the law itself. In a somewhat similar fashion, a firm that shares a labor market with discriminating firms should not be able to use as a defense that it was merely following their lead in setting wage differentials, if it forces women to accept those differentials through the mechanism of occupational segregation.

9. For a discussion of how wage realignment is to be accomplished—whether through a job evaluation scheme, an assessment of employee qualifications, or other means—see Principles Governing Wage Realignment, below. Most equal pay cases have looked at jobs rather than at people. See, e.g., *DiSalvo* v. *Chamber of Commerce of Greater Kansas City*, 416 F. Supp. 844, 853 (W.D.Mo. 1976), *aff'd*, 568 F.2d 593 (8th Cir. 1978), where the court said, "[T]he crucial issue is not what skills are possessed, but whether the duties actually performed require or utilize those additional skills." In contrast, the court in *Calage* v. *University of Tennessee*, 544 F.2d 297 (6th Cir. 1976), appeared to base its approval of a difference in salary at least in part on the differences in qualifications of the incumbents.

In *Kyriazi* v. *Western Electric Co.*, 461 F. Supp. 894 (D.N.J. 1978), where entry-level positions required virtually no qualifications but the employer consistently hired women into lower grades than men, the court had no trouble finding a violation of Title VII. However, determining what wage loss resulted—that is, how to adjust wages to negate the effects of occupational segregation—was more difficult.

On the other hand, given that discrimination has caused the employees to suffer a loss, the principle of Title VII is that they be "made whole" (*Albemarle Paper Co.* v. *Moody*, 422 U.S. 405 [1975]). As the court in *Rock* v. *Norfolk and Western Railway Co.*, 473 F.2d 1350, 1354 (4th Cir. 1973), said: "The rule is well-established that, where discrimination violations of the Act have been found the remedy granted must eliminate all residual effects of past discrimination to the greatest extent practical." Clearly the past, and indeed continuing, occupational segregation and resulting discrimination in compensation can be remedied only by a realignment on an entirely new basis where whether the position is a "woman's" or "man's" job does not enter into the computation of compensation in any way. This is essentially the notion of "front pay," an adjustment of wages that continues until the job structure has so aligned itself that occupational segregation ceases to exist. See, e.g., *James* v. *Stockham Valves and Fittings Co.*, 559 F.2d 310, 358 (5th Cir. 1977); *Patterson* v. *American Tobacco Co.*, 535 F.2d 257, 269 (4th Cir. 1976).

the women's jobs should be compensated at 95 percent of the rate paid to the men, the county paid them 70 percent of the male rate.

The Supreme Court held that it was not necessary to show that the men's and women's jobs were equal; that is, the coverages of the Equal Pay Act and Title VII are not coextensive.[10] The Court did not rule on the notion of "comparable worth"; no attention was paid to the value of the work to the employer or to the employees' qualifications. The essence of the decision was that if sex was impermissibly used as a factor in the wage-setting procedure, then Title VII was violated.

Similarly, in *IUE v. Westinghouse Electric Corporation*,[11] sex played a role in the wage-setting scheme. Originally, men in predominantly male jobs were paid a supplement over the wage paid to women in jobs with the same point rating, a policy that was discriminatory on its face. When Westinghouse was forced to end this practice, the women's jobs were simply reclassified downward, and work force segregation remained essentially unchanged.[12] In the *Westinghouse* decision the Court held wage realignment

---

10. In deciding that Title VII claims of sex discrimination in compensation are not limited to those cognizable under the Equal Pay Act, the Court said that "only differentials attributable to the four affirmative defenses of the Equal Pay Act are 'authorized' by the Act within the meaning of the Bennett Amendment" (452 U.S. 161, 171 [1981]). The Court did not reach the merits of the plaintiffs' claim; it addressed only the scope of Title VII, declaring that

> Respondents' claim is not based on the controversial concept of "comparable worth," under which plaintiffs might claim increased compensation on the basis of a comparison of the intrinsic worth or difficulty of their job with that of other jobs in the same organization or community. Rather, respondents seek to prove, by direct evidence, that their wages were depressed because of intentional sex discrimination, consisting of setting the wage scale for female guards, but not for male guards, at a level lower than its own survey of outside markets and the worth of the jobs warranted. The narrow question in this case is whether such a claim is precluded by the last sentence of § 703(h) of Title VII, called the "Bennett Amendment." (452 U.S. at 166, footnotes omitted)

The "comparable worth" theory takes several forms, but in essence the idea is to eliminate wage differentials due to sex segregation of the work force, whatever the source of that segregation. The "worth" of a job would be determined by the skill, training, responsibility, and similar factors required, independent of "market factors"; in particular, comparable worth as an attempt to bring the wages in female-type jobs such as nursing more into line with wages in male-type jobs such as engineering. The Court in *Gunther* specifically disclaimed any intent to decide whether Title VII embraces such a theory. Our version of wage realignment is based on similar principles—that is, that differentiation based on job segregation constitutes illegal discrimination, but only in those cases where an employer is culpable, at least in part, for the segregation. However, that the employer is culpable may follow simply from the pattern of setting wages. The short-term profit-maximizing strategy would be to pay all workers at the "female" job rate, in which case the work force would not be segregated, as has been shown above.

11. 631 F.2d 1094 (3d Cir. 1980), *cert. denied*, 49 U.S.L.W. 3954 (22 June 1981).

12. For example, grades 1–4 had 1 male and 182 females; grades 5–13 had 75 males and 31 females (30 in grades 5 and 6 and 1 in grade 9).

to be necessary because the wage structure, while ostensibly based on a job classification scheme, was tainted by the company's discriminatory acts. The realignment required in *Westinghouse* went beyond establishing equal pay for jobs classified by the company at the same grade level. Since a violation of Title VII had been established, the remedy included scrutiny of the grades assigned by the company to each job at issue in the case to determine whether it was or was not discriminatory.

The ruling in *Westinghouse*—that a change in grade in combination with sex segregation constituted sex discrimination—can be extended to cases where the initial establishment of a grade or salary level is combined with sex segregation. Under such an extension, the principle underlying the *Westinghouse* decision has wide applicability. A realignment of wages would be required in the presence of job segregation and resulting disparate average wages for men and women, whether or not a history of purposeful wage discrimination like that in *Westinghouse* could be established.[13] All that would be necessary would be a showing that the defendant, like the Smith Company in our simplified example, (1) had segregated its work force and (2) had taken its cue from the action of whatever outside forces are in play to set pay scales for females in the female-type jobs at a lower rate, so that (3) the differential in wages between men's occupations and women's occupations, though resembling the practice of most other companies (who currently discriminate), would be different from the differential a nondiscriminating company might establish between the same occupations.

In other words, the discrimination of having women in lower-paying jobs than similarly qualified men should be sufficient to establish the employers' liability for compensation claims under Title VII. The remedy of opening up access to all jobs but maintaining the existing wage structure is inadequate. To continue to pay according to the job's former status as a male- or female-type job constitutes continuing sex discrimination.[14] To

---

13. That is, in *Westinghouse* a conscious decision was taken to pay less for women's jobs than for men's jobs with the same point rating. However, we contend that no showing of such deliberate discrimination in the setting of wage rates should be required to establish liability in the presence of an employer-segregated work force and accompanying sex-based wage differentials.

14. This was the view of the court in *Brennan v. Sears, Roebuck and Co.*, 410 F. Supp. 84, 100 (N.D. Iowa 1976):

The disparity of job grades regarding division managers of the Fort Dodge store's men's and women's clothing divisions, positions which have in the past been held by men and women, respectively, indicates to the Court that at least *as to those* positions, the sex factor has influenced their grading. Therefore, were the Court directly faced with an existing pay discrepancy involving the Fort Dodge store division managers of men's and women's clothing, with the job grades of the defendant's plan being urged as a defense, that defense would be rejected. The nearly systematic placement of women-oriented jobs in a grade lower than the male-oriented jobs would force the Court to conclude that the grading had been affected by [the traditional notion of women's roles].

See also *Corning Glass Works v. Brennan*, 417 U.S. 188 (1974).

realign the wages is equivalent to the requirement of "front pay" that courts have in the past mandated.

An employer's defense based on an appeal to market forces or supply and demand should not be allowed to excuse it from the consequences of its own actions in segregating its work force; we have shown how "market forces" may discriminatorily influence wage rates and how discriminating employers both segregate and mimic the wage practices of other discriminating firms.[15] That such discriminating firms are currently in the majority and thus dominate "the market" is evidence that progress under Title VII requires more far-reaching remedies and deterrences, rather than a validation of the wage practices of segregating employers. "Everyone does it" has never been an acceptable defense of illegal employment practices.[16]

Our proposal for the application of Title VII to situations not covered by the Equal Pay Act has the advantage of focusing on the evil—occupational segregation and the accompanying wage differentials. By requiring wage realignment only when an employer has practiced occupational segregation, we exclude certain cases. If we have an all-female or all-male firm in which executives and secretaries are all of a single sex, we would not suggest that a realignment of wages is required.[17] Nor would realignment be proposed in cases in which the firm was not single-sex but in which the male-female division among employees was roughly the same across job categories, or in cases where male-type jobs were integrated by sex and female-type jobs were not.

Principles Governing Wage Realignment

Dropping the simplifying assumption that all workers can do all jobs means that we need an economically and legally adequate way of deciding what the realigned pay structure should look like. The proponents of limiting the scope of application of employment discrimination laws often cite with horror the prospect of government invasion of every workplace in an effort to achieve a massive restructuring of the economy.[18] However, this is not what is contemplated under the current proposal.

---

15. See, e.g., *Brennan* v. *Victoria Bank and Trust Co.*, 493 F.2d 896 (5th Cir. 1974). That the women "choose" the lower-paying jobs is not an adequate defense. In *James* v. *Stockham Valves and Fittings Co.*, 559 F.2d 310, 334 (5th Cir. 1977), the court refused to allow the defendant to rely on self-classification by the minority group as a justification for the occupational segregation, mentioning among other factors the perceived futility of seeking better jobs when the incumbents of those positions were all white males.

16. See note 8 above.

17. Obviously, if the other sex were excluded by the employer, a claim of denial of access would be cognizable.

18. Much of the debate accompanying the passage of the Equal Pay Act focused on the necessity to keep the Department of Labor from interfering in job evaluation

If an employer has been found guilty of practicing occupational segregation, every aspect of its personnel policies has already been quite thoroughly investigated. Once liability has been established, the further intrusion involved in bringing about an unbiased realignment of wages is relatively slight. Moreover, although the subsequent effects of realignment may be widespread, the immediate attention is focused only on the guilty employers, who can have little justification for continuing their present wage-setting practices, tainted as they are.

Nonetheless, it is evident that one reason for judges' reluctance to decide for the plaintiffs in cases asking for wage realignment under Title VII is their disinclination to supervise the process of realignment and their lack of confidence in their ability to distinguish, in a way that would hold up on appeal, between plans acceptable and those unacceptable under Title VII.

---

and the so-called market process. This was the rationale of *Lemons* v. *City and County of Denver*, No. 76-W-1156 (D. Colo. 1978), in which plaintiffs unsuccessfully sought pay for nurses comparable to that of engineers (and others with training of a similar duration and responsibilities of a similar magnitude) was unsuccessfully sought. Similarly, in *Christensen* v. *Iowa*, 563 F.2d 353 (8th Cir. 1977), the court abjured a role in adjusting wages that were held to be based on market factors. However, in *Corning Glass Works* v. *Brennan*, 417 U.S. 188 (1974), the Court concluded that the illegality of a pay differential originally based on the fact that men would not work at night for the rate paid women in the day was not cured by opening the night shift to women; instead, the day shift, which had been all-female due to market factors, had to be raised to the night rate. See also *Brennan* v. *Victoria Bank and Trust Co.*, 493 F.2d 896, 902 (5th Cir. 1974): "the fact that a woman may be willing to work for less than a man is not a valid basis for discrimination in compensation"; *Hodgson* v. *Security National Bank of Sioux City*, 460 F.2d 57, 63 (8th Cir. 1972): the "traditional notion that women, because of their principal roles as wives and mothers, must occupy an employment status second to men" does not justify different wages.

Job evaluation schemes normally take into account such things as the amount of time required to learn the job, the number of people supervised, educational level, working conditions, and physical and mental effort required for the job. Points are assigned to various factors to determine the wages, usually based on references to wages for a few key jobs that may have been set by comparison with "market wages" for those occupations. Since there is inherent subjectivity in evaluating a job, there is an opportunity for bias to enter in. For example, the training and experience required, the authority exercised, the level of responsibility, the lack of direct supervision, and other factors might indicate that a job usually called "executive secretary" should rate as high in a job evaluation scheme as what is usually thought of as a middle-management job; however, that is rarely found to be the case in actual evaluation schemes. Moreover, job evaluation schemes may be inherently biased by, for example, giving more points to temporary physical effort than to fatigue factors, to the advantage of men. See, e.g., *Hodgson* v. *Daisy Manufacturing Co.*, 317 F. Supp. 538 (D. Ark. 1970), *aff'd* in part and *rev'd* in part (on other grounds), 495 F.2d 823 (8th Cir. 1971). See also Ruth G. Blumrosen, "Wage Discrimination, Job Segregation and Title VII of the Civil Rights Act of 1964," *University of Michigan Journal of Law Reform* 12 (1979): 397 for a discussion of the discrimination inherent in job evaluation schemes.

Therefore, the arguments in favor of orders of realignment in certain cases are incomplete without a set of workable guidelines on the realignments required by these arguments.

A reasonable criterion to use in guiding realignment is that the realigned wages ought to have a pattern similar to the one they would have in a labor market in which sex discrimination was absent. When one considers the implementation of such a criterion in complicated cases in which there are many types of occupations and not everyone can do every job, a thought experiment might be helpful. Suppose that one day all women were to disappear from the labor market, in the process vacating all the jobs they had held. Assume that for each woman who left, a man of identical talent and knowledge entered the labor market.

Some of the newly entered men would presumably be hired to replace the vanished women in previously female-type jobs. Others might go to work in male-type jobs for which they were competent. We can now ask ourselves what the occupational wage pattern might look like in our reconstituted labor market, in which employers have been forced to give up sex discrimination by the disappearance of women on whom to inflict it.

As a first approximation, each of the previously female-type occupations would assume the wage of the male-type occupation closest to it in terms of worker requirements. Each such pair of jobs would have a common supply of labor, namely, all those who are competent to perform the pair of jobs and who are excluded by lack of competence from higher-wage jobs. A similar wage for any two paired jobs would make sense, exactly as in the simpler case described above, where there was only one pair of occupations. What would force through this first-order adjustment would be the difficulty in recruiting labor for the jobs formerly performed by women, since the men whom employers would be forced under our assumption to seek for those jobs would have alternative options not available to women (in the paired jobs, and in other previously all-male jobs requiring lower skills but paying higher wages than the previously female jobs).

As time went on, a second-order adjustment might be anticipated. We would expect that the number of workers whom managers would want to keep employed in the previously all-female jobs would decline because of the new necessity of paying them higher wages. This would cause a market realignment in which wages would sink for certain pairs of jobs, most significantly those in which the previously female job in the pair paid a great deal less than the previously male job, and in which the work force for the former was much larger than that for the latter.

Even later, a third-order adjustment would occur, with a redefinition of the duties of and requirements for particular jobs, as employers adjusted to the new wage pattern and rationalized their production processes to take account of it.

Wage Realignment and Job Evaluation

The realignment of wages in actual cases under the rubric of "comparable worth" would be the administered analog to the first stage in the process of adjustment to a sex-blind labor market described in the last section. The second-order and third-order adjustments we have described could be expected to follow along later through the operation of market forces, rather than through administered changes.

In our discussion of the first-order adjustment process, the essential element was the grouping of jobs into sets that could draw from a common pool. Practical methods of doing this must surely have a great deal in common with job evaluation schemes in wide use in American business. These schemes describe jobs in terms of their requirements for generalized abilities. They work by assigning, for each job under consideration, a numerical score to each kind of "ability" proportional to the amount or the quality of that ability that the job is assumed to require. The ability scores are then added up into a total score for each job. The reduction of a highly circumstantial job description to a single numerical score facilitates the comparison of jobs whose duties differ considerably in a qualitative way. Thus, the implementation of a job evaluation scheme in a comparable worth study takes the place of the pairing of male and female occupations in the illustrative discussion above. In principle, at any rate, the two procedures are quite similar.

Our analysis has put emphasis on worker characteristics rather than job characteristics. For at least some of the job evaluation schemes, the job characteristics included in the evaluation index have been chosen consciously or unconsciously by the designers of these systems because they imply the requirement for certain abilities in the incumbent worker. For example, the widely used Hay System awards points for the knowledge and problem-solving ability required of and the independence exercised by the worker.

Before any particular scheme is employed as a tool of analysis in a comparable worth case, it must be amended to exclude sex bias in job evaluation. It is doubtful whether any existing scheme could be used without amendment in this direction. (As an example, training material given in the past to Hay System job evaluators equates the skill necessary to operate a mimeograph machine with the skill necessary to "operate a typewriter.") Certainly, a great deal of further research would be required before any particular job evaluation system could be endorsed for the purposes of wage realignment. However, we can have some confidence that an appropriately designed scheme, not in principle different from job evaluation schemes currently in wide use in American business, could contribute to the achievement of a first-order approximation to the pattern that would emerge after discrimination had been ended.

Conclusion

If we assume, as did the Court in *Gunther*, that Title VII is applicable to cases of discrimination in compensation in other than equal work contexts, then we are led to the conclusion that occupational segregation by an employer requires wage realignment as a remedy. Once the employer has unlawfully channeled its employees into sex-typed jobs, Title VII does not permit compensation structures based on sex segregation in the market, which has the result that the "male jobs" are more highly paid than the "female jobs." Simply opening up jobs to all employees or applicants is an insufficient remedy for occupational segregation, in view of the courts' preference for nondisplacement of incumbents and other factors. What is needed is for wages to be realigned so that compensation levels do not reflect whether the job is a "male" or a "female" one.

Realignments based on a concept that goes beyond the simplicity of equal work for equal pay may seem to be a step into uncharted and difficult terrain. Yet the principles that can govern realignment are quite well known. The opening provided by *Gunther* may well permit the application of a nondiscriminatory wage structure to achieve a remedy on the wage side in cases of occupational segregation by an employer.

PART FOUR

Legislation and Litigation

11

Canada's Equal Pay for Work of Equal Value Law

RITA CADIEUX

When Parliament adopted the Canadian Human Rights Act in 1977, it introduced a bold new element into the long struggle of Canadian women for equality in the work force—a provision for equal pay for work of equal value, or, as it is usually termed in the United States, "comparable worth."[1] No longer could employers get away with paying women less by hiving them off, deliberately or not, in different classifications from men doing essentially the same work. Now women would be entitled to the same rewards as men wherever their jobs involved equal skills, effort, responsibility, and conditions.

Women's groups were jubilant, of course. But Canadians in general seemed scarcely to notice the change at the time. One might have expected heated debate when the matter came before the House of Commons Committee on Justice and Legal Affairs. The objections raised there were minimal. Tremendous support for the concept was expressed by representatives of women's organizations and major unions.

Parliament's intentions are clearly set out in Section 11 of the act (Appendix I). But there is a world of difference between adopting sound legislation and putting it into effect. One of the first tasks faced by members of the new Canadian Human Rights Commission in the months before the

---

1. In matters of employment, the Canadian Human Rights Act applies to the 11 percent of the work force that falls under federal jurisdiction. Other workers are under provincial jurisdiction, and only Québec among the ten provinces has enshrined the equal value concept in its human rights law. The "Canadian experience" related here is thus limited to the federal scene.

act came into force in March 1978 was to set up the mechanisms for its implementation. We took our motto from Ron Basford, then minister of justice, who had told the Commons committee considering the act:

> There will no doubt be some problems and, of course, some provincial jurisdictions have said that the problems are such that we should not adopt the concept. The federal government has adopted a different approach: that we should legislate the principle, and through the Commission and through its efforts at setting out guidelines, solve those problems.

Preparation for Implementation

Our first step was the preparation of a preliminary paper by the secretary-general of the commission, Martha Hynna, which raised questions about the application of the concept of equal value and stated the concerns of some of the organizations that would be affected. The paper outlined a number of ways of dealing with these questions and concerns, including the establishment of a task force representing various interests to present the commission with policy options. This was the course we adopted.

The chief commissioner asked me to chair the task force, which was composed of representatives of employers in the private and public sectors, unions, and women's groups and a legal advisor. The task force met during the month of December 1977 and presented its report at the end of February 1978. One of its recommendations was that "consultations should take place with a representative sample of employers, employer groups, employee associations, unions and women's groups, regarding these recommendations and the supportive reasoning before any guidelines or policy bulletins are issued." The commission undertook to organize such consultations and circulated the task force report as widely as possible to women's groups and to all employers and unions under federal jurisdiction, soliciting comments, suggestions, and briefs. The response was excellent, and questions raised in the report, as well as its recommendations, formed the basis for the discussions during these consultations early in 1978. We were then confident that we understood the concerns of those who were going to be most directly affected by Section 11. There were many concerns. Employers shook their heads over the problems involved in developing measurement techniques to evaluate dissimilar jobs. They resented the idea implicit in Section 11 that they could not continue paying the lowest wages the market would bear for certain jobs. They felt that the law of supply and demand was threatened.

Unions were not as enthusiastic as they might have been, either. Over the years, union negotiators have developed the collective bargaining process on the basis of many separate bargaining units with separate contracts. They had great difficulty reconciling this process with the possibility that wage rates might be arrived at outside the usual negotiations, on the basis of another unit's pay scale. They, too, doubted that dissimilar jobs could be evaluated on a common scale.

Employers' and unions' concerns were with the principle equal pay for work of equal value, not just with the details of implementation. Representatives of women's groups, in contrast, were enthusiastic about the principle; their concern was with effective implementation—in particular, the implementation of the part of Section 11 that allowed the commission to pass guidelines identifying factors that might justify different wages for men and women performing work of equal value. The task force report had identified certain factors that it considered reasonable. For example, a person who had been ill and was now working on a rehabilitation assignment might justifiably be paid at the former level, even though doing work of equal value to someone paid at a lower level, until able to resume his or her former duties. Women's groups were concerned that exceptions like this could be used to perpetuate old injustices. Moreover, they, like employers and unions, were interested in how work would be evaluated and particularly in how skill, effort, responsibility, and conditions of work would be assessed.

The Guidelines and the General Approach to Equal Pay

Following these consultations, the commission felt that it was in a position to rule on these contentious points. Guidelines were approved by the commission and issued in the *Canada Gazette* in September 1978 (Appendix II). These guidelines clarify the criteria set out in the act for determining the value of work—skill, effort, responsibility, and conditions of work—and list seven factors that may justify wage differentials so long as they are applied consistently and equitably to all employees, both male and female.

After this, the commission developed its approach and methodology concurrently with the investigation of complaints. Fortunately, the number of complaints was initially low, allowing us to refine our instruments of investigation. On the other hand, this slow start convinced us of the need to inform women of their rights under the legislation and to demystify the question of equal pay for work of equal value.

The Present Situation

Between March 1978 and November 1983, we received sixty complaints under Section 11, nineteen of which have been dismissed, three withdrawn, and fifteen settled. Twenty-two complaints are still under investigation, and one is awaiting tribunal. Most were group complaints, a good many of them filed by unions on behalf of their members.

These figures by no means represent the full measure of pay discrimination in Canada. The Canadian Human Rights Act applies in matters of employment to only a small part of the work force: the federal public service, employees of federal Crown corporations and agencies, and employees of federally regulated companies (e.g., the transportation and communications industry and banks). Even in this part of the work force, women and men are not yet getting equal pay for work of equal value. Few employers have taken it upon themselves to review their job evaluation and compensation systems and to modify them to comply with the act. It is, therefore, mainly through the complaint process that compliance has been achieved. While a few settlements have had some impact, the legislation has eliminated only a small fraction of existing discrimination in pay between men and women.

Statistics on women's work and pay are similar in Canada and the United States. The trend is the same, and, with a few years' delay, the figures are the same. I need not, therefore, elaborate on the statistics but will merely indicate the dimensions of the pay discrimination problem in Canada. From 1967 to 1977 there was a 70.6 percent increase in the number of women in Canada's labor force, compared with a 25 percent increase in the number of men. Women now account for more than 40 percent of the labor force, and this percentage is constantly growing. Nearly three-quarters of women between twenty-five and forty-four are expected to be in the labor force by 1989, compared with slightly over half at present.

The average salary of women working full-time in Canada is about 62 percent of the average salary of male full-time workers. There are several reasons for this difference, not all of them related to discrimination. What our commission has the power and duty to correct is that part of the difference that can be traced to discrimination on the basis of sex. The following figures suggest that such discrimination is still prevalent. At the end of May 1978, only about one-third of the women with master's degrees were in the $20,000-plus income bracket, compared with more than half the men. The median salary for a woman with a bachelor's degree and no previous work experience was $13,090—less than the $13,270 earned by a man with a one-year college diploma and no experience.[2]

Implementation

How do we proceed with an equal pay complaint? Let us say that a woman notifies the Canadian Human Rights Commission that she thinks she has a complaint. It must first be established that her job and those allied to it are performed mostly by women, and that the jobs with which she wants

---

2. Statistics Canada report, co-sponsored by the Women's Bureau of the Department of Labour: "Higher Education—Hired?" (August 1980).

hers compared are performed mostly by men. We say "mostly," without specifying a percentage, for the obvious reason that an employer could otherwise escape any equal pay complaint by hiring one or two women into the better-paid group.

Next it must be ascertained that the male and female groups in question work for the same employer, work in the same establishment, and come under federal jurisdiction. The definition of "establishment" opens up many problems. Does it mean the same building, the same firm, the same branch, the same region? Normally, we will accept the definition used in the employer's compensation system, so long as that definition is not intended to avoid paying men and women equitably. If the employer pays different rates for the same job in different regions, then the region is the establishment. If the employer uses a uniform scale in all of its workplaces, then the whole organization will be the establishment. The purpose of the equal pay section of the act is not to correct regional disparities, but differences in pay that are due to sex. And it may be noted that our legislation clearly states that putting one group in one place and another group in another place, so as to claim that they are in separate establishments, is not acceptable.

After preliminary investigation confirms that the complainant's situation can be dealt with as an equal pay complaint, the process of comparing the value of the jobs begins. The employer, the union, the complainant, and the human rights commission are all involved. First, the complainant (who may be an individual, a group, a union, or the commission itself) must clearly specify which groups are to be compared. Once the comparison group is identified, a sample of positions at all levels in the two groups is chosen. Although the sample is drawn at random, the employer and the union are invited to comment on its composition.

An exact picture of the various jobs is then drawn up by the commission's compensation experts. It is based on the actual work done, not on a paper job description. Investigators visit the workplace, see the work being done, interview the employees about their tasks, and talk to the employer. They make their assessment on the basis of the skill, effort, and responsibility required and the conditions under which the work is performed—the four criteria spelled out in the commission's guidelines. Each criterion can be broken down into components, and a value is assigned to each component. The relative value of two jobs emerges from the comparison. This is certainly not a new way of establishing "value": different categories of jobs are already implicitly or explicitly compared in every compensation system. What is different, under the act, is that internal equity is established without reference to the marketplace. The so-called market value is often distorted by society's perception of women's work as having limited value.

If it is found that the complainant group is being underpaid, a settlement is arrived at. Proposals and counterproposals are made as to the most equitable way of rectifying the situation. If it is not possible to reach an agreement through this process, the commission may decide to invoke a human rights tribunal, which, like a court, minutely reviews the job evaluation and, if it finds that sex discrimination exists, orders that the situation be corrected and that the complainants be compensated.[3] A tribunal's orders can be enforced—or challenged—in the federal court.

While the impact of the legislation has so far been limited, the publicity given to settlements has served to raise the awareness of both employers and employees. Some settlements have been considerable. These are summarized below.

Leona Mollis v. *the Treasury Board*

Our first important settlement, achieved early in 1980, involved nurses in two federal penitentiaries located in the Atlantic provinces. The complaint was initially filed by Leona Mollis, who claimed that her salary and the salaries of other nurses, all of whom were women, were lower than the salaries of "health care officers," all of whom were men, although they did work of equal value.

An examination of the job descriptions showed that the one for the health care officers was more complete and at least twice as long as that for the nurses. The choice of words used to describe the two positions differed, leaving the impression that health care officers had more responsible positions. But interviews with workers in the two groups, using the job descriptions as a starting point, showed that the descriptions were not accurate. The nurses and the health care officers performed the same work. Indeed, the nurses were better qualified but worse paid.

The resolution of this complaint affected only six nurses, but the commission enjoined the employer, in this case the Treasury Board of the federal government, to examine salaries in all penitentiaries where the same situation existed. This resulted in a subsequent salary adjustment for eighteen more nurses. Overall, the settlement involved an average wage adjustment of $1,000 annually for each of the twenty-four nurses affected and retroactive pay to April 1978 totaling $18,000.

When a new collective agreement was concluded for the male health care officers, an additional thirty nurses were placed in a discriminatory pay

---

3. Under the Canadian Human Rights Act, once a complaint has been substantiated, a voluntary settlement is attempted through a conciliation process. If a settlement is not achieved, the commission may appoint a human rights tribunal. Section 39(1) states: "The Commission may, at any stage after the filing of a complaint, appoint a Human Rights Tribunal to inquire into a complaint." Most of the time, however, tribunals are appointed when voluntary settlements agreeable to the parties and the commission have been impossible to achieve. Human rights tribunals are appointed by the commission from a panel of prospective members established and maintained by the governor in council.

situation. The Treasury Board therefore agreed to adjust their salaries to restore equality. The average adjustment was $200 per nurse.

In this case men and women were actually performing the same tasks. We have since achieved settlements in cases where the work performed by the complainants was different from the work of the comparison group.

Public Service Alliance of Canada v. Treasury Board
(The Librarians' Case)

The Public Service Alliance of Canada (PSAC), a union of government employees, lodged a complaint on behalf of members of the Library Services group (LS), 66 percent of whom are women, alleging that they were performing work of equal value to that of members of the predominantly male Historical Research group (HR), but were not receiving equivalent pay. This was the first complaint under Section 11 for which an intergroup comparison of employees performing dissimilar work had to be made.

Investigation of the complaint posed a number of problems. The employer used a separate evaluation plan to measure the value of jobs in each group, and neither plan was suitable for an intergroup comparison. So it was necessary to find a plan that would measure the value of the full range of jobs in both groups. The complainant, the respondent, and the commission agreed to use the Aiken Plan (a nine factor point rating system) with modifications to remove obvious sex biases.

Since there were more than 700 positions in the two groups, it was not feasible to examine each one; nor was it possible to make direct comparisons between positions. A sample of 25 HR and 31 LS positions was drawn for study. Job data were collected by means of questionnaires and interviews with incumbents of the positions and/or their supervisors. The jobs were then rated by a commission evaluation committee. Agreed ratings were obtained for all of the positions whose incumbents had responded, and these were related to salary data. Because the commencement dates of the LS and HR contracts did not coincide, salary figures were prorated over a twelve-month period to obtain comparable figures for the two groups.

Even with a sample of 56 positions, it was not possible to make a direct position-to-position comparison to determine whether there was discrimination and, if so, to what extent. The statistical method of regression analysis was used to make this determination. To this end, each position was plotted on a graph with midpoint salaries and evaluation points as the axes. Regression lines were drawn for each set of data points as shown in Figure 11-1. The vertical distance between the two lines at the average LS rating (292 points) is a measure of the average amount of discrimination for the group.

To obtain the amount required to eliminate discrimination at each level of the LS group, an average point rating for all positions at each level was

Figure 11-1

Comparison of Salaries Paid to Members of the Library Services (X) and Historical Research (O) Groups

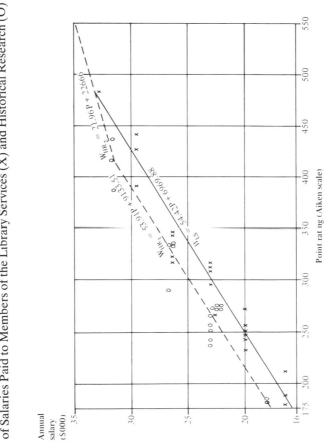

Note: Salaries are at midpoint of range. Not all data points are shown. For Library Services group, Wages = ($54.42)(points) + $6,969.88; r^2 = .945. For Historical Research group, to 425 points, Wages = ($53.91)(points) + $9,133.51; r^2 = .949. For Historical Research group, 425 to 550 points, Wages = ($21.96)(points) + $22,666.

Source: Canadian Human Rights Commission.

calculated. In graphic terms, the distance between the points and the HR salary line represents the amount. In mathematical terms, the average ratings were substituted in the HR salary equation and the result subtracted from the present LS salary at each level. (These data are presented in both forms in Figure 11-2.)

The analysis showed that the librarians' complaint was justified. As a result, their salaries were adjusted by up to $2,500 a year, and back pay of up to $5,900 was paid to each of them. Altogether, the salaries of 470 librarians were adjusted for a total of $2.3 million, including retroactivity to 1 March 1978, the date the act came into effect. Adjustments were also paid to members of the LS group who were employed at any time between 1 March 1978 and the date of the decision. Those who had retired or resigned had to apply in writing to the Treasury Board within six months of the decision in order to receive the retroactive increase. The ongoing cost of the LS settlement is approximately $900,000 per annum.

Following this settlement, there has been a voluntary wage settlement along similar lines for approximately fifty librarians employed by the Library of Parliament. A recent agreement between the National Research Council and its librarians can be seen as another effect of our settlement in this case. The negotiated agreement contained provision for the payment of equalization adjustments to the librarians.

The British Columbia Telephone Company

Another case worth mentioning involves the British Columbia Telephone Company. When the complaint was filed, the company had separate job descriptions and separate pay scales for building servicemen and building servicewomen, with lower rates of pay for the female group. The investigation showed that while certain duties were different, the work performed by the two groups was of equal value. The commission asked the employer and the union to get rid of the discriminatory differences in their next collective agreement. They did so, and the commission approved the settlement of the complaint. Under the new collective agreement, a single pay scale integrating male and female job descriptions applies to all employees in that category. New employees, whether male or female, will start at the same level.

As this settlement shows, the commission uses the collective bargaining route to settle equal pay complaints whenever possible. In such cases the settlement must be approved by the commission, as stipulated in the act.

Public Service Alliance of Canada v. *Treasury Board* (The General Services Case)

On 12 December 1979 the PSAC filed a complaint on behalf of the food, laundry, and miscellaneous personnel services subgroups of the federal

Figure 11-2

Library Services–Historical Research Complaint Adjustment of Salaries

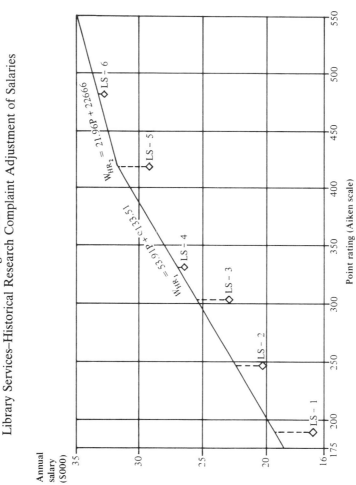

Note: Library Services wages were increased to the wage line for the Historical Research group. Annual adjustments for each group amounted to: LS-1 (189 points) $2,345; LS-2 (249 points) $2,237; LS-3 (302 points) $2,356; LS-4 (330 points) $345; LS-5 (418 points) $2,122; and LS-6 (480 points) $366.
Source: Canadian Human Rights Commission.

government's general services group. The PSAC alleged that its members in these subgroups, who were mostly women, were being paid less than workers in four comparable subgroups composed mostly of men.

The employees are distributed over twenty-two geographic zones, with up to thirteen levels in each zone. The classification system establishes that at any given level, regardless of occupational grouping, all general services employees are performing work of equal value. However, within each zone and at each level, the seven groups were each paid at a different rate. The investigation revealed that, with few exceptions, the four male-dominated groups were paid at higher rates than the three female-dominated groups.

The commission substantiated the complaint in May 1980 and asked the complainant and the respondent to come up with a proposal that would eliminate pay disparities in their next collective agreement, which was about to be negotiated. At the same time, the commission instructed its staff to begin seeking a settlement.

Representatives of the PSAC and the Treasury Board met several times in 1980. They also met with the commission's equal pay specialists to discuss possible methods of arriving at a settlement but were unable to reach one that was acceptable to all parties. The Treasury Board originally took the position that if the salaries of the female-dominated groups were adjusted to those of the lowest-paid male-dominated group, discrimination based on sex would be eliminated. The complainant, on the other hand, wanted the female-dominated groups to get the rate paid to the highest-paid subgroup. In early March 1981 the Treasury Board made another proposal based on the "averaging" concept—female-dominated subgroups would receive an increase at each level and in each zone corresponding to the percentage difference between the average pay rates of the male- and female-dominated groups.

This $13.6 million proposal was rejected by both the commission and the PSAC. The commission felt that the proposal would leave men and women performing work of equal value earning different wages and would open the door to innumerable individual or group complaints within each cluster of employees. It argued, moreover, that the proposed terms would not meet the requirements of Section 11.

In March 1981 a human rights tribunal was appointed to hear the complaint. Before the tribunal hearings took place, however, both parties reached a settlement that the commission approved in early March 1982. The settlement had two parts. The first was an agreement negotiated between the union and the Treasury Board, ratified in December 1981, and retroactive to December 1980 which corrected previous disparities by establishing a single pay rate for all seven subgroups, with incremental salary steps at each level. Employees were placed at the appropriate step in their salary range according to seniority. All employees had progressed to the maximum step of their ranges by the termination date of the contract in

January 1983, at which time the wage structure reverted to a single rate for each level. With the implementation of this contract, all employees at the same level, notwithstanding geographical differences, were guaranteed the same wages by the end of the contract period. During the life of the contract, the only wage differences were due to seniority.

The second part of the settlement involved the payment of a lump sum in compensation for the wages lost between 15 November 1978 (one year prior to the filing of the complaint) and 20 December 1980. The payment varied with the employee's level and subgroup but ranged from $1,361.00 to $12,129.11 per employee, for a total payment of close to $17 million. The amount of compensation for the retroactive period was arrived at, with the agreement of the parties, by comparing the regression pay line for each of the nationally female-dominated subgroups to the regression pay line for the four nationally male-dominated subgroups.

To determine the regression pay line, the zone rates for each level were averaged. These averages were then weighted by the national population for that level of the subgroup or subgroups represented. For each female subgroup, an adjustment, representing an hourly equivalent, was derived for each level from the distance between the male and the female regression line. Where the female line values are higher than the combined male line value, no adjustment took place.

This part of the settlement applied to all classes of employees in the compensated subgroups and levels of the general services group in departments and agencies for which the Treasury Board is the employer, providing they were employed at any time between 15 November 1978 and 21 December 1980. About 3,300 people were employed in the three female-dominated subgroups at the time of the settlement. Of these, 2,300 were women, so that the compensation settlement affected 1,000 men as well.

The commission approved the settlement because it was satisfied that past discrimination would be corrected by compensating those employees who had been underpaid because they worked in female-dominated subgroups or "women's jobs." In addition, the new collective agreement dissolved the subgroups involved in this complaint, introduced a new, single pay plan for the general services group, and established a new rate structure from which all previous pay differentials based on sex have been eliminated.

Public Service Alliance of Canada v. *Treasury Board* (Registered Nursing Assistants)

Another complaint stemmed from the unsuccessful attempt of two Registered Nursing Assistants (RNAs) in Deer Lodge Hospital to formulate a complaint under Section 11. Their contention was that they were performing work of greater value than that of orderlies but that they were receiving the same wages. When it was explained that such a complaint ("greater" value rather than "equal" value) could not be dealt with under Section 11, they sought another comparison job. The only one they could find was that of Specialist Orderly, which was classified at one level higher than their own in the same occupational group, Hospital Service (HS). Although this second complaint could with some difficulty have been dealt with under Section 11, it was considered preferable to file a complaint under Sections 7 and 10, alleging that the classification standard for the HS group discriminated against RNAs by undervaluing their work.

At the suggestion of the commission staff, the two RNAs contacted the classification section of the PSAC so that a group complaint could be filed on behalf of all RNAs in the HS group (they had been unsuccessful in obtaining support from the PSAC at the local level). This complaint specified two areas where it was alleged that the work of the RNAs was not correctly evaluated: Specific Vocational Training (SVT) and Responsibility for the Safety of Others (RSO).

All positions in the HS group are classified with a common evaluation plan that measures skill, effort, responsibility, and working conditions. These factors are subdivided into nine subfactors. SVT is a subfactor of "skill," and RSO a subfactor of "responsibility." On its face the plan is nondiscriminatory; however, the positions selected as benchmarks for the plan included one for RNAs, and it was the evaluation of this benchmark position that was at issue.

The scale for the SVT subfactor ranks all benchmark positions within a range of eight degrees. Orderlies and RNAs were rated at the same degree. Enquiries at community colleges and hospitals revealed that the formal training period for RNAs varies from province to province, with thirty-nine weeks as an average figure. Formal training for orderlies lasts two weeks, followed by a short but unspecified period of on-the-job training. It was thus quite clear that there was a significant difference between the two jobs in terms of the amount of formal training required. Less clear was the difference in the RSO subfactor. Both RNAs and orderlies were rated at the degree 2, and the Specialist Orderly at degree 3. On balance, it was considered that as far as "responsibility for patient safety" was concerned, the differences were neither clearcut nor sufficiently great to justify a change in the ratings.

The position of the Treasury Board staff was that the complaint was not proper, because a classification standard is not a "policy or practice that deprives or tends to deprive . . . an individual or class of individuals of any employment opportunities . . . on a prohibited ground of discrimination" as stipulated in Section 10 of the act. After a number of meetings, they agreed to review the standard while reserving their position on the complaint itself. The result of the review was that the SVT subfactor of the benchmark position for RNAs was increased by one degree, but the RSO subfactor was not changed.

For the reasons given above, these findings were acceptable to the commission. The upward adjustment of the SVT subfactor raised the benchmark position from level 5 to level 6. The settlement required the Treasury Board to review all RNA positions and reclassify those whose duties are comparable to those of the benchmark position, retroactive to one year prior to the filing of the complaint. All personnel occupying these positions were promoted retroactively, and former occupants were compensated for the period that they occupied them. Over two hundred positions were reclassified. The cost of settlement was estimated at $28,000, and the ongoing cost will be approximately $150,000 per annum.

This case presented the commission with an equal pay complaint that could not be entertained under Section 11 because of the wording of the act. It is interesting in that it demonstrates the commission's ability to make use of Section 10 in such cases.

Litigation

A complaint against the British American Bank Note Company was dismissed by a tribunal and by the federal court on the basis of jurisdiction. The commission's appeal of the latter decision was also dismissed. The commission appointed a Human Rights Tribunal in September 1983 to hear the complaint filed by the female clerical workers at the Glace Bay heavy water plant against Atomic Energy of Canada Ltd.

This is the extent of litigation to November 1983 in relation to the equal pay provisions of the act. No doubt there will be more litigation before the equal value concept is imbedded in all job evaluation and pay systems. But the commission takes deep satisfaction in knowing that we have been able to settle several complaints without resorting to tribunals at all.

Public Information and Consultation

The commission also has a mandate to develop and conduct information programs to foster public understanding of the act. We have therefore prepared various publications to explain our approach to the equal pay provisions, and we have taken every opportunity to explain to employer and employee groups what compliance entails.

We have pursued our policy of consulting with our constituency. We have, for example, contacted a number of employers and unions whose operation falls under our jurisdiction, as well as a number of women's groups, to solicit their opinions on additional equal wage guidelines that would take into account situations not presently covered where a discriminatory wage differential may exist. These new guidelines are described in the following section.

Additional Guidelines

In December 1981 the commission approved amendments to its Equal Wages Guidelines to cover two situations: a labor shortage in a particular job classification that results in a premium salary being paid to employees in that occupation, and a change in the work performed by a group of employees in a particular classification that causes a decrease in the value of the work, without the wages of the incumbents being reduced accordingly.

Because a wage differential may result from a combination of one or the other of these factors with sex discrimination, the invocation of these factors to justify unequal wages will be severely restricted. An employer who paid men and women different rates on these grounds would not only have to provide conclusive evidence that a labor shortage exists or a change in the work performed has occurred; he would also have to show that the differential applies between workers of the same sex as well as between workers of opposite sexes. An exemption granted under the labor shortage provision is subject to review after a fixed period of time, not to exceed one year. In addition, the work-devaluation exemption does not apply if the employer continues to hire employees and pay them at the old rate despite the devaluation of the job.

Conclusion

I believe that the concept of equal pay for work of equal value will, in time, be included in all Canadian human rights legislation. Widespread application of the concept will not create chaos in the country's pay system, as the pessimists say. It will, however, help ensure that women receive compensation that is appropriate to the value of their work, rather than compensation that reflects the fact that they have had fewer employment options than men.

The former head of the U.S. Equal Employment Opportunity Commission, Eleanor Holmes Norton, was once asked why she had predicted that the comparable worth issue would be the equal employment issue of the eighties. She replied: "Because it is the last large preserve of discrimination left untouched by Title VII in the United States. . . . Moreover, this turns out to be the form of discrimination that probably affects the largest number of Americans today, and that is women who work in sex-stereotyped jobs, almost 80 percent of all women, and, to a lesser degree, minorities as well."[4]

Large numbers of women will continue to find employment in the traditionally female jobs. In 1979, 62.6 percent of all Canadian women in paid employment worked in the clerical, sales, and service sectors. This

---

4. The MacNeil-Lehrer Report, September 2, 1980, Transcript Library #1287.

proportion has remained substantially the same for many years. Why shouldn't women work as secretaries and nurses and home economists and telephone operators and bank tellers, if they are good at it and find it satisfying? They do not need equal opportunities programs to get jobs in these fields. They are already trained and experienced and on the job, contributing their labor to society.

What they *do* need is for society to re-examine these jobs and their importance to the economy. We may find in some cases that women's labor in traditionally female jobs is being fairly compensated; in other cases we may find that it is not. We will never know unless we analyze those jobs from the perspective of the *value* of the work, and not on the basis of their market value. Women deserve to know what their work is worth in relation to the work men do—and they deserve to be paid for it.

Section 11 of the Canadian Human Rights Act will undoubtedly have an impact on the remuneration of women in the part of the work force to which it applies. It may eventually influence other jurisdictions to modify their legislation. After all, what it requires of employers is nothing more than a rationalization of their job evaluation and compensation systems.

In 1978, when we started, the public reaction to our work was disbelief; then came warnings that it couldn't be done. Since the librarians' settlement, however, the mood has been changing. The financial newspapers and others have carried very positive articles on the question of equal pay for work of equal value, and some consultants are urging employers to review their pay systems.

Five years of implementation is not long enough to allow us to predict the future impact of these legislative provisions, but it is long enough to allow us to state that the instrument we were given to correct wage disparities between men and women can be an effective one.

Appendix I
Section 11: Canadian Human Rights Act:

Equal wages
11. (1) It is a discriminatory practice for an employer to establish or maintain differences in wages between male and female employees employed in the same establishment who are performing work of equal value.

Assessment of value of work
(2) In assessing the value of work performed by employees employed in the same establishment, the criterion to be applied is the composite of the skill, effort and responsibility required in the performance of the work and the conditions under which the work is performed.

Separate establishments
(2.1) Separate establishments established or maintained by an employer solely or principally for the purpose of establishing or maintaining differences in wages between male and female employees shall be deemed for the purposes of this section to be a single establishment.

Different wages based on prescribed reasonable factors
(3) Notwithstanding subsection (1), it is not a discriminatory practice to pay to male and female employees different wages if the difference is based on a factor prescribed by guidelines issued by the Canadian Human Rights Commission pursuant to subsection 22(2) to be a reasonable factor that justifies the difference.

Idem
(4) For greater certainty, sex does not constitute a reasonable factor justifying a difference in wages.

No reduction of wages
(5) An employer shall not reduce wages in order to eliminate a discriminatory practice described in this section.

Disparité salariale discriminatoire
11. (1) Constitue un acte discriminatoire le fait pour l'employeur d'instaurer ou de pratiquer la disparité salariale entre les hommes et les femmes qui exécutent, dans le même établissement, des fonctions équivalentes.

Critères
(2) Les critères permettant d'établir l'équivalence des fonctions exécutées par des employés dans le même établissement sont les qualifications, les efforts et les responsabilités nécessaires pour leur exécution, considérés globalement, compte tenu des conditions de travail.

Établissements distincts
(2.1) Les établissements distincts qu'un employeur aménage ou maintient dans le but principal de justifier une disparité salariale entre hommes et femmes sont réputés, pour l'application du présent article, ne constituer qu'un seul et même établissement.

Disparité salariale non discriminatoire
(3) Ne constitue pas un acte discriminatoire au sens du paragraphe (1) la disparité salariale entre hommes et femmes fondée sur un facteur reconnu comme raisonnable par une ordonnance de la Commission canadienne des droits de la personne en vertu du paragraphe 22(2).

Idem
(4) Des considérations fondées sur le sexe ne sauraient motiver la disparité salariale.

Diminutions de salaire interdites
(5) Il est interdit à l'employeur de procéder à des diminutions salariales pour mettre fin aux actes discriminatoires visés au présent article.

Appendix I (*continued*)

"Wages" defined

(6) For the purposes of this section, "wages" means any form of remuneration payable for work performed by an individual and includes salaries, commissions, vacation pay, dismissal wages, bonuses, reasonable value for board, rent, housing, lodging, payments in kind, employer contributions to pension funds or plans, long-term disability plans and all forms of health insurance plans and any other advantage received directly or indirectly from the individual's employer.

Définition de «salaire»

(6) Pour l'application du présent article, «salaire» s'entend de toute forme de rémunération payable à un individu en contrepartie de son travail et, notamment, des traitements, commissions, indemnités de vacances ou de licenciement, primes, de la juste valeur des prestations en repas, loyers, logement et hébergement, des rétributions en nature, des contributions de l'employeur aux caisses ou régimes de pension, aux régimes d'assurance contre l'invalidité prolongée et aux régimes d'assurance-maladie de toute nature et des autres avantages reçus directement ou indirectement de l'employeur.

Appendix II
Equal Wages Guidelines and Amendment

27/9/78
Canada Gazette Part II, Vol. 112, No. 18

SI/TR/78-155
Gazette du Canada Partie II, Vol. 112, N⁰ 18

Registration
SI/78-155   27 September, 1978

CANADIAN HUMAN RIGHTS ACT

Enregistrement
TR/78-155   27 septembre 1978

LOI CANADIENNE SUR LES DROITS DE LA PERSONNE

Equal Wages Guidelines

Ordonnances sur l'égalité de rémunération

The Canadian Human Rights Commission, pursuant to subsections 11(3) and 22(2) of the Canadian Human Rights Act, is hereby pleased to issue guidelines as set out in the Schedule hereto respecting the application of section 11 of the Canadian Human Rights Act and prescribing factors justifying different wages for equal work.

La Commission canadienne des droits de la personne en vertu des paragraphes 11(3) et 22(2) de la Loi canadienne sur les droits de la personne, désire émettre des ordonnances conformément à l'annexe ci-après au sujet de l'application de l'article 11 de la Loi canadienne sur les droits de la personne et des facteurs justifiant la disparité salariale pour des fonctions équivalentes.

Dated at Ottawa, this 18th day of September, 1978

Fait à Ottawa le 18 septembre 1978

GUIDELINES OF THE CANADIAN HUMAN RIGHTS COMMISSION RESPECTING THE APPLICATION OF SECTION 11 OF THE CANADIAN HUMAN RIGHTS ACT AND PRESCRIBING FACTORS JUSTIFYING DIFFERENT WAGES FOR EQUAL WORK

ORDONNANCES DE LA COMMISSION CANADIENNE DES DROITS DE LA PERSONNE AU SUJET DE L'APPLICATION DE L'ARTICLE 11 DE LA LOI CANADIENNE SUR LES DROITS DE LA PERSONNE ET DES FACTEURS JUSTIFIANT LA DISPARITÉ SALARIALE POUR DES FONCTIONS ÉQUIVALENTES

Short Title
1. These Guidelines may be cited as the *Equal Wages Guidelines*.

Titre abrégé
1. *Ordonnances sur l'égalité de rémunération.*

Interpretation
2. In these Guidelines, "Act" means the *Canadian Human Rights Act.*

Interprétation
2. «Loi», la *Loi canadienne sur les droits de la personne.*

Guidelines
3. Subsections 11(1) and (2) of the Act apply in any case in such a manner that in assessing the value of work performed by employees employed in the same establishment to determine if they are performing work of equal value,

Ordonnances
3. Les paragraphes 11(1) et 11(2) de la Loi s'appliquent dans tous les cas où le travail exécuté par les employés d'un même établissement est évalué en vue de déterminer si ces employés remplissent des fonctions équivalentes.

Appendix II (*continued*)

(*a*) the skill required in the performance of the work of an employee shall be considered to include any type of intellectual or physical skill required in the performance of that work that has been acquired by the employee through experience, training, education or natural ability, and the nature and extent of such skills of employees employed in the same establishment shall be compared without taking into consideration the means by which such skills were acquired by the employees:

(*b*) the effort required in the performance of the work of an employee shall be considered to include any intellectual or physical effort normally required in the performance of that work, and in comparing such efforts exerted by employees employed in the same establishment,

(i) such efforts may be found to be of equal value whether such efforts were exerted by the same or different means, and

(ii) the assessment of the effort required in the performance of the work of an employee shall not normally be affected by the occasional or sporadic performance by that employee of a task that requires additional effort;

(*c*) the responsibility required in the performance of the work of an employee shall be assessed by determining the extent to which the employer relies on the employee to perform the work having regard to the importance of the duties of the employee and the accountability of the employee to the employer for machines, finances and any other resources and for the work of other employees; and

a) les qualifications requises pour l'exécution du travail d'un employé comprennent les aptitudes physiques ou intellectuelles nécessaires à l'exécution de ce travail et acquises par l'expérience, la formation, les études ou attribuables à l'habilité naturelle; la nature et l'importance de ces qualifications chez les employés qui travaillent dans le même établissement doivent être évaluées sans tenir compte de la manière dont elles ont été acquises;

b) l'effort requis pour l'exécution du travail d'un employé comprend tout effort physique ou intellectuel normalement nécessaire à ce travail; lorsqu'on compare les fonctions des employés d'un même établissement à cet égard,

(i) l'effort déployé par un employé peut être équivalent à celui déployé par un autre employé, que ces efforts soient exercés de la même façon ou non et

(ii) l'effort nécessaire à l'exécution du travail d'un employé ne doit pas normalement être considéré comme différent sous prétexte que l'employé accomplit de temps à autre une tâche exigeant un effort supplémentaire;

c) les responsabilités liées à l'exécution du travail d'un employé doivent être évaluées en déterminant dans quelle mesure l'employeur compte sur l'employé pour accomplir son travail, compte tenu de l'importance des exigences du poste et de toutes les ressources techniques, financières et humaines dont l'employé a la responsabilité;

Appendix II (*continued*)

(*d*) the conditions under which the work of an employee is performed shall be considered to include noise, heat, cold, isolation, physical danger, conditions hazardous to health, mental stress and any other conditions produced by the physical or psychological work environment, but shall not be considered to include a requirement to work overtime or on shifts where a premium is paid to the employee for such overtime or shift work.

4. (1) Subject to subsection (2), for the purposes of subsection 11(3) of the Act, the factors prescribed to be reasonable factors justifying differences in the wages paid to male and female employees employed in the same establishment who are performing work of equal value are the following, namely,

(*a*) different performance ratings, where these are given to the employees by means of a formal system of performance appraisal that has been brought to the attention of the employees;

(*b*) seniority, where a wage and salary administration scheme applies to the employees and provides that they receive periodic pay increases based on their length of service with the employer;

(*c*) red circling, where the position of an employee is re-evaluated and as a result is down-graded, and the wages of that employee are temporarily fixed, or the increases in the wages of that employee are curtailed, until the wages appropriate to the down-graded position are equivalent to or better than the wages of that employee;

(*d*) a rehabilitation assignment where an employer pays to an employee wages that are higher than justified by the value of the work performed by that employee while that employee recuperates from an injury or illness of limited duration;

d) les conditions dans lesquelles l'employé exécute ses fonctions comprennent le bruit, la chaleur, le froid, l'isolement, le danger physique, les risques pour la santé, le stress et toutes les autres conditions liées à l'environnement physique et au climat psychologique; elles ne comprennent pas cependant l'obligation de faire des heures supplémentaires ou de travailler par postes lorsque l'employé reçoit une prime à cet égard.

4. (1) Aux fins du paragraphe 11(3) de la Loi, les facteurs reconnus raisonnables pour justifier une disparité salariale entre les hommes et les femmes qui travaillent dans le même établissement et remplissent des fonctions équivalentes sont,

a) la rémunération fondée sur le rendement, lorsque les employés sont assujettis à un tel régime et font l'objet d'une évaluation dans ce sens après que cette condition ait été portée à leur connaissance;

b) l'ancienneté, lorsqu'un régime salarial stipule que les employés ont droit à des augmentations statuaires fondées sur leurs états de service;

c) la surévaluation des postes, lorsque le poste d'un employé a été réévalué et déclassé et que l'employé reçoit un traitement intérimaire ou que ses augmentations ont été bloquées jusqu'à ce que le traitement du poste ainsi déclassé devienne équivalent ou supérieur au traitement de l'employé en question;

d) l'affectation comportant des tâches allégées, lorsqu'un employeur verse temporairement à un employé un traitement supérieur à la valeur du travail exécuté pendant que l'employé se remet d'une blessure ou d'une maladie;

Appendix II (*continued*)

(*e*) a demotion pay procedure, where the employer reassigns an employee to a position at a lower level because of

    (i) the unsatisfactory work performance of the employee caused by

        (A) the deterioration in the ability of the employee to perform the work,

        (B) the increasing complexity of the job, or

        (C) the impaired health or partial disability of the employee or other cause beyond the control of the employee, or

    (ii) an internal labour force surplus that necessitates the re-assignment of the employee to a position at a lower level,

and the employer continues to pay to the employee the same wages that he would have paid if he had not re-assigned the employee to a position at a lower level;

(*f*) a procedure of phased-in wage reductions, where the wages of an employee are gradually reduced for any of the reasons set out in subparagraph (*e*)(i); and

(*g*) a temporary training position, where for the purposes of an employee development program that is equally available to male and female employees and leads to the career advancement of the employees who take part in that program, an employee is temporarily assigned to a position but receives wages at a different level than an employee who works in such a position on a permanent basis.

(2) The factors set out in subsection (1) are prescribed to be reasonable factors justifying differences in wages if they are applied consistently and equitably in calculating and paying the wages of all male and female employees employed in the same establishment who are performing work of equal value.

e) le mode de rémunération en cas de rétrogradation, lorsqu'un employeur attribue à un employé des fonctions moins importantes, à cause

    (i) d'un rendement insuffisant attribuable à une diminution de l'aptitude à exécuter le travail, une complexité de plus en plus grande du travail, ou des problèmes de santé, une incapacité partielle ou toute autre cause indépendante de la volonté de l'employé, ou

    (ii) un surplus de main-d'œuvre nécessitant la réaffectation de l'employé à un poste d'un niveau inférieur,

et que l'employeur continue de verser à l'employé le même salaire que s'il ne l'avait pas réaffecté à un poste moins important;

f) la méthode de réduction graduelle du salaire, lorsque le salaire d'un employé fait l'objet d'une réduction graduelle à cause de l'un des motifs mentionnés au sous-alinéa *e*)(i); et

g) l'affectation temporaire à des fins de formation, lorsque, dans le cadre d'un programme de perfectionnement, un employé est temporairement affecté à un poste et reçoit un traitement différent de celui des titulaires permanents; ces programmes de perfectionnement doivent être accessibles tant aux femmes qu'aux hommes et leur fournir d'égales possibilités d'avancement.

(2) Les facteurs mentionnés au paragraphe (1) sont considérés comme raisonnables et justifient une disparité salariale, s'ils sont appliqués rigoureusement et d'une manière équitable dans le calcul et le paiement des salaires des hommes et des femmes qui travaillent dans le même établissement et exécutent des fonctions équivalentes.

Appendix II (*continued*)

(*Extract from the* Canada Gazette Part II, dated January 13, 1982)

(*Extrait de la* Gazette du Canada Partie II, en date du 13 janvier 1982)

Registration
SI/82-2   13 January, 1982

CANADIAN HUMAN RIGHTS ACT

Equal Wages Guidelines, amendment

The Canadian Human Rights Commission, pursuant to subsections 11(3) and 22(2) of the Canadian Human Rights Act, is hereby pleased to amend the Equal Wages Guidelines issued by the Canadian Human Rights Commission on September 18, 1978*, in accordance with the schedule hereto.

Dated at Ottawa, this 14th day of December, 1981

SCHEDULE

1. Subsection 4(1) of the *Equal Wages Guidelines* is amended by deleting the word "and" at the end of paragraph (*f*) thereof and by adding thereto the following paragraphs:
"(*h*) the existence of an internal labour shortage in a particular job classification, where the employer is able to show that the wages paid to a group of employees in that classification are higher than

(i) the wages paid to a group of employees in that job classification that has filed a complaint under subsection 32(1) of the Act with respect to the payment of the higher wages, and
(ii) the wages paid to a group of employees in that job classification of the same sex as the group in respect of which the higher wages are paid; and

Enregistrement
TR/82-2   13 janvier 1982

LOI CANADIENNE SUR LES DROITS DE LA PERSONNE

Ordonnances sur l'égalité de rémuneration—Modification

La Commission canadienne des droits de la personne en vertu des paragraphes 11(3) et 22(2) de la Loi canadienne sur les droits de la personne, se fait un plaisir de modifier, par la présente, les Ordonnances sur l'égalité de rémunération rendues par la Commission canadienne des droits de la personne le 18 septembre 1978*, conformément à l'annexe ci-jointe.

Fait à Ottawa, le 14 décembre 1981

ANNEXE

1. Le paragraphe 4(1) des *Ordonnances sur l'égalité de rémunération* est modifié par suppression du mot «et» à la fin de l'alinéa *f*) et par adjonction de ce qui suit:
«*h*) l'existence dans l'établissement d'une pénurie de main-d'œuvre à l'intérieur d'une classification donnée, lorsque l'employeur peut démontrer que la rémunération versée à un groupe d'employés appartenant à cette classification est supérieure
(i) à la rémunération versée à un groupe d'employés qui appartient à cette classification et qui a déposé une plainte en vertu du paragraphe 32(1) de la Loi portant sur cette rémunération supérieure, et
(ii) à la rémunération versée à un groupe d'employés qui appartient à cette classification et qui est du même sexe que le groupe à qui la rémunération supérieure est versée; et

---

*SI/78-155, 1978 *Canada Gazette* Part II, p. 3695

*TR/78-155, *Gazette du Canada* Partie II, 1978, p. 3695

(*i*) a change in the work performed by a group of employees in a particular job classification that results in positions being re-classified at a lower level and the employer continuing to pay the group the same wages that he would have paid if positions had not been re-classified, where the employer is able to show that

(i) no person who is employed to perform the work of an employee in that group is paid wages equivalent to or better than wages paid to an employee in that group prior to the change, and

(ii) the group is paid wages that are higher than

(A) the wages paid to a group of employees in that job classification that has filed a complaint under subsection 32(1) of the Act with respect to the payment of the higher wages, and

(B) the wages paid to a group of employees in that job classification of the same sex as the group in respect of which the higher wages are paid."

i) une modification des tâches dans le travail d'un groupe d'employés appartenant à une classification donnée qui entraine le déclassement de postes et le versement par l'employeur au groupe de la rémunération qu'il lui aurait versé s'il n'y avait pas eu de déclassement, lorsque l'employeur peut démontrer

(i) que la rémunération de toute personne engagée pour exécuter le travail d'un employé qui appartient à ce groupe n'est pas égale ou supérieure à celle versée à un employé de ce groupe avant la modification,

(ii) la rémunération versée au groupe est supérieure

(A) à la rémunération versée à un groupe d'employés qui appartient à cette classification et qui a déposé une plainte en vertu du paragraphe 32(1) de la Loi portant sur cette rémunération supérieure, et

(B) à la rémunération versée à un groupe d'employés qui appartient à cette classification et qui est du même sexe que le groupe à qui la rémunération supérieure est versée.»

EXPLANATORY NOTE

(This note is not part of the Guidelines, but is intended only for information purposes.)
This amendment adds two factors to the reasonable factors justifying differences in the wages paid to male and female employees employed in the same establishment who are performing work of equal value.

NOTE EXPLICATIVE

(La présente note ne fait pas partie de l'ordonnance et n'est publiée qu'à titre d'information.)
Cette modification ajoute deux facteurs aux facteurs raisonnables justifiant la disparité salariale entre les hommes et les femmes qui travaillent dans le même établissement et remplissent des fonctions équivalentes.

12

A Review of
Federal Court Decisions
under Title VII of the
Civil Rights Act of 1964

MARY HEEN

The *Gunther* Decision

The federal equal pay statute, the Equal Pay Act of 1963, offers an effective means of remedying sex-based wage discrimination where men and women perform the same work. By its terms, however, it can do little to resolve the pervasive problem of wage discrimination in sex-segregated jobs, where men and women perform different work.[1] In attempting to develop, under existing federal antidiscrimination statutes, the expanded concept of equal pay for work of equal value, or comparable worth, it has been necessary to rely on Title VII of the Civil Rights Act of 1964, which prohibits all forms of employment discrimination on the basis of race, color, national origin, religion, or sex.[2] Nevertheless, until recently federal courts

---

1. Equal Pay Act of 1963, Pub. L. 88-38, 77 Stat. 56, 29 U.S.C. § 206(d). For a comprehensive review of the problem of wage discrimination and job segregation, see the National Academy of Sciences report to the Equal Employment Opportunity Commission: Donald J. Treiman and Heidi I. Hartman, eds., *Women, Work and Wages: Equal Pay for Jobs of Equal Value* (Washington, D.C.: National Academy Press 1981). See also Committee on Post Office and Civil Service, House of Representatives, Joint Hearings before the Subcommittees on Human Resources, Civil Service, Compensation and Employee Benefits, *Pay Equity: Equal Pay for Work of Comparable Value*, 97th Cong., 2d Sess., Parts I and II, Serial no. 97-53 (Washington, D.C.: U.S. Government Printing Office 1983).

2. Title VII of the Civil Rights Act of 1964, Pub. L. 88-352, 78 Stat. 255, 2 July 1964, see 42 U.S.C. § 2000e, *et seq.* For a pre-*Gunther* discussion of expanding the concept of wage discrimination under Title VII, see generally, e.g., Ruth Blumrosen, "Wage Discrimination, Job Segregation, and Title VII of the Civil Rights Act of 1964," *University of Michigan Journal of Law Reform* 12 (1979): 397; Cynthia E. Gitt and Marjorie Gelb, "Beyond the Equal Pay Act: Expanding Wage Differential Protections under Title VII," *Loyola University Law Journal* 8 (1977): 723; but see also E. Robert Livernash, ed., *Comparable Worth: Issues and Alternatives* (Washington, D.C.: Equal Employment Advisory Council, 1980); Bruce A. Nelson, Edward M. Opton, and Thomas E. Wilson, "Wage Discrimination and the Comparable Worth Theory in Perspective," *University of Michigan Journal of Law Reform* 13 (1980): 231.

were divided on the issue of whether Title VII's prohibition against discrimination in "compensation" is broader in scope than the Equal Pay Act.

In *County of Washington* v. *Gunther*, decided in 1981, the United States Supreme Court resolved the threshold legal issue of whether sex-based wage discrimination claims can be brought under Title VII without satisfying the equal work standard of the Equal Pay Act. In a significant but narrowly written opinion, the Supreme Court ruled that compensation discrimination claims brought under Title VII are not restricted to claims for equal pay for "substantially equal" work.[3] The Court recognized that Title VII represents a more comprehensive attack on discrimination than the Equal Pay Act, and that Title VII should be broadly interpreted as prohibiting the "entire spectrum" of practices that result in sex-based employment discrimination.

The *Gunther* decision represents a crucial first step toward development of the concept of comparable worth as a means of achieving pay equity through litigation. *Gunther* establishes that women may challenge systematic sex-based wage discrimination under Title VII without the necessity of showing that the employer has hired male workers at higher wages to perform substantially equal work. This means that litigation is not foreclosed when women are underpaid in jobs that are different from men's jobs. Title VII thus provides a potentially significant means of combatting the problem of the undervaluation of "women's work" in traditionally female occupations. Although many difficult issues remain to be resolved by the lower courts as post-*Gunther* pay equity litigation progresses, Title VII and the Equal Pay Act provide a legal framework for further development and resolution of such claims.

The Factual Background

Alberta Gunther worked as a guard in an Oregon county jail. The jail had a men's section and a women's section, and the guards were likewise segregated by sex. The duties of the male and female guards were similar, except that the female guards were responsible for fewer prisoners and, unlike the male guards, were required to perform clerical work. The female guards were paid substantially lower wages than the male guards.

Alberta Gunther and three of her co-workers filed a Title VII sex-discrimination case in federal district court against the county. They claimed that they were paid unequal wages for work "substantially equal" to that performed by male guards and, alternatively, that even if the jobs were not substantially equal, part of the pay differential was attributable to intentional sex discrimination.

---

3. *County of Washington* v. *Gunther*, 452 U.S. 967 (1981). Justice Brennan wrote the opinion of the Court, joined by Justices White, Marshall, Blackmun, and Stevens. Justice Rehnquist wrote a dissenting opinion joined by Chief Justice Burger and Justices Stewart and Powell.

The federal district court concluded after trial that the female guards' jobs were not "substantially equal" to those of the male guards. Each male guard supervised more than ten times as many prisoners as a female guard did, and the female guards devoted much of their time to less valuable clerical duties. The trial court held, therefore, that the jobs did not fulfill the equal work standard of the Equal Pay Act; that is, the jobs did not require substantially equal skill, effort, and responsibility under similar working conditions. Under that standard, the women were not entitled to equal pay. The trial court's conclusion was upheld on appeal, and the women did not seek Supreme Court review of that issue.

The district court also dismissed the women's alternative claim that the discrepancy in pay between the male and female guards was attributable in part to intentional sex discrimination. The court concluded that a sex-based wage discrimination claim could not be brought under Title VII unless the women showed that the jobs being compared satisfied the equal work standard of the Equal Pay Act. Because the court had held that the jobs were not substantially equal, it did not consider any of the evidence offered on the issue of intentional sex discrimination.[4]

On appeal, the Ninth Circuit Court of Appeals reversed, holding that the women were not precluded from suing under Title VII to protest discriminatory compensation practices merely because their jobs were not equal to the higher-paying jobs held by members of the opposite sex. The court of appeals instructed the district court to consider evidence offered by the women at trial that "a portion of the discrepancy between their salaries and those of the male guards could be ascribed only to sex discrimination." In a supplemental opinion issued in denial of rehearing, the court of appeals reiterated its conclusion that a wage discrimination claim can be brought "under some other theory compatible with Title VII" even if it could not satisfy the equal work standard. The court declined to decide what theories might be feasible. The court of appeals then remanded the case to the district court for consideration of the discriminatory compensation claim. At the same time, it observed that the women had already presented some "evidence of intentional sex discrimination that was not considered by the district court because the district court believed that disposition of the equal pay claims was the end of the inquiry."[5]

The Supreme Court upheld the decision of the court of appeals. As a result, the case was finally returned to the district court so that Alberta Gunther and her co-workers could attempt to prove their Title VII claim. As outlined to the Supreme Court, the women's proof would show that the county conducted its own survey of outside markets and the worth of the

---

4. *Gunther* v. *County of Washington*, 20 FEP Cases 788 (D. Ore. 1976).

5. *Gunther* v. *County of Washington*, 602 F.2d 882 (9th Cir. 1979), *petition for rehearing denied*, 623 F.2d 1303 (1980).

guard jobs; that the county survey indicated that the women should be paid approximately 95 percent as much as the male guards; that it paid them only 70 percent as much, while paying the male guards the full evaluated worth of their jobs; and that the failure to pay the women the full evaluated worth of their jobs was attributable to intentional sex discrimination. The Court declined to decide, however, whether "intentional" discrimination must be shown in all cases as an element of a Title VII compensation discrimination claim.

If the Supreme Court had ruled against Gunther and her co-workers, achievement of pay equity through litigation would have been virtually impossible. Their victory means that the courthouse door remains open to such claims, and therefore the decision has significance beyond the specific factual setting of that case.[6]

The Legal Issue

The legal issue resolved in *Gunther* is the narrow statutory question of whether the Bennett Amendment, found in the last sentence of Section 703(h) of Title VII,[7] restricts Title VII's prohibition of sex-based compensation discrimination to claims of equal pay for equal work. This issue required the Supreme Court to discuss the relationship between Title VII and the Equal Pay Act and to examine closely the language of the two statutes.

Title VII makes it unlawful for an employer "to discriminate against any individual" with respect to "compensation, terms, conditions, or privileges of employment, because of such individual's race, color, religion, sex, or national origin." In addition, Title VII prohibits discrimination not only with regard to "compensation," but also with respect to hiring, classification, assignment, promotion, and discharge.[8]

The Bennett Amendment, added as a "technical amendment" to Title VII during the last two days before its passage, provides:

> It shall not be an unlawful employment practice under this subchapter for any employer to differentiate upon the basis of sex in determining the amount of wages or compensation paid or to be paid to employees of such employer if such differentiation is authorized by the provisions of [the Equal Pay Act].

To determine what pay differentials are "authorized by" the Equal Pay Act, the Court examined the language of that statute. The Equal Pay Act provides as follows:

---

6. Subsequent to the Supreme Court's decision, the parties in *Gunther* settled the case; as a result, it was unnecessary for the district court to reach a decision on the Title VII claim.

7. 42 U.S.C. § 2000e-2(h).

8. 42 U.S.C. § 2000e-2(a)(1), (2).

No employer having employees subject to any provisions of this section shall discriminate, within any establishment in which such employees are employed, between employees on the basis of sex by paying wages . . . at a rate less than the rate at which he pays wages to employees of the opposite sex in such establishment for equal work on jobs the performance of which requires equal skill, effort, and responsibility, and which are performed under similar working conditions, except where such payment is made pursuant to (i) a seniority system; (ii) a merit system; (iii) a system which measures earnings by quantity or quality of production; or (iv) a differential based on any other factor other than sex.

The Court observed that the Equal Pay Act is divided into two parts: a definition of the violation, followed by four affirmative defenses. Although recognizing that the language and legislative history of the Bennett Amendment "are not unambiguous," the Court concluded that the term "authorized" in the Bennett Amendment refers only to the Equal Pay Act's four affirmative defenses, and not to the equal work standard. The affirmative defenses "authorize" employers to differentiate in pay even though such differentiation might otherwise violate the act.

Accordingly, claims for sex-based discrimination can be brought under Title VII even though no member of the opposite sex holds an equal but higher-paying job, provided that the challenged wage rate is not based on seniority, merit, quantity or quality of production, or any "other factor other than sex." As affirmative defenses, the employer has the burden of showing that the wage differential is based upon one of the four Equal Pay Act exceptions.

Post-*Gunther* Legal Issues

The *Gunther* decision answered the technical statutory construction question by concluding that the Bennett Amendment does not incorporate the equal work standard into Title VII, but does incorporate the Equal Pay Act's four affirmative defenses. Although the decision constitutes a very important first step toward development of a comparable worth or pay equity theory, it left many other questions unanswered. The Supreme Court expressly declined to decide the "precise contours of lawsuits challenging sex discrimination in compensation under Title VII," leaving for another day questions of how to prove and defend against such wage discrimination claims.

The contours of pay equity lawsuits await careful delineation by the lower courts. The ultimate resolution of post-*Gunther* legal issues will determine the efficacy of Title VII as a means of remedying wage discrimination in sex-segregated jobs. The conduct of post-*Gunther* litigation does not take place in totally uncharted territory, however. Over the last twenty years, courts have established standards for proving other types of Title VII claims, and for establishing Equal Pay Act defenses. Compensation discrimination claims asserted by women seeking pay equity should be analyzed, therefore, within the well-established Title VII theoretical framework, modified by the employer's burden of establishing any applicable Equal Pay Act affirmative defense.[9]

Proving a Title VII Compensation Discrimination Claim

An important question left unanswered by the Supreme Court's *Gunther* decision is what must be shown by plaintiffs (employees) to establish a *prima facie* case: that is, what plaintiffs have to show in order to establish a legally sufficient claim of Title VII compensation discrimination. Establishing a *prima facie* case does not necessarily mean that the plaintiffs win their case, but it shifts to the defendants the burden of contradicting the plaintiffs' evidence or otherwise defending against the claim.

The Ninth Circuit Court of Appeals held in *Gunther* that the women would have to show more than unequal wages for "comparable" work in order to establish a *prima facie* case, although it declined to decide what more must be shown. Because Gunther and her co-workers voluntarily assumed the burden of showing that the pay disparity was attributable to intentional sex discrimination, the Supreme Court was not faced with the necessity of deciding whether proof of unequal wages for comparable work is, by itself, sufficient to establish a *prima facie* case under Title VII. The Court accordingly declined to decide whether "intentional" discrimination must be shown in all cases as an element of a Title VII compensation discrimination claim. A showing of "intentional" discrimination in the Title VII context, it should be noted, does not require proof that the employer subjectively intended to harm or disadvantage women, but may refer to the employer's objective intent to treat women differently from men.

Under traditional Title VII analysis, there are three basic ways of establishing a discrimination claim: showing (1) overt discrimination, also called "*per se*" or "facial" discrimination; (2) disparate impact of a facially neutral policy or practice on the protected group; or (3) disparate treatment.[10] Overt discrimination cases are sometimes grouped with dispa-

---

9. See, e.g., Edith Barnett, "Comparable Worth and the Equal Pay Act—Proving Sex-Based Wage Discrimination Claims after *County of Washington* v. *Gunther*," *Wayne Law Review* 28 (1982): 1691–1700; Winn Newman and Jeanne M. Vonhof, "Separate but Equal—Job Segregation and Pay Equity in the Wake of Gunther," *University of Illinois Law Review* (1981): 285–91.

10. See generally, e.g., Barbara Lindemann Schlei and Paul Grossman, *Employment Discrimination Law*, 2nd ed., Washington, D.C.: Bureau of National Affairs, 1982, pp. 1–16. For an excellent practical introduction to Title VII for nonlawyers, see E. Richard Larson, *Sue Your Boss: Rights and Remedies for Employment Discrimination* (New York: Farrar, Strauss & Giroux 1981), pp. 31–75.

rate treatment cases, although distinct issues of proof, discussed below, require separate analysis.[11] A plaintiff may rely on any one or all of these theories to establish a *prima facie* case. As explained more fully below, the Supreme Court has required showing of "intent" or "discriminatory motive" only under the disparate treatment theory.

Under the facial or overt discrimination approach, the discriminatory motive—that is, the intent to treat women differently from men—is clear from the employer's policy or action itself. An additional showing of intent is therefore unnecessary. For example, an employer would be engaging in overt discrimination against women if it were to post a job notice stating "no women need apply," or establish a pay rate of ten dollars an hour for men and eight dollars an hour for women performing the same job, or pay lower pension benefits to women employees because of their greater average longevity.[12] An employer that refuses to hire women with preschool children, but does hire men with preschool children, would also be engaged in overt discrimination.[13] In these cases, the employer openly treats women differently from men.

Once such a discriminatory employer policy or action is shown, the *prima facie* case is established. The burden then shifts to defendants to contradict the existence of such a policy or to establish the defense that sex is a *bona fide* occupational qualification ("bfoq") for the job.[14] This defense has been construed by the courts as an extremely narrow exception. The employer must prove that there is a factual basis for believing that "all or substantially all women would be unable to perform safely and efficiently the duties of the job involved," and that "the *essence* of the business operation would be undermined by not hiring members of one sex exclusively."[15] Sex would be a bfoq for the job of wet nurse or sperm donor, for example, or for particular acting roles. The Supreme Court has also

---

11. One commentator has explained the distinction as follows: "Both facial [overt] discrimination and pretext cases are often referred to as 'discriminatory treatment' cases and require proof of intent to discriminate. . . . In facial discrimination cases, the existence of the requisite intent is apparent from the employer's act of classifying employees on a prohibited basis." Wendy W. Williams, "Firing the Woman to Protect the Fetus: The Reconciliation of Fetal Protection with Employment Opportunity Goals under Title VII," *Georgetown Law Journal* 69 (1981): 641, 669 and n. 176.

12. See *Arizona Governing Committee* v. *Norris*, 463 U.S. 000 (1983); *Los Angeles Department of Water and Power* v. *Manhart*, 435 U.S. 702 (1978).

13. See *Phillips* v. *Martin Marietta Corp.*, 400 U.S. 542 (1971).

14. The "bfoq" defense applies only in cases of discrimination on the basis of sex, religion, or national origin: 42 U.S.C. § 2000e–2(e). Presumably there is no defense to a *per se* race discrimination case.

15. *Dothard* v. *Rawlinson*, 433 U.S. 321, 333 (1977) (emphasis in original), quoting from *Diaz* v. *Pan American World Airways*, 442 F.2d 385, 388 (5th Cir. 1971) (flight attendant); *Weeks* v. *Southern Bell Tel. & Tel. Co.*, 408 F.2d 228, 235 (5th Cir. 1969) ("switchman" job).

recognized sex as a bfoq for the job of guard in a maximum security prison with a history of "rampant violence," where the state showed that use of women guards would pose a substantial security problem directly linked to the sex of the guard. Establishing sex as a bfoq is an extremely difficult showing for employers to make; consequently, few employers succeed in establishing a bfoq defense to a claim of overt discrimination.

Under the "disparate impact" theory, plaintiffs may challenge "employment practices that are facially neutral in their treatment of different groups but that in fact fall more harshly on one group than on others and cannot be justified by business necessity."[16] For example, minimum height and weight requirements for correctional officers that would disqualify over 41 percent of all women, but less than 1 percent of all men, have been held to have an impermissible disparate impact on women.[17] Proof of discriminatory intent is not required in a disparate impact case. As explained by the Supreme Court in *Griggs* v. *Duke Power Company*,[18]

> The Act proscribes not only overt discrimination but also practices that are fair in form but discriminatory in operation. The touchstone is business necessity. If an employment practice which operates to exclude [the protected group] cannot be shown to be related to job performance, the practice is prohibited.

Because Congress intended Title VII to reach "the *consequences* of employment practices, not simply the motivation," the employer's "good intent or absence of discriminatory intent does not redeem employment procedures or testing mechanisms that operate as 'built in headwinds' for [protected groups] and are unrelated to measuring job capability."[19]

Plaintiffs need only show that the challenged practice has a significant discriminatory impact in order to make out a *prima facie* case under this approach. The burden of proof then shifts to the employer to show that the practice is justified by a substantial and legitimate "business necessity." If this showing is made, plaintiffs are entitled to show that alternative practices would fulfill the "business necessity" with a less discriminatory impact."[20]

Under the disparate treatment theory, a claim arises if the employer treats some people less favorably than others because of their race, color, religion, sex, or national origin. In this type of case, the employer typically denies that it treats women less favorably than men. Proof of "discriminatory motive is critical, although it can in some situations be inferred from the mere fact of differences in treatment."[21] For example, in individual dispa-

---

16. See *International Brotherhood of Teamsters* v. *United States*, 431 U.S. 324, 335–6 n. 15 (1977).
17. *Dothard* v. *Rawlinson*, 433 U.S. 321, 329 (1977).
18. *Griggs* v. *Duke Power Company*, 401 U.S. 424, 431 (1971).
19. Ibid. at 432 (emphasis in original).
20. *Dothard* v. *Rawlinson*, 433 U.S. at 329–30 (1977).
21. *Teamsters* v. *United States*, 431 U.S. at 335 n. 15 (1977).

rate treatment hiring discrimination cases, the Supreme Court has outlined four elements of a *prima facie* case: (1) plaintiffs belong to a group protected by Title VII; (2) they applied for and were qualified to perform the job; (3) despite their qualifications, they were not hired; and (4) the position thereafter remained open and the employer continued to seek applicants.[22] Establishing these four elements constitutes "proof of actions taken by the employer" from which "discriminatory animus" may be inferred because "experience has proved that in the absence of any other explanation it is more likely than not that those actions were bottomed on impermissible considerations."[23]

Once the individual disparate treatment *prima facie* case is established, the burden of producing evidence shifts to the employer to "articulate some legitimate nondiscriminatory reason" for the action taken. Should the defendant carry this burden, through the introduction of admissible evidence, the plaintiff then has the burden of proving that the "legitimate reasons offered by the defendant were not its true reasons, but were a pretext for discrimination."[24] Showing pretext is a difficult factual burden for plaintiffs to sustain, however, because of the employer's control of information in the employment setting.

The *prima facie* showing for classwide disparate treatment differs from the showing made in individual cases. In a classwide disparate treatment case, plaintiffs challenge an employer's pattern and practice of discriminatory treatment of women. In a hiring case, for example, plaintiffs introduce statistical evidence of significant disparities between men and women in the employer's work force compared to the general labor force and other relevant labor pool data, and couple this statistical showing with evidence of individual instances of discrimination.[25] However, "[w]here gross statistical disparities can be shown, they alone may in a proper case constitute *prima facie* proof of a pattern or practice of discrimination."[26] The focus at the *prima facie* case stage is not on individual hiring decisions, but on a pattern of discriminatory decision making. In order to rebut a *prima facie* showing of classwide disparate treatment, the employer must demonstrate that the statistics used by the plaintiffs are either inaccurate or insignificant, and provide a nondiscriminatory explanation for the apparently discriminatory result.[27]

Compensation discrimination claims should be analyzed within the established Title VII theoretical framework. Theoretically, pay equity cases

22. *McDonnell Douglas Corporation* v. *Green*, 411 U.S. 792, 802 (1973).
23. *Furnco Construction Corporation* v. *Waters*, 438 U.S. 567, 579–80 (1978).
24. *Texas Department of Community Affairs* v. *Burdine*, 450 U.S. 248 (1981).
25. *International Brotherhood of Teamsters* v. *United States*, 431 U.S. at 334–40 n. 20, 357–62 (1977).
26. *Hazelwood School District* v. *United States*, 433 U.S. 299, 307–8 (1977).
27. *International Brotherhood of Teamsters* v. *United States*, 431 U.S. at 359–60 n. 46.

could be brought under any of the above approaches. Because disparate impact cases do not require direct or indirect proof of an intent to discriminate, it would be inappropriate for courts to require that all plaintiffs show "intentional" discrimination.[28] Moreover, *Gunther* does not preclude bringing wage discrimination claims under a disparate impact theory, under which facially neutral pay policies could be shown to have a discriminatory effect on women. Such policies could include a head-of-household pay bonus plan, for example, or utilization of a job evaluation plan that places special value on skills or job requirements (e.g., heavy lifting) that are associated with jobs traditionally held by men.[29] In *American Federation of State, County and Municipal Employees* (AFSCME) v. *State of Washington*, a ground breaking case, a federal district court held that a wage system based upon salary surveys conducted by the state had a disparate impact on women where the state's comparable worth studies found a 20 percent disparity between male and female jobs of comparable worth.[30] Pay equity litigators must also consider the practical necessity of familiarizing courts with the complex and often well-disguised forms of sex-based wage discrimination. As a matter of litigation strategy, therefore, cases with factual settings offering the greatest chance of success—that is, the most egregious examples of wage discrimination—should be brought first. If the strongest cases are brought first, courts will have less trouble perceiving the sex discrimination and, in the process, will become more familiar with the problem of job segregation and the undervaluation of women's work.

The strongest cases are those disparate treatment cases in which plaintiffs offer direct proof that the employer considered sex in establishing lower wages for jobs performed by women. The *Gunther* plaintiffs offered such direct proof of disparate treatment, which then would have put the burden on the employer to establish one of the Equal Pay Act's four affirmative defenses.

In *AFSCME* v. *State of Washington*, the district court also found disparate treatment in compensation from the following set of factors asserted by plaintiffs: (1) the failure of the state to pay predominantly female jobs the full evaluated worth of their jobs according to the state's own job evaluation studies, which since 1974 showed an average 20 percent disparity between

---

28. Some post-*Gunther* lower court decisions have, without analysis, required a showing of intentional discrimination. See, e.g., *Power* v. *Barry County, Michigan*, 539 F. Supp. 721 (W.D. Mich. 1982); *Blowers* v. *Lawyers' Cooperative Publishing Co.*, 27 FEP Cases 1222 (W.D.N.Y. 1981); see also *Connecticut Employees Association* v. *State of Connecticut*, 31 FEP Cases 191 (D. Conn. 1983).

29. Newman and Vonhof, *"Separate but Equal,"* pp. 289–91.

30. *AFSCME* v. *State of Washington*, 32 FEP Cases 1577 (W.D. Wash. September 16, 1983) (oral opinion). At this writing, written findings of fact and conclusions of law have not been issued by the court. See Plaintiffs, Proposed Findings of Fact and Conclusions of Law, pp. 52–57, submitted on October 14, 1983.

predominantly male and predominantly female jobs of comparable worth; (2) the perpetuation of a historically segregated job structure and discriminatory compensation system; (3) statistical evidence of a pattern of treatment showing a negative correlation between the wage and the percentage of females in a state job classification; (4) evidence of discrimination against other members of the protected class; (5) application of subjective standards in the salary setting system; (6) evidence of prior acts of discrimination, including the use of sex-segregated classified ads; and (7) admissions of discrimination, including admissions at trial of former state officials that the state's compensation system was discriminatory. The court concluded that "the evidence is overwhelming that there has been past historical discrimination against women in employment in the State of Washington and that discrimination has been manifested . . . by direct, overt and institutionalized discrimination." The court found the discrimination to be "pervasive" and "intentional."[31]

As mentioned above, disparate treatment can also be *inferred* from a series of events or an employer's pattern or practice of treatment. Although courts utilize well-established factual and statistical models for drawing inferences of intentional discrimination in hiring cases, analogous models have not yet been widely adopted for wage discrimination cases. Several such models have been outlined in post-*Gunther* cases but have limited applicability to the factual pattern presented by the individual case. For example, in *Briggs* v. *City of Madison*, a federal district court adopted the following model for a *prima facie* showing of wage discrimination: (1) plaintiffs are members of a protected class (2) who occupy a sex-segregated job classification (3) that is paid less than a (4) sex-segregated job classification occupied by men, and (5) that the two job classifications at issue (in this case public health nurses and public health sanitarians) are so similar in their requirements of skill, effort, and responsibility and in their working conditions that it can reasonably be inferred that they are of comparable value to an employer.[32] Although the court held that the plaintiffs, female public health nurses, had succeeded in establishing a *prima facie* case of wage discrimination, it limited the significance of the holding to the facts of that case, and ultimately ruled in favor of the defendant. The disparate treatment model developed in *Briggs* is therefore limited in its formulation to wage claims challenging differential treatment in very similar jobs.

In another post-*Gunther* case, *Wilkins* v. *University of Houston*, the Court of Appeals for the Fifth Circuit examined evidence that the university had engaged in a pattern or practice of discriminating against women employees in setting wages for professional and administrative positions. The district court, in a pre-*Gunther* ruling, had permitted plaintiffs to pursue

31. Ibid. at 1577.
32. *Briggs* v. *City of Madison*, 536 F. Supp. 435, 445 (W.D. Wis. 1982).

their compensation claim without requiring them to satisfy the equal work standard, but had nevertheless rendered judgment in favor of the university. The Fifth Circuit reversed the district court's judgment and held that the plaintiffs had successfully established their compensation discrimination claim with regard to the university's academic division. The Fifth Circuit reviewed the plaintiffs' showing of statistical disparities, coupled with instances of discriminatory treatment, under established standards for classwide disparate treatment cases:

> (1) a statistically significant, disproportionate number of women in the academic division were paid less than the minimum established by the pay plan for the level of their jobs; (2) all four of the employees in the academic division who were being paid more than the maximum for their job level were men; (3) . . . five of the eighteen women who were underpaid and two other women had their jobs reclassified into lower levels, while no jobs held by men were similarly reclassified; and (4) the university's equal opportunity officer testified that a purpose of the pay plan was to remedy sexually discriminatory compensation practices of the university.

Adapting the *prima facie* case model for hiring cases and applying it to the plaintiffs' compensation discrimination claim, the Fifth Circuit held that the plaintiffs had presented an unrebutted *prima facie* case of classwide disparate treatment.[33] The *Wilkins* and AFSCME decisions thus represent cases where successful proof of a compensation discrimination claim was accomplished under established Title VII standards.

Employer Defenses: Incorporating the Equal Pay Act Defenses into Title VII

Another major issue left open by the *Gunther* decision is what effect incorporation of the Equal Pay Act's fourth affirmative defense—"factor other than sex"—will have on Title VII pay equity litigation. The Supreme Court acknowledged in *Gunther* that the first three defenses are redundant

---

33. *Wilkins* v. *University of Houston*, 654 F.2d 388, 405–7 (5th Cir. 1981), *rehearing denied*, 662 F.2d 1156, *vac'd and rem'd on class issues, for further consideration in light of Pullman Standard v. Swint*, 456 U.S. 273 (1982) and *General Telephone Company of the Southwest* v. *Falcon*, 457 U.S. 147 (1982), *cert. denied on evidentiary issues*, U.S., 74 L. Ed 2d 47,57 (1982), *on remand, aff'd in part and vac'd in part and remanded*, 695 F.2d 134 (5th Cir. 1983); see also *Melani* v. *Board of Higher Education*, 561 F. Supp. 769 (S.D.N.Y. 1983); cf. Plemer v. Parsons-Gilbane, 32 FEP Cases 1351, 1353-1356 (5th Cir. 1983) ("It is not the province of the courts, however to value the relative worth of . . . differing duties and responsibilities given the absence of either evidence of a kind similar or that delineated in *Wilkins*, or any direct or otherwise clear evidence as to how the Company valued the positions.").

of provisions found elsewhere in Section 703(h) of Title VII,[34] but explained that the Bennett Amendment guarantees a consistent interpretation of like provisions in both statutes. The Court emphasized, however, that incorporation of the fourth defense "could have significant consequences for Title VII litigation."

Without explaining these possible consequences, the Court contrasted Title VII's broadly inclusive prohibition of discriminatory employment practices, which is intended to proscribe "not only overt discrimination but also practices that are fair in form, but discriminatory in operation," with the different design of the fourth Equal Pay Act affirmative defense, "to confine the application of the Act to wage differentials attributable to sex discrimination." The fourth affirmative defense was added to the Equal Pay Act, the Court noted, because of a concern that *bona fide* job evaluation systems used by American businesses would otherwise be disrupted.

> Under the Equal Pay Act, the courts and administrative agencies are not permitted 'to substitute their judgment for the judgment of the employer . . . who [has] established and employed a bona fide job rating system,' so long as it does not discriminate on the basis of sex [citation omitted] Although we do not decide in this case how sex-based wage discrimination litigation under Title VII should be structured to accommodate the fourth affirmative defense of the Equal Pay Act . . . we consider it clear that the Bennett Amendment, under this interpretation, is not rendered superfluous.

The Court expressly declined to predict what impact the fourth affirmative defense will have on Title VII wage discrimination litigation, while suggesting that it could have significant consequences with regard to employers who have set wages pursuant to *bona fide* job evaluation systems.[35]

A central issue that must be resolved, therefore, is what constitutes a *bona fide* job evaluation system that does not discriminate on the basis of sex. Underlying this issue is the question of whether market factors, which themselves may reflect sex discriminatory wage structures, should be subject to special scrutiny if incorporated into a job evaluation system. If the employer defense of "factor other than sex" is interpreted to include re-

---

34. Section 703(h), 42 U.S.C. §2000e–2(h) provides in relevant part (emphasis added):

> Notwithstanding any other provision of this subchapter, it shall not be an unlawful employment practice for an employer to apply different standards of compensation, or different terms, conditions, or privileges of employment pursuant to a *bona fide seniority or merit system, or a system which measures earning by quantity or quality of production* . . . provided that such differences are not the result of an intention to discriminate because of . . . sex.

35. 452 U.S. at 170–71.

liance on market factors or prevailing job rates, an unexamined incorporation of such factors into a job evaluation system could provide insidious
justification for paying women less. In contrast, rejection of market factors
as a complete defense would more properly acknowledge the role that sex
discrimination has played in setting the prevailing wage rates in certain
segregated job categories.

A case decided before *Gunther* illustrates the problems caused by
relying on market factors as a justification for paying women less. In *Christensen* v. *Iowa*, the Eighth Circuit Court of Appeals held that the University
of Northern Iowa did not discriminate when it paid secretaries less than
physical plant employees, even though the university's own internal job
study had placed the two job categories in the same labor grade and assigned
equal point values to the jobs. The university argued that adjusting the
system by providing for advanced step starting pay for many of the physical
plant employees, but not for clerical workers, reflected the different prevailing wage rates for such jobs. The Eighth Circuit accepted the university's
justification:

> We find nothing in the text and history of Title VII suggesting that
> Congress intended to abrogate the laws of supply and demand or other
> economic principles that determine wage rates for various kinds of
> work. We do not interpret Title VII as requiring an employer to ignore
> the market in setting wage rates for genuinely different work classifica-
> tions.

The Eighth Circuit concluded that the women had failed to make a Title VII
prima facie case and that market factors could be considered by employers
when the work classifications are *different*,[36] even though it is clearly established that employers cannot rely on the "market price" as a basis for paying
women lower wages than men under the Equal Pay Act.[37]

The Court in *Gunther* did not express any view regarding the continuing
validity of the *Christensen* case.[38] However, the Eighth Circuit's decision was
based in part upon an extremely narrow view of Title VII, which the
Gunther decision arguably corrects. The court in *Christensen* rejected the
argument that reliance upon market rates impermissibly carries over the
effects of past discrimination in the marketplace into the wage policies of the
university, relying on the notion that Title VII was intended to ensure equal
job *opportunities*. Since the women were theoretically free to change jobs,
the Eighth Circuit concluded that equal opportunity was not at issue and

---

36. *Christensen* v. *Iowa*, 563 F.2d 353 (8th Cir. 1977).

37. See, e.g., *Corning Glass Works* v. *Brennan*, 417 U.S. 188, 205 (1974).

38. See n. 8 of the Court's opinion in *Gunther*, but see also Justice Rehnquist's
dissenting opinion, 452 U.S. at 204, suggesting the continuing validity of the *Christensen* case.

therefore that the women had failed to show a violation of Title VII. A similarly limited view of Title VII was urged upon the Supreme Court by the county in *Gunther*—that is, that Title VII could be relied upon for hiring and assignment cases, but that the Equal Pay Act equal work standard should apply to Title VII sex-based wage discrimination cases. The Supreme Court rejected such a narrow approach to the definition of equal employment opportunity as inconsistent with the express congressional determination that a "broad approach" is essential to overcoming and undoing the effects of discrimination. This suggests that the *Christensen* case would be decided differently under the logic of *Gunther*. Nevertheless, the question of the extent to which "market factors" may be relied upon by employers in establishing a "factor other than sex" defense remains a troublesome issue not resolved by *Gunther*.

Faced with a related question in a post-*Gunther* Title VII equal pay case, *Kouba* v. *Allstate Insurance Co.*, the Ninth Circuit Court of Appeals applied what it described as a "pragmatic" standard of "reasonableness," which "protects against abuse yet accommodates employer discretion." The court held that the employer must "use the factor [other than sex] reasonably in light of the employer's stated purpose as well as its other practices."[39] The employer, an insurance company, used prior salary to determine the wages of its new sales agents. The trial court held that the company's method of computing wages constituted unlawful sex discrimination under Title VII, and that use of prior salary did not constitute a "factor other than sex" within the meaning of the Equal Pay Act's fourth affirmative defense. This conclusion was consistent with well-established Equal Pay Act law that resort to prior salary or "market rate" as a basis for setting starting rates is not an acceptable justification for wage differentials.[40] On appeal, although the court of appeals shared the lower court's "fear that an employer might manipulate its use of prior salary to underpay female employees," it rejected the trial court's approach, which required the employer to demonstrate that it had made a reasonable attempt to satisfy itself that the factor causing the wage differential was not the product of sex discrimination. The court of appeals instead adopted an approach that focused on the employer's business reason for using the factor: "An employer thus cannot use a factor which causes a wage differential between male and female employees *absent an acceptable business reason.* Conversely, a factor used to effectuate some business policy is not prohibited simply because a wage differential results" (emphasis added). The court of appeals expressly left for another day the task of formulating a standard to distinguish between unacceptable business reasons and acceptable ones, observing that not

---

39. *Kouba* v. *Allstate Insurance Co.*, 691 F.2d 873, 876–877 (9th Cir. 1982).
40. See Barnett, "Comparable Worth and the Equal Pay Act," p. 1692.

every reason making economic sense is acceptable. The trial court was instructed that before finding a violation on remand, it must evaluate the business reasons asserted by the employer and find that they "do not reasonably explain its use."[41]

Although the court of appeals adopted a "reasonableness" standard to evaluate the employer's asserted business reasons, it failed to define the employer's burden of establishing such an affirmative defense. More importantly, the *Kouba* court failed to apply appropriate Equal Pay Act precedent in analyzing the "factor other than sex" defense. This departure from precedent in *Kouba* has been criticized as "unnecessarily calling into question the established and well understood law under [the Equal Pay Act]."[42]

Unlike the *Kouba* case, *Briggs v. City of Madison* compared jobs that were different in content, and therefore the court was required to interpret the application of the fourth affirmative defense to a pay equity claim. Nevertheless, by holding that the employer rebutted the plaintiffs' *prima facie* case with "evidence of its perception that the retention of sanitarians required raising their salary ranges," the district court ignored the heavy burden of establishing an affirmative defense.[43] The employer's subjective evidence clearly could not satisfy the affirmative Equal Pay Act burden of demonstrating that a "factor other than sex" provided the basis for the wage differential. The court in *Briggs* thus misapprehended the clear evidentiary consequences of *Gunther's* holding.

Bringing Post-*Gunther* Pay Equity Cases

The reluctance of courts to enter the "controversial" area of comparable worth is clear from the Supreme Court's careful limiting language in *Gunther*. The Court maintained that the women's claim in *Gunther* was not based on the "comparable worth" concept, and characterized it as follows:

> [The women's] claim is not based on the controversial concept of "comparable worth," under which plaintiffs might claim increased compensation on the basis of a comparison of the intrinsic worth or difficulty of their job with that of other jobs in the same organization in our community. Rather, [the women] seek to prove, by direct evidence, that their wages were depressed because of intentional sex discrimination, consisting of setting the wage scale for female guards, but not for

---

41. *Kouba* v. *Allstate Insurance Co.*, 523 F. Supp. 148 (E.D. Cal. 1981), *rev'd* and *rem'd*, 691 F.2d 873 (9th Cir. 1982).

42. Barnett, "Comparable Worth and the Equal Pay Act," p. 1692; see also discussion of *Kouba* in *Bence* v. *Detroit Health Corporation*, 000 F.2d 000, 32 FEP Cases 434, 438–39 (6th Cir. 1983).

43. *Briggs* v. *City of Madison*, 28 FEP Cases 739 at 750.

male guards, at a level lower than its own survey of outside markets and the worth of the jobs warranted.[44]

The Court noted that Gunther's claim did not require a court to make its own "subjective assessment of the value of the male and female guard jobs or to attempt by statistical technique or other method to quantify the effect of sex discrimination on the wage rates."[45]

Although the Court expressly declined to define the scope of future lawsuits, the cautious language of the opinion suggests that post-*Gunther* litigation must be very carefully structured. Otherwise, the door opened by *Gunther* could be closed by unfavorable resolution of the legal issues discussed above.

Two cases discussed below provide factual models from which an initial approach for future cases may be developed: (1) wages inconsistent with the employer's own job evaluation system and (2) substantial wage disparities between jobs that are quite similar, but not "substantially equal," combined with other evidence of sex discrimination. A third case, comparing wages for dissimilar jobs without systematic job evaluation evidence, represents an approach that failed before *Gunther* was decided; it provides an example of an approach that has little chance of immediate success. All three cases arise in the context of historically sex-segregated job structures.

Wages Inconsistent with the Employer's Own Job Evaluation System

A case that was pending on a petition for review by the Supreme Court at the time review was granted in *Gunther* provides a compelling factual model. As in the Supreme Court's characterization of the *Gunther* plaintiffs' claim, *International Union of Electrical, Radio, and Machine Workers (IUE)* v. *Westinghouse Electric Corp.*,[46] was based upon a theory of intentional undervaluation of womens' jobs, resulting in pay rates below their evaluated worth to the employer. The plaintiffs—the union and a class of past and present female production, maintenance, and warehouse employees at a New Jersey Westinghouse plant—claimed that the present discriminatory wage structure was the direct descendant of past overt discrimination against women.

The plaintiffs in the IUE case pointed first to the employer's history of intentional sex discrimination. In the 1930s Westinghouse analyzed and assigned points to each job on the basis of a gender-neutral job-rating system, although the jobs were sex-segregated, and then deliberately set lower wage rates for jobs occupied by women than for those with equal

---

44. *County of Washington* v. *Gunther*, 452 U.S. at 166.
45. Ibid. at 181.
46. *IUE* v. *Westinghouse Electric Corporation*, 19 FEP Cases 450 (D.N.J. 1979), 631 F.2d 1094 (3d Cir. 1980), *cert. denied*, 452 U.S. 967 (1981).

ratings held by men. The point ratings were based on the employer's evaluation of the knowledge and training required and the specific demands and responsibilities of the jobs.

The employer's 1939 *Industrial Relations Manual* described the system as follows:

WAGE RATES FOR WOMEN

The occupations or jobs filled by women are point rated on the same basis of point values for Requirements of the Job and Responsibility, with the same allowance for Job Conditions, as are the jobs commonly filled by men. . . .

The gradient of the women's wage curve, however, is not the same for women as for men because of the more transient character of the service of the former, the relative shortness of their activity in industry, the differences in environment required, the extra services that must be provided, overtime limitations, extra help needed for the occasional heavy work, *and the general sociological factors not requiring discussion herein.*

The rate or range for Labor Grades do not coincide with the values on the men's scale. Basically, then, we have another wage curve or Key Sheet for women below and not parallel with the men's curve.[47]

The system of pay differentials through sex-segregated key sheets continued until 1965, the effective date of Title VII.

Plaintiffs claimed that when the pay scale was unified in 1965, the new wage scale embodied the deliberately discriminatory policy of the prior plan. Although the key sheets were combined into one sheet, the employer created new labor grades at the bottom of the old grades and assigned almost all of the predominantly women's jobs to the new bottom-ranked grades. The women maintained that the system of sex-based pay differentials instituted in the 1930s had therefore continued to the present, modified only in form.

Because the plaintiffs did not attempt to show that the "men's" and "women's" jobs were "substantially equal," the trial court ruled against them. On appeal, the Third Circuit Court of Appeals held that even though the alleged facts could not support an Equal Pay Act claim, because the jobs compared were not substantially "equal," the plaintiffs should be given an opportunity to present to the trial court their Title VII claim based upon intentional discrimination. As in the *Gunther* case, only the threshold issue was considered by the Third Circuit decision. When the Third Circuit's

---

47. Westinghouse Industrial Relations Manual: Wage Administration, November 1, 1938 and February 1, 1938, cited in Brief for Appellants, Appendix, 110–62, 158. *IUE* v. *Westinghouse Electric Corporation*, 631 F.2d 1094 (3d Cir. 1980). *See* Newman and Vonhof, "Separate but Equal," pp. 292–96.

conclusion had been confirmed by the *Gunther* decision, the case was returned to the district court for trial of plaintiffs' claims. Before going to trial, however, the plaintiffs obtained a favorable settlement from the employer, including back pay and prospective upgrading of their jobs.[48]

Substantial Wage Discrepancies between Similar but Not Substantially Equal Jobs

Decided before *Gunther*, the *Taylor* v. *Charley Brothers Co.*[49] case provides an early example of a case where a federal district court found, after trial, that although the jobs compared are not substantially equal, a portion of the male-female wage differential could only be attributed to intentional sex discrimination. The employer was therefore held to be liable under Title VII. The union was also held to be liable because of its acquiescence in the wage discrimination.

The plaintiffs, women warehouse employees of a wholesale grocery supplier in Pennsylvania, sued their employer for discriminating on the basis of sex by maintaining sex-segregated job classifications, by failing to consider female applicants for certain job categories and promotions, and by paying women less for work of comparable value to the employer.

Jobs in the warehouse were divided into two departments. Department 1, composed of men only, included dry grocery and general warehouse work. Employees in this department handled canned and bottled foods, dog and cat food, perishable foods, such as fruits and vegetables, frozen food, meat, and dairy products. Department 2, composed of women, with the exception of two male forklift operators, included a health and beauty aids division and a repack division. Employees in health and beauty aids handled drugstore or toiletry items, film, panty hose, and merchandise such as mops, light bulbs, pails, and other household items. Repack division employees handled cigarettes and other tobacco products, candy, spices, gravy and soup mixes, and certain store supplies.

The district court found that from 1964 until 1980 no woman was hired into Department 1 and that, until recently, the employer did not even consider applications from women when job openings occurred in that department. Similarly, the company did not interview men for openings in Department 2.

The court found that most of the jobs in the two departments were not "substantially equal," but that the jobs were all characteristic of laborer's work. However, the court also found that the hourly wage differential of $1.70 (pre-1980) or $1.45 (post-1980) could not be justified on the basis of the different content of the jobs in the two departments. It could only be

---

48. *IUE* v. *Westinghouse Electric Corporation*, 28 EPD ¶32, 645 (D.N.J. 1982) (settlement tentatively approved).
49. *Taylor* v. *Charley Brothers Co.*, 25 FEP Cases 602 (W.D. Pa. 1981).

attributed to intentional sex discrimination, as evidenced by the longstanding policies of segregating women from men in the work force and assigning substantially lower wages to those women who were performing jobs substantially equal to jobs performed by men. The court summarized the evidence of intentional discrimination as follows:

> Defendant Charley Brothers' intention to discriminate against women in setting their wage rates lower than men may be inferred from the fact that it had not undertaken any evaluation which would have indicated the value of the jobs held by either men or women; from its pattern and practice of segregating women within a single department within the company; from its pattern and practice of only considering women job applicants for openings in that department; and from various discriminatory remarks made by company officials.[50]

The court adopted the job evaluation performed by the plaintiffs' expert according to criteria of the American Association of Industrial Management, and rejected the evaluation performed by the employer's expert. Except for a few job categories where the work was "substantially equal," the court concluded that women in Department 2 should earn about 90 percent of what the men earn in Department 1. Thus, the court concluded that women were assigned lower wages because they were women, and not because of the content of their jobs.

In summary, in the *Charley Brothers* case, the type of work being performed by women was similar to that performed by men, although not necessarily "substantially equal" within the meaning of the Equal Pay Act. The results of a job evaluation study, which indicated that the women were underpaid, combined with other evidence of sex discrimination, resulted in a finding that the wage differential violated Title VII.

A High-Risk Approach: Comparing Wages for Dissimilar Jobs without Systematic Evidence

In the pre-*Gunther* case of *Lemons* v. *City and County of Denver*,[51] a class of nurses (more than 97 percent of them women) employed by the city of Denver challenged the city's job classification and pay plan. Under the plan, employees were assigned a job class, and then "related" job classes were clustered around a "key" class. The key classes included "Graduate Nurse I" and "Licensed Practical Nurse I." Each "key" class was subject to an annual Denver area wage survey to determine what the private sector paid for a corresponding job. The key classes were established so that easy comparison could be made with jobs in the private sector.

---

50. Ibid. at 614.
51. *Lemons* v. *City and County of Denver*, 17 FEP Cases 906 (D. Col. 1978), 620 F.2d 228 (10th Cir.), *cert. denied*, 449 U.S. 888 (1980).

The nurses' Title VII claim was based on the proposition that nursing positions, predominantly held by women, were underpaid by the city and the community in comparison with other predominantly male jobs of equal worth to the employers. Arguing that sex-discriminatory wage policies prevailing in the community should not be perpetuated by the city, the nurses maintained that the nursing "key" class should be discontinued, and that they should instead be paid on an existing scale that the city maintains for professionals and administrators, the "General Administrative Series."

The nurses charged that their jobs required greater training and skill than many other male-dominated city jobs—for example, tree trimmers, sign painters, and real estate appraisers—that were compensated at a higher rate. However, they presented no systematic job evaluation evidence to support their claims.

The city maintained that there was no discrimination against nurses on the basis of sex, that it was operating the system in good faith, and that the wages it set for nurses were set to meet competition. The city also argued that it was bound by the city charter to give like pay for like work and that it was following the charter.

The Tenth Circuit Court of Appeals upheld the district court's judgment in favor of the city: "The courts under existing authority cannot require the City within its employment to reassess the worth of services in each position in relation to all others, and to strike a new balance and relationship. Also, this cannot be done in total disregard of conditions in the community." Quoting the *Christensen* case, the court concluded that Title VII does not require an employer to ignore the market in setting wage rates for genuinely different work classifications.

The *Lemons* case attempted a direct attack, without adequate supporting data, on the problem of undervaluation of women's work. The district court described it as "pregnant with the possibility of disrupting the entire economic system of the United States of America." This kind of approach raises the specter of involving federal courts in the process of restructuring the wage-setting process. The lesson of the *Lemons* case is that a claim of undervaluation of women's work should be supported by the results of well-designed job evaluation studies and other evidence that shows that the employer discriminates on the basis of sex. Such evidence is crucial where the jobs being compared are dissimilar.

Conclusion

The *Gunther* case provides pay equity litigators with the possibility of attacking sex-based wage discrimination caused by the undervaluation of "women's work." *Gunther* answered one important question, but left open many others. The *Gunther* case did not resolve the following major issues:

What are the *prima facie* case requirements for Title VII compensation discrimination claims?

What effect will incorporation of the Equal Pay Act's fourth affirmative defense have on Title VII litigation? Will "other factor other than sex" be interpreted to include reference to market factors or prevailing job rates as a justification for paying women less? Or will reliance on market factors be rejected as an employer defense?

What constitutes a *bona fide* job evaluation system that does not discriminate on the basis of sex? Where the employer has not utilized a job evaluation system, will plaintiffs be entitled to present their own job evaluation as evidence?

The future of pay equity litigation depends upon how these and other questions are answered by courts during the next several years. The dissenting opinion in *Gunther* predicted that the Court's decision will be treated like a restricted railroad ticket, "good for this day and train only."[52] To prove that prediction wrong, post-*Gunther* cases must be very carefully structured to permit development of the "comparable worth" concept without unduly limiting the Title VII theories under which such claims can be brought.

Before filing a "comparability" lawsuit under Title VII, possible cases should be examined to determine whether the following factors are present:

1. A systematic job evaluation study
   • Wages paid for jobs held predominantly by women are inconsistent with results of a job evaluation study *conducted by the employer.*
   • Alternatively, the results of a systematic job evaluation study conducted by the potential plaintiffs' experts reveal a sex-discriminatory wage structure. (This situation is not as advantageous to plaintiffs as the one described above, but not all employers have conducted job evaluation studies.)
2. Comparison of wages for similar jobs
   • There are substantial pay disparities between "similar" jobs; that is, the jobs being compared are characteristic of a particular *type* of work. For example, pay rates for different assembly line jobs or for different forms of laborer's work are compared, rather than pay rates for secretaries and truck drivers.
3. Other evidence of sex discrimination in a sex-segregated workplace
   • Discriminatory statements have been made by the employer.
   • There is evidence of pattern and practice discrimination against women in hiring and assignment of work.

---

52. *County of Washington* v. *Gunther*, 452 U.S. at 183 (Rehnquist, J., dissenting, quoting *Smith* v. *Allwright*, 321 U.S. 649, 669 (1944) (Roberts, J., dissenting)).

At this stage of pay equity litigation, cases should have at least two, and preferably all three, of the above categories of evidence. With only one or none of the above factors, the case would have little chance of immediate success and could result in inhibiting further development of the "comparability" concept under Title VII. In contrast, by bringing the strongest cases first, women begin the gradual process of educating the courts and employers to recognize and remedy the interrelated problems of job segregation and sex-based compensation discrimination. Such an approach provides the possibility of achieving pay equity through litigation.

13
The Role of Labor

LISA PORTMAN, JOY ANN GRUNE, AND EVE JOHNSON

The Structure and Activities of the Labor Movement

Samuel Gompers once compared the labor movement, composed of hundreds of autonomous unions and related organizations, to a rope of sand. Fortunately, the ninety-five unions banded together as the American Federation of Labor and Congress of Industrial Organizations—the AFL-CIO—are stronger than a rope of sand. This federation represents nearly 14 million workers, 26 percent of them female.[1] Three large unions—the Teamsters, the National Education Association, and the United Mine Workers—are outside the AFL-CIO, and there are an undocumented number of smaller, unaffiliated unions.

The unions within the AFL-CIO are diverse, representing professional employees, unskilled workers, highly paid workers, and those who earn little more than the minimum wage. Some unions have a preponderance of women members; some have none or only a few. In spite of this diversity, the issue of comparable worth—or pay equity—has won support in the short time since it surfaced on the national scene; attesting to this is the fact that many unions and the AFL-CIO itself have passed convention resolutions endorsing pay equity.[2]

---

1. *Union Membership and Employment* (Washington, D.C.: AFL-CIO Research Department, 1980).

2. Joy Ann Grune, *Manual on Pay Equity: Raising Wages for Women's Work* (Washington, D.C.: Committee on Pay Equity, 1980), published by the Conference on Alternative State and Local Policies, 2000 Florida Ave., N.W., Washington, D.C. 20009; see also *Highlights of Recent Labor Union Activity* (Washington, D.C.: National Committee on Pay Equity, 1983).

The main function of unions is to bargain for improved hours, wages, and working conditions for their members. Historically, however, the labor movement has expanded its activities to include a wide-range of social reforms in areas such as public education, civil rights, Social Security, the minimum wage, equal pay, and affirmative action. In the 1980s the labor movement is the vanguard of the comparable worth struggle.

Although all affiliated unions can participate in supporting comparable worth through the AFL-CIO, only a few are actively involved in the campaign. It is an important issue for most unions whose members are predominantly female and for those representing workers subject to wage disparities. Philosophical support is offered by unions whose members or industries are not directly affected by the issue. Building trade unions, for example, have few female members and are therefore rarely confronted by salary discrepancies whose adverse effects are felt chiefly by women. Such unions participate in the pay equity struggle by endorsing AFL-CIO policy resolutions and actions. The reluctance of some unions to participate directly in pay equity activities is discussed below.

Women's Rights

The labor movement played a leading role in effecting the passage of the Equal Pay Act of 1963 and the Civil Rights Act of 1964. Labor was not then, nor is it now, in agreement with a narrow interpretation of the "substantially" equal work provision of Title VII of the Civil Rights Act. Nevertheless, its view of working women at that time was not much different from that of society as a whole. The stereotypical notions that women's work was secondary to men's and that women workers needed special protective legislation, prevailed.[3] Furthermore, the value of women's work in women's occupations, relative to the value of men's work in men's occupations, was discussed by labor in terms much like those used by government, industry, and education.

Protective legislation—enacted for the express purpose of safe guarding the health of women workers but subsequently recognized as an impediment to their financial well being—was supported by the AFL-CIO until, at its 1973 Convention in Bal Harbour, Florida, it endorsed the Equal Rights Amendment.[4] Since that time the AFL-CIO and individual unions have been victorious in numerous equal pay cases, establishing nondiscriminatory wage scales and acquiring back pay for their members. The unions' attack on unequal pay was not entirely altruistic, it should be noted, since both unions and employers were held liable if signed contracts were found to

---

3. *UAW Policy: Convention Resolutions Relative to Women Worker's Rights* UAW Women's Department (Detroit, 1968).

4. *AFL-CIO Proceedings*, Bal Harbour, Florida, 1973.

be in violation of the Equal Pay Act. Although the equal pay fight has been won in principle, violations, of course, still exist.

The Coalition of Labor Union Women

In addition to the AFL-CIO, affiliated national unions, and unaffiliated unions and associations, the labor movement includes trade and industrial departments, state, county, and city labor councils, world organizations, and special institutes—all of which may also deal with comparable worth issues. The pay equity work of one such group—the Coalition of Labor Union Women—has been particularly noteworthy. Union women were instrumental in the founding of the National Organization for Women, the Women's Equity Action League, and other feminist organizations, but they perceived a need for an additional organization specifically for union women. With such an organization in mind, a group of union staff women met in 1973, in an airport in Chicago, and outlined a plan for the Coalition of Labor Union Women. CLUW's founders hoped for a turnout of 800 women at the organization's first convention a year later; over 3,000 attended. Today CLUW has 8,000 members, and its president, Joyce Miller, vice-president of the Amalgamated Clothing and Textile Workers Union (ACTWU), was selected to be the first woman on the previously all-male AFL-CIO Executive Council.

Pay equity is one of CLUW's priorities, and CLUW is an effective proponent of the principle. CLUW's volunteer counsel (all CLUW officers serve gratis), Winn Newman, is a leading figure in pay equity litigation. He served as counsel for the International Union of Electrical Workers (IUE) when it litigated its landmark case against Westinghouse and is currently special counsel for the American Federation of State, County and Municipal Employees (AFSCME) in its suit against the state of Washington. Both he and CLUW have published materials and held national conferences on comparable worth.

Approaches to Antidiscrimination Issues

The AFL-CIO approaches antidiscrimination efforts through many avenues. First and foremost is collective bargaining, often coordinated with litigation. Education is important for staff and rank-and-file members, as is the gathering and dissemination of information. The federation has also sought new legislation and attempted to broaden the interpretation of existing legislation.

Collective Bargaining. Collective bargaining is central to union activity; it is what unions do best. Collective bargaining is the process through which employees represented by a labor union negotiate wages, benefits, and working conditions with their employer. The resulting agreement is a legally enforceable contract that prevents employers from reneging on promises. Through decades of contract negotiation, mechanisms have been developed that can correct many discrimination problems and ameliorate others. Contracts can, for example, promote plantwide seniority so that women can move out of low-wage women's departments when openings occur in higher-paid ones; they can require employers to re-evaluate job classifications to upgrade certain work grades and titles, allowing women in those slots to move to better-paying categories; they can allow workers to use the grievance procedure and arbitration to correct some inequities; and they can require a reassessment of hiring practices that assign women to low-pay, low-opportunity jobs.

Education.   Education programs for adult union members are numerous. Classes meet in university and community college facilities, union halls, churches, union residential schools, at the George Meany Center for Labor Studies, and at work sites.[5] The programs may be as sophisticated as a thirteen-week course at the Harvard University Labor Program or as simple as a stewards' training course at a local union hall. New ideas are translated into teaching materials that eventually reach large numbers of workers. Some courses are designed particularly for women.[6]

Gathering and Disseminating Information.   The AFL-CIO and the larger unions maintain research departments to keep abreast of economic issues affecting their members. Data are available from the Labor Department, the Bureau of Labor Statistics, other government agencies, universities, and industry, and this information may be disseminated through the labor press and special pamphlets.

Legislation.   Individual unions and the AFL-CIO have been involved in many legislative campaigns at national, state, and local levels. As mentioned above, the AFL-CIO has made a complete turnaround on the Equal Rights Amendment and now not only endorses it but devotes resources toward its ratification.

Pay Equity

Labor unions have been among the leaders of the movement for pay equity. The AFL-CIO, some of its affiliated unions, CLUW, and independent unions have used a variety of tactics in this cause. Unions that have done pay equity work include but are not limited to: the American Federation of State, County and Municipal Employees (AFSCME); the Service Employees International Union (SEIU); the International Union of Electrical, Radio and Machine Workers (IUE); the United Electrical Workers

---

5. Annual catalogues of the George Meany Center for Labor Studies, Silver Spring, Md., 1972–1981.

6. For a detailed discussion of labor education for women, see Barbara Wertheimer, ed., *Labor Education for Women Workers* (Philadelphia: Temple University Press, 1981).

of America (UE); the Communications Workers of America (CWA); the United Auto Workers (UAW) 65; the National Union of Hospital and Health Care Employees (1199); the American Nurses Association (ANA); the American Association of University Professors (AAUP); the Telecommunications International Union (TIU); and the National Education Association (NEA). Most of these unions have substantial numbers of members in predominantly female jobs, such as clerical, library, nursing, and electrical assembly work.

The movement for pay equity owes a great deal to the determination of labor unions. Comparable worth as a measure of wages made its first known appearance in the United States in the 1940s when the War Labor Board ruled that the General Electric Company and the Westinghouse Corporation had ignored their own job evaluation studies and reduced the wages for women's work by up to one-third. The case had been filed by the UE, and the union's victory resulted in wage increases for thousands of female electrical workers. Other unions—for example, the UAW—were active in the broad coalition that struggled for seventeen years for the passage of the 1963 Equal Pay Act, which originally included comparable worth language.[7]

The roots of the contemporary movement for pay equity can be found in the IUE's efforts since 1969 to litigate structural wage inequities under Title VII of the 1964 Civil Rights Act.[8] The IUE, CLUW, and other organizations supplemented this work by education, research, lobbying, and testifying at congressional and agency hearings that Title VII is applicable to wage discrimination associated with job segregation. In the case of the IUE's Title VII Compliance Program, the international union led the way in formulating an approach to structural wage inequities and organizing local and member support and participation. In other unions it was the state and local affiliates who took the initiative and later received support from the international headquarters.

Once under way, the development of pay equity activities within a union is shaped by the dynamic exchange between members and staff on the one hand, and among local, state, and international levels on the other. In addition, the union is acting and reacting within a larger environment in which employers often resist pay equity demands through well-financed and well-organized campaigns in the workplace, in the courts, and in the legislatures.

AFL-CIO Policies

Like many of its affiliated unions, one of the AFL-CIO's first official steps in supporting pay equity took the form of adopting a resolution at a

---

7. Dorothy Haener, Testimony on behalf of the UAW to Senate and House Labor Committee, April 1983.

8. Winn Newman and Carole Wilson, "The Union in Affirmative Action," *Labor Law Journal*, June 1980.

national convention. AFL-CIO resolutions are particularly important because they are policy statements that represent the positions of 95 labor unions. At its November 1979 convention, the federation endorsed the following statement on equal pay for work of comparable value:

WHEREAS: The differential between men's and women's wages continues to grow, and men now make 175% of the women's earnings; and

WHEREAS: Over 80% of women workers are segregated into "female" occupations that are different in content from "men's" jobs, but in many cases are not different in the skill, effort and responsibility required; and

WHEREAS: Low rates for women tend to bring down the wage rate for men as well as women; therefore be it

RESOLVED: That the AFL-CIO encourages all efforts, such as that commissioned by the EEOC, to determine whether appropriate job measurement procedures exist or can be developed to reevaluate women's jobs according to their "real worth" without regard to sex so that the wage rates paid will truly reflect skill, effort, responsibility and working conditions; and be it further

RESOLVED: That the AFL-CIO treats job inequities resulting from sex and race discrimination like all other inequities which must be corrected, and urges its affiliates to adopt the concept of equal pay for work of comparable value in organizing and in negotiating collective bargaining agreements.

Two years later, the AFL-CIO unanimously adopted a second and stronger resolution:

Working women continue to suffer from widespread wage discrimination in the workplace. Full-time women workers earn 50¢ for every dollar earned by full-time men in the work force.

A 1981 EEOC-commissioned study completed by the National Academy of Sciences confirms that enormous wage differential results from discrimination against women.

The AFL-CIO calls upon its affiliated unions:

—To work through contract negotiations to upgrade undervalued job classifications, regardless of whether they are typically considered "male" or "female" jobs.

—To initiate joint union-employer pay equity studies to identify and correct internal inequities between predominantly female and predominantly male classes.

The AFL-CIO urges its affiliates to recognize fully their obligations to treat pay inequities resulting from sex discrimination like all other inequities which must be corrected and to adopt the concept of "equal pay for comparable work" in contract negotiations.

The AFL-CIO will take all other appropriate action to bring about true equality in pay for work of comparable value and to remove all barriers to equal opportunity for women.

The 1981 statement is more specific in calling on affiliated unions to "work through contract negotiations to upgrade undervalued job classifications" and to "initiate joint union-employer pay equity studies." It also says the AFL-CIO will take "all other appropriate action," which includes litigation. This strengthening of the federation's position was undoubtedly due to a combination of factors, among them the increasing activity of working women, unions, and other organizations in support of comparable worth, favorable court and strike settlements, the Supreme Court's conclusive decision that Title VII is not restricted in its application to equal work situations, and continuing education, debate, and lobbying within the labor movement on the proper role of unions in promoting pay equity.

In testimony submitted to the Equal Employment Opportunity Commission (EEOC) in 1980, Lane Kirkland, president of the AFL-CIO, affirmed the importance of the issue and stated the essence of the labor movement's position:

> Experience demonstrates that the system for setting wages, and establishing other terms and conditions of employment that best meets workers' needs is collective bargaining. No single step is more likely to bring greater equity to the wage setting process than the spread of union organization to every worker who wants a voice in his or her own working situation. The AFL-CIO and its affiliates are devoting their energy and resources to that task. It is difficult for us to envisage a more fruitful contribution to the public good.[9]

In view of the statistics showing that women's wages increase dramatically when they organize, this is a cogent point. Kirkland went on to state that strategies other than collective bargaining must also go forward. In particular, he urged the EEOC to move vigorously, but carefully and systematically, to consolidate its developing legal position in the courts. He suggested that the Commission turn its attention to the most straightforward cases— *Westinghouse*, for example—in which there is no need for the Commission

---

9. Lane Kirkland, Testimony. Hearings before the United States Equal Employment Opportunity Commission on Job Segregation and Wage Discrimination, Washington, D.C., 1980. (Available on microfiche from EEOC).

to provide a basis for comparing different jobs and their worth. The *employer* has provided a standard of comparison.

Union Tactics

Organizing, collective bargaining, internal education, job evaluation studies, and litigation have been the basic tools used by unions to win wage equity increases for women workers. When unions feel that public sentiment, membership support, or existing laws and their enforcement are not strong enough to permit them to achieve their goals, they also lobby, draft legislation, build coalitions, engage in education of the public, and financially support equity activities. The selection of tactics, as well as the way they are combined and weighted, varies among unions and changes over time. The examples of union activities offered below are not exhaustive. They were selected because, in combination, they portray the range of approaches unions have taken.

Job Evaluation Studies

The proper role of job evaluation in wage setting has been debated within the labor movement. Historically, organized labor has been skeptical of job evaluation systems because employers have used them to perpetuate discrimination and justify existing wage rates. The AFL-CIO went on record against their use as early as 1955 because employers were using them as "objective standards" for setting wages in order to supplant collective bargaining in wage determination.[10] John Zalusky, an AFL-CIO economist, states that "the range of potential human error and mismanagement [in job evaluations] begs for decisions by agreement at the bargaining table or by a disinterested party through a grievance procedure. Certainly the issue is too important to be left to the judgement of consultants or management technicians."[11]

On the other hand, unions have used job evaluation successfully in a wide range of situations. They have lobbied successfully with other organizations for state and local legislation requiring wage and job studies in public employment; District 1199 and the Connecticut State Employees Association, for example, succeeded in securing legislation mandating such a study in that state. The new CWA collective bargaining agreement with AT&T on behalf of members in the Bell System calls for a joint labor management occupational job evaluation committee at each operating telephone company. These committees will research, develop, and make recommendations on job evaluation plans. IUE won a major court case, *IUE* v. *Westinghouse*, and several out-of-court settlements by arguing that the

---

10. John Zalusky, "Job Evaluation: An Uneven World," *AFL-CIO Federationist* (April 1981).
    11. Ibid.

General Electric Company, Westinghouse, and other employers had deliberately used lower pay scales for all women employees in clear violation of their own job evaluation results. Because of these victories, new contracts often contain substantial increases in wage rates for predominantly female electrical assembly jobs.[12] Other unions, such as AFSCME, District 65 of the UAW, the Maine State Employees Association, and the Civil Service Employees Association in New York have negotiated joint labor-management wage and job studies. The study results are used by unions in bargaining, litigating, and organizing, as has been done, for example, in Washington State, San Jose, Connecticut, New York, Maine, Los Angeles, Florida, and Minnesota. Other unions have performed small, inexpensive studies of their own to buttress bargaining demands, as AFSCME did in Humboldt County, California.[13] Critical to these successes has been the union's step-by-step involvement, from the selection of a technical consultant, through the study design, to the application and evaluation of the results.

Traditional job evaluation systems have been identified as a major source of discrimination against women because they leave out or undervalue the factors that are often found in women's work, such as manual dexterity and repetitive lifting. Unions, often jointly with management, have developed and applied less biased job evaluation plans, which identify the extent of wage depression for women's jobs and set the stage for bargaining demands. Job evaluation has been extremely important to unions in documenting wage discrimination, to the point that some management consultants are advising clients to avoid job evaluations if they do not already exist, lest the company become vulnerable to legal action.

The evolving union position on the role of job evaluation appears to be guided by three basic questions: (1) Are the systems unbiased as far as is humanly possible? (2) How will they relate to collective bargaining? (3) Do they perpetuate discriminatory wage rates? Job evaluation studies are not a substitute for collective bargaining. They can be expensive, time-consuming, and technically complex, and they are vulnerable to employer domination. But if unions are at least equal participants with management, these studies, as the last decade shows, can document wage depression for undervalued jobs and serve as important organizing tools for increasing commitment to pay equity. By calling on its members to "initiate joint union-management pay equity studies," the AFL-CIO has officially accepted the role of job evaluation in wage setting, with the important condition that labor be a full participant.

---

12. Newman and Wilson, "The Union in Affirmative Action."
13. *A Survey of State and Local Government Initiatives on Pay Equity* (Washington, D.C.: National Committee on Pay Equity, 1983).

Collective Bargaining

Collective bargaining has been used by unions to negotiate job evaluation studies and to provide wage equity increases to occupants of undervalued jobs. In San Jose, when the city refused to correct the wage discrimination identified by a job evaluation study, AFSCME members struck for
eight days. The city agreed to commit $1.5 million to upgrade jobs, above
and beyond general salary increases. (This strike is described in more detail
below in the AFSCME case study.)

The National Union of Hospital and Health Care Employees (1199),
negotiated a contract with the state of Connecticut that provides a pay
equity fund equal to 1 percent of the health care workers' payroll. This is the
first step in a continuing effort to provide equal pay for work of comparable
value to the predominantly female hospital and health care workers in the
state.

SEIU has negotiated upgradings in job classifications, across-the-board
(as opposed to percentage) wage increases, and higher entry-level wages in
order to raise salaries for undervalued jobs. (These accomplishments are
described in more detail below.)

Collective bargaining is the heart of union activity. Successful bargaining for wage equity increases usually requires prior research, education,
organizing, and training.

Litigation

When education, organizing, research, and bargaining fail to produce
agreement with the employer on wages, the union has several options.
These include reducing its demands, bringing public pressure to bear on the
employer, striking, filing charges with government agencies, and litigation.
Labor unions, and especially the IUE and AFSCME, have borne a large
share of the responsibility for developing a legal strategy for the enforcement of comparable worth under Title VII and Executive Order 11246.

The IUE was a pioneer in this area. Its work, and that of AFSCME, is a
model for union use of antidiscrimination laws to strengthen the union, the
members, the contract, and the environment for comparable worth. Not
only have the IUE's out-of-court settlements and legal victories brought pay
increases and back wages to its members; more generally they have established wage discrimination associated with job segregation as a clear violation of the law.

In most cases, IUE began with research on wage and job structures and
found that the employer had ignored its own study results and set women's
wages below the worth of the jobs. When collective bargaining failed to
produce agreement, the union turned to the National Labor Relations
Board, and when necessary, filed charges or a lawsuit. Other unions—most
notably AFSCME—have used EEOC charges to strengthen their hands at
the bargaining table.

Although few unions have invested in an aggressive Title VII enforcement program, victories in the *Westinghouse* and *Gunther* cases have been extremely important in the development and viability of pay equity initiatives (see Chapter 12). By establishing some comparable worth inequities as clear violations of the law, these victories put pressure on employers. They are also important symbolic victories, confirming working women's feelings that the undervaluation of their work is wrong, and they provide a legal context and vocabulary in which these feelings can be validated.

In addition to their length and expense, court cases can have the disadvantage of removing the issue from the workplace to the courts, from workers to lawyers. Litigation is not a substitute for education, research, organizing, or bargaining; it is a tool, and, if used properly, it can complement other union activities.

Education and Organizing

A union's ability to raise wages for predominantly female jobs depends, in the final analysis, on the commitment of its members, staff, and leaders. Bargaining for pay equity, like all bargaining, requires staff energy, money, time, educational resources, and expertise. Pay equity advocates have therefore carried out education, training, and organizing geared to members, staff, and leaders at international, state, and local levels.

Unions themselves have prepared educational programs and materials on all aspects of pay equity to mobilize their members, including convention resolutions, workshops at union conventions and women's conferences, seminars for lawyers, newspaper coverage, pamphlets, and manuals. This educational work is designed to pave the way for bargaining and to meet member needs as tactics are refined. The mobilization of union members around contract demands enhances the effectiveness of the negotiating committee at the bargaining table. Should a strike be necessary, there is no substitute for a well-educated, well-organized, and enthusiastic membership united in their determination to move toward wage equity. It is particularly important that members be actively organized for pay equity. The struggle for comparable worth seeks to reverse the historical undervaluation of women's labor and the trivialization of women workers. The process of winning wage equity can be as empowering for women as the wage victory itself, for the process and the victory bring about shifts in the balance of political and economic power in the workplace. Male co-workers must be educated and organized to support re-evaluations of the wage-setting process for undervalued jobs, some of whose occupants are men. All workers must guard against attempts by employers to remedy the wage gap by illegally reducing male wages. The support of men in the workplace is necessary, not only for the pay equity fight itself, but also to prevent unnecessary divisions that may weaken the union's power to represent all its members fairly.

Because of the growing appeal of pay equity to women workers, and the growing support it is receiving from men, unions such as AFSCME and SEIU are beginning to use comparable worth in their promotional materials and organizing drives. It is possible that pay equity may be the catalyst that brings labor unions and working women together in a new partnership that takes as its right the dignity and value of women's labor.

Wider Efforts

Although unions' traditional responsibility is to negotiate for wages, benefits, and working conditions, they do take part in larger social, political, and economic struggles and rely on a variety of tactics in order to do so. This involvement may be motivated by a desire to advance the unions' primary goals or by a sense of responsibility to the wider society.

Thirteen international unions and CLUW are members of the National Committee on Pay Equity, a coalition of individuals and organizations including work force representatives, women's and minority organizations, lawyers, researchers, state and local government agencies, and working men and women. Unions have been members of local and state coalitions, in Michigan and California for example, and have lobbied successfully for comparable worth legislation in a number of states.[14] On the federal level, union representatives have lobbied and testified for enforcement of Title VII and Executive Order 11246.

These activities have been critical, for unions usually bring power and resources when they decide to broaden their efforts. Unions have helped to lead the way in litigation, new legislation, organizing, and bargaining. The development of a national policy like pay equity is an expensive undertaking. Although women's and civil rights organizations can contribute people, ideas, and determination, they are often short on money, lawyers, and technical assistance, also essential ingredients for policy development and implementation. Unions are particularly important when the government fails to play a leadership role.

Union Reluctance to Promote Comparable Worth Policies

Although the number is increasing, not all unions that represent workers in predominantly female occupations have actively advanced equal pay for work of comparable value for reasons located outside and inside the labor movement. Comparable worth is a sex discrimination issue as well as a bargaining issue. Enforcement agencies of the federal government, such as the EEOC and the Office for Federal Contract Compliance Programs (OFCCP), have not encouraged union participation in enforcing antidiscrimination laws; in fact, in the past, these agencies often held unions legally

---

14. Bureau of National Affairs Special Report, *The Comparable Worth Issue* (Washington, D.C.: Bureau of National Affairs, 1981).

and financially responsible for discrimination along with the employers, even when the union had tried to bargain and litigate to eliminate it. After much lobbying, this practice was changed during the Carter administration when the EEOC declared that good faith efforts to end discrimination relieved the union of culpability. The government's rejection of unions as allies in enforcement made many unions view sex discrimination laws as legal and financial threats, rather than as tools enabling them to represent workers better.

Some unions, such as the International Ladies Garment Workers Union (ILGWU), represent workers in the secondary segment of the economy, characterized by intense competition, low profits, and low capital investment. Although the ILGWU, which is 80 percent female, claims to have reduced the wage gap between the male and female garment workers in its membership, it has not reduced the gap between its members and, say, auto or steel workers. To date, comparable worth advocates have not addressed interindustry wage differentials. The ILGWU instead is promoting stronger labor laws and regulations to deal with the economic vulnerability of workers in its industries.

Some unions leaders have said that comparable worth has the potential to divide male and female workers. Without effective education and organizing, such a division in the ranks could jeopardize unionization efforts or weaken unions, especially during negotiations.

Union skepticism toward job evaluation has also led to a reluctance to initiate pay equity activities. As noted above, the AFL-CIO is on record as encouraging joint labor-management studies. In order to conduct such a study, however, a union must have the staff, technical expertise, and possibly legal counsel that equal participation requires.

To the best of our knowledge, only one labor union has been found guilty by the courts in a pay equity case. In *Taylor* v. *Charley Brothers Company*, women employees of a wholesale grocery supplier in Pennsylvania charged the company with sex discrimination, including paying women less than men for work of comparable value.[15] The Teamsters, who represent female and male workers at the company, were later charged as well. The women had approached the Teamster business agent with their salary complaints, but he did not represent their interests to the satisfaction of the women or the court. In 1981 the Western District Court of Pennsylvania found in the women's favor. The next year the company and the union settled while the case was on appeal. Charley Brothers agreed to provide approximately $1.1 million in back pay to 250 women, to institute preferential hiring procedures for some heavier warehouse jobs, and to equalize or narrow wage rate differentials between predominately male and predominately female jobs. The Teamsters agreed to these arrangements, which

---

15. *Taylor* v. *Charley Brothers Co.*, 25 FEP Cases 602.

were incorporated into the collective bargaining contract. The Teamsters Union also agreed to distribute $50,000 over three years to their women members.

Case Studies

Let us now look at the pay equity efforts of several AFL-CIO affiliated unions in greater detail.[16] These are not the only unions working on the issue; they were chosen because their approaches to pay equity illustrate the various paths available.

The American Federation of State, County and Municipal Employees, AFL-CIO

AFSCME has over one million dues-paying members. The vast majority of these are state and local public employees, with a few federal and nonprofit workers. White-collar and professional employees account for approximately 30 percent of the members. Four hundred thousand of AFSCME's members are female. Half of these women are in one occupation: clerical work. The others are food service workers, teacher aides, social workers, librarians, and so on.

Comparable worth became an issue for AFSCME around 1974, when the Washington Federation of State Employees and other organizations requested and participated in a comparable worth study of public employment in the State of Washington.[17] AFSCME represents some state employees in Washington but is forbidden by state law to bargain for wages. The study, which has been updated twice, showed a pattern of underpayment for predominantly female jobs (see Chapter 7). In September 1981, AFSCME filed sex discrimination charges with the EEOC, and in July 1982, filed suit against the state in federal court.

The international union began an educational campaign on pay equity in the 1970s. The international office, which includes a women's activities department, aids affiliates in their research, organizing, bargaining, and litigation. State and local levels of the union have run their own educational programs for members.

AFSCME has relied heavily on job evaluation studies as a prelude to negotiating wage equity increases. It has lobbied or negotiated for and participated in job evaluation studies of the state civil service systems in Washington, New York, Florida, Minnesota, Michigan, Wisconsin, Maine,

---

16. Unless otherwise indicated, information on union activities was collected through conversations with union staff and from printed material, such as press releases, memoranda, and newsletters.

17. Norman D. Willis and Associates, *Comparable Worth Study* (Seattle: 1974).

and elsewhere. In addition, AFSCME locals in Humboldt County, California, Hennipen County, Minnesota, and Pennsylvania (see Chapter 8) conducted small studies of their own for use in bargaining.

In 1979 over two-hundred clerical workers, members of Local 101 in San Jose, held a "sick-out" until the city agreed to a joint labor-management job evaluation study. The study showed that predominantly female jobs were paid 15 percent less, on the average, than traditionally male jobs of comparable worth. In negotiations, the city was reluctant to implement the study results and sought to take equity increases out of the fund for general salary increases. Rallies, public educational programs, a march, the filing of EEOC charges, and eventually a strike were necessary to win implementation. In this first such action for implementation of comparable worth, municipal employees struck for eight days in July 1981 and then ratified a contract that provides for across-the-board wage increases of 7.5 percent the first year and 8 percent the second year for 2,000 city workers. In addition, wage equity increases were allocated for predominantly female jobs totaling $1.5 million and ranging from 5 to 15 percent over two years.[18]

In 1981 AFSCME began a major litigation program. It filed EEOC charges against Washington State, Hawaii, Connecticut, Wisconsin, Los Angeles, and Chicago. In most of these jurisdictions, the complaints were filed because the public employer refused to implement the findings of a study that found women's jobs underpaid relative to their worth.

In Washington State, AFSCME Council 28, under the leadership of Executive Director George Masten, has been successful in pressing its case on behalf of state employees who were identified as receiving, on average, 20 percent less pay than male workers in jobs of comparable skill, effort, and responsibility. In the fall of 1983, Federal Judge Jack Tanner ruled that the Washington State salary schedule showed pervasive discrimination. In his oral decision, Tanner cited violations of Title VII of the Civil Rights Act: "The evidence is overwhelming that there has been past historical discrimination against women in employment in the state of Washington and that discrimination has been manifested, according to the evidence, by direct, overt and institutionalized discrimination."[19]

AFSCME is represented on the board of the National Committee on Pay Equity; its state and local affiliates have worked for comparable worth in coalition with other organizations; and it has lobbied at the state and federal levels for new pay equity laws and more effective enforcement of existing ones. This large national union has also played a part in promoting equitable pay as an issue in local and state elections and as an important plank in national political party platforms.

---

18. Bureau of National Affairs, "EEO Notes," *Fair Employment Practices Summary of Latest Developments*, 426 (July 1981): 5.
19. *AFSCME* v. *State of Washington*, 32 FEP Cases 1577.

The International Union of Electrical, Radio and Machine Workers, AFL-CIO

The IUE represents 300,000 members. Approximately 35 percent of these are females who work in the electrical equipment manufacturing industry. Many employers have maintained sex-segregated labor grades for decades and continue paying women doing assembly work at rates below those of men doing unskilled common labor.[20]

At its 1972 convention the IUE initiated a Title VII Compliance Program because it found that collective bargaining was often not sufficient to remedy sex discrimination. The program involved the education of members and staff and research on jobs and wages by sex and race. If the employer refused to bargain, the IUE filed charges with the NLRB along with complaints under Title VII and/or Executive Order 11246. In addition, the IUE has worked closely with federal agencies. Under the Carter administration, these efforts resulted in adoption by the EEOC of a "Resolution on Title VII and Collective Bargaining" which encouraged union participation in antidiscrimination efforts.

IUE has filed many EEOC charges against employers, including General Electric, Westinghouse, and White-Westinghouse, for wage discrimination against predominantly female jobs. Most charges resulted in out-of-court settlements calling for wage increases and back pay. Because of these IUE accomplishments, employers are more willing to negotiate, local unions are more likely to initiate comparable worth efforts, and grievance machinery has become better equipped to handle pay equity problems. The IUE has also filed *amicus* briefs in support of other comparable worth causes.

IUE v. *Westinghouse*, a key comparable worth case, was won by the union, and a settlement was approved by the U.S. District Court of New Jersey on 26 February 1982. About 600 present and former members of Local 449 at a Westinghouse lamp plant in Trenton received back pay from a fund of $75,000, and about 85 workers, mostly women, have been upgraded.[21]

The IUE is represented on the board of the National Committee on Pay Equity. Its representatives have done extensive traveling and speaking on behalf of pay equity and presented testimony at congressional and agency hearings.

The Communications Workers of America, AFL-CIO

CWA represents over 600,000 people in the telecommunications industry, of whom 85 percent are employed by AT&T. Half of the members are

20. Carole Wilson, *Pay Equity for Women* (Washington, D.C.: Union for Democratic Action Education Fund, 1981).
21. *IUE* v. *Westinghouse Electric Corporation*, 23 FEP Cases 588.

females employed in clerical or traffic (operator) jobs. Many jobs are being eliminated or changed by the introduction of new technology.

CWA passed at its 1980 convention a resolution urging the EEOC to "adopt and enforce positive and progressive rules on comparable worth." It also submitted testimony to the EEOC at its April 1980 hearings on wage discrimination and job segregation. The union has educated members and staff on the issue through its national, regional, and women's conferences. It is represented on the Board of the National Committee on Pay Equity.

Most of CWA's pay equity work has occurred in connection with its negotiations with the telephone company. They negotiate one national contract every three years. In 1975 CWA participated in a classification study concentrating on clerical jobs in an effort to introduce consistency and order into AT&T's large and unwieldly collection of job titles. In the 1977 contract, a new classification system upgraded all the predominantly female jobs.

The 1975 reclassification study set the stage for the 1980 negotiations, in which other jobs were upgraded and a six-member labor-management Occupational Job Evaluation Committee was established to research and design a new job evaluation system for nonmanagement employees. After agreeing on rules of behavior and general objectives, the committee field-tested different methods of job analysis in fourteen jobs and selected a system that emphasizes interviews with workers. The compensation factors selected and the scoring system have been evaluated by a ten-member committee representing management and union members, balanced in terms of sex, race, and job category. The new job evaluation system was field tested and final recommendations were to be made in May 1983. Unfortunately, the break up of AT&T put a stop to this pioneer venture, and CWA is now beginning anew negotiations with each of the regional systems.

CWA was originally skeptical of job evaluation, but a decade of investigation led it to adopt a job evaluation approach to deal with pay discrepancies and the wage problems introduced by technological change. For CWA, worker participation in the development and implementation of job evaluation is the critical factor.

The Service Employees International Union, AFL-CIO

SEIU has 625,000 members. A third are health industry workers, a third are janitors, and a third are public employees. Fifty percent of the members are women who work as nurses, clericals, and aides in both the private and the public sectors.

A comparable worth resolution was passed at SEIU's 1980 convention. The Women's Advisory Committee, women's conferences, and union publications have been forums for educating union members and staff on this issue. SEIU is represented on the board of the National Committee on Pay Equity and has lobbied at state and federal levels for new pay equity legislation and the enforcement of existing laws.

SEIU has relied less than the other unions discussed here on job evaluation studies. It is troubled by the possibility of employer control and by the technical complexities often involved. SEIU tends to represent smaller units than AFSCME or CWA and finds job evaluations less feasible in these small units. In Oregon, where SEIU represents state employees, Local 503, which includes professional, technical, and clerical workers, has successfully lobbied for a joint labor-management re-evaluation of all state jobs.

SEIU has negotiated job reclassifications to upgrade the classification and pay of female-dominated jobs. In Santa Clara County, California, Local 715 negotiated a contract in July 1981 that provided for a general 16.5 percent increase for two years and additional increases of 5 to 10 percent for the clerical unit. An entry-level clerk under this agreement receives a 19 percent wage increase over two years. The contract also sets up a grievance procedure for individual challenges to classification decisions. The grievance committee consists of representatives of labor and management and a neutral party.

SIEU also advocates across-the-board dollar increases as a way of reducing the wage gap within its units, because it believes that percentage increases tend to preserve the job hierarchy and perpetuate wage disparities. Local 503 in Oregon won across-the-board increases after extensive discussion in the bargaining unit about how this would benefit undervalued female jobs.

Finally, school secretaries in Minneapolis struck in 1981 because they wanted their entry-level salaries raised to that of janitors in the school district. Local 284 won increases averaging 20 to 25 percent for the secretaries.

Many of the health care workers represented by SEIU are employed in nursing homes and in low-paid firms where the labor force is overwhelmingly female. Comparable worth analysis typically focuses on inequities within one firm, not among firms or industries, and this requires that there be a number of men in the unit for wage comparison purposes. This requirement is difficult to meet in nursing homes. It remains to be seen how SEIU, or any other union, will overcome this problem.

Future Actions

Through education, training, and organizing programs, the labor movement will continue to teach its members what comparable worth means and how to implement it.[22] To achieve equal pay for work of comparable value, more union leaders and staff members will have to become committed to the

---

22. Thomas R. Donahue, Secretary-Treasurer of the AFL-CIO, *Remarks to the National Labor Organization Meeting of the National Committee on Pay Equity* (Washington, D.C.: 1983).

cause so that they, in turn, can educate working women who do not as yet realize that they are discriminated against and have remedies available to them. It is likely that this educational work will be taken by more unions and will result in more workplace agitation for comparable worth.

Unions will continue to be at the forefront of the pay equity fight, not only as a moral imperative, but also as a political necessity since its federal government allies have left the field. The EEOC and the OFCCP are no longer developing comparable worth enforcement mechanisms. Unions will continue to file charges before the NLRB and EEOC when they believe the employer is maintaining discriminatory practices. We can expect to see more labor participation in joint union-management job evaluation studies. Unions will continue negotiating new studies and investigating employers' job evaluations and their relation to actual wages. More will insist that employers pay according to their own evaluation, as in *Westinghouse*.

The labor movement's preferred operational mode will continue to be collective bargaining, which is as it should be. Because of education, organizing, and the growing number of studies, all of which create momentum, we can expect to see more contracts providing for wage increases for undervalued jobs. Unions will probably also make greater use of reclassification as a way of increasing wages. The labor movement, including CLUW, will continue to spread contract language protection to working women by organizing them and will begin to support groups that are taking steps to organize themselves.

The vigor of the labor movement's attack on pay inequities will depend on the resources it can afford to commit to the battle. If union members want action on comparable worth, there will be action. If they find other issues more compelling—keeping jobs, for example—comparable worth and affirmative action programs may sink lower on the priority list.

Labor's continued initiative in fighting for pay equity and related issues is essential. Unions alone have the legal right to represent employees. They have knowledge of plant practices and first-hand experience with classification and wage determination processes. Unions also have the technical and material resources that many other friends of pay equity lack.

But pay equity cannot be addressed by labor alone. Coalitions must form around this issue, as they have around other important issues. The National Committee on Pay Equity and state- and city-wide coalitions are proof that such varied constituencies as labor, women, minority groups, legal experts, academics, professionals, and politicians can work collaboratively in the development of this important national policy. Comparable worth has captured the imagination and often the resources of a wide range of interest groups. Although coalition building is difficult, this diversity may be the movement for pay equity's greatest strength. In the past, unions have played a critical role in welding together many groups in a common cause. Comparable worth presents an opportunity for them to do so again.

14

Comparable Worth under Various Federal and State Laws

VIRGINIA DEAN, PATTI ROBERTS, AND CARROLL BOONE

Title VII of the Civil Rights Act of 1964 has been widely identified as a law that might be interpreted to prohibit employers from discriminating against women by undercompensating their traditional occupations. Following the *Gunther* decision of 1981 (see Chapter 12 for a full discussion), federal courts can be expected to entertain and consider the merits of increasing numbers of comparable pay claims. However, it is a mistake for comparable worth advocates and strategists to define and carry on their activities only within the confines of Title VII. Activities are already going on in other arenas, and many other activities are possible. Legislation affecting comparable worth falls into several categories: (1) laws that outlaw sex-based discrimination in pay setting by private and public employers, including both fair employment practice (FEP) laws and equal pay acts (EPAs); (2) laws that broadly outlaw sex discrimination, including equal rights amendments (ERAs); (3) laws and regulations governing the employment policies and practices of private employers who contract with governments; (4) civil service laws governing wage-setting practices and policies for a particular group of public employees; and (5) laws on collective bargaining.

This chapter reviews the status of state laws in these five areas and federal civil service in order to suggest possible legislative action on comparable worth or legal action where laws are already in place. Comparable worth is used only in the limited legal sense of corrective action aimed at discrimination resulting from occupational segregation and unfair salary-setting practices, not in the wider political sense as is sometimes used in this volume.

State Equal Pay Acts, Fair Employment Practice Laws, and Equal Rights Acts

Most current legislative activity has centered on the passage of civil service laws on comparable worth for state workers, who are usually a large proportion of a state's total work force (see Chapter 15). Other sources of potential activity are enforcement proceedings under state FEP laws and state EPAs whose language is broader than that of the federal Equal Pay Act (federal EPA) and requires equal pay for jobs of "comparable worth" or "comparable character." Favorable court rulings under the language of such laws will make them possible models for law reform efforts in other states.

While Title VII and the federal EPA are the only major federal laws that provide rights and remedies for individual workers with regard to wage discrimination, most states also have equal pay and fair employment practice laws that address this form of discrimination. (See Appendix.) For instance, thirty-nine states have equal pay laws, fifteen of which use broader language than the Federal EPA, specifically referring to "comparable" work. And no provision in the federal EPA excuses noncompliance with any state equal pay standards that are higher than those set forth in the federal law. A few state EPAs exclude claims when a remedy is available under the federal EPA, but this would not be the case in a comparable worth fact situation; that is, the federal law clearly does not provide a remedy in those situations. A case interpreting the Alaska EPA specifically addresses this issue: *Rinkel* v. *Association Pipeline Contractors Inc.* allowed a woman to pursue an equal pay claim under its law even though her federal EPA suit had been denied because the federal law covered only similarly situated jobs, and the woman was alleging that a unique job that she occupied would have been paid better had it gone to a male worker.[1]

With regard to the relationship between Title VII and state FEP laws, Congress expressly provides that state statutes defining sex discrimination more comprehensively than Title VII are not pre-empted or superseded by Title VII. Two sections address this issue:

> 42 U.S.C. 2000h-4: Nothing contained in any title of this Act shall be construed as indicating an intent on the part of Congress to occupy the field in which any such title operates to the exclusion of State laws on the same subject matter, nor shall any provision of this Act be construed as invalidating any provision of State law unless such provision is inconsistent with any of the purposes of this Act, or any provision thereof.

> 42 U.S.C. 2000e-7: Nothing in this subchapter shall be deemed to exempt or relieve any person from any liability, duty, penalty, or punishment provided by any present or future law of any State or political subdivision of a State, other than any such law which purports to require or permit the doing of any act which would be an unlawful employment practice under this subchapter.

These specific provisions of Title VII make it clear that state FEP laws can be

---

1. Alaska Superior Court, 20 EPD 30,222 (1979).

as important as Title VII in the development of case law defining unfair employment practices as including comparable pay. When "comparable" pay disparities are specifically cited in a state's FEP law, as they are in Alaska, case law developments can provide models for legal arguments as well as for legislative reform.

Finally, now that the ten-year effort for ratification of a federal ERA has come to a close, it will be as important to clarify rights and remedies under state ERAs as to develop new federal strategies. Sixteen states have their own ERAs, which should provide strong protection from discriminatory classifications based on sex.

These three areas of law—EPAs, FEPs, and ERAs—are described below.

Equal Pay Acts

The equal pay movement in the United States began twenty-four years before the federal EPA was passed in 1963 and has always included some level of awareness and concern about the pay disparities that women workers experience in jobs dissimilar, but comparable in effort, skill, and responsibility to men's jobs. The language of many state EPAs passed both before and after the federal act either includes specific comparable work language or uses language that is arguably broader than the narrow equal work standard, which courts have interpreted as applying only to jobs that are "equal" or "substantially identical." Earlier versions of the federal equal pay bill, first introduced in 1945, embodied a "comparable work" standard, and a 1942 War Labor Board order addressed intraplant sex-based wage inequities for "comparable quality or quantity of work."[2]

By 1982 thirty-nine states and Puerto Rico had enacted equal pay laws. The specific language of these laws varies. Only five of the thirty-nine state EPAs are identical to the federal act, which confines violations to the narrow equal pay for equal work standard. Sixteen specifically allow comparisons of comparable jobs. The rest vary widely, some using language that is arguably similar to the federal standard, and others using language that is arguably broader. Table 14-1 summarizes these state laws.

Though little litigation interpreting the broader state EPAs is reported, the language of these laws and the growing contemporary concern about comparable worth should increase interest in them. None of the EPAs have been passed as part of the contemporary legislative effort for comparable worth; nonetheless, those that appear to be broader than the federal EPA— and specifically those that refer to "comparable" skills, requirements, or character—should be available to challenge comparable worth inequities. Women workers may wish to pursue comparable pay claims under these broader state statutes.

---

2. 109 Congressional Record 9197; War Labor Board, General Order No. 16, adopted 24 November 1942, 24 War Labor Rep. (BNA) XII.

Table 14-1

Selected Characteristics of State Equal Pay Laws

State[1]	Year Enacted/ Amended	Equal Pay Standard[2]	Comparable Pay Standard	Other Standard	Cannot Reduce Wages to Compensate	Employment Agreement No Defense
Alabama	1949					
Alaska[3]	1962					
Arizona	1955/1977			yes[4]		yes
Arkansas	1949		yes[5]	yes[5]		
California	1963			yes[4]		yes
Colorado	1949			yes[6]		
Connecticut	1969/1973			yes[6]		yes
Delaware						
Florida	1966	yes		yes[7]		
Georgia			yes[8]			
Hawaii	1959			yes[9]		
Idaho	1969		yes[8]			
Illinois	1943			yes[10]		
Indiana	1965	yes				yes
Iowa					yes	
Kansas	1978				yes	
Kentucky	1966		yes[8]		yes	yes
Louisiana						
Maine	1954		yes[8]			
Maryland	1966		yes[11]		yes	yes
Massachusetts	1934		yes[11]			yes
Michigan	1919			yes[12]		
Minnesota	1969	yes			yes	
Mississippi						
Missouri	1963			yes[4]		
Montana	1919			yes[13]		
Nebraska	1967		yes[8]		yes	
Nevada	1975	yes			yes	yes
New Hampshire	1947			yes[14]		yes[15]

Table 14-1(*continued*)

State[1]	Year Enacted/ Amended	Equal Pay Standard[2]	Comparable Pay Standard	Other Standard	Cannot Reduce Wages to Compensate	Employment Agreement No Defense
New Jersey	1952			yes[16]		
New Mexico						
New York	1937			yes[16]		
North Carolina						
North Dakota	1965		yes[8]		yes	yes
Ohio	1959	yes			yes	yes
Oklahoma	1965		yes[8]			
Oregon	1955		yes[11]		yes	yes
Pennsylvania	1947	yes	yes[17]		yes	yes
Rhode Island	1946			yes[14]		
South Carolina						
South Dakota	1966		yes[8]			
Tennessee	1974		yes[8]		yes	yes
Texas[1]	1919			yes[18]		yes
Utah						
Vermont	1974	yes				
Virginia	1943					
Washington	1965			yes[12]		
West Virginia			yes[11]		yes	yes
Wisconsin	1959			yes[19]		
Wyoming						

1. All state equal pay acts cover private and public sector employers and employees except for that of Texas (A.R.C.S. Title 117, Art. 16825), which covers only public employment.
2. Florida (see also item 7), Indiana (A.I.C. § 22-2-2-4), Minnesota (M.S.A. § 181.67), Nevada (NRS. 608.017), Ohio (O.R.C.A. § 4111.17), Pennsylvania (after 1968) (P.S.A. 43 § 336.3), and Virginia (C.V. § 40.1-28.6) have the same language as the federal Equal Pay Act: "No employer having employees subject to any provision of this section shall discriminate, within any establishment in which such employees are employed, between employees on the basis of sex by paying wages to employees in such establishment at a rate less than the rate at which he pays wages to employees of the opposite sex in such establishment for equal work on jobs the performance of which requires equal skill, effort and responsibility, and which are performed under similar working conditions"

3. Alaska's EPA, which required equal pay for "work of comparable character or work," was repealed in 1980. At the same time, however, identical language was added to the state fair employment practice law (A.S. § 18.80.010) as an enumerated unlawful practice.

4. Arizona (A.R.S. § 23.340), California (Labor Code § 1997.5), and Missouri (A.M.S. § 290.400) require equal pay for the "same classification."

5. Arkansas has two equal pay laws. The 1955 law (A.S. § 81.624) requires equal pay for "comparable work." The 1977 law (A.S. § 81.333) requires "equal compensation for equal services" and repeals "all laws and parts of laws in conflict thereof."

6. Colorado (C.R.S. § 8-5-05) and Connecticut (C.G.S. § 31-75) prohibit discrimination in wages "solely on account of sex" and "solely on the basis of sex," respectively.

7. Florida has two equal pay laws. The 1969 law uses the federal EPA standard (F.S.A. § 448.07) (see item 2). The 1973 law (F.S.A. § 724.06) requires "equal pay for equal services."

8. The Georgia equal pay law (C.G.A. § 54-100), although it uses the federal EPA language in its section on prohibited acts, gives the enforcing agency the authority to "insure that all employees are receiving comparable pay for comparable worth on jobs which have comparable requirements relating to skill, effort and responsibility," in another section. Idaho (I.C. § 44-1702), Kentucky (K.R.S. § 337.423), Maine (26 M.R.S.A. § 628), and Oklahoma (O.S.A. § 198.1) require equal pay for "comparable work on jobs that have comparable requirements relating to skill, effort and responsibility." Nebraska (R.S.N. § 48-1219) uses federal EPA language in the prohibited acts section and calls for equal pay for "comparable work on jobs which have comparable requirements" in the policy section. North Dakota (N.D.C.C. § 34-06.1-03) and South Dakota (S.D.C.L. § 60-12-15) require equal pay for "comparable work on jobs which have comparable requirements relating to skill, effort and responsibility, but not to physical strength." Tennessee (T.S.A. § 50-321) requires equal pay for "comparable work on jobs the performance of which requires comparable skill, effort and responsibility and which are performed under similar working conditions."

9. Hawaii (H.R.S. § 387-4) prohibits "discrimination in any way in payment of wages . . . as . . . between the sexes."

10. Illinois (48 I.A.S. § 4a) prohibits an "unequal wage for equal work."

11. Maryland (A.C.M. Art. 100 § 55A) requires equal pay for work of "comparable character or work." Massachusetts (149 M.C.L.A. § 105A) uses the phraseology "like or comparable character or work." Oregon (O.R.S. § 652.220) and West Virginia (W.V.C. § 21-58-1) prohibit discrimination in wages for "work of *comparable character*, the performance of which requires comparable skills."

12. Michigan (M.C.L.A. § 750.556) and Washington (R.C.W. § 49.12.75) prohibit sex-based wage discrimination for persons "similarly employed."

13. Montana (M.C.A. § 39-3-104) requires equal pay for "equivalent services or for the same amount or class of work or labor."

14. New Hampshire (N.H.R.S. 275:37) prohibits discrimination "in the payment of wages as between the sexes, or . . . [unequal] rates . . . for equal work or work on the same operations."

15. New Hampshire allows discriminatory wage rates if they have been collectively bargained.

16. New Jersey (N.J.S.A. § 34:11-56) prohibits discrimination "in any way in the rate or method of payment of wages . . . because of sex." New York (M.C.L.N.Y. Labor Law § 199.2) prohibits discrimination "in the rate . . . of pay . . . because of sex."

17. In 1955 Pennsylvania passed a law requiring equal pay for "work under comparable conditions on jobs the performance of which requires comparable skills." In 1968 that language was repealed and replaced by federal EPA language (see also item 2).

18. Texas (A.R.C.S. Title 117, Art. 6825) requires "same compensation" for "same kind, grade and quantity of work."

19. Wyoming (W.S. 27-4-301) requires equal pay for the "same work."

Yet the fact that there are so few comparable worth cases reported under these laws suggests that the enforcement mechanisms that currently exist are weak; that few working women know about and pursue their rights and remedies under these laws; or that the existing procedures for recording and reporting decisions under these laws, when the claims are pursued in administrative agencies, are weak or lacking. Further information about these shortcomings and their causes is needed.

Fair Employment Practice Laws

Typically, FEP laws prohibit discrimination in employment on the basis of race, color, religion, sex, and age. Many of the laws include language prohibiting discrimination in "compensation" or acts that "limit, segregate, or classify" an individual on the basis of sex or other protected categories. These phrases are also included in the federal law and demonstrate legislative intent to address sex-based wage discrimination claims.

Most, but not all, FEP laws provide that individuals aggrieved under the law can file a charge with an enforcement agency established by the law. Following attempts to resolve the issue informally, the agency can issue a formal finding and order back pay and other remedial action. The agency finding can be appealed to a state court.

New York passed the first state FEP law in 1945, following eight years of study and wartime regulation of discriminatory practices within the state. The law prohibited discrimination on the basis of race, creed, color, or national origin. Sex was added as a protected category in 1965. Twenty-four more states passed similar laws before the federal Civil Rights Act of 1964 was enacted. Between 1964 and 1982, sixteen more states passed FEP laws, bringing the total to forty-one. Three of the states that do not have FEP laws have equal pay laws, two of which have comparable worth language.

The federal law and most state laws are patterned after the original New York Human Relations Act. While these laws have come to be known generically as "fair employment practices" acts or laws, individual state laws are called by a variety of other titles as well, including human relations or human rights acts or laws, civil rights acts or laws, acts or laws against discrimination or antidiscrimination laws. Characteristics and dates of enactment of state FEP laws are summarized in Table 14-2.

A few FEP laws include language that provides additional guidance relating to sex-based wage discrimination. Utah's Anti-Discrimination Act defines discrimination in matters of compensation as "the payment of differing wages or salaries to employees having substantially equal experience, responsibilities and competency for the particular job."[3]

The South Carolina Human Affairs Act adds language, often found in the EPAs of other states that prohibits employers from reducing the wage

---

3. U.C.A. § 34-35-6.

rate of any employee in order to comply with provisions of the act relating to age.[4] At this time, the language does not specifically apply to sex. The South Carolina Act also provides that it is not unlawful to "apply different standards of compensation, different terms, conditions or privileges of employment pursuant to a bona fide seniority or merit system or a system which measures earnings by quantity or to employees who work in different locations provided that such differences are not the result of an intention to discriminate . . . [or] if such differentiation is authorized by the provisions of § 6(d) of the Fair Labor Standards Act of 1938, as amended (29 U.S.C. 206(d))."

Alaska's is the only FEP law that includes specific comparable worth language. It provides that it is unlawful for "an employer to discriminate in the payment of wages as between the sexes, or to employ a female in an occupation in this state at a salary or wage rate less than that paid to a male employee for work of comparable character or work in the same operation, business or type of work in the same locality."[5] This language was added by a 1980 amendment to the law at the same time that the state's EPA, which included identical language, was repealed. A case challenging pay differentials between state public health nurses and state physician's assistants is now moving through the administrative agency that enforces Alaska's FEP law.

Legislatures have considered bills that would have added comparable worth language to their FEP laws in legislative sessions in 1978 (Michigan), 1981 (Oregon), and 1983 (California and Pennsylvania). The Michigan bill provided that

> an employer in this state shall not maintain differences in wages between male and female employees who are performing work of equal value. . . . The [State Civil Rights] Commission shall determine the value of work performed, [considering] the composite of the skill, effort and responsibility required in the performance of the work and the conditions under which the work is performed. Sex shall not constitute a reasonable factor in justifying a difference in wages.[6]

The bill introduced in the 1981 Oregon legislative session would have amended the state FEP law to make it specifically unlawful for an employer

> (A) In any manner to discriminate between employees in the payment of compensation for work which requires comparable skills, efforts, responsibilities under comparable working conditions because of an employee's race, religion, color, sex, national origin, marital status or age if the employee is 18 years of age or older and under 70 years of age.

---

4. G.L.S.C. a1-13-10 (1972).
5. A.S. § 18.80.010.
6. Michigan H.G. 6697 in 1978 and Michigan S.B. No. 279 in 1981.

Table 14-2

Selected Characteristics of State
Fair Employment Practice Laws

State[1]	Year Enacted/ Year Sex Added	Specific Language on Compensation	Specific Language on Classification and/or Segregation	Specific Language on Comparable Worth
Alabama[2]				
Alaska	1953/1972	yes		yes[3]
Arizona	1965	yes	yes	
Arkansas				
California	1959			
Colorado	1957	yes		
Connecticut	1947/1967	yes	yes	
Delaware	1953	yes	yes	
Florida	1967/1972			
Georgia	1978	yes	yes	
Hawaii	1963	yes	yes	
Idaho	1961	yes	yes	
Illinois	1961		yes	
Indiana	1961/1971			
Iowa	1963		yes	
Kansas	1953	yes	yes	
Kentucky	1966/1977	yes	yes	
Louisiana[4]				
Maine	1965/1973	yes		
Maryland	1951	yes	yes	
Massachusetts	1964/1965	yes		
Michigan	1964	yes	yes	
Minnesota	1955/1969	yes	yes	
Mississippi				
Missouri	1961	yes[5]	yes	
Montana	1947	yes		
Nebraska	1965	yes		
Nevada	1961/1965	yes	yes	
New Hampshire	1965/1971	yes		
New Jersey	1945/1970	yes		
New Mexico	1949/1969	yes		
New York	1945/1965	yes		
North Carolina	1977			
North Dakota	1979	yes		

(B) To compensate any employee at a rate less than the rate paid other employees for work which requires comparable skills, efforts, responsibilities under comparable working conditions.[7]

The Oregon bill further provided that a pay differential was not unlawful if "based in good faith on a collective bargaining agreement," and that "no employer shall reduce employees' salaries" to comply with the provision on comparable worth.

---

7. Oregon H.G. 2969.

Table 14-2 (*continued*)

State[1]	Year Enacted/ Year Sex Added	Specific Language on Compensation	Specific Language on Classification and/or Segregation	Specific Language on Comparable Worth
Ohio	1959			
Oklahoma	1963	yes		
Oregon	1949/1955	yes		
Pennsylvania	1955/1969	yes		
Rhode Island	1949/1971	yes	yes	
South Carolina	1972	yes	yes	
South Dakota	1972			
Tennessee	1967/1972	yes	yes	
Texas				
Utah	1953			yes[6]
Vermont	1963/1971			
Virginia				
Washington	1949/1969		yes	
West Virginia	1967/1977	yes		
Wisconsin	1945/1961	yes		
Wyoming	1965	yes		

1. All FEP laws include private and public sector employment except for those of Georgia, Texas, and North Carolina, which cover only the public sector.
2. Alabama has no FEP law, but in 1976, 1978, 1979, 1980, and 1982, the state budget bill included a clause forbidding discrimination based on race or sex in *state employment*.
3. Alaska's is the only FEP law that specifically mentions "comparable" work pay disparities as a discriminatory employment practice.
4. In 1981 an FEP bill was introduced in the Louisiana legislature but died during the legislative session.
5. Guidelines to Missouri's FEP act provide that "wage schedules . . . must not be related to or based on sex of employees."
6. Utah's FEP law defines "discrimination in matters of compensation" as "the payment of differing wages or salaries to employees having substantially equal experience, responsibilities and competency for the particular job."

State Equal Rights Amendments

Claims under Title VII and state FEP laws and EPAs may be strengthened by alternative claims regarding state constitutional protections set forth in states that have their own ERAs. Sixteen states have constitutional provisions that prohibit sex discrimination. Each state's provisions differ somewhat in wording and scope; their characteristics are summarized in Table 14-3. Because sex-based discrimination claims have usually been brought in federal court under Title VII, few state courts have decided yet whether it is unconstitutional to pay women's work less than men's work of comparable value under modern state ERAs.[8]

---

8. However, the Utah Supreme Court held that paying male police officers more than female police officers did not violate the state's *1896* ERA, in 506 P.2d 809.

Table 14-3
State Equal Rights Amendments

State	Year Enacted	Requires State or Government Action	Wording Like Federal ERA	Court Review Standard Used
Alaska	1972			medium
Colorado	1973	yes	yes	high
Connecticut	1974			medium
Hawaii	1972	yes	yes	high
Illinois	1970	yes*		high
Maryland	1972		yes	high
Massachusetts	1976		yes	high
Montana	1977			low
New Hampshire	1974	yes	yes	none‡
New Mexico	1973		yes	none‡
Pennsylvania	1971		yes	high
Texas	1972		yes	low
Utah	1896			low
Virginia	1971	yes†		low
Washington	1972		yes	high
Wyoming	1890	yes		none‡

*Covers action by state, local governments, and school districts.
†Covers governmental action only.
‡No case law concerning standard of review.

Advocates and planners recommend that the first comparable worth claims represent the strongest possible cases. Such a case might involve (1) discrimination by a state government agency (2) in a state with a modern ERA worded like the proposed federal ERA (3) where courts have already established that a high standard of judicial review is required.

The following subsections present a method for deciding whether to bring a comparable worth pay discrimination claim under a particular state ERA.

State Action Requirement

Some state ERAs cover only actions by the states themselves or other government agencies, not actions by private employers. Others include sex discrimination by local governments as well. For example, the Colorado constitution provides that "Equality of rights under the law shall not be denied or abridged by the state of Colorado or any of its political subdivisions on account of sex." Montana has the only state ERA that also specifically prohibits discrimination by "any person, firm, corporation, or institution."[9] When the constitutional provision does not specify, most courts infer a "state action" requirement. Therefore, a claim against a state employee compensation system that pays predominantly female jobs less

---

9. Colo. Const. Art. II, § 29, 1972; Mont. Const. Art. II, § 4, 1973.

than predominantly male jobs of comparable worth is preferred because it avoids possible litigation on the jurisdictional issue of the state action requirement.

Any comparable worth litigation against a state as employer meets the state action requirement. State civil service systems are the target of many Title VII suits challenging comparable worth pay disparities. Where the state is not directly involved, however, courts can often find the required "state action." For example, the Washington State courts have held that such a requirement was met in a case where the defendants were an interscholastic sports association including public schools as members (*Darrin* v. *Gould*), and a professional basketball team that leased the Seattle Coliseum (*McLean* v. *First Northwest Industries of America, Inc.*).[10]

Federal ERA Legislative Intent

In terms of case law development, the strongest comparable worth cases will be those brought under modern ERAs whose wording is like or similar to that of the proposed federal ERA. These states are most likely to rely on the legislative history of the federal ERA.

Nine of the state ERAs have language that closely follows that of the proposed federal ERA ("Section 1. Equality of Rights under the law shall not be denied or abridged by the United States or by any state on account of sex"). Fourteen of the provisions have passed since 1970 and, therefore, share a legislative history with the proposed federal ERA. The two exceptions, the Utah and Wyoming ERAs, were passed in 1896 and 1890 respectively.

Many legislative revisions and court decisions under state ERAs have eliminated blatant discrimination, such as laws prohibiting employers from hiring women for jobs requiring heavy lifting. However, modern wage compensation systems do not usually overtly classify jobs according to sex. Therefore, courts considering wage discrimination claims based on comparable worth will be required to look beyond the neutrality of a compensation law or practice to its practical effect.[11]

Standard of Judicial Review

The judicial standard used by the court determines how closely the court looks at the law or action being challenged as discriminatory. The most important factor in predicting the outcome of a discrimination claim based

---

10. *Darrin* v. *Gould*, 54 P.2d at 891 (1975); *McLean* v. *First Northwest Industries of America, Inc.*, 600 P.2d 1927 (1979).

11. Whether the *County of Washington* v. *Gunther* decision requires the presence of direct or indirect intent is an issue that the Supreme Court left open and commentators are speculating about. See Winn Newman and Jeanne M. Vonhof, "'Separate but Equal'—Job Segregation and Pay Equity in the Wake of *Gunther*," *University of Illinois Law Review*, (1981): 269–331.

on comparable worth raising the ERA doctrine is whether state courts have already clearly established a high standard of judicial review that exceeds the standard applied by courts under the equal protection clause of the Fourteenth Amendment of the federal Constitution.

A *low* standard of review means that the court will not generally overrule a gender-based law or practice if the state presents any rational reason for it. Early sex discrimination cases brought under the federal equal protection clause applied this standard. The practical consequence is that very few classification schemes would be held unconstitutional, because the courts would probably find that the defendant government did not enact laws *solely* for the purpose of discriminating against women.

A *medium* standard of review requires the state to show that the classification serves important governmental objectives and is substantially related to the achievement of those objectives. More recent court decisions raising sex discrimination under the equal protection clause have applied this standard, resulting in practice in a lesser degree of judicial scrutiny than is applied to race, national origin, or alienage cases.

A *high* standard of judicial review requires, at a minimum, that courts apply the same legal test that federal courts now apply to race discrimination: the state can justify distinctions between the sexes only by showing that there is a compelling interest served by the discriminatory legislation and that there is no less discriminatory method that could achieve the same purpose.

Under a high standard, a state would have to demonstrate that the discriminatory compensation law or wage-setting practice was the *only* means of achieving a legislative purpose related to a compelling state interest. For example, the purpose of the Washington State Civil Service Law is "to establish . . . a system of personnel administration based on merit principles and scientific methods governing the . . . classification and pay plan."[12] Under the high standard of review, the state could be required to show that its method of setting wages is closely related to the stated "compelling" purpose of the law. Even if it were able to demonstrate the required relationship, it would have to show that there is no other method that could accomplish the same purpose with less discriminatory results. The practical consequence of this high level of scrutiny, at least as applied in race discrimination claims, is that a government classification showing differential impact is almost certain to be held unconstitutional.

Existing federal laws against sex discrimination were enacted by Congress under the authority of the equal protection clause of the Fourteenth Amendment that provides "No State shall . . . deny to any person within its jurisdiction the equal protection of the laws." State laws against discrimination were enacted by legislatures under similar general state constitutional

---

12. RCW 41.06.010.

provisions. Because of the general wording, Congress and state legislatures also have the authority to reinterpret these constiutional provisions—modifying or limiting their application to sex discrimination. The more specific wording and legislative history of the federal and strong state ERA's create a constitutional foundation stronger and clearer than the equal protection clause and suggest the highest degree of scrutiny.

Therefore, theoretically, a claim under a strong state ERA has several distinct advantages over a claim under state or federal FEP law because the constitutional provisions in ERAs are not merely the equal protection clause of the Fourteenth Amendment applied to sex. At a minimum, the strongest state ERAs should give government workers already protected against job-related sex discrimination a stricter standard of review for their claims. This stricter standard would increase the likelihood that courts would find it discriminatory to perpetuate past discrimination by basing women's wages on prevailing rates.

Executive Orders—State and Local Laws

Like the federal government, state and local governmental entities, such as cities and counties, frequently have executive orders, laws, ordinances, or statutes regulating contractors with whom they do business. The details of these orders vary considerably from one locale to another, with different terms defining whom the code applies to, what type of affirmative action program is required, who is to enforce it, the extent of its review and recordkeeping requirements, and its general effectiveness. Since there is such diversity, only a few examples can be mentioned.[13] Comparable worth proponents are beginning to look toward this area of the law in order to raise the issue of pay disparity for governmental entities and private employers alike.

Recent fluctuations in the application and implementation of federal Executive Order 11426, as amended with regard to comparable worth, are an indication of the wide range of possibilities available to executive branches and legislatures seeking avenues to address sex bias in the pay-setting practices of private-sector employers who do business with their governments. They are also an indication of the interrelationship between the language of such laws and their interpretation and implementation by the government officials who are to carry them out.

Whether these state or local laws regulating government contractors will have any significant impact on pay disparities will probably depend on whether they have been vigorously enforced against other, more widely acknowledged forms of sex discrimination. The addition of specific language

---

13. For a more extensive review of various state and local ordinances, see the *Employment Practices Guide*, Commerce Clearing House.

addressing comparable worth will, of course, also be helpful. A number of the laws seek to remedy the problem of underutilization of minorities and women in certain job classifications. While such laws do not directly confront the issue of comparable worth, they do focus on the critical underlying question of occupational segregation.

San Francisco's Non-Discrimination in Contract Ordinance, for example, requires the contractor, subcontractor, or supplier to agree not to discriminate. It regulates advertisements and requires the posting of notices of job openings. The Human Rights Commission, the enforcing agency, also has access to employment records for the purpose of investigating whether or not the employer is in compliance with the provisions of the ordinance. Failure to comply may result in a fine as well as disqualification from all future contracts.[14] The commission has the power to promulgate rules and regulations, which are to be, as far as practicable, similar to those adopted under federal Executive Order 11426.[15]

A unique proposal has been adopted by Madison, Wisconsin's City Council.[16] The current Affirmative Action Plan for the City of Madison Vendors includes the usual provisions barring discrimination along with affirmative action goals, but the plan adopted on November 15, 1983, specifically addresses the problem of wage discrimination and pay equity. Though the Plan's language was weakened from earlier drafts, which called for comparable pay for comparable positions,[17] the final plan looks toward "making progress toward achieving wage parity."[18] Such parity is defined as ". . . the extent to which salary distribution approximates the representation of women, minorities and handicapped persons in the workforce."[19]

This straightforward approach to wage equity, that is linking up overall salary distribution with the percentage of the target population, is innovative, and is designed to reduce the wage gap between men and women and between whites and minority group members through salary redistribution, independent of regulations concerning underutilization in specific classifications and equal opportunity generally.

Regulating private employers who do business with state and local governments is one way in which rule-making bodies can reach beyond the

---

14. San Francisco Administrative Code, Non-Discrimination in Contracts, Chapters 12 and 13. Available from San Francisco Human Rights Commission, 1095 Market Street, San Francisco, Ca. 94103.

15. Ibid. at 12B(2)(9).

16. Madison, Wisconsin, Affirmative Action Plan for City of Madison Vendors, adopted 15 November, 1983. Available from Affirmative Action Office, City-County Bldg., 210 Monona Ave. Rm. 515, Madison, Wisconsin 53710.

17. Madison, Wisconsin, Draft Affirmative Action Plan for City of Madison Vendors. See fn. 12, Section VI-D.

18. Affirmative Action Plan, supra fn 12 at IX.A.1, Goals and Timetables.

19. Ibid.

confines of their own employment settings to reduce sex bias and the wage gap in the private sector.

Civil Service Laws

Most of the legislative activity currently taking place in the area of comparable worth focuses on the reform of civil service laws affecting state workers. There has been some similar activity at the local level, where governing boards of municipalities and school districts have instituted comparable worth studies or pay policies for their employees.

Legislation has been enacted providing for pilot or preliminary studies to look at a few job classes; other laws require studies evaluating and classifying all the jobs in the state's civil service system. Some states have enacted legislation that establishes "pay equity" or "comparable worth" as state policy, leaving the details to collective bargaining or action by the executive branch or both. Legislation has required the collection of information on comparable worth from the jurisdiction itself or from other jurisdictions or the collection of statistics and personnel data relevant to comparable worth within the jurisdiction. A few state legislatures have mandated the allocation of money for pay equity adjustments. Even when studies and data collection do not lead directly to wage adjustments, the resulting information is available to working women, employers, and collective bargaining representatives, and it can be the groundwork for future action either by the legislature in collective bargaining or as evidence in litigation.

Federal Civil Service Laws

The Civil Service Reform Act of 1978[20] establishes that federal management policy is to be implemented according to certain merit system principles, including one that says: "Equal pay should be provided for work of equal value."[21] This and other changes in the law represent the most comprehensive reform of the federal work force since the passage of the Pendleton Act of 1883.[22]

The civilian work force covered by the federal merit system numbers over two and a half million employees, with a payroll of over $46 billion.[23] The Reform Act of 1978 is the first codification of the merit system. Interestingly, though the new code expressly includes the equal value standard, rather than the more narrow equal work one, the scanty legislative history indicates that no changes in the current law were intended.[24] In fact, the

---

20. 5 U.S.C.S. § 2301.
21. 5 U.S.C.S. § 2301(b)(3).
22. U.S. Code, Congressional and Administrative News, 95th Congress, 2d Session [1978] Legislative History, Senate Report No. Pub. L. 95-969, p. 2723.
23. Ibid., p. 2724.
24. Ibid., p. 2741.

director of the Standards Development Center of the Office of Personnel Management has stated that "the key to our equal value system was its single job evaluation plan attribute," and the Reform Act merely restates this statutory principle.[25]

The issue of job worth arose for the federal government in the early 1800s when workers petitioned the Congress to raise their pay because other nongovernment jobs of equal difficulty and responsibility were paid more. In 1923 the Classification Act was passed, which mandated that work involving similar duties, responsibilities, and qualifications be paid the same. As the classification system developed, a single measurement was applied to all federal white-collar jobs, professional, administrative, technical, and clerical. One set of grade levels, GS-1 through GS-18, was then applied to all these jobs.[26]

Blue-collar jobs are not included on this yardstick and are evaluated on a different basis, making cross-occupational comparison difficult. Whereas white-collar workers are graded under the General Schedule, the Federal Wage System is used for trade, craft, and laboring jobs. The Postal Service, encompassing 25 percent of the federal labor force, is covered by four separate classification systems. Whereas the Federal Evaluation System uses a factor method, the Federal Wage System covering nearly half a million blue-collar workers "combines a single job evaluation system with local varying wage rate." The principle that has controlled the setting of blue-collar wages since 1861 is "that federal blue collar wages should equal as nearly as possible locally prevailing private sector wage rates for similar work."[27] For white-collar workers, in contrast, wage rates are nationwide.

Though no major litigation challenging the Civil Service Commission on comparable worth pay disparities has come to light, there is no reason to assume this will not develop. Federal employees are protected under Title VII of the Civil Rights Act and other employment discrimination laws after a final agency action on an employment discrimination claim. The House of Representatives Subcommittee on Compensation and Employee Benefits, Human Resources and Civil Service held joint hearings in September and December 1982 on pay equity issues, including wage discrimination in the federal sector and its relationship to classification schemes.[28] Some federal

---

25. Paul A. Katz (director of the Standards Development Center, Office of Personnel Management), "Why Not Equal Pay?" *Women in Action* 9, no. 8 (Nov./Dec. 1979): 1.

26. Ibid.

27. Donald J. Treiman, "Job Evaluation: An Analytic Review—Interim Report to the EEOC," staff paper (Washington, D.C.: National Academy of Sciences, 1979), pp. 17, 19, and 23.

28. *Pay Equity: Equal Pay for Work of Comparable Value* (2 vols.), Joint Hearings before the Subcommittees on Human Resources, Civil Service, Compensation and Employee Benefits of the Committee on Post Office and Civil Service,

workers have already complained about pay disparities. Federally Employed Women, an organization promoting opportunity and equality for women in government, testified at both the Wage Discrimination Hearings held by the EEOC and the congressional hearings mentioned above about the concentration of women in the lowest-paid jobs in the federal sector; for example, where 84.0 percent of employees in the clerical field are women, only 8.9 percent in the professional category are. FEW argues that the classification system was tailored to fit categories that are fifty years old and influenced by sex bias.[29]

State Civil Service Laws

Many states have civil service classification schemes based on the premise of external and internal equity in pay relationships; jobs with the same value—in relationship to each other and to other jobs in the workplace—are paid the same. The concept and the job evaluation systems that implement it have been used for decades by both private and public employers. However, the application to identifying and eliminating internal and external (labor market) sex bias is new. In fact, comparable worth advocates are finding that existing job evaluation systems can create and perpetuate internal sex bias by the selection and weighting of the factors that are the basis for the evaluation.

As a result, the movement for comparable-worth-oriented job evaluation studies is two-pronged, calling first for the adoption of job ranking as a method of assigning value or salaries and second for the improvement of existing job evaluation methods to reduce or eliminate sex bias. Both goals can be addressed by legislative reforms of civil service pay-setting policies. It is important to keep in mind, however, that legislation is only one way to accomplish this kind of reform. So far, more comparable worth studies have been negotiated in collective bargaining than have been legislated (see Chapters 13 and 15).

Most laws regulating pay setting for public employees include language barring discrimination in pay setting and expressing a commitment to the "merit principle" or to "scientific methods" of job classification.[30] In fact,

---

House of Representatives, 97th Congress, 2d Session, 16, 21, 30 September and 2 December 1982, Serial no. 97-53 (U.S. Government Printing Office: Washington, 1983).

29. Dorothy Nelms and Lynn Revo-Cohen (Federally Employed Women), testimony at *Hearings before the United States Equal Employment Opportunity Commission On Job Segregation and Wage Discrimination*, Washington, D.C., 28–30 April 1980 (Washington, D.C.: U.S. Government Printing Office), pp. 625–30.

30. For example, see Alaska, A.S. § 39.25.010: a system of personnel administration "based upon the merit principle [which] includes integrated salary programs based on the nature of the work performed and a position classification plan based on

efforts to make pay-setting policies more objective will probably improve the pay position of women's classifications whether or not comparable worth is an articulated objective. Even when civil service laws call for prevailing wage surveys or a benchmark system, the selection of jobs surveyed and benchmarked, as well as the establishment of the pay relationships of the unsurveyed jobs that make up the majority of the classifications, is at the discretion of the civil service administrative agency. Much can be done within that system to eliminate sex bias in wage setting.[31]

Finally, some states have recognized a right to legal remedy for employees affected by an action by the civil service or personnel agency that violates the requirements of the civil service law.[32] To the extent that civil service laws create individual legal rights and remedies, they can be used like an FEP law or EPA as an avenue for judicial remedy of inappropriate classification or pay setting. Moreover, one of the advantages of this avenue is that civil service laws are primarily a directive to agencies, and do not require enforcement by aggrieved individuals, although they can be used by such individuals. Another advantage of civil service laws is that they represent (or create) a commitment on the employer's part to comparable worth. Negotiations and collective bargaining are made easier when both employer and union representatives support comparable worth and have only to determine how it should be accomplished.

Local Civil Service Laws

Local governments' approaches to comparable worth are similar to state-level activity. Sometimes personnel departments initiate improved job

---

the principle of like pay for like work"; Hawaii: a system of personnel administration based on "merit principles and scientific methods governing classification of positions"; Indiana: a classification plan shall group all positions based on "their duties, authority, and responsibilities"; Maryland, Art. 64A 16: "each class shall embrace all positions similar in respect to the duties and responsibilities pertaining thereto and the qualifications for the fulfillment thereof"; Washington 41.06. 010 (state civil service law), 28B.16.010 (state higher education personnel law): a [system] of personnel administration based on "merit principles and scientific methods governing classification and pay plan."

31. For instance, see "Pay Equity Policy Meets Prevailing Wage Law in SF," *Comparable Worth Project Newsletter* (Winter 1981), p. 23.

32. See *State* v. *King*, 413 N.E. 2d 1016 (Ind. App. 1980): county employees win increases in court by challenging violation of personnel act; *Iowa Department of Social Services* v. *Iowa Merit Employment Department*, 261 N.W.2d 161 (1977): employees unsuccessfully challenge classification in state court; *Murphy* v. *Administrator of Division of Personnel Administration*, 386 N.E.2d 211 (Mass. 1979): employees could seek reclassification pursuant to state law in court. Some state civil service laws specifically provide for such a cause. See Massachusetts law G.L.A. 30 49: "Any manager of employee objecting to any provision of the classification affecting his office or position may appeal in writing to the personnel administrator and shall be entitled" to a departmental hearing upon such appeal and then to a hearing before the civil service commission. Collective bargaining agreements also include procedures for grieving an improper classification.

classification systems without legislative directives.[33] Sometimes the issue is raised and resolved in collective bargaining, as it was in San Jose. And sometimes legislative bodies for city and county governments and for school and public utility districts are passing laws requiring job classification studies, revising their pay policies to incorporate the principle of comparable worth, or both.

In November 1981 the San Francisco Board of Supervisors adopted a policy of "pay equity" for city workers, though how this policy will be carried out is yet to be defined. When Local 400 of the Service Employees International Union sought pay equity increases for city clerical workers the following spring, the San Francisco Civil Service Commission responded that city charter language mandating prevailing wage surveys prevented the commission from implementing the new policy. Discussions have continued, but no actual changes in policy have taken place in the two years following adoption of the policy.

Laws Governing Collective Bargaining

While federal and state laws governing collective bargaining do not directly require comparable worth, they are as important as the laws that do. Much comparable worth activity takes place at the bargaining table. Collective bargaining laws will either encourage or discourage union organizing and collectively bargained comparable worth studies and pay adjustments.

Some labor relations laws give civil service laws priority over collectively bargained agreements; others provide that bargained agreements can override civil service laws. More and more unions are taking the position that comparable worth studies should be a joint effort of labor and management, including workers representing the affected job classes.

Activists who lobby for civil service laws reform need to know how collective bargaining laws and civil service laws interface in order to design legislation to fit the particular jurisdiction. In Connecticut, for example, the comparable worth law provides that the studies it mandates will be implemented in collective bargaining. The California law provides that the data collected will be presented to the state legislature and to employee bargaining representatives. Minnesota's comparable worth law requires that the money allocated by the legislature for pay adjustments be earmarked for collective bargaining units in proportion to the number of undervalued women's jobs in those units.

A related category of labor relations law comprises those provisions that protect "concerted activity" by unionized and nonunionized workers to improve their working conditions. These laws protect efforts by the many unorganized women in women's occupations to raise comparable worth issues and establish comparable worth committees in their workplaces.

---

33. For example, Renton, Washington, and St. Louis, Missouri, have done so.

"Concerted activity" around comparable worth will also be protected by such laws when it is part of a union organizing drive. We will consider these aspects of labor relations laws in more detail below.

Laws That Protect Employees Seeking Comparable Worth Pay

Broadly speaking, "collective bargaining" refers to the organized efforts of two or more employees to negotiate with their employer regarding wages and other terms and conditions of their employment. (See Chapter 13 for a discussion of the role of comparable worth in organizing and bargaining.) These activities are protected, prohibited, or ignored by a variety of federal, state, and local laws, ordinances, regulations, executive orders, attorney general opinions, and interpretative court and arbitration decisions. Although these laws generally refer to the process of employer-employee negotiations through an authorized bargaining unit that is a union or labor organization, they sometimes protect individual or "concerted activities" that do not, or are not intended to, mature into collective bargaining agreements. Workers who individually or collectively plan to raise the issue of comparable worth should first familiarize themselves with applicable labor laws. This knowledge is essential for planning strategies and actions that take advantage of already existing procedures and protections and are not against the law.

It is difficult to generalize about laws that affect collective bargaining and concerted activities. Such employee activities may be lawful or unlawful, depending on whether the employer is private or public (and if public, whether it is the federal, state, or municipal government); whether the employer voluntarily agrees to bargain collectively; whether a specific activity, such as "striking," is legal; and whether an authorized bargaining unit exists. Under different laws, a collective bargaining agreement to pay equal wages for comparable work as a corrective action to existing discriminatory practices may be null and void as a violation of public policy, subject to legislative approval, or unenforceable in court.

Definitions

Applicable laws frequently employ the following terms, which are clarified here: "collective bargaining," "exclusive representative," "bargaining unit," "organizing," "concerted activities," and "meet and confer."

Under state and federal laws, "collective bargaining" refers to negotiations between an employer and labor organizations authorized to represent employee members. The authorized labor organization or union is called the "exclusive representative," or "bargaining agent," and, generally, where an exclusive representative has been authorized, the employer cannot bargain with any other group or individual. The employees who are represented are referred to as the "bargaining unit."

Organized employee activities that are not part of these negotiations are referred to as "organizing" or "other concerted activities." The "concerted activity" of employees where there is not a recognized bargaining unit may or may not be protected by law. The term "concerted activity" is inherited from criminal law. If the facts of a criminal case fit under the definition of concerted activity, a person involved in the alleged criminal activity may be an "accomplice" or part of a "conspiracy." At one time the organizing activities of employees seeking increased wages or improved working conditions were considered criminal, and this is still true under certain circumstances: public employee collective bargaining is prohibited by law today in North Carolina and Virginia, and thirty-eight states prohibit most, if not all, public employees from striking. Only in Montana have courts interpreted the statutory "right to concerted activities" as including the right of public employees to strike. A few state laws provide for mandatory strike penalties. The Kentucky Department of Personnel, for example, subjects striking employees to disciplinary action, including dismissal. Other states limit the right to strike in various ways. Such states frequently limit or prohibit strikes by "essential" employees, such as police or firefighters or impose certain procedural requirements, such as mandatory mediation, before public'employees can strike.

Comparable-worth-related concerted activities often result when employees want to organize in order to bargain collectively for pay equity adjustments and there is no official bargaining agent (see definition below), or when an outside labor organization is challenging a recognized bargaining agent that is unwilling to negotiate for such pay adjustments. Sharing information about wages with co-workers is an example of a concerted activity. When concerted activities are protected by law, it would be an unfair labor practice to retaliate against employees who shared this information. Where they are not protected, employees dismissed or disciplined for such activities have no legal recourse.

Concerted activities that are formalized by the establishment of an official representative bargaining unit are called "collective bargaining." The legal use of "collective bargaining" is narrower than the common use of the term. It refers to the ongoing process of negotiation between an employer and an organized group of employees represented by an *official* (authorized by law) bargaining agent, which may be a union or an employee. (Some atypical state laws specifically allow an individual employee to bargain. Washington State, for example, allows academic employees of community college districts to negotiate with their districts on their own behalf but denies this privilege to other state employees.)

Written collective bargaining agreements are negotiated to determine wages paid and other terms and conditions of employment, including health and life insurance, retirement benefits, training, and working conditions. As women have joined unions, collective bargaining agreements have started to include reproductive health benefits, child care, flexible working hours, sick leave to take care of family members, maternity and paternity leaves, affirmative action, job evaluation studies based on comparable worth, and comparable worth pay equity adjustments.

At least ten states have laws applying to some or all public employees that mandate only that the employer "meet and confer" (or "consult") with employee representatives at reasonable intervals and discuss their recommendations. These laws do not obligate the public employer to accept the recommendations presented, not do they require a written "collective bargaining agreement." Federal laws governing most federal civil service employees are "meet and confer" rather than collective bargaining laws.

Some state laws and the federal law covering civil service employees make certain issues mandatory subjects of bargaining and exclude others, or permit but do not mandate bargaining, or permit employer and employee to "meet and confer" about wages and working conditions. Under some of these "mixed" laws, including those covering federal employees, wages are not required subjects for bargaining.

Application of Federal and State Laws
Private Industry

Almost all employees in private industry are covered by federal labor laws. The most important, the National Labor Relations Act (NLRA), was passed in 1935 to protect an employee's "right to self organization, to form, join, or assist labor organizations, to bargain collectively through representatives of their own choosing, and to engage in other concerted activities, for the purpose of collective bargaining or other mutual aid or protection" (§7). This act makes it unlawful for employers to "interfere with, restrain, or coerce employees in their exercise of these rights" (§8(a)). A later amendment also protects the rights of employees not to participate in collective bargaining or other concerted activities (§7). Private employees have a "right to strike" under the NLRA.

Federal Government Employees

A single federal law, the Civil Service Reform Act of 1978, covers federal workers. This act established the Merit Systems Protection Board, which is similar in function to the National Labor Relations Board in that its purpose is to safeguard the merit system and federal employee rights. However, the bargaining rights of federal employees are much more limited than those of public employees under the NLRA and are similar to those of public employees covered by "meet and confer" laws.

State and Local Government Employees

Much recent comparable-worth-related collective bargaining activity is concentrated in the area of state and local government employment. Public employees who work for units of state or local government may or may not be covered by a maze of state and local labor laws and regulations.[34]

As of January 1981 thirty-nine states, the District of Columbia, and the Virgin Islands had statutes or executive orders covering some or all employees. Of these, twenty-three states, the District of Columbia, and the Virgin Islands had comprehensive public employee bargaining laws. All of these comprehensive laws *mandate* collective bargaining, except those of Kansas and Missouri, which require employers to "meet and confer"; and Washington State, which *mandates* collective bargaining for local government employees and teachers, *permits* it for community college teachers and Port District employees, and *mandates* (by executive order) that state employers "meet and confer" (but not bargain for wages) with state civil service employee bargaining representatives.

Even in states without such laws, public employee collective bargaining may be addressed by executive order, attorney general opinions, personnel board policies, or state court decisions. For example, an executive order mandates collective bargaining rights for employees in the executive branch of state government in Illinois. A Louisiana attorney general opinion permits collective bargaining for all public employees. Collective bargaining is permitted for New Mexico state employees under a state personnel board rule.

State courts have disagreed about the meaning of statutory silence regarding public employee bargaining rights. Court decisions have upheld such rights where no laws existed in Arizona, Arkansas, and Colorado. In Tennessee, however, courts have interpreted the absence of law as prohibiting bargaining altogether.

Mississippi is the only state that has no laws, regulations, executive orders, or court decisions addressing the issue of whether public employees have a right to bargain collectively. Three states—North Carolina, Texas, and Vermont—have laws that prohibit collective bargaining by public employees; and a Utah attorney general's opinion has ruled that state employees cannot bargain collectively.

Coverage

The differences in coverage under state collective bargaining laws are many. Even laws within each state vary considerably. Some laws are limited

---

34. An excellent source of current information on state laws is published and regularly updated by the Bureau of National Affairs, Washington, D.C. 20037. The BNA publishes a "Summary of State Labor Laws," as well in-depth analyses of topics including the test of laws, executive orders, personnel policies, and attorney general opinions and summaries of cases interpreting them. These materials may be ordered from the BNA or found at any law library, and some other libraries, in the *Government Employee Relations Report* RF-203.

to or exclude employees of specific administrative units: all state employees, all civil service employees, all classified civil service employees, local employees, municipal employees, city water works employees, transit workers, school district employees, community college employees, university employees. Michigan law, for example, mandates collective bargaining for all public employees except state civil service employees. Washington State has a "meet and confer" provision for state civil service classified employees, but not for those who are exempt from civil service. Collective bargaining is mandated for all local public employees (only) by Nevada statute.

Eleven other states have comprehensive labor relations laws limited to specific occupational groups: teachers, school administrators, firefighters, police. Montana has a separate law covering nurses. Sixteen states have enacted separate labor relations laws governing public school teachers.

Ten states have a single collective bargaining law, modeled after the NLRA, that protects the bargaining rights of "public" employees. Even these laws, collectively referred to as "public employees relations acts" (PERAs), have not been uniformly applied or interpreted. Some PERAs allow local governments to choose not to be placed under the jurisdiction of state collective bargaining provisions. Delaware law, for example, covers employees of local governments only if the local governments elect coverage.

Degree of Protection Provided

State protective labor laws vary extensively, and some protect the employer more than they do the employee. The legal protection provided ranges from a complete ban on organizing and bargaining activities, including strong penalties against striking, to laws paralleling the NLRA and requiring both parties to bargain collectively in good faith and to negotiate a written agreement concerning wages and other terms and conditions of employment.

Other state laws allow public employers to bargain collectively but place no obligation on them to do so. Permissive bargaining laws are still stronger than "meet and confer" laws. The degree of protection afforded by the latter depends largely on the persuasive abilities of organized employees, since they neither require negotiation nor recognize collective bargaining agreements. Sometimes a law will combine permissive and mandatory features. Alabama, for example, permits collective bargaining for firefighters and mandates "meet and confer" for teachers.

Inclusion of Wages as a Bargaining Subject

Protective bargaining laws will, of course, be of little assistance to employees seeking comparable worth pay adjustments if the applicable law does not include salaries and wages within the "scope of bargaining." Three states—Minnesota,[35] New Jersey, and New Mexico—do not include wages or salaries among the defined bargaining subjects. Thirty-eight states, however, specifically include wages and salaries within the scope of bargaining rights for some, if not all, employees. In six states, wages are mandatory bargaining subjects for municipal employees in cities, counties, political subdivisions, and municipal corporations, as well as teachers and community college district academic employees, but not for state civil service employees or four-year higher education personnel.

Conditions Governing Wage Agreements

Even if wages are a permissible subject of collective bargaining, wage agreements may be subject to state civil service laws or legislative funding approval. Even state laws that require a public employer to bargain collectively about wages frequently include a provision that makes the resulting agreement conditional on other laws, regulations, or decisions. The Washington State bargaining law for civil service employees, for example, provides that any matter delegated to the civil service system shall not be bargainable; a wage-setting system based on a survey of prevailing rates is included in the civil service law. Wisconsin, Idaho, Massachusetts, Delaware, and California laws are also limited by the state civil service law.

Recently, California civil service law was amended in 1981 for most state employees and in 1983 for those in higher education to allow comparable worth pay adjustments. A Rhode Island attorney general opinion advised that a bargaining agreement may obligate the governor to propose changes in the merit system law or change personnel rules with regard to bargainable subjects such as classification and wage plans. Under Wisconsin and Connecticut law, the provisions of a labor agreement supersede civil service law and other statutes related to wages.

Even if wage agreements are not in conflict with state civil service or merit system laws, they may be subject to ultimate rejection by the legislature or local funding body; the California law allowing comparable worth pay adjustments is subject to approval by the legislature in the annual budget act. This is not to say that bargaining collectively for comparable worth pay within the public sector is inadvisable, but the bargaining unit must be simultaneously involved in communicating with and educating the funding authority.

---

35. However, employee bargaining units will negotiate with the state to determine which classifications receive what amount of moneys under the 1982 comparable worth amendment to the Minnesota Civil Service Law, MS 43 A.01.

Unit Determination

Another factor that affects bargaining for comparable worth pay is the applicable law, regulation, or practice concerning bargaining unit determination. Bargaining for comparable worth is most likely to win support where a majority of members of the bargaining unit will benefit from it. Therefore, it is most likely to succeed where bargaining units represent employees within occupational groups rather than administrative units. Some states, such as Hawaii, designate bargaining units by statute. In Hawaii all "nonsupervisory white collar employees" are included in a single statewide bargaining unit. In addition to the disadvantages of including a wide variety of job classifications, this kind of law makes communication and organizing difficult because the bargaining unit is spread all over the state. The Alaska law, which defines bargaining units as administrative departments or agencies, presents the same problems. Most laws set certain criteria for unit determination and provide that disputes will be resolved by the state employee relations or personnel board.

Common criteria for unit determination are: efficiency of operation; common community or interest; history of bargaining; similar duties, skills, and working conditions; and desires of employees. Therefore, most state laws would allow a bargaining unit made up of "predominantly female" job classifications unless someone challenged the unit, perhaps on the basis of historical bargaining unit make-up.

Only the 12 per cent of all women workers who are unionized can take advantage of collective bargaining laws or agreements that can be used to bring about comparable worth pay adjustments. Women who desire comparable worth will need to give serious consideration to organizing as a means of strengthening their position with employers, legislators, and courts.

Conclusion

Proponents of comparable worth should not limit their legal strategies to those available under Title VII of the Civil Rights Act. Some state equal rights amendments, fair employment practices acts, and equal pay acts, while often untested, may offer stronger legal remedies than Title VII. Action under these laws may apply to the private as well as the public sector. For public sector employees at all levels, civil service laws offer comparable worth possibilities either through interpretation of existing laws or enactment of new ones. It is also possible for new laws or executive orders to extend comparable worth requirements to government contractors. Employers in the public or private sector should also be aware of their options under collective bargaining, since comparable worth can be introduced at the bargaining table as well. It is important to explore all options for implementation and to choose those which best suit the legal and political situation.

Appendix

State Equal Pay and Fair Employment Practice Laws and Code Citations

15 of 39 State Equal Pay Laws mandate equal pay for comparable work; all 41 State FEP Laws prohibit sex discrimination in employment.

State	Equal Pay Law Code Citation	Date Enacted	FEP Law Code Citation	Date Enacted	Date Sex Added If Known
Alabama					
Alaska	A.S. § 23.10.155	repealed 1973	A.S. § 18.80.010	1953	1972
Arizona	A.R.S. § 23.340	1955/1977	A.R.S. § 41.1461		
Arkansas	A.S. § 81-624/§ 81.333	1949			
California	Cal. Labor Code § 1197.5	1963	Cal. Govt. Code § 12940	1959	
Colorado	C.R.S. § 8-5-05	1949	C.R.S. § 24-34-301	1957	1967
Connecticut	C.G.S. § 31-75		C.G.S. § 46a-51	1947	
Delaware			19 D.C.A. § 710	1953	
Florida	15 F.S.A. § 448.07 § 725.06	1969/1973	F.S.A. § 23.161-167	1967	1972
Georgia	C.G.A. § 54-100	1966	C.G.A. § 89.1707	1978	
Hawaii	H.R.S. § 387-4	1959	5 H.R.S. § 378-1	1963	
Idaho	I.C. § 44-1702	1969	11 I.C. § 67-5909	1961	
Illinois	48 I.A.S. § 4a	1943	P.A. § 81-1216	1961	
Indiana	A.I.C. § 22-2-2-4	1965	A.I.C. § 22-9-1-1	1961	1971
Iowa			I.C.A. § 601A.1	1963	
Kansas	K.S.A. § 44-1205	1978	K.S.A. § 44-1001	1953	
Kentucky	K.R.S. § 337.423	1966	K.R.S. § 344.030	1966	1977
Louisiana					
Maine	26 M.R.S.A. § 628	1954	5 M.R.S.A. § 4551	1965	1973
Maryland	A.C.M. Art. 100 § 55A	1966	A.C.M. Art. 49B § 1-28	1951	1965
Massachusetts	149 M.C.L.A. § 105A	1934	151B M.C.L.A. § 4	1964	
Michigan	M.C.L.A. § 750.556	1919	M.C.L.A. § 37.2201	1964	
Minnesota	M.S.A. § 181.67	1969	M.S.A. § 363.01	1955	1969
Mississippi					
Missouri	A.M.S. § 290.400	1963	A.M.S. § 296.010	1961	

Appendix (*continued*)

State	Equal Pay Law		FEP Law		
	Code Citation	Date Enacted	Code Citation	Date Enacted	Date Sex Added If Known
Montana	M.C.A. § 39-3-104	1919	M.C.A. § 49-2-301	1947	
Nebraska	R.S.N. § 48-1219	1967	R.S.N. § 48-1116	1965	
Nevada	N.R.S. § 608.017	1975	N.R.S. § 613.330	1961	1965
New Hampshire	N.H.R.S. § 275-37	1947	N.H.R.S. § 354-A	1965	1971
New Jersey	N.J.S.A. § 34:11-56.2	1952	N.J.S.A. § 10:5-1	1945	1970
New Mexico			N.M.S.A. § 28-1-1	1949	1969
New York	M.C.L.N.Y. Labor Law § 199.a	1937	M.C.L.N.Y. Human Rights Law § 290	1945	1965
North Carolina			G.S.N.C. § 143-422	1977	
North Dakota	N.D.C.C. § 34-06.1-03	1965	N.D.C.C. § 34-01-19	1979	
Ohio	O.R.C.A. § 4111.17	1959	O.R.C.A. § 4112.99	1959	
Oklahoma	O.S.A. § 198.1	1965	O.S.A. § 25-1101	1963	
Oregon	O.R.S. § 652.220	1955	O.R.S. § 659.110	1949	1955
Pennsylvania	P.S.A. 43 § 336.3	1947	P.S.A. 43 § 956	1955	1969
Rhode Island	G.L.R.I. § 28-6-17	1946	G.L.R.I. § 28-5-1	1949	1971
South Carolina			G.L.S.C. § 1-13-10	1972	
South Dakota	S.D.C.L. § 60-12-15	1966	S.D.C.L. § 20-13-1	1972	
Tennessee	T.S.A. § 50-321	1974	T.S.A. § 4-21-101	1967	1972
Texas	A.R.C.S. Title 117, Art. 6825	1919			
Utah			U.C.A. § 34-35-6	1953	
Vermont			V.S.A. T.21 § 495	1963	1971
Virginia	C.V. § 40.1-28.6	1974			
Washington	R.C.W.A. § 49.12.75	1943	R.C.W.A. § 49.60.010	1949	1969
West Virginia	W.V.C. § 21-58-1	1965	W.V.C. § 5-11-1	1967	1977
Wisconsin			W.S.A. § 111.31	1945	1961
Wyoming	W.S. § 27-4-301	1959	W.S. § 27-9-101	1965	

15

Developments in Selected States

ALICE H. COOK

Historians of social reform in the United States have always had to weigh the relative contributions of the states and the federal government. Since the days of the New Deal, the federal government has clearly established its pre-eminence in this field, after having left it almost entirely to the states during the first 150 years of its history. Yet it is important to note that in respect both to wage and hour legislation and to civil rights statutes covering employment, the federal government has fallen in line only after a substantial number of states have moved on these issues.[1]

The Bureau of National Affairs *Special Report* on comparable worth, which appeared in October 1981, contained a section on state and local action on this issue. It noted, *inter alia*, that fourteen states had equal pay laws framed in terms of comparable worth, some of them dating from early post–World War II days.[2] This raised the question of whether some states were running well ahead of the federal government in this regard. Might the Reagan administration's revitalization of the doctrine of states rights, ironically, encourage more states to act in the very area from which the administration itself was in retreat? More realistically, were the concerned groups backing comparable worth legislation limiting its application to public employment, or were they endeavoring to develop and administer a concept of comparable worth applicable to all wage earners—public and private— within state boundaries?

Just at this point the Industrial Relations Center at the University of Hawaii was commissioned by the state legislature to undertake a study of comparable worth, preliminary to more clearly defined action on the part of

Acknowledgment: This chapter is a revision of a paper presented at the 1983 spring meeting of the Industrial Relations Research Association, Honolulu. An early version appeared in the conference *Proceedings* (Madison: Industrial Relations Research Association, 1983). Both the chapter and the paper are summaries of a report submitted to the Hawaii legislature in February 1983: Alice H. Cook, *Comparable Worth: The Problem and States' Approaches to Wage Equity* (Honolulu: Industrial Relations Center, University of Hawaii at Manoa, 1983).

1. Ronnie J. Steinberg, *Wages and Hours: Labor and Reform in Twentieth-Century America* (New Brunswick, N.J.: Rutgers University Press, 1982).

2. Bureau of National Affairs, *A BNA Special Report: The Comparable Worth Issue* (Washington, D.C.: BNA 1981).

the state.[3] The Center supplied some funds to enable me to look at a number of state programs during the summer of 1982. I went on to augment this investigation by corresponding with agencies in other states as well, so that the report that went to the Hawaii legislature and interested support groups carried information on seventeen states.[4]

I found four main approaches to the study and implementation of pay equity: legislation, unilateral action of state personnel offices, collective bargaining between the state and unions representing various units of its employees, and litigation, undertaken for the most part by unions of aggrieved employees. I shall deal with experiences in each of these categories in this chapter.

First, however, it is worth noting that many of the initiating parties have taken the preliminary step of making a study of job segregation in the employment area to which they direct attention. These studies have usually also included a survey of concomitant wage differentials between occupations dominated by male and female employment. Several such studies have been instituted by legislation and presumably were meant to be followed by implementing acts framed to correct demonstrated inequities. The Illinois and Kentucky studies are examples.[5] Some studies have been undertaken by

---

3. Hawaii Legislature, House Resolution 208, HD1, 1982.

4. The states visited were: Connecticut, Maine, Maryland, Massachusetts, Michigan, New Jersey, New York, and Pennsylvania. The states on which information was gathered by correspondence and telephone were: Alaska, California, Idaho, Illinois, Kentucky, Minnesota, Nebraska, Washington, and Wisconsin. A total of seventeen were covered in the report to the Hawaii legislature.

A 1983 Princeton University B.A. has gathered information on seven additional states: Florida, Hawaii, Iowa, New Mexico, North Carolina, Oregon, and Vermont. The author's focus is mainly on areas where advocacy groups have been active in initiating studies themselves or in lobbying for legislation. She reports that bills have been introduced in Oregon and Iowa but expects that only Iowa will eventually adopt legislation. She notes that in Florida AFSCME and the state have negotiated a one-year contract to establish a joint committee to study comparable worth. Of the seven states examined, New Mexico alone has taken steps to upgrade women's salaries: "In March, 1983, the state's legislature passed a 3.3 million dollar appropriation, most of which will go to upgrade the salaries of the lowest paid employees, 86 percent of whom are women. The governor [is reported] strongly to support the measure and is 'certain' to sign it into law, according to the executive director of the State's Commission on the Status of Women." Diane deCordova, "A State of Action: The Pursuit of Pay Equity in the States" (B.A. dissertation, Princeton University, 1983), p. 96.

5. The bill adopted by the Illinois legislature in 1982 asked the Status of Women Commission to carry out a study of a sample of male- and female-dominated occupations to determine whether a wage differential exists and, if so, how great it is. The commission in turn employed Hay & Associates to do a study using twenty-four benchmark classes. At the same time, the Kentucky General Assembly adopted a concurrent resolution "directing a comprehensive study by the Legislative Research Commission into the comparable worth issue among the jobs of state employees." The study is scheduled to be completed in mid-1983.

commissions on the status of women;[6] some by consultants under contract to unions; some by personnel offices; some by such internal agencies as affirmative action offices, wage classification sections, or legislative research bodies. Many, if not most, of the reports have been public documents, widely available to the concerned parties.

Some of these studies, for a variety of reasons, have never been implemented. A series of studies and reports in Nebraska establish wide discrepancies between men's and women's wages that continue to exist. The Nebraska Women's Legislative Caucus is endeavoring to get the Legislature to consider remedial action.[7] The Michigan study carried out by the Women and Work Office of the state's Department of Labor came out at a time when Michigan's record high unemployment rate obscured all other considerations.[8]

Another, less rigorous kind of preparation for action is the public hearing, conducted at the state capital or widely distributed locations within a state. Hearings have the advantage of including a broad body of local and even individual experiences with pay discrimination and with efforts to deal with it. Their publication assures them a certain amount of continuing influence and supplies information to other jurisdictions concerned with the problem. Assemblywoman May Newburger set up a hearing on pay inequities in the state of New York for the summer of 1983. California's Commission on the Status of Women joined with the Department of Industrial Relations, the Department of Fair Employment and Housing, and the Fair Employment and Housing Commission to conduct hearings in several locations throughout the state in 1981 as preparation for its legislation of the same year. Testimony from these hearings has been published in nine volumes.[9]

The failure of studies to result in the implementation of a comparable worth program through either legislation or collective bargaining cannot

---

6. DeCordova's research was mainly directed to discovering initiating groups, including advocacy as well as research organizations. She addressed inquiries to all the active state commissions on the status of women and concludes that such groups and their voluntary counterparts are almost invariably the moving factors in achieving comparable worth programs.

7. In late 1982, however, it was reported that the State Commission on the Status of Women was holding legislative hearings in several cities and that a task force was working "with the Commission on the Status of Women, the Personnel Department, labor unions and other concerned groups to address the pay equity problem" Cheryl Long, "Equal Pay for Work of Comparable Value" (Lincoln, Neb.: Pay Equity Task Force, 1981), p. 4.

8. Arthur Young & Co., *A Comparable Worth Study of the State of Michigan Job Classifications* (Detroit: Arthur Young & Co., 1980). This report is obtainable from the Office of Women and Work, Department of Labor, 309 N. Washington, Box 30015, Lansing, MI 48909.

9. *Hearings on Pay Inequities and Comparable Worth*, various dates (Sacramento, 1981).

help but generate high levels of frustration. In some states, including Wisconsin, Washington, and Michigan, litigation has followed such failures as disappointed women have turned to their representative organizations to take up the struggle in the courts.

Studies, of course, are also used to prepare for litigation. They are, however, usually of a more general sort, representing a collection of historical and statistical data from governmental and scholarly sources to demonstrate an alleged pattern and practice of discrimination. Briefs *amici curiae* further broaden the informational and support base for such programs.

As noted earlier, efforts to establish comparable worth programs have taken a number of forms. Let us direct our attention now to each of these in turn.

Legislation

The *BNA Special Report* called attention in 1981 to the fact that several states had long since adopted legislation calling for equal payment of men and women judged by standards of "comparable worth" or "comparable work."[10] Massachusetts was one of the first, with a law adopted in 1945, California the most recent, with its 1981 statute. This legislation appears to be divisible into two categories: that adopted after the new national concern with "pay equity" or "comparable worth," a date I somewhat arbitrarily set as 1979, when the first national pay equity conference was held,[11] and that adopted earlier, either before or after the federal Equal Pay Act (EPA) of 1963. Most of the latter legislation applies equally to the private and public

---

10. The states with comparable worth statutes include Alaska, Arkansas, California, Georgia, Idaho, Kentucky, Maine, Maryland, Massachusetts, North Dakota, Oklahoma, Oregon, South Dakota, Tennessee, and West Virginia: *BNA Special Report*, pp. 115–19. Six of these statutes were adopted before the federal Equal Pay Act (1963), and eleven since then. One state, Pennsylvania, replaced a comparable worth law of 1955 with the federal language in 1968. Only California adopted its statute after 1979; it did so in 1981.

11. This conference, called by a self-constituted organization, the National Pay Equity Conference, included representatives of the Women's Bureau, the Equal Employment Opportunity Commission, several trade unions, and state commissions on the status of women, as well as lawyers from a number of advocacy groups, scholars, and activists. The conference was addressed by Eleanor Holmes Norton, then chair of the EEOC; Carin Clauss, solicitor in the Department of Labor, responsible for cases arising from the Office of Federal Contract Compliance Programs (OFCCP), which administers Executive Order 11246 as amended by Executive Order 11345; representatives of various job evaluation consulting firms; and lawyers active in wage litigation. The National Committee on Pay Equity emerged as a permanent organization from this conference. Its proceedings were edited and published: Conference on Alternative State and Local Policies, Committee on Pay Equity, *Manual on Pay Equity: Raising Wages for Women's Work*, ed. Joy Ann Grune Washington, D.C.: 1979.

sectors, and most of it has been disregarded. Massachusetts has had no experience whatever with implementing the law, according to its attorney general's office. Moreover, at the time of my visit to Boston, a state legislator was drafting a new bill without reference to the law already on the books.[12]

The "new era" legislation tends to deal exclusively with the state employer and with pay equity in state employment. An exception is Alaska, which in 1949 adopted a "Wage Discrimination against Women" statute forbidding an employer to pay a woman a lesser wage rate than that paid to a man for "work of comparable character or work in the same operation." In 1980 this law was repealed, but identical language was inserted it into the state Fair Employment Practices (FEP) statute's enumeration of unfair labor practices.[13] Although many states have FEP laws proscribing sex discrimination, Alaska's is the only one that includes specific comparable worth language (see Chapter 14).

Where did the comparable worth language in the pre-1979 statutes originate? The federal Women's Bureau, which never ceased from its founding day to the present to advocate equal pay—however variously defined—has produced over the years "an impressive body of statistical data, documenting wide differentials in wages paid to men and women in all occupations."[14] Mary Anderson, the bureau's first head, at one time chaired a national equal pay organization. In 1952—eleven years before the federal EPA became a reality—the Bureau consolidated the activities of some twenty large national organizations into a united campaign for passage of a federal law. My belief is that the Women's Bureau in the period between and immediately after the wars put out a model draft of state equal pay legislation that a number of states adopted without much debate and on the bureau's good authority.

The laws adopted and the bills drafted after 1979, on the other hand, are the products of a new era of comparable worth legislation, one informed by a new shelf of studies; animated by a national campaign of associated women's organizations; encouraged by the agencies engaged in administering equal pay legislation for the federal government; aided by the introduction of new measurement techniques developed by professionals in job evaluation; and encouraged by the outcome of a number of federal cases, headed by the Supreme Court's decision in *County of Washington* v. *Gunther.*[15]

---

12. Aide to Barbara Gray, Committee on Pay Equity, Massachusetts legislator, personal communication, July 1982.

13. A.S. 1962, § 23, 10.155 (1949).

14. Morag MacLeod Simchak, "Equal Pay in the United States," *International Labour Review* 193 (1971): 549.

15. *County of Washington* v. *Gunther*, 101 S. Ct. 2242 (1981).

It is these new laws and bills that concern us in appraising the present status of comparable worth legislation in a number of states. For the most part these bills or statutes are specific in purpose and scope. They direct state departments of personnel or other appropriate agencies to examine, or re-examine, their job and wage classification systems for evidence of sex bias and to undertake further studies that will provide the basis for a reconstruction of these systems such that they will be bias-free and will allocate wages solely according to job content and job requirement.

Several states have drafted legislation, and some of these have passed bills, that authorize studies of the present systems of payment in relation to job-segregated areas of state employment. Illinois by law and Kentucky by joint resolution of the two houses of the legislature have authorized studies and appropriated funds to allow an expert consultant to carry out the necessary surveys. The draft legislation on which the New Jersey legislature will vote in late 1983 or early 1984 covers all public employees in the state and would thus cover towns, villages, cities, and counties as well as the state itself. This bill is of special interest because it is the product of considerable study by the State Commission on the Status of Women and the State Commission on Sex Discrimination in the Statutes, which together formed a task force on comparable worth made up of representatives of state employee unions, the state's Affirmative Action Office, scholars from Rutgers University, representatives of autonomous women's organizations, and others with special interest in the subject. The task force helped draft the legislation and committed its various organizational affiliates to support of the program. The bill itself calls for a study to be conducted under the supervision of a similar task force that would have fifteen members and include representatives of the legislature as well. The bill's sponsor, Senator Wynonah Lipman, has ensured that an appropriation of $100,000 will accompany the passage of the bill.[16]

Beginning in 1979, Connecticut adopted a series of three bills related to comparable worth. The first mandated a study of sex segregation; the second authorized an evaluation of jobs in state service through a study of benchmark jobs; and the third, passed in 1981, called for an evaluation of every position on the state roster. The director of the Labor Relations Department established an advisory committee to oversee the study and included on it three representatives of the private sector as well as delegates from women's organizations, labor unions, and both houses of the legislature. The State Commission on the Status of Women, which in Connecticut is a creature of the legislature and acts in an advisory capacity to that body, was responsible for much of the initiatory work that resulted in the legislation.

---

16. Alma Saravia, executive secretary, New Jersey Commission on Sex Discrimination in the Statutes, personal communication, 30 June 1983.

Implementation to correct any inequities disclosed in these studies is in the hands of the collective bargaining representatives of the state and the various unions representing its employees. Three such units have already dealt with the problem by agreeing to establish equity funds that accrue through payments of 1.0 percent to 1.9 percent of payrolls until the job evaluation studies are completed. At that time payments to the discriminated categories will begin and will continue until equity with their higher-paid, male-dominated counterparts has been attained.

California amended its equal pay law in 1981 to require its Department of Personnel Administration to review and analyze "existing information, including those studies from other jurisdictions relevant to the setting of salaries for female-dominated jobs" and to make this information available "on an annual basis to the appropriate policy committee of the legislature" and the bargaining parties.[17] This law pertains only to female-dominated categories in state employment, defined as those job titles where women make up more than 70 percent of the employees. Several state departments and a coalition of women's organizations, Women in Politics, were responsible for the research, hearings, and lobbying activity that preceded the adoption of the law.

Minnesota amended its statutes on compensation in 1982 to require its "Commissioner of Employee Relations to submit a list of male- and female-dominated classes, paid less than other classes with the same number of Hay points" and empowered its "Legislative Commission on Employee Relations to recommend an amount to be appropriated for comparability adjustments to the full legislature." The recommended amount "may assume full implementation of comparable worth . . . in one biennium or over a longer period of time."[18] In May 1983 the legislature enacted the first appropriation of $21.7 million for pay equity adjustments.

The state of Washington offers a classic example of the failure of a thoroughgoing study (made in 1974) to result in immediate implementation. The two successors of the governor who had ordered the study were unenthusiastic about supporting its recommendations, although the discrepancy between male- and female-dominated occupations evaluated as comparable ran about 20 percent. When the legislature sought to deal once more with the issue in 1982, it was unable to come up with a formula that would satisfy both women's organizations and trade unions, although both were eager for legislative action. Finally, in June 1983, nine years after the original study, the legislature passed and the governor signed enabling and appropriation bills that will allow comparable worth adjustments to begin.

Helen Remick, a consistent proponent of the study and its implementa-

17. Government Code, State of California, § 19827.2.
18. Minnesota Council on the Economic Status of Women, "Update: Pay Equity for State Employees" (St. Paul: Council, 1982).

tion during the long period of delay, had turned her attention away from legislation to the state's personnel code, which in Washington, as in most states, gives personnel departments wide latitude to initiate and operate systems of job classification and compensation under general directions of equity. The initiative for implementing a comparable worth program, therefore, might well come from a personnel director or a civil service commission. Indeed, this is precisely what seems to have happened in two states covered in this study.

Unilateral Action of the State Personnel Office

Personnel departments took the initiative in introducing revisions of classification and compensation systems in Idaho and Nebraska. The initiatives took place before the "new era" and apparently without pressure from advocacy groups, either unions or women's organizations, but in both cases the effect has been to institute criteria and to follow up with wage adjustments consistent with the goal of comparable worth. In both states a legislative base existed in laws calling for nondiscrimination in the payment of wages.[19]

Idaho's Civil Service Commission has the responsibility to "determine the relative worth of each job classification" and has done so using a method developed by Hay and Associates, which assigns value points to each job as a measure of its worth. The state compensation specialist then developed a method of attaching salaries to these points through in-state surveys. When she noted that women's salaries lagged considerably behind those of men in comparable categories, these discrepancies were ordered corrected. The result was that women's salaries increased by an average of 16.2 percent while men's increased 6.8 percent. Secretarial salaries increased between 20 and 30 percent.[20]

In Nebraska, as noted above, the plan of an outside consultant employed by the Personnel Department, was severely criticized by both an internal legislative agency and the Status of Women Commission. At this point the Personnel Department, according to a press report, "began work on a job classification system that may help erase the sex-related value factors."[21]

---

19. Idaho adopted a law in 1969, "Discriminatory Payment of Wages Based upon Sex Prohibited" (I.C. § 44-1702), that forbids an employer to pay any employee in any occupation in the state at a rate less than the rate at which he pays any employee of the opposite sex for comparable work on jobs which have comparable requirements relating to skill, effort and responsibility. The Nebraska statute (R.S.N. § 48-1219, 1967) calls for equal pay for equal work, but its FEP law (1965) calls for equal pay for comparable work on jobs with comparable requirements.

20. Maxine Matlock, State Compensation Specialist, personal communication, 4 November 1982.

21. Nancy Hicks, "Is Women's Work Really Worth Less?" *Lincoln Star*, 8 October 1982, p. 11.

Pennsylvania had much earlier, in 1955, set up an all-inclusive classification system that the state personnel director reports was aimed at eliminating sex differentials and establishing a compensation system based on internal equity throughout the entire job range, regardless of the location of state facilities—that is, without bending to local market conditions, a consideration that often operates to lower women's wages. As evidence that the state had essentially achieved the goal of comparable worth, the director pointed out that the system itself has never been seriously challenged by the unions, which began to bargain with the state at a much later date.[22] The unions did in 1979 ask a group of scholars at Temple University to undertake a study of certain male- and female-dominated occupations. The resulting study of eleven selected and matched jobs found, by two different measures, a substantial wage discrepancy between male- and female-dominated occupations. The study has not been followed up in collective bargaining, however. (See Chapter 8).

Collective Bargaining and Employee Representation

While most state personnel systems were established long before collective bargaining between states and their employees was legalized,[23] the problem of integrating collective bargaining rights with civil service laws has often led to frustration, and sometimes even to an impasse, in dealings between unions and personnel or labor relations directors. The element of equal employment opportunity has further tended to complicate labor relations.[24]

Nevertheless, collective bargaining has now existed long enough in a number of states that a certain degree of maturity and expertise has come to characterize the approach taken by the unions and the state as employer to new problems (see Chapter 13). One of the unions most active in advocating comparable worth is the American Federation of State, County and Municipal Employees (AFSCME). In addition to putting this issue on its bargaining agendas in many states, cities, and school districts throughout the

---

22. Interview with Charles Sciotto, Director of Personnel, State of Pennsylvania, and with state directors of compensation, classification, and labor relations, Harrisburg, 7 September 1982.

23. Some twenty-eight states have legalized collective bargaining for state employees. Many of these laws have included management rights provisions and other restrictions on the subjects of bargaining that go considerably beyond those in the private sector as laid down in the National Labor Relations Act and in state acts modeled on it. While some states bargain with employees even though no law exists to regulate the practice, unions find it very difficult under such circumstances to organize and to maintain sufficient membership strength for bargaining.

24. Alice H. Cook, *Equal Employment Opportunity, the Merit System and Collective Bargaining in Public Employment in the State of Hawaii* (Honolulu: Industrial Relations Center, University of Hawaii, and the state Department of Personnel, 1979).

country, AFSCME has set up a special legal staff in its Washington head-quarters to litigate such issues. We will turn to this aspect of implementing comparable worth in a later section.

AFSCME is not alone among public employee unions in raising this issue in collective bargaining. A number of Civil Service Employees Associations—some with a loose affiliation to AFSCME, others independent—have done so aggressively. The Service Employees International Union, state Nurses Associations, the American Federation of Teachers, the Communications Workers of America, and the National Education Association, as well as groups of librarians and clerical workers, have also placed comparable worth high on their bargaining agendas.

In both Maine and New York, unions have bargained with the states for agreements to conduct a comparable-worth-oriented study of classifications and compensation. Funds for these studies were also bargained out and were in both cases provided by the states. In Maine the study is set up under a joint labor-management committee whose major task is to lay out the parameters of the study and employ a consultant to carry it out with their active cooperation. The committee, established in the late summer of 1982, spent its first months in self-education, both on the subject of comparable worth and on techniques of job evaluation. At this writing it is negotiating with an outside consultant to undertake the study. The New York study, the parties agreed, is to be conducted under the direction of the Center for Women in Government, a part of the State University of New York.

Expert consultants are the first to assert that their function in job evaluation studies is limited to classification. The assignment of wages to these classifications is the responsibility of the collective bargaining partners (or, where employees are not represented by unions, of the employer unilaterally). Wage agreements in Connecticut are all the products of negotiation, as is the case also in California and Minnesota. In Maine and New York, the wage results of the studies now about to begin must be the product of bargaining.

The exact source of funds, their appropriation, and the way in which they will be earmarked for achieving pay equity will, of course, vary from state to state. In Minnesota, the legislature appropriates a total sum to be applied to comparability adjustments, and it is assigned to the various bargaining units according to the number of underpaid classes represented, with the understanding that these funds may be spent only on these classes and for this purpose.

Should bargaining over comparable worth break down, three alternatives are open to the parties: mediation, arbitration, and striking. To be sure, difficulties exist in the public sector over both arbitration and the use of the strike, though a few public employers accept both.[25] The fact that all

---

25. The problem with arbitration arises under the doctrine of state sovereignty, which would deem it inappropriate for a private individual, such as an arbitrator, to

three have been employed in comparable worth disputes merits some attention.

Mediation

In mediation, an outsider familiar with the specific issue in dispute and with labor-management relations in general endeavors to help the parties find their own solution to their problems. In Colorado Springs, for example, management was convinced that wage discrimination existed. The city had originally used a single-factor evaluation system but then tried to base salaries on market indicators, with the result that in one year the clerical staff received no increases. Eleanor Holmes Norton, recently chair of the federal Equal Employment Opportunity Commission, was called in to mediate. The problem was, given an established discrepancy between men's and women's remuneration, to determine how much of the difference should be attributed to discrimination and therefore corrected. Norton helped the parties to arrive at an agreement that 80 percent of the difference fell into this category and should be corrected, a decision with which the city council then concurred. The plan that emerged foresaw a four-year implementation period, with the first year's adjustment being 50 percent of the measured inequity.[26]

Arbitration

Arbitration may be of two kinds: one determines issues of interests; the other, of rights. The former is somewhat less acceptable to the public employer than the latter because of its effect on state sovereignty.

Arbitration of "interests" is relatively uncommon, for it deals with arbitration of the terms of the contract itself. Some public law requires this, however, when parties are at impasse in negotiation. Where "interest arbitration" is required, the issues have to do with clauses of the contract or the specific amounts of wage adjustments. Customarily unions go on strike at such point of impasse in the hope of enforcing their demands upon the employer. In public employment labor relations, even in jurisdictions where strikes are permissible, certain categories of employees—usually police and firefighters—are nevertheless forbidden to strike. As a *quid pro quo* for this denial of right, some states provide for "last offer" or other forms of arbitration. While it is not impossible as women enter these occupations, that an arbitrator may be faced with a comparable worth issue, my research has so far failed to discover such an instance.

Arbitration of "rights" takes place when one of the parties to a contract,

---

substitute his judgment for that of the sovereign state. As for public employee strikes, only a few states, among them Pennsylvania and Hawaii, have legalized their use as a last resort, after all methods of adjudicating the differences between the parties have failed.

26. *BNA Special Report*, p. 37.

usually the union, alleges that the other has violated or misinterpreted its wording or intent. Unless an arbitrator is expressly forbidden to deal with questions of job evaluation or wage assignment, he or she may do so. The vast amount of arbitration of wage rates in the private sector that took place under National War Labor Board rules in World War II set all the precedents necessary for allowing arbitrators to deal with the resolution of disputes over proper wage rates for particular classifications. Indeed, decisions of this kind, resting on the arbitrator's "best judgment," have probably settled as many wage and job classification disputes as have job evaluation plans.

Strikes

Where binding arbitration is not available or where negotiations over contract terms are at an impasse, unions may and do engage in strikes in order to achieve their demands. The most widely publicized "comparable worth" strike took place in San Jose, California, in the summer of 1980 and resulted in negotiations leading to substantial wage increases for the clerical workers who had gone on strike. In addition, they accepted a pay parity program to be realized over a two-year period.

Nurses in both public and private employment in several localities have prepared legal briefs or other studies to back up their claims for improvements in their pay scales. In some California towns they have resorted to strikes in an attempt to realize these demands. In San Jose four private hospitals in 1982 were struck for several weeks, but without success.[27]

Litigation

An appeal to the courts is, in theory, a measure of last resort. It is an attempt to enforce an action through judicial edict that has not been achieved by legislation or collective bargaining. Costly and drawn out, judicial remedies can rarely be undertaken by individuals who are not substantially assisted by an advocacy organization with a legal staff and financial reserves equal to the task.

The organization most committed to the use of litigation in the attainment of comparable worth is AFSCME, the major labor union in public employment. Determining its strategies and carrying most of its cases is Winn Newman, an attorney who has written widely on the issue and his experience in the courts.[28] He has initiated legal action against the states of Washington, California, and Wisconsin, as well as several cities.

27. *New York Times*, 14 February 1982, p. A38.
28. Winn Newman and Carole Wilson, "Statement of International Union of Electrical, Radio and Machine Workers, AFL-CIO-CLC," before the United States Commission on Civil Rights hearings in *Affirmative Action in the 1980s: Dismantling the Process of Discrimination*, submitted 11 March 1981; Winn Newman, "Compara-

Very few litigants have had recourse to state law, even when it is worded so as to require comparable worth in both the public and the private sectors.[29] Indeed, attorneys with whom I have discussed the matter believe that following *Gunther*, the way is clear to press cases under Title VII of the Civil Rights Act of 1964 and that a clearcut interpretation by the federal bench supporting a comparable worth case under that statute would be considerably more important than any victory that could be won in a single state.

Unlike current legislation on comparable worth, litigation has not been limited to the public sector. At least three cases have dealt with particular aspects of the question, giving rise to the expectation that the federal courts will be dealing broadly with the issue in the near future. The best-known of these is *IUE* v. *Westinghouse*, for which the Supreme Court refused *certiorari*, thus letting stand the decision of the circuit court in support of the union's case. The union had traced inequities in women's compensation to special "women's rates" established during World War II in defiance of National War Labor Board rulings calling for comparable pay for women. Two other cases are making their way through the federal courts. *Kouba* v. *Allstate* deals with the issue of whether women's lower salaries in previous employment justify lower pay in current employment. A circuit court has overturned the district court ruling that an employer must correct such market-based inequities. A district court ruled in *Taylor* v. *Charley Brothers Co.* that a wholesale grocer could not justifiably assign men and women to sex-segregated work groups at different pay when they were doing substantially the same work.[30]

Implementation and Costs of Comparable Worth

Current legislation and much ongoing collective bargaining and litigation in this area are chiefly concerned with adjusting pay inequities for

---

ble Worth—'A Job Inequity by Any Other Name . . .' " (paper presented to the University of Wisconsin Law School Center for Equal Employment and Affirmative Action, 30 November 1979); Winn Newman and Jeanne M. Vonhof, " 'Separate but Equal'—Job Segregation and Pay Equity in the Wake of *Gunther*," *University of Illinois Law Review* (1981): 269–331.

29. A case presently before the Alaska State Commission for Human Rights was brought by public health nurses as a class seeking to establish that they are comparable to physician's assistants (mainly male) who receive a rate of pay four ranges above those of nurses. The case was heard in October 1983, and a final ruling is expected in early 1984. Several tests were made of the Pennsylvania law when it contained comparable worth language. The judges in these instances decided that the law meant "equal pay for equal work" and so ruled. This interpretation may have contributed to the legislature's decision to change the law's wording.

30. *I.U.E.* v. *Westinghouse*, 23 FEP Cases 588; *Kouba* v. *Allstate Insurance Company*, 26 FEP Cases 1273; *Taylor* v. *Charley Brothers Company*, FEP Cases 602.

women in public employment. A recurring question is how high the costs of comparable worth schemes will run. Can states deal with them in a period when budgets are tight and federal subsidies diminishing? In at least one notable case brought by nurses before the federal district in Denver, the judge refused to deal with the issue of comparability in large part because to do so would rock the national economic boat.[31] The cost to the employer is inevitably a cogent factor, threatening in many instances to override considerations of equity.

Written into the comparable worth study programs of a number of states is the requirement that the task force and its consultant present the legislature or the governor with an estimate of the cost of putting the recommended program into operation. In New York State, the negotiated study of the classification and wage assignment patterns in the state must come up with estimates of the cost of phasing in comparable worth under various alternative measures. In California, a state now committed to achieving sex equity in compensation, a legislative analyst was able to say only that an "indeterminate additional annual cost [will accrue] to the General Fund." The analyst pointed out that ultimate determination on this point must rest with the governor as employer and with the appropriate employee organizations through the collective bargaining process, pursuant to the Employee Relations Act. The coalition of support groups for the bill, Women in Politics, through its Employment Task Force noted that implementation funds might be restricted by what the legislature appropriates for salary increases. The likelihood is that whatever the additional costs, they will be spread over a number of legislative sessions until equity is reached.[32]

Although Idaho, which has reportedly achieved gender equity in compensation, did not report a total figure for costs, its state compensation specialist noted that "the amounts of adjustment necessary in female-dominated occupations ran between 10 and 30 percent."[33] These adjustment costs appear to have been absorbed by a single appropriation.

The Minnesota bill included a procedure for making comparability adjustments, beginning in the biennium following adoption of the legislation. The Legislative Commission on Employee Relations is directed to recommend to the legislature an amount appropriate for comparability adjustments. This amount may assume full implementation in one biennium

31. The case was *Lemons* v. *City of Denver*, 620 F.2d 288 (10th Cir., 1980). However, it reached the Denver circuit before the Supreme Court's decision on *Gunther*, which clearly permitted federal courts to consider broader interpretations of Title VII than those laid down in the Equal Pay Act.

32. Analysis of Assembly Bill no. 129 (Lockyer) as amended in senate, 24 August 1981, 1981–1982 session, 27 August 1981; and Women in Politics news release, undated, addressed to all senate members, "Subject SB 456 (Carpenter), A Matter of Pay Equity."

33. Maxine Matlock, personal communication, 4 November 1982.

or over a longer period of time. When funds are appropriated, money is assigned for this specific purpose to the various bargaining units, based on the number of underpaid classes each represents. The actual distribution of salary increases within each unit is negotiated through the standard collective bargaining process. Minimum costs would be incurred in bringing the salary of each female class up to the lowest salary for a male job with the same or fewer Hay points ($17.9 million per year); maximum costs, based on bringing each female class up to the highest salary for a male job with the same or fewer Hay points, would amount to $39.8 million per year. The legislature appropriated for the 1983–85 biennium a salary supplement of $178 million. The minimum expenditure for pay equity would represent approximately 20 percent of the appropriation, while the maximum would require 45 percent.[34]

In the end, costs will depend on the evaluation system used and its factors and factor weights. It will also depend on the definition of "female-dominated class," for that definition will expand or contract the number of classes and hence the number of individuals affected.[35] The method selected to implement a comparable worth standard will also affect ultimate total costs. Peggy Owens, in a report for the Sondheim Commission in Maryland,[36] tabulated projected costs in three localities that have undertaken or will shortly undertake comparable worth payment adjustments (see Table 15-1).

Whatever the cost, as Nancy Perlman, former chair of the National Committee on Pay Equity, points out, "It is critical to remember that the cost of correcting discriminatory practices is not justification for violating the law."[37] In the *Manhart* case, where an employer sought to justify charging women more for insurance on pension premiums than men on the

---

34. The calculations appear to be based on studies carried out by the Legislative Audit Commission Survey of October 1978.

35. Some states will set sex imbalance at a point somewhere above the proportions of the sexes employed in state offices or in the state's labor force. Most frequently, bills and statutes have defined a female- or male-dominated class as one in which the gender imbalance is 70:30 or more. Thus, "mixed" categories are those with a gender mix between 31 and 69 percent.

36. The Sondheim Commission was appointed by the governor of Maryland to examine the degree to which state salary levels are competitive in attracting and retaining a qualified and productive labor force. It was not specifically charged to look into the issue of comparable worth and in fact did not do so despite strong representations by the State Commission on Women and the efforts of several women legislators. The pressure did, however, have the effect of producing a staff report by Peggy Owens, " 'Comparable Worth': A Summary of the Available Information on Comparable Worth" (Baltimore: Sondheim Commission, 1982).

37. Testimony before the U.S. Congress, House Subcommittee on Compensation and Employee Benefits, conducted in September 1982 and reported in BNA, *Daily Labor Report*, no. 180 (16 September 1982): E-1–3.

Table 15-1
Cost of Comparable Worth Payments

	Current Status of Program	*Projected Cost*	*% of Payroll*
Colorado Springs	Year 1 of 4-year implementation program	$1.7 million over 4 years	2.6% each year
San Jose	Year 2 of 2-year bargaining agreement	$1.6 million over 2 years	0.7% each year
Washington State	Under study	$64.9 million annually	5.0% each year

Source: Peggy Owens, " 'Comparable Worth': A summary of the Available Information on Comparable Worth" (Baltimore: Sondheim Commission, 1982), p. 8.

grounds that the overcharge was a means of recovering anticipated costs, the Supreme Court ruled that "the cost of correcting discriminatory practices is no justification for violating Title VII."[38]

Summary

The "new era" activity on comparable worth in the states is directed mainly to the state as employer, although New Jersey flings its net to cover other public employees within the state as well. The activity begins typically with a study of the degree of job segregation into sex-dominated occupations and then proceeds to relate wage differentials to these categories. Much of the job evaluation work that is the key to determinations of comparability is being carried out by outside consultants who are experts in this field. The assignment of wages to the reclassified categories is the work of the collective bargaining partners where union activity is legal in public employment. Where it is not, the personnel departments or civil service commissions proceed on their own to put the recommendations into operation. Funds for studies have usually been part of the enabling legislation.

Several states have been careful to set up advisory committees made up jointly of employee and management representatives to outline and oversee job evaluation studies in the expectation that by doing so they will secure a firm base of support for the studies' outcomes. Others have included more broadly constituted task forces in order to achieve a wider representation of legitimate interests, including those of the legislature, in the entire procedure preliminary to final reports and recommendations.

---

38. *Los Angeles Department of Water and Power* v. *Munhart*, 435 U.S. 702, 716–17 (1978).

Legislation may not be necessary to initiate studies and even implementation, since most civil service legislation is founded on a concept of equity that can be read to cover comparable worth. At least one state has proceeded on this basis. Other alternatives to legislation in the achievement of comparable worth are collective bargaining and the techniques developed in the private and public sectors for reaching agreements with the help of mediators and arbitrators. Where these resources are unavailable or insufficient, some states permit strikes in public employment. At least one such strike, in San Jose, was successful.

Where studies have demonstrated inequities and no remedial action has ensued, unions have resorted in several states to litigation. These cases are being argued under the compensation provisions of Title VII of the Equal Employment Opportunity Act, where the decision in *County of Washington* v. *Gunther* ordered courts to try charges going beyond the limits of equal pay for equal work.

In a period of tightening budgets, implementation costs are inevitably a major consideration. New York's agreement, for example, requires that a projection of these costs accompany the job evaluation study. Several states have estimated that comparable worth costs will run from less than 1 percent to about 5 percent of present payrolls. The variations depend, of course, upon the degree of discrepancy found to exist between comparable male- and female-dominated jobs. With perhaps one exception, the states committed to realizing equity are planning to do so over a number of years, an understanding shared by the employees' representatives. The Supreme Court has reminded us that cost alone does not justify delaying the realization of equity.

PART V

Conclusion

16

Technical Possibilities
and Political Realities:
Concluding Remarks

HELEN REMICK AND RONNIE J. STEINBERG

Comparable worth contradicts fundamental economic assumptions, stretches legal interpretations, challenges stereotypes of women workers, and causes scrutiny of accepted management tools. It questions some of our deepest beliefs about the nature and value of work. This volume explores some of the controversies generated by comparable worth; we hope it will stimulate readers to ask questions about and seek answers to a wide range of other topics as well. What follows builds on the major themes of this book by examining definitions of comparable worth; assessing various criticisms leveled against the policy; identifying related policy issues; and offering some general insights about the route by which comparable worth will become an institutionalized part of equal employment policy.

Culture and the Undervaluation of Women's Work

Occupational segregation is endemic to every culture. Cultural beliefs underlying the differentiation of men's and women's work are so strong (though obviously changeable) that widespread debate on a comparable worth policy would have been unthinkable twenty—perhaps even ten—years ago. The concept of comparable worth was introduced as "equal pay for work of equal value" at the close of the Second World War. The Equal Pay Act, passed only twenty years ago, in 1963, without a comparable worth standard, was as radical a reform as the political system could then tolerate.

In these twenty years, the economic contributions of women have become more important, not only because of the increased number of women working for pay, but also because of the decreased earning power of men, increased divorce rates, increased expectations about standards of living, and women's increased self-esteem. These trends have translated into women's increased political power, which allows them to frame and pressure for political reforms.

These changes in our cultural beliefs have left their mark on social science scholarship as well. In the academic community, each of a number of fields studying the determinants of occupational position and wages has developed its own set of theoretical constructs and has passed through a number of intellectual phases: first identifying the legitimate labor market bases for the wage differential between men and women; then showing the differentiation to be based substantially on factors that can be linked to what Title VII characterizes as discrimination; and, more recently, proposing policies to close that portion of the wage gap that can be linked to discrimination.

There are two main approaches to assessing wage inequity: an *a priori* approach, which uses a packaged system of factors and factor weights for the purpose of evaluating jobs within a specific firm, and a *policy-capturing* approach, which uses a statistical analysis of the individual firm as the basis for generating factor and factor weights for job evaluation. Each approach has technical strengths and weaknesses, and both must be tempered by political realities. For example, *a priori* systems have the advantage of making explicit the values used in evaluating jobs; these systems ask for years of education and experience, level of monetary responsibility, amount of heavy lifting, and so on. They already have weights assigned to the various degrees to which these factors are present in a job (see Treiman, 1979, for examples of systems). The systems thus allow employer and employee alike the opportunity to study the underlying value system of the evaluation instrument in an accessible, nonmathematical framework. Chapter 7, about Washington State, presents the results of such a study. As discussed at length in that chapter and in Chapter 4, the major limitations of these systems are their resistance to modification, general lack of flexibility or responsiveness to firm-specific factors, and probable bias.

Procedures labeled as policy capturing make fewer assumptions than *a priori* ones about what the firm should value because they build an evaluation system that is firm-specific. The procedure involves applying detailed questionnaires to each job, and then using multiple regression techniques to determine which elements of jobs are correlated to pay practices for that firm (see Chapter 8 for a detailed example). Depending on the overall composition of jobs within a firm, a policy-capturing analysis might, for example, show that the amount of interpersonal interaction was an important determiner of salaries and specifically, that persuasion was worth twice as much as in salary dollars as giving information. The kinds of job elements analyzed for in policy capturing are similar to or the same as those in *a priori* procedures, but in policy capturing systems the weighting, or importance, is determined in terms of the individual firm, and in *a priori* systems the consulting firm selling the system has predetermined the weights.

The factors used in the two kinds of systems are similar because *a priori* systems were, at some point, derived through a multiple regression (policy-capturing) study of pay policies across a sample of firms that produced an average picture of compensation. Because what is valued in work changes over time, the policies of individual firms vary, and consultants base new systems on old ones, *a priori* systems will only approximate the pay policies for any given firm or institution. While no research has been done to measure the discrepancies caused by the above factors, correlations between pre-existing salaries and the results of *a priori* applications tend to range above 0.8; that is, these systems describe, or "capture," existing firm-specific wage policies quite well without special tailoring to any given employer.

The choice in particular work settings between the two approaches to evaluation most likely will be made for political reasons. In some settings, certain consulting firms will be preferred because of previous working relationships or local reputation. *A priori* systems will be preferred where they are seen as more understandable and explainable. On the other hand, regression models are more likely to be preferred in settings with strong tastes for sophisticated mathematical models and computers (regression virtually cannot be done without computers) and for firm-specificity. Decisions may hinge on such diverse issues as how the firm's personnel staff feel about computers (and even whether they have one), or how mathematically sophisticated the managers and union leaders are.

The level of objectivity in measurement of either kind of system should not be confused with the mistaken view that there is or can be objectivity about values. Both approaches are ways of systematizing value systems, and both can capture discrimination embedded in an existing classification system. Both are geared to describe *what is* in the firm or in some other labor market. Neither starts from scratch in prescribing *what should be*. Rather than emphasizing differences between the approaches, comparable worth advocates should address the larger goal of developing guidelines for minimally biased systems of job evaluation.

Do we now need a single operational definition for comparable worth? At this point in our understanding of how work is valued and how we measure it, we think not. Rather, we need to focus our efforts on developing a set of general standards to be met and a range of acceptable techniques to meet them. As Ronnie Steinberg writes in Chapter 1, there can be no absolute standard of comparable worth to be applied in all situations. Standards must be derived partly from market wages and partly from firm-specific management and labor decisions about what features of jobs should be compensated. Whatever the technique, it must apply a job-content-based standard of worth consistently and accurately to job descriptions modified to capture fully the content of historically female work so as to establish a fair and legitimate wage for particular types of work.

The diversity that exists in the approaches to salary setting allows one to assess whether any one method or approach shows less bias than others. To date, studies using a number of different methods show surprisingly similar results: all demonstrate the systematic undervaluation of work done by women. We need not have a single means of setting salaries as long as the many ways are free of systematic bias against women.

Criticisms of Comparable Worth

As the goal of comparable worth has evolved from a political demand into a policy with serious economic consequences for employers, opponents have developed a number of arguments against it. Critics have argued, for example, that comparing dissimilar jobs is like comparing apples and oranges—which, they contend, is impossible to do. They assert as well that implementing a policy of comparable worth will undermine the free enterprise system, both because it involves setting wages arbitrarily and because the financial costs of implementation will be so great. They contend that a comparable worth policy will simultaneously increase inflation and unemployment. Finally, they say that integration of jobs and increased promotional opportunities alone will solve the problems of occupational segregation. Each of these arguments rests on a powerful truism as well as on a distorted understanding of both the measurement of wage discrimination and of eliminating it through the implementation of a comparable worth policy.

Apples and Oranges

A *Fortune* magazine article described comparable worth as "a fallacious notion that apples are equal to oranges and that prices for both should be the same." (Smith, 1978:58). The apples-and-oranges comparison refers to the supposed impossibility of finding a method to describe, evaluate, and establish equivalencies among dissimilar jobs. However, both suggestions—that no method for comparing dissimilar jobs can be found and that apples could not be equal to oranges—are themselves fallacious.

Of course, any particular apple may not be equal to any particular orange, nor are all apples identical. Yet there are general characteristics of fruit, such as the number of calories, the vitamin and mineral content, and so on, that make it possible to compare specific apples with specific oranges. Along some of these dimensions of comparison, the apples and oranges compared may, in fact, be equivalent, and therefore be of equal value.

Likewise, certain dissimilar jobs may comprise functional tasks and characteristics that, from the employer's point of view, are equivalent in value. Job evaluation systems describe and analyze jobs in terms of an array of underlying features such as prerequisites, tasks, and responsibilities. While far from perfect, these systems have been and continue to be used to classify dissimilar jobs, especially in large firms and at the management level. It is surprising, then, that the same employer groups that have supported job evaluation systems when they have been used to create and justify an existing organizational hierarchy and wage structure contend that such systems cannot be used to compare male-dominated and female-dominated jobs within that wage structure.

The Free Market

Critics also contend that comparable worth will destroy the free market as the basic mechanism for setting wages. This argument assumes, first, that wages are largely set through the impersonal forces of supply and demand and, second, that this is the best possible way to set wages. Government intervention will sabotage the invisible hand. This criticism of comparable worth policy is troublesome on three counts: it misrepresents the intent of comparable worth policy; it inflates out of all proportion the deleterious consequences to the market of establishing government-backed labor standards to protect employees against wage discrimination; and it assumes that the market now functions impersonally and fairly.

The goal of comparable worth policy is to pay a fair market wage to jobs historically done by women. This means that the wage rate should be based on the productivity-based job content characteristics of the jobs and not on the sex of the typical job incumbent. In other words, as noted in Chapter 1, comparable worth advocates seek to disentangle and remove discrimination from the market. The laissez-faire doctrine underlying the free market ideology assumes that employers and employees bargain as equals. Comparable worth policy can contribute toward a more smoothly running marketplace. Ironically, by giving less powerful women the power resource of a legally backed right to be paid at a nondiscriminatory wage rate, comparable worth policy removes a market imperfection (i.e., inequality between employers and some employees) that impinges unfairly on groups with less market power. Theoretically at least, by interfering in the free market we re-establish *laissez-faire* as the organizing principle guiding social relations in the labor market. (Steinberg, 1982).

The concern that specific social reforms will destroy the free enterprise system is not new. As far back as the 1890s, employers testified in the Massachusetts legislature that a particular law would lead to chaos in the productive process, that it would cause employers to move out of the state, that it would destroy the harmony between employers and employees, and that it would lead the country into socialism. The law was a child labor act prohibiting young children from working more than eight hours a day. Of course, none of the disastrous consequences materialized (Brandeis, 1935).

As this example suggests, government does interfere with the free market for the protection of employees. "Society" has always established limits on the actions that can be taken in the marketplace when such actions have gone beyond what is considered fair and appropriate. State child labor laws are one example, and we also have the Fair Labor Standards Act, the Occupational Health and Safety Act, and Title VII of the Civil Rights Act of 1964.

We interfere with the free market all the time in at least two other ways. First, government intervenes in the free market to protect employers. For example, the federal government provided funds to Chrysler, Amtrak, and Lockheed when it was seemingly necessary to keep these major companies from bankruptcy. Second, employers themselves repeatedly interfere with the free market. Price fixing, wage setting, and control of a particular product market are not necessarily the activities of personally evil individual employers; rather, they are often rational economic responses designed to minimize risk, reduce costs, and increase profits, thus allowing firms to remain in business.

An interesting example of employer collusion in wage setting is drawn from the comparable worth case *Lemons* v. *City of Denver* (22 FEP Cases 959). In the city of Denver, nurses were paid less than gardeners or tree trimmers. The nurses presented evidence that administrators of all the local hospitals met annually to set the salary levels that would be paid to nurses in the Denver metropolitan area. The judge failed to comment on the wage- and price-fixing activities of the hospital administrators when, as Mary Heen notes in Chapter 12, he ruled against the nurses. Under these circumstances, it would be virtually impossible for an individual nurse to bargain a "free market" wage.

The Cost

Critics of comparable worth policy also argue that the financial costs of adjusting female wages up to male standards would be prohibitive: employer advocacy groups have presented estimates that range from $2 billion to $150 billion (Newman and Vonhof, 1981:309). But the assumption underlying these estimates is that *all* wage discrimination in *all* work organizations is going to be rectified all at once and tomorrow. This assumption has no basis in history; nor does it reflect the approach thus far taken *within* work organizations to correct for systematic undervaluation or for other forms of discrimination.

Most legal reforms that impact upon the labor market have been implemented in stages: either the scope of coverage is initially restricted and gradually expanded to cover a larger proportion of employees over time, or the legal standard is introduced in steps (Steinberg, 1982). The first federal minimum wage law—the Fair Labor Standards Act—for example, called for an increase of the minimum hourly wage rate from 25 cents in 1938 to 40 cents in 1943 (ibid., ch. 4). Similarly, Title VII of the Civil Rights Act of 1964 limited initial coverage to work organizations in the private sector with at least a hundred employees and included a schedule extending coverage over a fiv-year period, so that by 1968 the law covered employers with at least twenty-five employees. In 1972 the law was amended to cover state and local government employ and firms with fifteen or more employees.

Even in those cases where pay equity adjustments have been made, corrections have been introduced a step at a time. In Minnesota, for example, the legislature appropriated 1.25 percent of its personnel budget, or $21.7 million, for pay equity adjustments. This represents the first of several appropriations needed to remove the undervaluation of women's work uncovered through a state study. The allocation of the first adjustments to specific undervalued job titles will be made according to a formula negotiated by labor and management. In the San Jose, California, comparable pay agreements, the city agreed to allocate $1.5 million for pay equity adjustments of 5 to 15 percent over a two-year period to begin the process of correcting for wage discrimination. Several of the bargaining units representing Connecticut public employees have negotiated "pay equity funds" in anticipation of the results of the third of three classification studies, as Alice Cook notes in Chapter 15. These pots of money represent a very small fraction of the state's wage bill; yet they offer a way of gradually building up the financial resources necessary to remove wage discrimination from the classification system.

Moreover, should comparable worth policy become incorporated into Title VII, it would no doubt be implemented as are policies designed to correct for other forms of employment discrimination. Currently, work organizations found to be in violation of the law must present a plan for eliminating discrimination that includes *reasonable* goals and timetables based on the probable availability of employees and the probable rate of turnover. Similarly, to comply with a comparable worth policy, firms would first have to determine the scope and form of wage discrimination in their organization. They would then have to develop a plan for removing it. As was true for San Jose, there is no reason to believe that a firm would be required to correct all inequities immediately if doing so would have serious financial consequences. Rather, the cost of implementing comparable worth policy will probably be spread out at the very least over the next two decades. While no doubt costly, the length of this implementation process should reduce the impact of its cost for any year or even any decade. The goal of the proponents of comparable worth is to balance fairness with fiscal responsibility.

Inflation and Unemployment

Comparable worth policy has been attacked as stimulating both inflation and higher unemployment. This pairing is interesting in that conventional macroeconomic theory holds that there is a tradeoff between unemployment and inflation. Again, critics overstate their case: comparable worth may prove modestly inflationary, but the degree of inflation will be a function of the rapidity of implementation. Similarly, unemployment may increase, but the extent of the increase will be a function of the degree of competition prevalent in the specific labor market in which any group of women works.

Increased Inflation

Opponents contend that equal pay for work of comparable worth will be inflationary because the increase in wages will not be the result of gains in productivity. Rather, employers will simply pass the additional labor costs on to consumers in the form of higher prices. While implementing comparable worth may, at some point, be inflationary, it is not at all clear that it would have a serious impact on the rate of inflation. At worse, if *every* employer in the United States eliminated the *entire* male-female wage gap *tomorrow* and nothing else changed, it is estimated that inflation would increase at a rate of approximately 4 percent over a ten-year period (Jonathan Ratner, personal communication, 1981). This is the maximum; since the process of adjusting wages will take at least several decades and will not eliminate all of the wage gap, it is clear that the impact on the inflation rate will be considerably less than the preceding estimate.

Increased Unemployment

Critics suggest that equal pay for work of comparable worth will result in higher unemployment because employers will substitute capital or technology for labor. Unemployment, however, is only likely to increase in those labor markets that are perfectly competitive—that is, those in which the forces of supply and demand operate without institutional constraints (Ratner, 1980). Agricultural workers and unskilled blue-collar workers, for instance, work in highly competitive markets.

But most women work in less competitive labor markets. Many work in white-collar and service jobs in large work organizations such as AT&T, IBM, Westinghouse, and the public sector. These work forces are characterized by well-developed internal labor markets with a large number of interconnected job titles in which the total number of positions is impervious to the fluctuations of the external labor market (Doeringer and Piore, 1971, ch. 2). Since the competition for these internal labor market jobs is largely restricted to employees within a firm, it is less likely that changing the wage rate will result in substantially higher unemployment, although it may raise the unemployment rate slightly (Ratner, 1980). This pattern was documented in Australia as the government eliminated lower minimum wages for women (Gregory and Duncan, 1979).

Finally, some women work in a third type of labor market, a so-called monopsonistic labor market. In this situation, the firm has a virtual monopoly in the community over the hiring or firing of a particular type of worker. For instance, many clerical and food service workers have limited geographical mobility and are restricted to working for one or a few employers. Since wages are not set in a competitive labor market, there is no reason to conclude that adjusting wages will result in an increase in unemployment. It has even been suggested that introducing comparable worth would accomplish the same changes as directly breaking down this monopoly. General economic theory would predict a decrease in unemployment under these circumstances (Ratner, 1980). Consequently, whether or not unemployment would increase would be a function of the degree of competition in the labor market.

The problems raised by critics of comparable worth policy—that you cannot compare apples and oranges, that it will undermine the free enterprise system, that it will prove too costly to implement, and that it will increase inflation *and* unemployment—at best rest largely on distorted facts and ungrounded assumptions and at worst use familiar symbols to play on the fears and insecurities of employees. Comparable worth policy addresses a very specific source of the wage gap: the artificial depression of wages paid for women's work. Like other labor and equal employment policies, it will no doubt be implemented slowly, both within firms and across firms. A realistic understanding of the dimensions of the problem, its cost, and its economic consequences will no doubt unfold as we begin to correct for it over the next two decades.

Integration of Jobs

Opponents of comparable worth frequently tout the integration of the work force as a better solution to the salary differentials between men and women. When most people speak of integration, they mean bringing women into male-dominated jobs by eliminating the few remaining barriers to their entry. It would then be totally up to the women to pursue these new careers if they wished to improve their earning power. While this process is, of course, important, full integration requires that men enter female-dominated fields as well. While some women are motivated by economic reasons to seek nontraditional work, these same reasons discourage men; because of the low wages and low status of female-dominated occupations, men have no incentives to seek this work.

Moreover, the segregation of our work force is so extensive that fully two-thirds of all men and women would have to change fields of employment to bring about an equal distribution of the sexes across all occupations. The sheer numbers involved point out the impossibility of integration alone as a reasonable solution. For example, almost 20 percent of the U.S. work force are clerical workers, virtually all of whom are female. Obviously only a small portion of the 5 million typists can become one of the 800,000 carpenters. The emphasis on women seeking men's jobs also raises questions about the men doing this work: are they to be asked to give up their jobs so that women may have them; if so, do we retrain them to be typists, and at whose expense?

There has been a tendency in several recent lawsuits to focus on eliminating discrimination at the entry level as the key to closing the wage gap; both *IUE* v. *Westinghouse* (23 FEP Cases 588) and *Taylor* v. *Charley Brothers Co.* (25 FEP Cases 602) make this point. In some employment situations, overt discrimination by the employer does occur at entry; at both Charley Brothers and Westinghouse, the jobs in question required no previous training, and the employer chose employment assignments. In many, perhaps most, employment situations, however, previous education, training, and experience are required by the employer, and potential employees indicate their preferences by applying for the specific jobs for which they have already acquired the necessary skills. Given the skill requirements of many jobs, successful implementation of the integration strategy would require extensive retraining programs similar to those funded under the Comprehensive Employment and Training Act, or more recently, the Job Partnership Training Act (Haignere and Steinberg, 1983). Without subsidized retraining programs, women must either retrain at their own expense (if they have the resources to do so) or compete with men for less skilled, higher-paid jobs in order to improve their economic well-being. While these strategies have some potential for solving the earnings problems of a few individuals, they are simply inadequate as an approach to a systemic problem.

One implicit message in the push for an integration strategy to equal employment is, once again, that women are the cause of their own exploitation; if they had just chosen the correct field of work, they would be making a reasonable wage. After all, if women's jobs are not systematically underpaid, then their assigned wages are a fair measure of the true worth of the jobs and of the workers in them. Many factors go into the choice of an occupation, and these factors affect both the hirer and the applicant. Whatever the reasons, these factors are obviously difficult to modify. In any case, men's jobs should not be the only ones that can be done with dignity and fair pay. Our society needs nurses, day care workers, waitresses, and typists. It is unreasonable to underpay these workers simply because they had the misfortune not to be born male and not to choose traditionally male jobs.

Promotion

Like those who push for an integration strategy, proponents of increased promotional opportunities as a solution to salary differentials fail to address the systematic undervaluation of women's work. Their arguments share two other features with the integration position: they shift the blame for their low wages to women, and they have an unrealistic view of actual opportunities.

Jobs with promotional opportunities are often contrasted to dead-end jobs. Yet for most of us, careers consist of a series of dead-end jobs. Many of us have gotten better jobs only by changing employers. Few jobs fit the fast-track model so often cited as typical, and not every worker is interested in fast-tracking. More often, we seek or settle for jobs that at least partly satisfy our needs for intrinsic satisfaction and/or extrinsic reward. Most clerical workers are not potential company presidents held down by sexist policies, nor are most nurses hospital administrators in disguise. Rather, they are often persons who like what they do, take pride in doing it well, and only wish for fair compensation for their efforts. They often aspire more to the crafts and trades model of a fair journey-level salary with low promotional expectations than to the business administration model, where one is a failure if one does not reach the top. We allow engineers, college professors, and carpenters to practice their professions for years with no promotional opportunities, and we compensate them with adequate salaries on which to support families and prepare for retirement; many nurses, clerks, and librarians ask only for the same rewards for their labor.

In some situations promotion is not a viable solution to low wages because opportunities are so scarce. Bridge jobs between job groups (e.g., clerical and professional) may not exist or may be inappropriate; for example, in a university setting there is no appropriate promotional line between secretaries and professors. Even where bridges are possible, one needs to be aware of the probability of advancement. Just because one woman has made the jump from clerical to professional work does not mean that all women, or even a second woman, will be able to. We need some sense of how much promotional opportunity there must be (e.g., 5 percent or 20 percent or 70 percent of all workers advance) to represent a realistic chance of promotion. Low-probability opportunities can sometimes be more damaging than no opportunities. Where there are no opportunities, management and the women workers understand the barrier. Once one or two are let across to the next level, it is easy for management and workers to blame the remaining women for their plight: if they were only somehow different, better, more ambitious, then they too could succeed.

We must also analyze the nature of the advancement and what it means in terms of the utilization of workers' potential; we question the values of systems where college-educated clerical workers must "promote" to less skilled custodial or delivery driver jobs in order to increase their earnings. Surely their employers are not maximizing the use of their abilities.

When they exist, promotional ladders can be a trap for workers. For example, in the higher education civil service system of the state of Washington, there are at least fourteen salary grades for clerical workers. The top salary of the highest position is almost 2.5 times that of the entry level of the lowest position, and this ladder is clearly one of the longest in the state system. One can keep very busy climbing this ladder, only to find that the top still pays less than entry-level positions in the trades or professional jobs. Promotional opportunity alone is obviously not enough to guarantee a living wage.

Although the creation of bridge jobs and the opening up of promotional opportunities must be part of any comprehensive equal opportunity program, the creation of ladders of any length will not remove the sense that one is being undercompensated for the value of one's work at any given level of achievement. Nor will the entry of a chosen few to higher-level jobs. The issue to be addressed by comparable worth is fair compensation, whatever one's job.

Comparable Worth in a Societal Context: Related Policy Issues

Comparable worth cannot be considered out of the context of work in general; labor is exchanged for wages, and comparable worth addresses the basis for the setting of wages. Wage setting is influenced by how we perceive elements of work and by how we perceive the person who does it. These two factors interact, complicating any analysis of work. Take, for example, the way we pay people who have jobs requiring intermittent work. Firefighters do not spend every moment fighting fires; while they wait for emergencies to happen, they may do limited work around the station, watch television, cook meals for one another, and so on. Yet we perceive their primary work to be that of firefighter, regardless of what percentage of their time is spent in that activity. Contrast the firefighter to the jail matron in the *Gunther* case. When the matrons were not busy with prisoners, they performed clerical work. These additional duties were then weighted into the "value" of their work, resulting in the *lowering* of their wages relative to jail guards, who had no assigned duties to perform when they were not busy with their prisoners. Perhaps the matrons should have refused the extra duties in order to keep their wages higher. Or firefighters' wages should be lowered to reflect the time they spend as cooks.

Women's status in the home also influences the perceived value of their paid work as well as expectations about what they can do in the workplace. Despite the changes we have gone through in the last fifteen years, in most families the bulk of responsibility for child care and household work falls upon the woman. Although the influx of women into the workplace has increased the work load (or perceived work load) of both the husband and wife—since many husbands are expected to do more at home now than in the past—being a father is not the same as being a mother, and being a husband is not the same as being a wife. Part of the adjustment to working wives has been the elimination of some tasks; witness the growth in fast food chains as women have entered the labor market and divorces have increased. Women also accommodate household demands by working part-time, but working part-time has important consequences for the value of their work.

Part-Time Work

Many women, especially those with young children, prefer part-time to full-time employment. Shorter work hours are their only way of dealing with the many demands in their lives. For mothers of school-aged children, work during school hours may be best; work hours for mothers of younger children are often chosen to fall outside the work hours of the husband, so that he can take care of the children while she works, and vice versa.

The increase in the number of working women has caused a shift in the peak working hours of many service industries. Grocery stores, for example, are quiet on weekdays from nine to four, when the few shoppers are primarily women with small children and people of retirement age. The stores are crowded in the early evening and on weekends. Retail stores follow much the same pattern of use. This concentration of hours of heavy use has caused many employers to create part-time, peak-hour jobs and to cut back in the number of full-time positions. The fact that women are more willing to accept part-time work than men are is causing a rapid feminization of these kinds of jobs.

Women's tendency to choose part-time work as a solution to role demands presents interesting compensation issues. Traditionally, part-time workers receive poorer benefit packages and lower hourly wages than full-time workers, even within the same firm; the authors of Chapter 9 added a factor for part-time work to their analysis of wages to account for these measurable effects. Economists tend to explain the lower compensation in terms of lower return to the employer for training and lower commitment by the employee. But are part-time workers really less productive and therefore worth less? Or is this a *post hoc* rationalization justifying a lower wage for female workers? Particularly for tedious jobs, our experience has shown two half-time workers to be more productive than one full-time employee.

Because most part-time workers are women, we must use care in sorting out how much of the lower pay is due to the sex of the workers and how much to their relative productivity. Part-time workers often have attributed to them the same kind of stereotypes attributed to women in general: they lack job commitment, they have no need for good wages or benefit packages, they offer no payoff for on-the-job training, and so on. Lower wages to part-time workers may represent a negative acknowledgment of the cultural value placed on women's work inside the home, an averaging together of low wages with the even lower return on mothering and housework. (This possibility should be familiar to academics seeking part-time tenure-line positions. The acceptability to the department of part-timers often hinges on what one does with the rest of one's time. If one is also employed elsewhere, a part-time commitment is acceptable; but part-time appointments are often denied to those devoting the rest of their time to family duties.)

Job evaluation systems do not take into account part- or full-time status; equal work would be judged to be of equal worth. The changes brought about by comparable worth leave us with several research questions. To what extent is the lower compensation for part-time workers due to the sex of the majority of the workers? If part-timers were paid like full-time workers, what would be the effect on their relationship to work? If women's work were paid comparably to men's work, would it change employers' perception of part-time workers, and would women be more or less likely to seek part-time work?

Child Care

For whatever cultural reason, child care is seen as a woman's issue and as women's responsibility. The problems of women as mothers needing to arrange care, as workers making low wages, and as day care providers are intertwined in a fashion that makes easy solutions unlikely.

Most women work in low-paying jobs. Their lower earning power within the family unit makes it more likely that they, rather than husbands, will stay home to take care of children when the children are sick or the child-care provider is unavailable. Women are more likely than men to have sole custody of children, ensuring total responsibility for their care. Low wages limit the amount of money women—especially single heads of households—can pay for child care.

Moreover, child-care providers are forced to charge low fees for their services or price themselves out of business. Hence, most are women who often cannot afford to do this work for long. Few find large day care centers to be profitable enough to develop or maintain. There is certainly no financial incentive to expand into the much needed but more expensive services of off-hours and sick child care. The low earnings of these workers tend to cause high turnover, thus increasing the pressures on the mothers of the children they care for.

Our cultural value system puts tending and teaching children near the bottom of worth scales. And yet developmental psychologists assert that the future well-being and cognitive development of human beings are determined in early childhood. While our society pays lip service to our youth, we assign very little monetary worth, and therefore importance, to the work of nurturing children, whether performed by mothers or child-care workers. It is difficult to ascertain whether caring for children is depreciated because women do it, because children are the recipients, or, most likely, both.

If women were paid comparably to men, they and their families would be able to pay more for child care, which would, in turn, increase the earnings of child-care providers. This latter increase would probably encourage or enable more persons to provide child care, thus increasing options and stability for women employed in other fields. Less certain is whether the increased earning power of women would change the relationships within the family enough to even out responsibility for children beween husband and wife.

The Process of Change

Because of the interrelatedness of wage setting and attitudes about work and perceptions of gender roles, it is obvious that change will not be easy. Efforts to bring about change must take place in the broad context of social justice efforts. The theoretical basis for change will have to be drawn from many disciplines. New policy on comparable worth will have to be made with consideration for the larger context of the roles of men and women in our society and the ways in which these contextual factors affect labor market choices and behavior.

In Chapter 1, we noted that there have been three identifiable stages in the development of comparable worth policy: a first stage, during the 1970s, marked by a number of identifiable, isolated activities; a second stage, which culminated in 1981, during which comparable worth was presented as a legitimate policy to address systemic undervaluation; and a third stage during which many public jurisdictions and private firms are identifying the extent of wage discrimination in their salary structures and developing feasible implementation plans for eliminating it.

We are in the midst of stage three. Many of the initiatives categorized and described by Alice Cook in Chapter 15 represent public sector efforts at bringing about change. Comparable worth activities have proliferated since 1980. If we add up the initiatives identified by Cook's and those cited in a study recently completed under the auspices of three organizations (Dean, et al., 1983), we can count over eighty state and municipal government efforts ranging from information gathering (including hearings), to job evaluation studies, to the enactment of comparable worth legislation, to the specification of enforcement efforts, and, finally, to comparable pay adjustments. Indeed, we learn of new initiatives at the rate of approximately two to three a week.

We now have enough experience in this area to identify a series of conditions necessary to move from information gathering to pay equity adjustments within a jurisdiction. At the center of the change process is the completion of a job evaluation study—to identify the extent of undervaluation as well as to pinpoint disparities on a job-by-job basis. (A notable exception to this pattern is the state of New Mexico, where $3.3 million was appropriated in 1983 to upgrade the lowest-paid job titles, an overwhelming majority of which are female-dominated, without the completion of a study.) In almost all jurisdictions, efforts to undertake a study were initiated by organized groups of women and spearheaded by either the state commission on the status of women or a local or national union. Unions and state commissions and/or state legislative task forces on the status of women have combined forces to press for a study in Washington State, Connecticut, Minnesota, and Maine, to cite a few instances. Unions alone have proven instrumental in New York State and in several municipalities.

In every case of pay equity adjustments, the study design included an advisory committee—often a joint labor and management committee—that influenced, monitored, and reviewed the study. In Washington State and Connecticut, for example, the committee assisted the consultant in the process of assigning evaluation points to jobs. In San Jose, the Women's Committee of Local 101 of the American Federation of State, County and Municipal Employees trained union members in filling out job description questionnaires.

Finally, after the study results were announced, these organized constitutent groups had to exert substantial pressure in multiple institutional arenas to gain salary adjustments in undervalued job titles. In Connecticut the unions have combined collective bargaining with litigation and legislation. In the state of Washington, years of unsuccessful pressure culminated in 1982 in a lawsuit by the union against the state, which was followed by legislative commitment to implementation in 1983. In San Jose the local union tried negotiating with the city manager and filing a complaint with the regional office of the Equal Employment Opportunity Commission. The members won their demands when they went out on strike.

We believe that the parameters of a national comparable worth policy are presently being formulated at the state and municipal levels. Studies are still needed because although there is growing awareness of wage discrimination in general, there is no political consensus about which jobs are undervalued and by how much. Interest groups must combine their strategies in order to build a case for a reform that not only affects relatively powerless groups of employees, but challenges the theoretical operating principles of the U.S. political economy. These efforts should result in an eventual consensus in favor of comparable worth, which should, in turn, decrease significantly the need for large-scale, costly, and highly technical studies. It should also, over the next decade, simplify the process of bringing about pay equity adjustments.

Conclusion

The reform of equal employment policy to encompass the right to equal pay for work of comparable worth will not happen in a political vacuum. Rather, as so much of the material in this book indicates, it is growing out of the efforts of groups of working women, exerting pressure through their organizations, to win a new set of legally backed employment rights.

This process of change started small. In its short history, success has stimulated further success. For example, court cases established precedents for eliminating the most flagrant instances of intentional sex discrimination in compensation. Once these precedents were in place, they served as a resource for employee groups pressing for changes in their workplace and as a foundation for further legal precedents that outlawed more subtle forms of wage discrimination.

Similarly, collectively bargained agreements implementing pay equity adjustments are not only significant to the employees they cover; they also are powerful models for other employees seeking to eliminate wage discrimination in their employment contracts. Firm-level studies of compensation systems provide not only the information needed to correct a specific wage structure, but also material for educating women workers and the general public about the contours of wage discrimination. As proponents of comparable worth build up a body of scientific evidence, establish legal precedents, and introduce pay equity into contracts, they negate the arguments of critics of comparable worth. Criticisms are best addressed when the policy is implemented effectively.

Moreover, as more firms adopt comparable worth, the resultant salary adjustments will permeate the wage structure of local labor markets. Through the process of pressure, innovation, imitation, and adjustment, the wages paid for work done primarily by women will catch up with the reality that women represent a large, permanent, and highly productive set of employees. These concrete actions will, no doubt, eventually transform a highly charged and controversial political demand into a routine and institutionalized feature of equal employment policy.

References

Brandeis, Elizabeth. 1935. *Labor Legislation: History of Labor in the United States.* Vol. 3: 1896–1932, ed. John R. Commons. New York: Macmillan.

Dean, Virginia, et al. 1983. "State and Local Government Action on Pay Equity: New Initiatives." Paper commissioned by the National Committee on Pay Equity.

Doeringer, Peter B., and Michael J. Piore. 1971. *Internal Labor Markets and Manpower Analysis.* Lexington, Mass.: D. C. Heath.

Gregory, Robert G., and Ronald C. Duncan. 1979. "The Relevance of Segmented Labor Market Theories: The Australian Experience of the Achievement of Equal Pay for Women." Manuscript.

Haignere, Lois and Ronnie Steinberg. 1983. "New Directions in Equal Employment Policy: Training Women for Non-Traditional Occupations." Working Paper no. 13. Albany, N.Y.: Center for Women in Government.

Newman, Winn, and Jeanne M. Vonhof. " 'Separate but Equal'—Job Segregation and Pay Equity in the Wake of *Gunther.*" *University of Illinois Law Review* (1981): 269–331.
Ratner, Jonathan. 1980. "The Employment Effects of Comparable Worth Policy." Working Paper no. 4. Albany, N.Y.: Center for Women in Government.
Smith, Lee. 1978. "The EEOC's Bold Foray into Job Evaluation." *Fortune* (11 September):58–64.
Steinberg, Ronnie J. 1982. *Wages and Hours: Labor and Reform in Twentieth Century America.* New Brunswick, N.J.: Rutgers University Press.
Treiman, Donald J. 1979. *Job Evaluation: An Analytic Review.* Washington, D.C.: National Academy of Sciences.

Contributors

JAMES R. BEATTY is Professor and Chair of the Department of Management at San Diego State University. He is an accredited personnel diplomate with the Personnel Accreditation Institute, a seminar leader for the American Compensation Association, a consultant in team building and human resources management, and a statistical expert witness in discrimination cases.

RICHARD W. BEATTY is Professor of Organization Behavior and former head of the Management and Organization Division at the University of Colorado. Dr. Beatty has testified in several comparable worth cases, and during 1982/83 he was the George A. Ball Distinguished Professor of Business Administration at Ball State University. He is the author of *Personnel Administration: An Experiential Skill-Building Approach* and *Performance Appraisal: Assessing Human Behavior at Work.*

BARBARA R. BERGMANN is Professor of Economics at the University of Maryland. She has served on the staff of the Council of Economic Advisors and the Brookings Institution.

CARROLL BOONE served on the 1974 advisory committee to the Washington State Comparable Worth Study. She recently completed law school and was a legal researcher and law clerk on the landmark comparable worth case, *AFSCME (Holmes)* v. *State of Washington.*

RITA CADIEUX has been the Deputy Chief Commissioner of the Canadian Human Rights Commission since 1977. She has worked in various social programs of the Canadian federal government since 1962 and was Director of the Office of Equal Opportunity at the Canadian Broadcasting Corporation from 1975 to 1977.

ALICE H. COOK is Professor Emerita at the New York State School of Industrial and Labor Relations, Cornell University. She is the co-editor of *Women and Trade Unions in Eleven Industrialized Countries,* another volume in this series on women in the political economy.

VIRGINIA DEAN is Coordinator and co-founder of the Comparable Worth Project. An attorney specializing in labor and employment law, she provides technical assistance, training and legal representation for workplaces and labor organizations addressing sex-based wage discrimination.

PAULA ENGLAND is Associate Professor of Sociology and Political Economy at the University of Texas at Dallas. She and George Farkas are currently writing a book on households, employment, and gender to be published in 1985. Dr. England has served as an expert witness in Title VII and Equal Pay Act litigation.

MARY W. GRAY is Professor and Chair of the Department of Mathematics, Statistics and Computer Science at the American University in Washington, D.C. She is also an attorney and has been involved in litigation concerning discrimination in employment and education.

JOY ANN GRUNE is a founder and Executive Director of the National Committee on Pay Equity. She has been a university instructor at the University of Pittsburgh and on the staff of 9 to 5: National Association of Working Women; the Service Employees International Union; and the Labor and Humanities Project of the AFL-CIO.

HEIDI I. HARTMANN is Study Director of the Committee on Women's Employment and Related Social Issues in the Commission on Behavioral and Social Sciences and Education, National Research Council/National Academy of Sciences. In a previous position with the NRC/NAS, she served as Research Associate for the Committee on Occupational Classification and Analysis, and co-edited the Committee's final report to the U.S. Equal Employment Opportunities Commission on the issue of comparable worth: *Women, Work and Wages: Equal Pay for Jobs of Equal Value.* Dr. Hartmann is a member of the editorial board of *Feminist Studies*, a scholarly journal of research and theory on women and gender.

MARY HEEN is Staff Counsel of the American Civil Liberties Union Women's Rights Project. Her responsibilities include all aspects of trial and appellate litigation, public education, and administrative advocacy, with special emphasis on employment discrimination. She was principal author of the brief *amici curiae* submitted in *Gunther* on behalf of the ACLU and thirteen other civil rights and women's organizations.

RUSSELL JOHANNESSON is Professor of Industrial Relations and Organizational Behavior at Temple University. He has been a consultant to the Department of Labor, Health Education and Welfare, Department of Justice, Civil Service Commission, State Farm Insurance Company, General Electric, Armco Steel, and National Cash Register.

EVE JOHNSON is a registered representative of Ferris & Company, a member New York Stock Exchange. She is a founding member of the National Committee on Pay Equity, and is currently representing Women's National Democratic Club on its executive board. Ms. Johnson is the former Coordinator of Women's Activities for the American Federation of State, County, and Municipal Employees.

KAREN SHALLCROSS KOZIARA is Professor of Industrial Relations and Organizational Behavior at Temple University. She has been a Woodrow Wilson Fellow and Fulbright Professor at the Royal University of Malta and is currently on the executive board of the Industrial Relations Research Association.

DAVID PIERSON is a consultant with Towers, Perrin, Forster, and Crosby in their Philadelphia office with a specialization in compensation. He was formerly on the faculty of the School of Business Administration, Temple University.

LISA PORTMAN is Assistant Director of the George Meany Center for Labor Studies in Silver Spring, Maryland. She has been Editor for *Ammunition*, a United Auto Workers magazine, and the Program Coordinator for the Institute of Labor and Industrial Relations for the University of Michigan, Ann Arbor. Ms. Portman is a Task Force Chairperson for the Coalition of Labor Union Women.

HELEN REMICK is Director of the Office for Affirmative Action at the University of Washington, Seattle. She has been actively involved with comparable worth in the State of Washington since 1976. Her interest in women's wages was kindled during early work experience as secretary, bookkeeper, receptionist, retail sales clerk and clerk typist.

PATTI ROBERTS is a co-founder of the Comparable Worth Project. She has served as Directing Attorney of the Women's Litigation Unit of San Francisco legal services program and held local and national offices in the National Lawyers Guild.

PATRICIA A. ROOS is Assistant Professor of Sociology at State University of New York at Stony Brook. She was a staff member of the National Academy of Sciences Committee on Occupational Classification and Analysis, which produced *Women, Work and Wages: Equal Pay for Jobs of Equal Value.*

SHARON TOFFEY SHEPELA is Professor of Psychology, Director of Research at the Counseling Center (a career counseling center for adult women) and Director of the Women's Research Institute of Hartford College.

RONNIE J. STEINBERG is Director of the Program on Comparable Worth for the Center for Women in Government at the State University of New York at Albany. She is author of *Wages and Hours: Labor and Reform in Twentieth Century America* (1982) and editor of *Equal Employment Policy for Women: Strategies of Implementation in the United States, Canada, and Western Europe.*

DONALD J. TREIMAN is Professor of Sociology at University of California, Los Angeles. He served as Study Director for the National Academy of Sciences Committee on Occupational Classification and Analysis and co-edited the Committee's report, *Women, Work and Wages: Equal Pay for Jobs of Equal Value* (1981). He is currently serving as consultant to the Center for Women and Government on a study of the comparable worth of public sector jobs in New York State, and as a member of the State of California Comparable Worth Task Force.

ANN VIVIANO is a Supervising Psychologist and Administrator at Shield Institute in New York. She is currently President of the Academic Division of the New York State Psychological Association. Dr. Viviano was previously Assistant Professor of Psychology at Pace University.

Index

307

Wage realignment as correction of discrimination, 163–72

Washington State: comparable worth study, 13, 17, 101–6, 138, 273–74, 282; Equal Rights Amendment, 249–50; Promotional opportunities in civil service, 295–96

Washington, State of v. *AFSCME. See AFSCME* v. *Washington State*

Westinghouse, and National War Labor Board, 7–9. *See also IUE* v. *Westinghouse*

Westinghouse v. *IUE. See IUE* v. *Westinghouse*

Wilkins v. *University of Houston, xi,* 207–8

Willis Study of Comparable Worth. *See* Washington State: comparable worth study

Women's Bureau, United States Department of Labor, 9, 271

Working conditions: and job evaluation, 73–74, 82–88, 113–14, 130–35; in nursing, 90–91

DATE DUE		
DEC 0 8 1991 NOV 2 3 2000		
MAR 3 NOV 2 8 2001		
DEC 1 4 OCT 2 8 2002		
MAR 2 1 1995 NOV 1 8 2002		
NOV 3 0 1997 NOV 1 3 2002		
DEC 1 7 1998		
MAR 2 1 1999		
MAR 2 1 1999 OCT 3 1 2000		